SKYMATES, VOLUME TWO:

THE COMPOSITE CHART

by

Steven Forrest & Jodie Forrest

ACKNOWLEDGMENTS

We'd like to thank the following people for friendship, support, insights, patience, practical assistance, or for opening their lives and homes to us:

The Forrest astrological apprenticeship program members, Jane Alexander, Joyce Allen, the Blue Sky Ranch community, Lynn Bell, Maridel Bowes, Linda Carson, Ceci y Chella de La Casa del Astrólogo en México, Janette DeProsse, Basil Fearrington, Hadley Fitzgerald, Kristin Fontana, Bunny Forrest, Nan Geary, Martha Goenaga, Wells Gordon, Mary Kay Hocking, Barbara Jensen, Cheryl Jones, Rhiannon Jones, Carl Kennison, Michelle Kondos, Steve Lautermilch, Rob Lehmann, Eileen Lehn, Catherine Losano, Manda the Cat (four new paws), Mark McDonough, Michael Mercury, Patricia Morales, the Nalbandian family, Rafi Nasser, Vinessa Nevala, Barbara Niepelt, Dorothy Oja, Lina Pratt, Keron Psillas, Pyanfar the Cat (four of the original Seven Paws), Michael Rank, Jose Manuel Redondo, Evelyn Roberts, Mary Beth Rodin, Savannah Scarborough, Phil Sedgwick, Tim Smith, Jane St. Clair, Brian Trent, the late Vincent the Cat (three of the original Seven Paws), and the two mystery women who appeared out of nowhere in the deep desert and whose hands are in the cover artwork.

We'd like to thank the following couples, "Skymates" all:

Scott Ainslie and Barb Ackemann, Willard and Bobbie Aldrich, Cyril Beveridge and Sinikka Laine, Maryska Bigos and Jeff Hamilton, Lynda Bunnell and Tom Stone, Nick and Karen Callen, Keith Cleversley and Lia Roldan, Bob and Ingrid Coffin, John and Barbara Connor, Paul Cory and Laura Haywood-Cory, Mike and Carol Czeczot, Mitch Easter and Shalini Chatterjee, Sue and Tommy Field, Chris Ford and Jo Wright, Kelli and David Fox, Ginger Gaffney and Glenda Fletcher, Karen Galey and Steve Briggs, Tracy Gaudet and Rich Leibowitz, Wolf and Martina Green, Robert and Diana Griffin, Dave and Donna Gulick, Dave Jaquish and Rhonda Schaller, Bill Janis and Shannon Glass, Judy and John Johnston, Dan and Teri Kee, Kittisaro and Thanissara, Alphee and Carol Lavoie, Luis Lesur and Barbara Kastelein, Jim and Sharon Mullaney, Ray Palmerini and Cheryl Carter, Starr and Mike Perry, Dag and Sharon Rossman, Eric Silver and Adela Rios, Cristina Smith and Sanford Wolcott, Trudie Styler and Sting, Tem Tarriktar and Kate Sholly, Joyce Van Horn and Kathy Jacobson, Ed and Paula Wansley, Jeff and Jan Ward, Kate and Joel Wechsler, James Weinberg and Mary Beth Cysewski, Charles and Cindy Wyatt, Scotty Young and Diane Swan, and Tom Young and Kristin Gooch.

Most of all we'd like to thank Ingrid Coffin, our fellow desert rat, for everything and then some.

FOREWORD

Perilously close to the beginning of our marriage, we tempted the Fates by writing a book about the astrology of love, sex and intimacy. That was the first edition of *Skymates,* which Bantam Books published in 1989. We were happy enough with that book, but years of working astrologically with our clients' relationships taught us that there was a lot more to know. A couple of decades of using astrology in our own intimate processes taught us even more. We really felt that we were ready to update Skymates, but we quickly realized that putting what we had learned into print was going to take us two volumes, not one.

In 2002, our own Seven Paws Press published *Skymates, Volume One: Love, Sex, and Evolutionary Astrology.* That book covered most of the elemental tools of synastry: deciphering the relationship message of the individual birthchart, working with interaspects and understanding house transpositions.

The present volume completes the picture with a consideration of the composite chart. As with *Volume One,* those of you who have the old Bantam edition of *Skymates* will occasionally encounter a familiar passage. Rest assured that the book you are holding in your hands is a substantially new piece of work. The material is deeper—and frankly, some of that depth comes from the freedom of not writing to fit the "dumbed-down" strictures of a mass market publisher. Furthermore, in response to popular demand, we've included a very extensive "cookbook" section. To get a head start in interpreting your own composite charts, you can simply look up the meaning of any planet in any sign or any house. They are all there, plus the Nodes of the Moon. Beware though: there are perils connected with piecemeal interpretation! We are proudest of the parts of the book that teach you how to think like an astrologer, pulling the messages of the individual configurations together into a single ironical, ambivalent, complicated whole—something that better resembles a modern relationship, in other words!

The whole is, famously, greater than the sum of the parts. Two birthcharts can tell us a lot about two people—how they see each other, how they interact. But always, when two souls dare to love each other, when they go through the doorway of romance and face the vexing, magnificent, wild country that lies beyond it, they create something new. Something bigger than themselves is born. And, together, they ride that beast through a landscape of darkness and heavenly light.

Turn the page; meet the real beast with two backs.

Thanks for joining us for another journey. And thanks for helping us live that double Aquarian life prophesied in our own composite chart.

—Steven Forrest and Jodie Forrest
Chapel Hill, NC
May 27, 2004

SKYMATES, VOLUME TWO: THE COMPOSITE CHART

By Steven Forrest and Jodie Forrest

Table of Contents

INTRODUCTION: WHAT IT'S ALL ABOUT

"Hungry?"

"Oh, I guess I could eat . . ."

Anyone who has ever been in a relationship that lasted more than five or six weekends knows about that tired, lackadaisical place all couples sometimes go.

"Feel like making love?"

"It would be OK, if you really want to . . ."

Forget it, right?

Boredom is part of life. If we have what it takes to make a relationship work, we'll accept boredom, flatness, and *ennui* as part of the deal sometimes. You had them before you were a couple and, if you break up, you'll have them still. They're part of *you*, and they are part of your lover too. You both bring them to the table. Being in a relationship won't make them go away. Falling in love briefly masks them, but when the hormonal fog clears, those dull feelings are still on the landscape.

Still, if that's *all* you feel together, your relationship is in serious trouble.

Skymates Two: The Composite Chart, in a nutshell, is a book about how couples get into that dismal place—and, merrily, how they can get out of it again.

There is a bag of tricks involved with reading composite charts, and we'll be exploring it in great detail. But here is the whole idea in a few words:

Couples, just like individuals, are free to make their own choices. Astrology enforces very little on anyone. There is tremendous wiggle-room in the symbolism. For any astrological question, there are right answers and wrong answers—and many shades of gray in between.

If an individual, in his or her freedom, elects to spend life watching television instead of living the life he or she was born to live, he or she will become bored, flat, and dull.

Exactly the same thing happens to couples.

Every couple, like every individual, is on the earth for an evolutionary reason. And that path is a path of fire: travel it, and we feel alive. For each individual and for every couple, there is a "right" way to live—and "rightness" here is not so much a moralistic perspective as an existential one. It's more about how we live than about what we believe. A Sagittarian *individual*, for example, needs plenty of opportunities for amazement and wonder in life: passionate education, culture-shock, and a feeling that tomorrow won't be a re-run of yesterday. For a *couple* with a composite Sagittarian Sun, it's exactly the same: put them in a predictable suburban life-style, run it for a few years, and they'll be having conversations along the lines of the one you read at the beginning of this chapter. They'll be on the road to divorce, in other words.

And the deepest tragedy is that they probably won't even really know why.

Enter the Shrinks: *"There's Something You're Not Dealing With . . ."*

Faced with the erosion of passion and connectedness, a modern couple will often seek help from psychotherapy and psychotherapeutic perspectives. In many cases, this is a wise and effective move. Intimacy is elusive, and it must be renewed daily. The *parts of ourselves with which we are not intimate* can take a deep bite of the closeness in our relationships too. If, for example, I am alienated from my own anger, I will surely have a difficult time dealing with my mate's anger as well. Furthermore, I'll probably see anger in my mate that isn't really there at all—it's actually just my own swallowed anger mirrored back to me. That's what shrinks call *projection.*

If, because of childhood trauma or bad religion, my sexuality is damaged, that issue will cast a long shadow over the bedroom.

If I am depressed, our relationship will be susceptible to depression too.

In all of these real-world situations, it is very possible that the arsenal of therapies a modern psychological counselor brings to the table might be very helpful. Psychological astrology can be deeply relevant here as well—that's a big part of what *Skymates One* was about. Make no mistake: this is not a book about denying personal responsibility for what happens in our relationships. There's probably nothing else in the world that so effectively brings our "inner work" to the surface as staying in a committed bond. We're all imperfect beings, and those imperfections rise up to challenge and guide us forward when we dare to love as humble adults. That material is revealed in the analysis and comparison of the two birthcharts, not in the composite chart.

With all that said, let's recognize that not all problems that a couple faces can be understood quite so psychologically. Psychological theory can be so penetrating and so effective that we run the risk of believing in it too uncritically. *With the composite chart, we enter a third dimension: you, me, and what we are together.* You might be the fundamental source of some challenge we're facing together. Or the problem might originate with me. But, just possibly, it has nothing directly to do with either one of us. Perhaps its origins lie in the mysterious space between us.

This "space between" is the natural domain of the composite, and we need to understand it precisely. Here, for starters, is what it is *not*: it is not my reaction to your "stuff," or your reaction to my "stuff." Those dimensions can be understood through birthchart comparison: interaspects, house transpositions, and so on—the techniques covered in the first *Skymates* volume. The "space between" really transcends each of us as individuals. It is like a third person in the relationship, with its own nature, intentions, and idiosyncratic needs. As the birthchart sketches the soul-intentions of an individual, the composite chart sketches the soul-intentions of the couple. As the birthchart maps the energy-body of an individual, the composite chart maps the energy-body of the couple.

A few paragraphs back we imagined a couple with their composite Sun in Sagittarius, with its implicit need for adventure and change. If an individual Sagittarian fails to "feed the Sun," that person will descend into pettiness, anxiety, and a feeling of being lost. It's the same for the couple. They need to be stretched too. Like the individual, they need to get out of their box.

Now let's complicate the picture. Maybe this composite Sagittarian couple, *as individuals*, are both cautious, conventional, stay-at-home types with 401K plans, smoke detectors, and a burglar alarm. The idea of quitting their jobs and spending six months serving as volunteer teachers in an Ecuadoran village wouldn't cross their minds in a thousand years. And yet that might be exactly what they need to survive as a couple. As an entity, they need more adventure and cross-cultural experience than they need as separate individuals. If they don't get it, *the Sun they share begins to die*—the relationship loses its zest. Their appetite for life is replaced by a soporific appetite for food or television.

And they wonder where their love went.

Conventional psychology could not help them find the answer. Worse, it would be inclined to seek an answer where none existed: *in the domain of something they're not dealing with.* They could be shoe-horned into imagining "deep psychological issues" in a way that reflected their psychologist's belief-system far more vividly than it reflected their actual realities. As we saw a little while ago, that psychological domain can be very productive in intimate counseling! But now, with the composite chart, we recognize that there is a vast area in the mystery of human love to which conventional psychological thinking is utterly blind. The whole is, famously, greater than the sum of the parts. For this couple, the problems—and their solutions—might exist in that wholeness they create together, and only be visible there. It might, in other words, not be visible through interaspects or other birthchart technicalities—but leap out when we contrast their boundary-busting composite chart with the staid life they have created.

Spirits at the Table; Spirits in the Bed

Just about all of us fantasize about hitting the lottery and spending the rest of our lives sipping piña coladas in some tropical paradise. But most of us know that given a little while, we'd be miserable there. A happy life requires more evolutionary grit. We need challenges; we need something to sink our teeth into. That's true of individuals, and it's true of couples as well. "And they lived happily ever after" is not only a transparent fiction, given the demanding realities of human love; it is also a monumentally bad idea. There's not much evolutionary momentum in being a bliss ninny—and, paradoxically, without evolutionary momentum we're not even very happy . . . once the piña colada wears off.

A birthchart and a composite chart both describe the same things: an optimal evolutionary path, the tools we have for the job, and what it looks like if we blow it. As couples or as individuals, knowledge of that path is astrology's precious gift to us. In terms of understanding, all we really have to add to the stew is an expanded, post-patriarchal view of human spirituality: we are not here to "transcend the flesh." We are not here to "avoid worldly temptation." The spiritual life—and the spiritual relationship—don't just mean sitting in a yoga position thinking pure thoughts with a belly full of organic bean sprouts. The "path" is wildly, delightfully more diverse than that. Each couple, like each individual, has its own way of fulfilling the soul contract. Two people might succeed in doing deeply spiritual work together—and both think they are atheists. Or fail, and both be devoutly religious—but never have spent that year in the Ecuadoran village.

We fall in love. We hear the proverbial violins. Mother Nature, ever smarter than we are, tricks us into forming a bond that can only break if our hearts break too. Little do we know what we have signed up for! Love will push us to our edges and beyond. But underlying the daily conversation, the spiderweb of mundane details, the bills, the dreams, the cats and the kids, there is a divine plan—a contract the souls made long ago, in another world. To fulfill it is joy. To abrogate it is folly—loneliness, lostness, anger and sorrow. And, woven into the astrological symbols of the composite chart, is the text of the contract and some advice from the angels about how to get it right.

In the pages that follow, we'll learn how to read that precious message.

PART ONE: THE COMPOSITE CHART

CHAPTER ONE: NUTS AND BOLTS

The whole is greater than the sum of the parts, or so goes the old proverb. And it's true, especially in affairs of the heart. When two people commit themselves to loving each other, the *whole* of that couple is something new, something distinct from either of the individuals.

Two shy little mice get married and quickly begin throwing elaborate dinner parties. Two aggressive extroverts get together and move to the backwoods of Alaska. The changes are not always so shocking, but the point is that the "meta-personality" of a couple does not always derive logically from the personalities of the individuals. Sometimes that meta-personality appears to have a mind of its own.

Every couple, then, is a threesome: you, me, and what we are together. Unraveling the sometimes Byzantine politics of this "eternal triangle" is the third and final step in the synastry pyramid we began exploring in our first volume of this series, *Skymates: Love, Sex and Evolutionary Astrology.* In that book, we explored the first step in that pyramid: dissecting each of the individuals separately, as if each existed in a vacuum. We also presented the second step: analyzing the interactions of the two birthcharts. Now, in this volume, we complete the picture by recognizing that, in love, there is always an invisible third party, casting its votes, throwing its tantrums, offering its insights, just like the two visible lovers. That ghostly but powerful presence is symbolized by the composite chart.

Working With the Composite Chart

The invisible third party in every partnership may be impossible to see, but it reveals its nature and its hidden agenda very clearly in the composite. Arbiter, deadlock-breaker, wild card, it moves behind the scenes to establish the framework of energy, attitude, and synchronicity within which the two lovers navigate for as long as they remain together.

What does a composite chart look like? Exactly the same as an ordinary birthchart.

How do you interpret one? Basically, by exactly the same rules you use with individual birthcharts—except that you need to remember that now you're talking about the personality of the couple, an entity separate and distinct from either of the flesh-and-blood human beings who compose it. (For a quick refresher on the basic meanings of signs, planets and houses as they relate to birthcharts, please see the first volume of *Skymates*, or *The Inner Sky*.)

Constructing the Composite Chart

How is the composite chart constructed? In essence, it is an *averaging* of the two birthcharts. The point precisely midway between your Sun and mine is our composite Sun. The midpoint of your Moon and mine is our composite Moon. If your Mercury lies toward the end of Scorpio and mine lies toward the end of Capricorn, the point exactly halfway between them—late Sagittarius—is the location of our composite Mercury.

The Houses are a little more complicated, and there is more than one theory about how to create them. In the approach that we favor, we find the composite Midheaven—the point halfway between your Midheaven and mine—and we use that, along with the place where the couple first met, as the basis for calculating the rest of the Houses. The pages that follow contain more details about this approach. If you're fainthearted when it comes to arithmetic and don't have a computerized calculation program, you'll find websites and an address at the end of this book where you can order computerized composite charts, or the software to set them up yourself.

As always in astrology, setting up the charts is merely a mechanical process, interesting for some, daunting for others, boring for most. The challenge—and the reward—lies in learning to cajole insight and understanding out of those primordial symbols of earth and sky. That's what this book is really about.

Origins

Whoever first came up with the idea of composite charts is one of astrology's unsung heroes. We have no idea who it was. The technique became popular in the early 1970s with the publication of John Townley's groundbreaking book, *The Composite Chart* and, shortly thereafter, Robert Hand's book, *Planets in Composite*. Neither man claims to have invented the basic idea, only to have refined it. Townley, in his book *Composite*

Charts: The Astrology of Relationships, traced the technique back to Germany in the 1920s. Dr. Walter Koch, who originated the popular Koch system of House division, apparently knew of it, but we have no particular reason to believe he created the idea.

The exploration of the importance of planetary midpoints seems to have been a special province of German astrologers, and so it's a reasonable guess to think we have them to thank for the technique. Reinhold Ebertin, especially, is associated with the midpoint theory, known generally as Cosmobiology. His most widely read book is *The Combination of Stellar Influences,* which came out in 1949. It is not about the composite chart *per se,* but it contains the germs of the techniques upon which it is based—it's a short step from noticing the sensitivity of a point midway between your natal Venus and your natal Mars to wondering if there might be some intimate significance to the point midway between *your* Venus and *mine,* or your Mars and mine.

Baldur Ebertin, Reinhold's son, has continued the work. Elsbeth Ebertin, the mother of Reinhold and grandmother of Baldur was also a serious professional astrologer. She edited the astrological magazine *Blick in die Zukunft (A Glance into the Future)* for over twenty years, starting in 1917, and wrote several books herself. It's plausible to hypothesize that the intellectual foundations of the composite chart lie in Germany between the two World Wars.

Two points are definite: the core of the technique lies in understanding the significance of midpoints; and everything else about composite charts is currently a muddle of competing approaches! In the rest of this chapter we'll first learn to think precisely about midpoints, then we'll explore some of the fuzzy areas, making some recommendations about the technical choices that have proven themselves most reliable in our own counseling practice.

So What's a Midpoint?

Have a look at Figure 1 on page 10. In this natal chart, Mars lies at 10 degrees of Virgo and Venus lies at 10 degrees of Libra. Halfway between them is their midpoint: 25 degrees of Virgo.

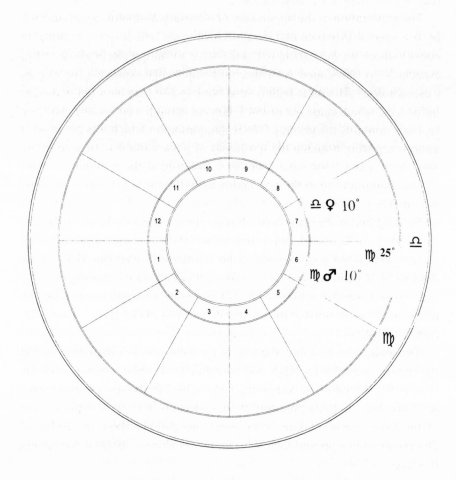

If you go around the chart "the long way," you could create another midpoint opposite the first, at 25 degrees of Pisces. But don't do that. Always use the shorter angle.

If my Moon lies in 15 degrees 59 minutes of Capricorn, and your Moon lies in 15 degrees 58 minutes of Cancer, that's obviously a very precise opposition. But their midpoint would be in 15 degrees 58.5 minutes of Aries. It wouldn't be in Libra, because that angle is *slightly* wider.

For most astrologers nowadays, the computer will do the arithmetic. But it still helps you achieve a more visceral feeling for the workings of the composite chart if you visualize how those midpoint positions are derived.

So what does a midpoint mean? The answer is about what you would think—it is a kind of "averaging" of the two planetary energies. Working with midpoints within the context of a natal chart is a big subject, and our friend Basil Fearrington has written and self-published an excellent and very concise booklet about it called *The Midpoint Manual* (Basil Fearrington, 15 North Conestoga Street, Philadelphia, PA 19139, bfearr@aol.com, www.BasilFearrington.com). With that text, and perhaps Ebertin's classic, *The Combination of Stellar Influences*, you can enter a fascinating and still rather cutting-edge realm of astrological theory. We won't go into it all in detail here, since much of it ranges beyond what we need to know in terms of composite charts, but here's a taste from *The Midpoint Manual*, about natal midpoints:

> *Let's use the Venus/Mars midpoint . . . What does Mars do when it contacts another planet or position? It energizes, heats, and stirs up what it touches. Here Mars is stirring up Venus. Think about it: what happens when romance (Venus) gets stirred up and becomes heated and energized (Mars)? It becomes passion, doesn't it? The Venus/Mars midpoint symbolizes many things that all fall under the umbrella of sexual passion and desire.*
> *—Basil Fearrington*

With the composite chart, we would never combine Venus and Mars, however. It would only involve combining *my Venus with your Venus*, or *my Mars with your Mars*. So, in a sense, the planetary energies stay very pure and one-dimensional. But we need to be careful about going too far with that idea. Unless your Mars and mine are both in the same house and sign, making the same aspects in the chart, they are rather different creatures.

And our composite Mars is yet a third creature, different from yours and different from mine, alien to both of us, but ever-present in our relationship.

Once we've gone through the process of finding the midpoints between your planets and mine, we've got a list of planetary positions. We can learn quite a lot from it from it, but really to get to the heart of the matter, we need to place those planets in the context of a chart. We need an Ascendant and a Midheaven. We need houses. And that's where a variety of viewpoints enter the picture.

Systems of House Division

One of the first headaches faced by a student of astrology lies in choosing which of several systems of house division to use. Most systems, but not all, agree on the location of the Ascendant and the Midheaven—Meridian houses will give you a funny Ascendant, and the Equal House system, which comes in two versions, gives you a choice between a Midheaven that floats like a loose cannon somewhere up near the top of the chart, or an Ascendant that does the same thing somewhere over on the chart's left hand side. All the varying systems place the cusps of houses two, three, five, six, eight, nine, eleven and twelve in different places, leading to much contention among astrologers.

To us, one point is evident: the very existence of all this controversy suggests that there is really no ultimate right answer to the question of which house system is "correct." Perhaps all or most of them work in slightly different ways, or perhaps there is a "right" one that is simply awaiting the right genius to discover it.

The majority of astrological teachers tend to solve this dilemma via "papal bull." We won't do that to you! Try several systems, working with the charts of more than a few people you know very well. Let the experience speak to you. Pick the house system that works best for you with those charts.

We've done that, and we've chosen the Placidus system, which we'll be using throughout the rest of this book. In our hands, it seems to be the system that is most consistently resonant with the sorts of questions we ask, in terms of both the birthchart and the composite chart.

Where are the cusps?

Intuitively, we might think that the most logically consistent way to proceed with the creation of the houses in a composite chart would be to take the midpoint of your Ascendant and mine, the midpoint of your second house cusp and mine, the midpoint of your third house cusp and mine, and so on. This system has many adherents, but there are some problems with it.

A few paragraphs back, we looked at an example where two people's Moons were in a nearly exact opposition. One was in 15 degrees 59 minutes of Capricorn and the other in 15 degrees 58 minutes of Cancer. We noted that their composite Moon would be in 15 degrees 58.5 minutes of Aries. It would be there, rather than in Libra, because that's the *slightly* shorter angle between those two Moon placements. But if you are imagining a tossed coin balancing momentarily on its edge and ready to fall either way, you are on the right page!

Without getting too deeply into the spherical trigonometry that underlies house systems, it suffices to say that for two people born at different latitudes, this can get very messy. We might find that the midpoint of their Ascendants gives a composite Ascendant at 15 degrees Pisces—but the midpoint of their second house cusp falls at 15 *Libra* (when common sense about the natural order of the signs suggests it should be Aries). The reason is that with near-oppositions, the coin could fall either way, depending on even slight differences of birth-latitude.

Many astrologers use this system anyway. They get around the problem of the zodiac sometimes getting out of whack through the simple device of just arbitrarily putting it back in order! They find the composite Ascendant in the usual way, and they let it "rationalize" the rest of the houses. In the example above, they would put that second house cusp at 15 Aries, even though the pure mathematics would say 15 Libra.

This is not the method we favor, but it works pretty well. Typically, the differences between it and the way we do it are small. That makes it easier to live with the problem, but harder to resolve it.

A slight variation on this system is to begin with the Midheaven rather than the Ascendant, and let the Midheaven rationalize the other houses.

With a computer program doing your calculations, know this: *if you're not prompted to enter a location (city and state or country) for the composite chart, you have opted for some variation of the system described above*. A few harrowing minutes with the dreaded manual of your computer program at least ought to let you know what the program is doing, and probably allow you to toggle between an Ascendant-based calculation and one based on the Midheaven.

Again, this system is not the one we favor, but as with house systems, we encourage you to let your own experience be your guide. We'll tell you what *we* think, but we won't tell you *what* to think!

Location, Location, Location!

Here's how the system we use works:

You calculate the composite Midheaven, which is simply the midpoint of the two natal Midheavens. Then you set up the rest of the houses based on that Midheaven, but *for the place where the couple first met.*

A variation on this approach is to use the composite Ascendant as the base instead of the Midheaven.

Again, a little time with the manual should reveal how your computer is "thinking."

If your composite chart calculation requires you to enter a place, know that it's one of these two systems in play.

The Midheaven-based and location-based system we employ with our clients, and which we will use throughout this book, is simply the one that has proven most consistently relevant to the realities people are actually experiencing—at least as we observe those realities!

Enough of This Open-Mindedness!

There is one techie piece about which we are adamant. We encourage you never to use the place where the couple is currently living as the basis of their composite chart. *Always use the place where they first met.* Often the two places are the same, of course, and the question becomes moot. But in the modern world, it is not unusual for a couple to have met in college in Miami, but then moved to Los Angeles. In such a case, use the Miami chart!

Astrology is absolutely consistent in its focus on beginnings. That is perhaps the keystone of the entire system: that the planetary patterns at the *beginning* of something describe the nature and intentions of the entity, be it a person, a business or an idea. We do speak of transitory forces affecting that initial chart, but they would have no meaning in a vacuum. They always need the chart of the "first breath" as something upon which they can act.

There is no reason to make an exception for the composite chart.

There are some truly profound issues at stake behind this seemingly rather picky issue. A birthchart—and, as we will be seeing on the following pages, the composite chart—gives us perspective on the soul's history and its present evolutionary intentions. It describes karmic wounds from long ago, patterns of strength and weakness that might be repeated, and much about the actual underlying purpose of the life. *It is a sacred document, reflecting the effects on the present of a long past which, by definition, cannot be changed, and which gives meaning to the present.* To us, it is ludicrous—and, frankly, it is tempting to say almost blasphemous—to imagine a couple could change all that by moving to Los Angeles!

So, for the really deep perspective, stick with the chart based on the place of the partners' first meeting.

With all that said, let's add that re-doing the composite chart for the place the couple is currently located is not a taboo, so long as you understand what you are seeing. Most astrologers, ourselves included, routinely "relocate" birthcharts in order to get a fix on what kinds of energies will be emphasized in a new place. That's an effective and helpful technique, but it doesn't erase the birthchart. It works more like "permanent transits" in the new place. Ditto for the relocated composite chart.

But We Met on the Internet!

You'll run into that theme a lot nowadays. Two people living hundreds of miles apart have actually developed quite a complex relationship long before they actually set eyes on each other. Frankly, unlike most of the rest of what we write about in these pages, we haven't had very wide experience with this issue. Currently, we are torn between two techniques:

Number One. Sooner or later, those two people will meet in person. Go ahead and treat everything in the conventional way, setting up the chart for the point of their first meeting.

The possibility of using astrological "magic" to "choose the optimal place" for the meeting arises here. But be careful! Say that God's plan is that you have a brief but highly instructive affair with each other, and much is learned and no harm is done—but instead you "elect" a place for the first meeting that emphasizes home, commitment, and biological fertility!

It might, in other words, be best to let things take their natural course in terms of where you first get together, then set up the chart and learn from it.

Number Two. If I'm in New York and you are in Maryland, then somewhere in the wilds of New Jersey there is *a physical point precisely halfway between us.* You can set up a chart for that point, as if the couple had met there. Theoretically, the idea is that this is exactly what we really do anyway—except that in a conventional composite chart, the "midpoint of our locations" probably lies about a foot from my heart and a foot from yours, right between us.

Finding this location-midpoint is actually very easy if you have access to modern astrological computer programs. In the synastry section, you'll see an option for another kind of joint chart called either a "relationship chart" or a "Davison chart." It's a simple, intuitive technique, which in our experience simply isn't as powerful as the composite chart. Such a chart is set up for the physical place midway between our two birth places, and for the moment in time precisely halfway between your birth-moment and my own. Enter the data, set up the Davison chart—then jot down the latitude and longitude it has calculated. Start over, using that as "the place where the couple met."

We Met in Paris, But Didn't Really Get Together Until . . .

You'll hear that one a lot too. In general, go for the earliest meeting, provided the two people were even dimly aware of each other! If one of them remembers the meeting, but the other one in all honesty does not, chances are good that the best chart will be the one for the place where they first truly became conscious of each other.

When you are not sure which location to use, set them both up and see which one resonates best with their realities and self-perceptions.

What About Other Kinds of Relationships?

You have a composite chart with the person who happens to sit next to you on the flight to Chicago. You have one with the check-out girl at the grocery, and one with your uncle who comes from the planet of bow ties and bourbon whiskey. You have one with your dog. Your cat has one with you.

If we know these charts, we will see them in action—maybe you and that person on the flight to Chicago are a Gemini with five planets in the third house. If so, you'll talk all the way to the Windy City. And then of course never see each other again.

The rule of thumb is fairly obvious: *the more significant the relationship, the more important the composite chart, and the more nuanced will be its material and psychological expression.*

Naturally, our significant sexual relationships tend to be among our most spiritually and psychologically evocative human connections. The principles we describe in these pages tend to work most vividly there, although with a bit of commonsensical translation, they'll work with other forms of relationship as well.

Multiple Composites

What about relationships among three or more people? That is a very complex subject. The entire basis of composite theory lies in the simple process of finding the midpoint between two points on the zodiac.

But what is the "midpoint" between *three* such points? What, in other words, is the sound of one hand clapping?

Try to visualize it. Intuition can do it—approximately. But not really rigorously. That creates a big problem in terms of trying to come up with composite charts for families, multiple-partner relationships or multiple-person friendships.

Here's a technique worth exploring. Define Aries as 0 degrees through 30 degrees, Taurus as 30 degrees through 60 degrees, and so on. That way a planet in, say, 19 degrees of Cancer would be located "109 degrees" along the ecliptic. (The beginning of Cancer would be 90 degrees. Add the 19 degrees to arrive at the 109 degrees.) That way, you convert all the planetary positions to a 360 degree system, based on the start of the zodiac in Aries.

To find, for example, the composite Mercury of three people, convert all their Mercury positions into this 360 degree notation. Add up those three numbers. Divide the result by three. Take that number and convert it back into a degree of the zodiac. If your answer were 277 degrees, that would mean that their composite Mercury was in 7 degrees of Capricorn.

Similarly, establish the composite Midheaven, and use the place where the group first came together for determining the house cusps.

This is called a "group chart" in many of the current computer calculation programs. We've had pretty good luck with it, but there are some logical issues around it, as we've described. Taste and see!

Other Kinds of Joint Charts

There are many other ways to join two or more charts. In this volume, we concentrate on the composite chart for the simple reason that, in our opinion, it is the most evocative, relevant and powerful of all these techniques. Among the other possibilities, the most intuitively obvious choice is probably also the composite chart's chief rival. That one is simple event chart set up for the birth of the relationship.

The First Meeting Chart. Jodie and Steve met a little before 2:00 p.m. on December 16, 1981. The chart is Venus-ruled (Taurus rising) and has an eighth house Sagittarian Sun conjunct Neptune and Mercury, with Jupiter almost exactly on the cusp of the "House of Marriage." It's very clearly a chart that speaks of serious intimacy and commitment, and it even makes that rather obvious Mercury/Neptune reference to "mystical" writing and publishing!

This technique works quite well, in other words, and most of the approaches to reading the composite chart could also be translated into the context of interpreting event charts such as these. They have one tragic flaw, however: *it is exceedingly rare that two people are looking at their watches when they first meet.* Total strangers have little motivation to note the time they meet—and even if we're hearing the proverbial violins, looking at our watches is usually the furthest thing from our minds! Thus, very typically, this promising technique founders on the lack of accurate data.

The Davison or "Relationship" Chart. We mentioned this technique above. It's another "real-time" chart, except that it's set up for a place exactly midway between the two birth places, and for a moment of time exactly midway between the two birth dates. It has relevance and power. We simply don't find its message quite as trenchant as that of the composite chart. We encourage you to explore it anyway if you find its logic compelling.

By the way, even though it's common to hear the Davison chart and the relationship chart described as synonymous, there is a slight technical distinction between them. In the true Davison chart, the space-and-time midpoints are calculated based on a strict mathematical "mean" of the data, whereas in the relationship chart, the spherical trigonometry of "Great Circles" is used for establishing the place that lies midway between the two birth places. The results are typically very close, so knowing which technique is right is difficult. Our experience with these charts is too limited to warrant a comment about which method is preferable.

The Coalescent Chart. Again, we have no experience here. What is a coalescent chart? According to Matrix Software's Winstar II program's Help file, "Each planet in the coalescent chart is calculated from a different harmonic, which is a result of the angular difference of the two positions of that planet in the two charts being compared. The resultant harmonic number is multiplied by the degree number of either person's planet (the result will be the same) to arrive at the degree of the coalescent planet." If you can figure out what that means, go ahead and give it a try! As usual, our aim is to write about what we *do* know, and refrain from commenting on the rest.

CHAPTER TWO: A FEW EXAMPLES

Let's look at some composite charts, just so you can see what we're talking about. A picture is worth a thousand words . . .

First, we'd like to tell you about our sources. Couples' meeting places were researched on the Internet and come from official websites, bios or interviews. All the birth data for the charts we use in this book have a Rodden Rating of "A" or higher, with the exception of Duke Ellington's chart, which has a Rodden Rating of "C."

What are Rodden Ratings? The late astrologer Lois Rodden spent the last 40 years of her life collecting birth data for other astrologers. Mark McDonough, president of AstroDataBank Company, worked with Lois for six years to organize her data into a vast CD-ROM database, distributed as a software product, "Lois Rodden's AstroDataBank." We love it for both reference and research, not to mention those late night dinners with our astro-buddies when we get a sudden urge to look up someone's birth chart. Here's what www.astrodatabank.com says about the Rodden Ratings:

> "AA, A, and B data are the only data that should be used in astrological studies. Data rated 'AA' (from birth certificate or birth record) are the most accurate obtainable. Data rated 'A' (from memory) are usually accurate, but there are exceptions. Politicians and entertainers are notorious for giving misleading birth dates and times, except when consulting their astrologer. 'B' data (from biographies) are similarly accurate because authors who give times are likely to have obtained the data from the subject, the subject's immediate family, or from a birth record.
>
> Data rated 'C' (caution) are not reliable, since they have no direct link to their source. In all cases where there is no source or data classification, the data can only be considered hypothetical. Similarly, data that is quoted 'from *The Mountain Astrologer* magazine' or 'from Rodden' is a quote from a reference and not a direct source. Where did these reference sources get the data? If that is not known, these data must be given a data source of 'original source not known' and a Rodden Rating of

'C.' All rectified data are also rated 'C.' Some astrologers consider rectified times more accurate than birth times. Unfortunately, there is no consensus on how to rectify birth times. Thus, one astrologer's ultra-accurate rectified time may contradict another astrologer's ultra-accurate rectified time. Until there is a standard and proven rectification method, you should treat all rectified data with caution."

Other Rodden Ratings are: DD, "dirty data," with two conflicting sources; X, data with no time of birth; and XX, data without a known or confirmed date. But again, everything we're using is rated "AA" or "A," except for Duke Ellington's birthchart's Rodden rating of "C." Ellington's chart was rectified from an approximate time by the late well-known astrologer and author Ronald Davison (inventor of the Davison chart), and we would tend to trust his work.

Duke Ellington was born to middle-class African-American parents on April 29, 1899 at 1:25 a.m. in Washington, DC. Please see page 23 for his birthchart. His official website (www.dukeellington.com) says: "By the time of his passing, he was considered amongst the world's greatest composers and musicians. The French government honored him with their highest award, the Legion of Honor, while the government of the United States bestowed upon him the highest civil honor, the Presidential Medal of Freedom. He played for the royalty and for the common people and by the end of his 50-year career, he had played over 20,000 performances worldwide."

That paragraph doesn't capture the grace and presence of Ellington's Venus-ruled Taurean Sun, nor the cool, enigmatic, urbane demeanor of his Aquarian Ascendant and Moon-Saturn conjunction in Sagittarius. He all but epitomized the style and elegance of the Big Band era. In his teens he began to dress with such precocious flair that he was nicknamed "Duke," and the name stuck. His middle school taught flawless manners as a point of pride, and that manners could help carry the students past prejudice. Later, that style and those manners would help Ellington move at ease among all walks of life, social classes, types of musicians—and help land him numerous gigs. We do well to learn to use our second house planets as resources, and Ellington had both Venus and Mercury in Aries in the second house.

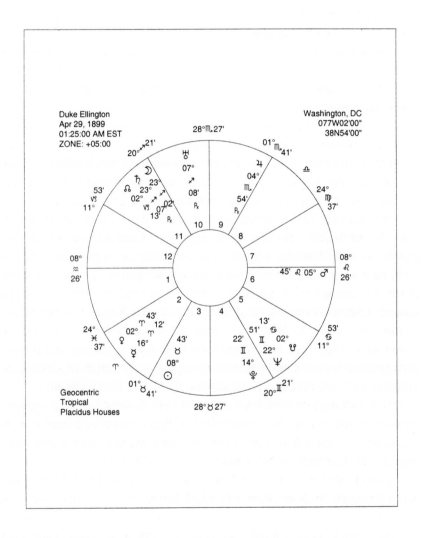

Duke Ellington
Apr 29, 1899
01:25:00 AM EST
ZONE: +05:00

Washington, DC
077W02'00"
38N54'00"

Geocentric
Tropical
Placidus Houses

He soaked up influences and inspiration from anywhere and everywhere, wrote incessantly and composed over 900 songs—third house Sun, and a Moon-Saturn conjunction's need for achievement. He was a team leader—eleventh house Moon-Saturn conjunction—whose band produced polished performances, even when some of them were subject to various forms of anti-social behavior and bickering. With each individual player in mind, he wrote parts that made all their solos shine (Aquarian Ascendant and eleventh house Moon). His band played all over the world—eleventh house Sagittarian Moon again—and with such jazz luminaries as Miles Davis, Cab Calloway, Dizzy Gillespie, Ella Fitzgerald, Tony Bennett and Louis Armstrong.

Yet Ellington was very much his own person. His mother, Daisy Ellington, told him he was blessed and special. Many mothers feel that way about their children. Yet Daisy also told Duke that he must allow nothing to stop him, that he must ignore all the supposed barriers and naysayers around him, and that he could do anything anyone else could do—heady and daring advice for an African-American child born in the Washington, D.C. of 1899, and perfect for Ellington's Aquarian ascendant. His granddaughter, Mercedes Ellington, has said that the highest compliment Duke paid was to call someone was "beyond categories," because he hated labels and categories of any sort (Aquarian Ascendant). He wrote some groundbreaking work, including "Black, Brown and Beige: A Tone Parallel to the History of the Negro in America," an orchestral piece in three movements. That work may sound tame by today's standards, but its first performance was a smashing success in the very different climate of January, 1943 (Aquarian ascendant ruled by a tenth house Uranus).

His granddaughter Mercedes also said that, musically, Duke's genius must have led him to feel lonely and isolated, and that meeting Billy Strayhorn must have been a great joy for them both. Strayhorn's chart is on page 25. He was born on November 29, 1915 at 4:15 a.m. in Dayton, OH.

He and Ellington were very different. When the confident Ellington was still a teenager, he dropped out of school, formed his own band, and used to send a friend ahead to his gigs to announce "Make way for the Duke!" But the conservatory-trained Strayhorn was shy as a young man, later becoming warm and gregarious, although he remained very modest and unassuming. We suspect that his humility may have come from his Sun and Venus in his second house, the house where we are learning about self-esteem, as well as from his Virgo Moon. Yet the tenth house position of his

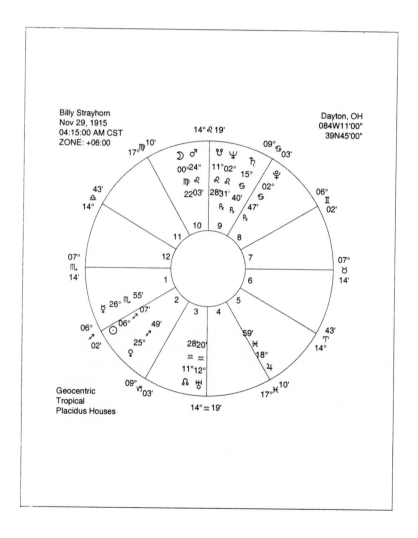

Moon and its conjunction to his Scorpio Ascendant's co-ruler, Mars in Leo, must have made him yearn to excel at his work, despite his self-effacement. He probably loved to perform, too, with a fifth house Piscean Jupiter, yet Strayhorn didn't cut anything like Ellington's imposing figure; he was short, slight and bespectacled. When he met Ellington at one of his performances in Pittsburgh in December 1938, the twenty-three-year-old Strayhorn had been playing the local music scene for years, but still had a day job as a drugstore clerk. The fortyish Ellington was so impressed with Strayhorn's rendition of Duke's "Sophisticated Lady," as well as with Strayhorn's own compositions, that he asked the young man to visit him in New York City. Strayhorn composed a piece inspired by Ellington's directions to his apartment: "Take the A Train." It would become world famous as Ellington's band's theme song.

Although neither man was certain exactly what Strayhorn's role would be, he joined Ellington's band, and within a year had made himself indispensable arranging, composing, and covering the piano chair if Ellington needed it done. They were collaborators for almost 30 years, devoted to one another, their music, and Ellington's band. Strayhorn learned so fast—first house Mercury—and their musical styles had melded so seamlessly that today's scholars say that Strayhorn's role has been underestimated, and that it's hard to tell who actually wrote what.

That's what scholars think. What did the poised and self-contained Ellington think? He said, "Billy Strayhorn was my right arm, my left arm, and all the eyes in the back of my head. My brainwaves are in his head and his in mine." Volume Seven of Ken Burns's *Jazz* documentary has some remarkable footage of Ellington talking about Strayhorn. To paraphrase that footage, Ellington said that he might be on the road in Los Angeles and get stuck on something he was composing, and rather than tough it out, he'd phone "Strays." Ellington would say that he was doing something in E flat, and he had a guy walking up a road and didn't know if the guy should turn right or left or do a U turn. First, Strayhorn would say, "Oh yes, I know what you mean" (empathic Scorpio Ascendant), and then "I'm sure that you could do that better than I" (the humility of the Virgo Moon and the second house Sun and Venus). But, added Ellington, looking both amused and respectful, all the while Strayhorn was thinking how he could outdo Ellington (Strayhorn's Moon-Mars conjunction, and Mars in Leo in the tenth house square his first house Scorpio Mercury). Then the two of them would discuss the piece for a while and come up with virtually the same solution, simultaneously.

Their composite chart is on page 28. The entity formed by their relationship is a second house Aquarian with a Sun-Venus conjunction and with Venus also conjunct Mercury, the Sun trine a tenth house Libra Moon, and Sagittarius rising with Uranus and Jupiter conjunct in Capricorn in the first house.

First, their composite Sun is in Aquarius, whose archetypes are the Exile, the Truth-sayer, the Non-conformist, and the Genius. Given the phenomenal quality and quantity of their music, the archetype of the Genius makes a lot of sense here, and that's certainly how Ellington is regarded. The natural expression of this relationship breaks the rules and thinks outside of the box. What rules did they break? That's hard to say from a distance, but one comes to mind: "relationships should always be totally equal in every possible way." Strayhorn, a virtually equal collaborator, seemed quite content to let Ellington be the star. Ellington had the big name. Ellington was "the guy." That inequality in their relative fame must have come in part from the difference in their ages, and from the fact that Ellington was already well-known when he met Strayhorn. For all we know, they had bitter disagreements over calling the band "The Duke Ellington Orchestra." But we doubt that was the case. Feuding musicians generally don't collaborate as well and as seamlessly and for as long as these two did, nor take such pleasure in their work together. And here's a strong response to that second house Sun: they had *confidence* in their work together, confidence in the relationship, confidence in one another. Mutual affection was there too; their composite Sun was conjunct Venus in Aquarius, the goddess of love and the creative arts in the sign of the Genius. Shared creativity fed their relationship. Their communication must have helped facilitate the composing process, with Mercury also conjunct Venus. And what a Mercury in Aquarius way Ellington used to describe that process: he had "a guy walking down the road and didn't know if the guy should turn right or left or do a U turn."

What about their composite Libran Moon? Libra is a Venus-ruled sign, and the heart of their relationship was in the arts, in their music. The music of that period was quintessentially Libran, too: stylish, polished, elegant and balanced. Bands wore suits; singers wore sequined gowns. Sophistication mattered. Their composite Moon was in the tenth house, and they shared a Libran public identity through performing their music with

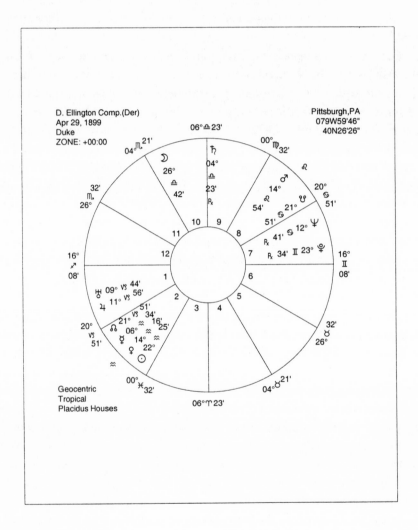

D. Ellington Comp.(Der)
Apr 29, 1899
Duke
ZONE: +00:00

Pittsburgh,PA
079W59'46"
40N26'26"

06°♎23'

04°♏21'

☽ 26° ♎ 42'

♄ 04° ♎ 23' ℞

00° ♍ 32'

♌

♂ 14° ♌ 54'

☋ 21°

20° ♋ 51'

32' ♏ 26°

♋ 51'

℞ 41' ♋ Ψ 12°

10

9

8

℞ 34' ♊ 23' ♇

11

12

7

16° ♐ 08'

6

16° ♊ 08'

1

♅ 09° ♑ 44' ♃ 11° ♑ 56'

2

5

21° ♑ 51' ☊ 06° ♒ 34' ☿ 14° ♒ 16' 25'

3

4

32' ♉ 26°

20° ♑ 51'

♀ 22°

⊙

♒

04° ♉ 21'

Geocentric
Tropical
Placidus Houses

00° ♓ 32'

06° ♈ 23'

their orchestra. Here's a classic good response to the composite tenth house Moon: finding the right work for each person and supporting one another in that work. The acclaim that their music earned must have been profoundly gratifying to them, too.

All that performing involved a lot of traveling, which must have nourished their composite Sagittarian Ascendant, the mask of the gypsy. A couple with this composite Ascendant needs to take risks, to take leaps of faith, to engage fully and heartily with life and not be Sister Prudence—all the more so with the chart ruler Jupiter in the first house and conjunct Uranus. Ellington took a risk inviting Strayhorn to visit him in New York City on the strength of one meeting, and Strayhorn took a risk in going, and in writing "Take the A Train" to take with him. In the light of their composite Sagittarian Ascendant, that tune takes on a whole new meaning!

Let's look at another composite chart, that of Arnold Schwarzenegger and Maria Shriver. Schwarzenegger was born on July 30, 1947 at 4:10 a.m. in Graz, Austria. Shriver was born on November 6, 1955 at 5:12 p.m. in Chicago, IL. They met at a tennis match in Forest Hills, NY. Please see their birthcharts and composite chart on pages 30, 31 and 32.

Schwarzenegger is a second house Leo with a Sun-Saturn-Pluto conjunction, a sixth house Capricorn Moon, and Cancer rising with Mercury conjunct the Ascendant and Venus in Cancer in the first house. A weaker response to his Sun-Saturn-Pluto second house stellium could have left him insecure and lacking in confidence, and a weaker response to his sixth house Capricorn Moon could have him feeling underemployed, subservient and somehow lesser than his colleagues. He's said to have been a rather shy boy—Cancer Ascendant. However, whatever one may think of Schwarzenegger's politics or personality, he's now a strong-willed, self-made man, who's used Saturnian shrewdness and persistence and Plutonian insight, as well as Leonine presence and Venusian charm, to get where he is today.

Longtime friends have said that his childhood goals were to move to America, become an actor and marry a Kennedy. To those ends, he trained as a bodybuilder despite his parents' opposition. When his father said he could go to the gym only three times a week, Arnold built a gym at home. There's his sixth house Capricorn Moon finding a way around the obstacle: if he couldn't go to the tools, he would bring the tools to him. After a string of victorious European bodybuilding competitions, in 1968 he moved to America, as he had planned, with a duffel bag of clothes and about twenty

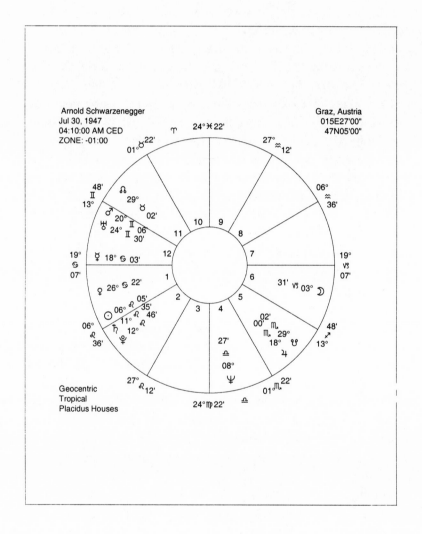

Arnold Schwarzenegger
Jul 30, 1947
04:10:00 AM CED
ZONE: -01:00

Graz, Austria
015E27'00"
47N05'00"

Geocentric
Tropical
Placidus Houses

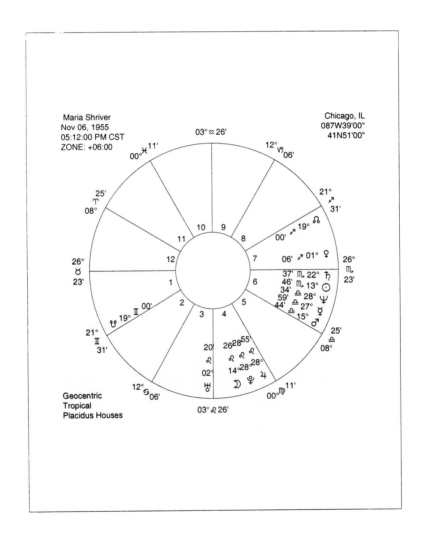

Maria Shriver
Nov 06, 1955
05:12:00 PM CST
ZONE: +06:00

Chicago, IL
087W39'00"
41N51'00"

03° ≈ 26'

00° ⋇ 11'

12° ♑ 06'

25'
♈
08°

21°
♐
31'

00' ♐ 19° ☊

26°
♉
23'

06' ♐ 01° ♀

26°
♏
23'

37' ♏ 22° ♄
46' ♏ 13° ☉
34' ♎ 28° ♆
59' ♎ 27° ☿
44' ♎ 15° ♂

♋ 19° ♊ 00'

25'
♎
08°

21°
♊
31'

20'
♌
02°
♅

26° 28° 55'
♌ ♌
14° 28° 28°
☽ ♀ ♃

00° ♍ 11'

12° ♋ 06'

03° ♌ 26'

Geocentric
Tropical
Placidus Houses

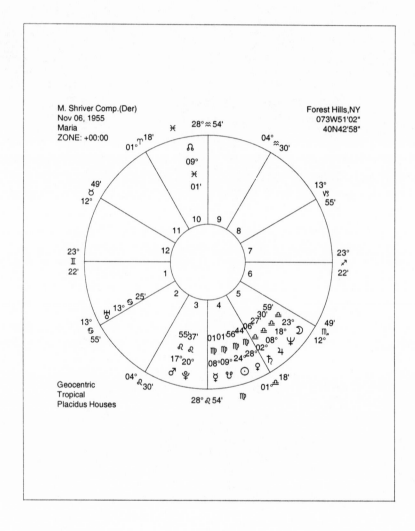

M. Shriver Comp.(Der)
Nov 06, 1955
Maria
ZONE: +00:00

Forest Hills,NY
073W51'02"
40N42'58"

Geocentric
Tropical
Placidus Houses

dollars. He could barely speak English. Placing second in his first American Mr. Universe competition in 1968 galled him, despite his various international wins (Leo Sun), so he trained harder (Sun-Saturn conjunction and sixth house Capricorn Moon) and won Mr. Universe in 1970 for the first of seven times, defeating one of his boyhood idols, Reg Park. Schwarzenegger has said: "It is one thing to idolize heroes. It is quite another to visualize yourself in their place. When I saw great people, I said to myself, 'I can be there.' (sixth house Capricorn Moon)"

In 1970, he got his first movie role. Although it got off to a rocky start from his accent and his last name, his acting career continued. In 1977, his autobiography, *Arnold Schwarzenegger: The Education of a Bodybuilder* was a big success, probably helped by his role as himself in 1974's *Pumping Iron*. Note that first house Mercury and publication—although becoming an author hadn't been on his list of goals, it certainly helped him accomplish them. In 1978 he met Maria Shriver, the niece of John F. Kennedy, Robert Kennedy and Teddy Kennedy. The attraction was immediate. He's supposed to have told her mother, Eunice Kennedy Shriver, "Your daughter has a great body." That Sun-Pluto conjunction is not hesitant about potentially charged statements!

Maria Shriver is a sixth house Scorpio with a Sun-Saturn conjunction, a fourth house Leo Moon and Taurus rising. With five planets in the sixth house, a Sun-Saturn conjunction, and her primal triad all in fixed signs, she was extremely serious and focused about her work, and she'd set goals of her own. She wanted to become a network news anchor by the time she was thirty, and she wasn't in a big hurry to get married. Moreover, she admired her parents' marriage and wanted a strong marriage of her own: fourth house Leo Moon. She has said that she was pretty sure when she met Arnold that she would marry him. On the day they met, she asked him to spend a weekend with her family at the Kennedy family compound in Cape Cod (fourth house Leo Moon—she introduced him to the clan right away). She liked Arnold and so did her family; they all thought he was funny and unaffected, and she admired his drive—that much fixity can recognize a person of equal resolve. He liked her intelligence and willingness to speak her mind. But she was on a career track, moving up in her profession. In 1985, she got the anchor job on the CBS Morning News. She and Arnold married in 1986 after an eight-year courtship, long by today's standards, but quite natural for two goal-oriented and careful Saturn types. She kept working in high-profile jobs for CBS and NBC until Arnold's victory in the California gubernatorial election.

Their composite chart is a fourth house Virgo with a Sun-Venus conjunction, a fifth house Moon-Neptune conjunction in Libra, and Gemini rising. The composite Sun in Virgo isn't surprising for two such hard-working people. This couple needs to *grow*, both as individuals and as a couple. They'll relish and should support anything that promotes their personal or professional growth. Even so, they need to avoid too much critical nit-picking. To that end, even if they don't work together, it would be wise for them to have some ways in which they can serve their larger community. Shriver comes from a political family, and Schwarzenegger's been elected to office. They have both worked extensively in front of cameras. Arnold's been the honorary weight-lifting coach for the Special Olympics, founded by Maria's mother, since shortly after they met. Moreover, their composite Sun is in the fourth house. They need a home, a hearth, a fastness where they can retreat from all the details of their busy lives, a sense of being rooted in one place. They also need a sense of extended family. The couple has four children, and Schwarzenegger married into the close-knit Kennedy family. We don't know how the couple feels about living in Sacramento versus Los Angeles, but we're sure that they'd do well to have some land where they felt profoundly at home and where they and their relatives can "nest." They have a Sun-Venus conjunction, often seen in the composite charts of couples who are either in love, engaged in creative work together, or both. Remember their immediate mutual attraction, despite their natal Sun-Saturn caution? The Sun-Venus conjunction is often seen in the charts of people who are close friends. Two people with a composite Sun-Venus conjunction simply *like,* as well as love, one another, and the balm of that Venusian fondness can be applied to many a rough spot.

Meanwhile, their Moon-Neptune conjunction in Libra reflects not only the glamour that surrounds them, but also their ability to work through their differences. Arnold's a Republican and Maria is a Democrat, from what amounts to a Democratic dynasty. Each needs to feel reciprocated in what he or she gives to the other and to the relationship. Shriver wasn't enthralled with the idea of Schwarzenegger's running for governor, but she has said that when she realized how much he believed in it and wanted to do it, she wanted to be as supportive of him as he'd always been supportive of her and her goals and career.

Their children are natural teachers for one of the needs of their fifth house Moon: the ability to play. Hard-working though their composite Virgo Sun is, they need some time for inspired silliness, and relaxation or creativity as its own reward. With their composite Moon in the house of romance, they also need to remain wonderfully attentive to each other.

Their composite Ascendant in Gemini indicates a need for a lively, *interesting* life together, not just busyness for its own sake. Their high comfort level with the media is a big plus here, as are Arnold's focus on education and Maria's news programs. In a joint TV appearance on *Oprah*, they were poised and articulate. Shriver has said that when they met, she thought she would have a challenging life with him, and an interesting one. That's grist for the mill for a composite Ascendant in Gemini.

The third composite chart we'll examine here is that of actors Nicolas Cage and Patricia Arquette. They met in the late 1980s and dated briefly, then met again in 1995 and married shortly thereafter. They divorced amicably in 2001, have remained friends, and speak respectfully of one another. Please see their birthcharts and composite charts on pages 36, 37 and 38.

Born January 7, 1964 at 5:30 a.m. in Harbor City, CA, Nicolas Cage is a first house Capricorn with a wide Mercury-Sun-Mars conjunction, a tenth house Libra Moon, and Sagittarius rising. He's the nephew of Francis Ford Coppola, but wanted to prove he could succeed without the famous name, so he changed his last name to Cage in 1983 (a self-willed first house Capricorn Sun-Mars: accomplishing the Capricorn "great work" alone). We were amused to read that his first successful role was in childhood, when he pretended to be his own "Cousin Roy" in order to menace a bully who'd been taking his snacks (first house Capricorn Sun-Mars again). He studied acting as a teenager and dropped out of high school for acting work; there's the Sagittarian Ascendant's taste for experience, as well as the first house Capricorn Sun's drive and focus. He's been drawn to "Method" acting, which involves the actor's creating as complete a biography of his character as possible, to help him identify with the character (tenth house Libra Moon) and therefore more fully embody the role. He's taken some unusual parts as eccentric characters in quirkish films, rather than parts that would seem to make the most sense for his career track—that's a tenth house Moon decision, to take a part because you *feel* like doing it. He's quite willing to experiment (Sagittarian Ascendant, and Venus in Aquarius). He likes to improvise; director David Lynch calls him the "jazz musician of

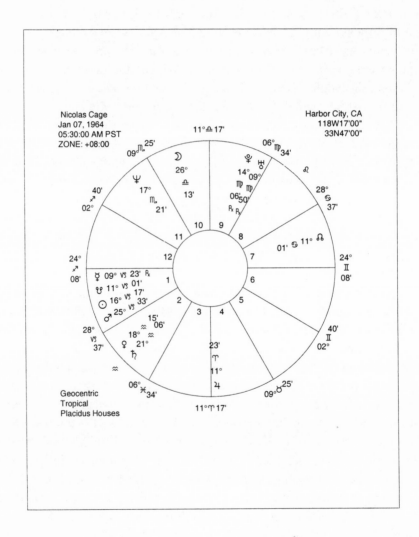

Nicolas Cage
Jan 07, 1964
05:30:00 AM PST
ZONE: +08:00

Harbor City, CA
118W17'00"
33N47'00"

11°♎17'

09°♏25'

06°♍34'

☽ 26°
♎ 13'

♀ 14°♍09'
♅
06°♍50'
℞ ℞

♌

28°
♋ 37'

♆ 17°
♏ 21'

01' ♋ 11° ♌

40'
♐ 02'

24°
♐ 08'

24°
♊ 08'

☿ 09° ♑ 23' ℞
☋ 11° ♑ 01'
☉ 16° ♑ 33'
♂ 25° ♐

15'
06'
♒

40'
♊ 02'

28°
♑ 37'

18° ♒
♀ 21°
♄

23'
♈
11°
♃

09°♉25'

06°♓34'

11°♈17'

Geocentric
Tropical
Placidus Houses

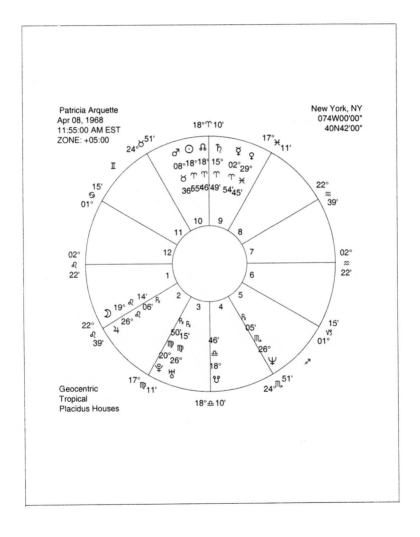

Patricia Arquette
Apr 08, 1968
11:55:00 AM EST
ZONE: +05:00

New York, NY
074W00'00"
40N42'00"

Geocentric
Tropical
Placidus Houses

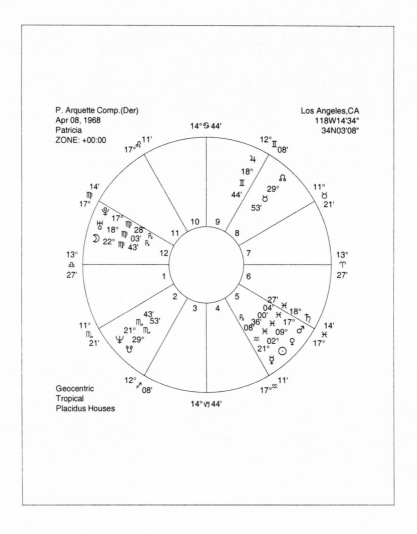

acting" (Sagittarian Ascendant, first house Mercury, and Venus in Aquarius). Cage likes classic sports cars (Sagittarian Ascendant and Sun-Mars conjunction) and comic books, which he says are modern mythology (Sagittarius Ascendant again).

Patricia Arquette was born on April 8, 1968, at 11:55 a.m. in New York City. She's a tenth house Aries with a first house Leo Moon and Leo rising. Saturn conjuncts her Sun from her ninth house. Also from a family of actors or those in acting-related professions, she grew up in a commune in northern Virginia (tenth house Aries Sun; she probably had a public identity in the community through her family's commune, even at that age). At age fifteen she ran away from home (a gutsy triple Fire primal triad) to move in with her older sister, fellow actress Rosanna Arquette (the first house Moon tends to stay connected to family). By age 18 she was getting acting roles (tenth house Aries Sun and Mars). She has great range as an actress, able to move easily from comedy to drama to terror (first house Leo Moon, and Venus in Pisces). She's also truthful and direct (Aries Sun, first house Moon) and says her acting goal is to work on movies that she really likes. She's also said that she wants to be the sort of artist who takes risky projects—Mars in Taurus in the tenth house. She has a nurturing side, too (first house Moon), handing out poison ivy remedies on the set, and being involved in the search for a cure for breast cancer since she lost her mother to that disease in 1997.

The couple's composite chart is a fifth house Pisces with a Sun-Venus conjunction, and Mars and Saturn (in the sixth house) widely conjunct Venus, Libra rising and a twelfth house Moon-Uranus-Pluto conjunction in Virgo. With that Piscean fifth house stellium and a Libran Ascendant, we can expect these two to have a highly romantic story (and one that perhaps would be hard to live up to, given the inevitable Saturnian realities of day-to-day living . . .). With their composite Moon-Uranus contact, we can also expect that story to be an unconventional one, and with Mars's involvement in the composite fifth house Piscean stellium, perhaps an impulsive one.

When they met in a Los Angeles deli, Cage was so smitten with Arquette that he told her he loved her and was going to marry her. She turned him down. Undaunted, he asked her for a quest, for things he could do to prove his love for her—composite fifth house Sun-Venus-Mars in Pisces! She thought he was a little strange, but took a napkin and made a list of dragons he would have to slay, including getting her J.D. Salinger's autograph and a black orchid. He began working his way through the list, buying a

Salinger letter and spray-painting an orchid black (there are no black ones in nature). At that point she agreed to go on a trip with him, but not to marry him. Still, she got unnerved and broke it off within a few weeks. They dated other people, and Nicolas had a son, Weston, with actress Christina Fulton. He and Patricia ran into each other in 1995, eight years after their first meeting, and *in the same deli where they'd first met* (fifth house Piscean stellium goose-bump material!). Not long afterwards, she called him and proposed, and they got married on her twenty-seventh birthday. They lived in a fake castle with Gothic decor—composite Moon-Uranus-Pluto conjunction in Virgo. Again, although they divorced in 2001, they refer to each other respectfully and affectionately and have remained friends.

CHAPTER THREE: THE ETERNAL TRIANGLE

It's the year 2100. National defense claims larger and larger portions of every country's budget. Communication exists but could be improved. Arms talks and peace talks accomplish little. The deadlock frustrates the politicians as much as the populace, but no one knows how to get out of the impasse.

Then one day, astronomers pick up signals from approaching extraterrestrials, ordering us to surrender . . .

If we didn't panic in such a situation, it would be hard to imagine something more likely to unite us, force us to work out our differences and introduce change and growth into our relationship.

Couples operate the same way. A dyad, a system with two parts, can easily become locked into polarization. "You say yes; I'll say no. You want a schedule; I want to be spontaneous. You want to sleep with the window shut; I want to sleep with it open." The tendency for partners to drift into that combat zone is powerful, and damaging if allowed to continue unchecked.

No need to wait for the spaceships to arrive. In synastry, the third force is *the dynamics of the relationship itself,* represented by the composite chart. Ideally the composite chart helps cast a tie-breaking vote, assisting in the resolution of conflicts between two people. It functions as a mediating entity.

Sometimes the nature of that composite chart aligns itself with one or the other person, and sometimes with neither of them. A variety of different "political" situations can arise, depending on the inclination of the composite chart. Maybe the "extraterrestrial force" backs one side. Perhaps it terrorizes both parties, inciting a stampede out of the partnership, much as Orson Welles's radio broadcast of H. G. Wells's *War of the Worlds* provoked a panic-stricken exodus of listeners who believed that Martians really were invading the Earth.

Let's examine a few of those political balances of power formed between two birthcharts and their composite chart. We'll take some imaginary, constructed examples, and some real ones. Please remember, however, that few composite charts fall *precisely* into the following categories. They are intended only as general guidelines to help you organize your analysis.

Culture Shock

Vickie is a fourth-house Cancer with a Cancer Moon and Pisces rising. She's a reserved, gentle young woman who raises award-winning orchids. Much of her time is tranquilly spent in a fragrant greenhouse, coaxing incredible blooms from her plants. At an orchid show, Vickie meets Nathan when their flowers tie for first prize. Nathan owns a greenhouse fifty miles away; he's a twelfth-house Capricorn with Pisces rising and a first-house Pisces Moon. These dreamy, introverted people are surprised and pleased when they strike up a friendship that quickly deepens into love. But their friends are flabbergasted when Vickie and Nathan take a safari down the Amazon together in search of rare orchid specimens. Six months ago, the prospect of even getting the shots needed for such a journey would have traumatized them. What happened?

Vickie and Nathan's composite chart shows the Sun and Moon both in Aries and the first house, with Aries rising. The *logic of their relationship itself* demands that they as a couple share adventurous experiences, face challenges, and enthusiastically engage themselves with life. Fourth-house Cancer or twelfth-house Capricorn experiential food, which would sustain them as individuals, will starve them as a steady diet if they stay together.

But if Vickie forces herself to live in a gung-ho world that is completely alien to her, she will feel crazy, cut off from her fourth-house Cancer center—just as crazy as Nathan will feel if he bends over backward to live a lifestyle equally foreign to his twelfth-house Capricorn energy.

Their composite chart, wildly at odds with their birthcharts, shows that Vickie and Nathan are in *Culture Shock*. To maintain that kind of bond requires incredible adjustments from both partners. Can such a couple stay together? Certainly, if each person is willing to make those compromises, and if their lives are structured so that each person has enough time alone to be able to recharge. It's difficult to stay sane when cut off for too long from the experiences symbolized by one's birthchart.

Couples in Culture Shock need three kinds of experiences, one kind for each partner and one for the couple itself. In our example, Vickie might take time alone in her greenhouse, Nathan on the road to orchid shows, and the two of them together on those Arian safaris. Each type of experience—his, hers, and that of the couple—should be granted equal importance for the happiness of Vickie, Nathan, and their relationship.

If you and your mate are in Culture Shock, recognize that too much togetherness is not what you need. Be generous about allotting one another "space," autonomy, separate friends, hobbies, vacations, or apartments. But be sure to create an area in your lives where you participate together in the experiences indicated by the composite chart, or your bond will not be fed. Value the gift of Culture Shock: it can keep you from becoming too set in your ways.

The Nicolas Cage-Patricia Arquette composite chart, discussed in the previous chapter, is an example of Culture Shock. Cage has a first house Capricorn Sun conjunct Mars and Mercury, a tenth house Libra Moon and Sagittarius rising. He needs to accomplish Capricornian Great Works that will involve courage, will-power, following his own choices without being swayed by a need for approval, and possibly leadership (Sun-Mars conjunction in Capricorn in the first house—this must be a bit like living in the head of a hammer!). He has an emotional need for a career where he can express himself subjectively and artistically, quite possibly while working with others (tenth house Libra Moon). He has a big appetite for new experiences and adventures (Sagittarius rising and a first house Mercury).

Meanwhile, Arquette is a tenth house Aries with a first house Leo Moon and Leo rising. She needs to develop courage and spirit and take risks in the area of life we call career and public identity, where her vocation, astrologically, is Warrior, Heroine, Pioneer and Daredevil. All of the above is also supported by her Sun's ruler, her tenth house Mars. She has the emotional needs of the Performer—all the creativity and the need for positive feedback—and needs to learn to act on her feelings (first house Moon) and follow her gut. Her initial presentation (Ascendant) should be warm, demonstrative, soulful and heart-centered, whereas Cage's should be gypsy-ish, articulate, strong, daring and willful.

Are you sensing some similarities? Here are two self-willed, gutsy, accomplishment-oriented, creative people.

Yet their composite chart has a fifth house Pisces Sun-Venus conjunction, with Venus also conjunct Mars and Saturn in the sixth house, Libra rising, and a twelfth house Moon-Uranus-Pluto conjunction. With the Piscean Sun and twelfth house Moon, their relationship needs a basis in mysticism, in silent, shared meditative space, in time spent perceiving the Divinity in one another. Time to free-float in inner space. Time "touching souls," as Joni Mitchell would say. Certainly there's romantic, knight-in-shining-armor energy here, with Venus and Mars in the stellium, and with

Libra rising. Their fifth house composite Sun needs to maintain that romantic energy, to maintain a sense of cherishing and wonder. It needs as much of a fairy-tale romance as possible. Yet even with their fairy tale-ish beginning, and with their composite Virgo Moon's need to express competence echoing their individual charts, and with all the best intentions in the world, their relationship may have been difficult for them to maintain, even without the fishbowl of Hollywood added to the mix. Why? Because this is Culture Shock. Simply put: how long can a first house Capricorn Sun-Mercury-Mars, and a tenth house Aries Sun, inhabit a fifth house Pisces Sun and twelfth house Moon composite "space" together without each person's feeling depleted and needing a time out?

Their bond must have been very strong. They've remained friends, and Arquette has said, "He is (a man) I have . . . really, really respected . . . I believe in him in this greater sort of forever, dignity and nobility way."

The Feudal System

Will is a fifth-house Gemini with a Leo Moon and Aquarius rising. Linda is a Taurus with a Cancer Moon and Sagittarius rising. Their composite chart shows a fifth-house Gemini Sun, a Leo Moon, and an Aquarian Ascendant. In other words, their composite chart looks much like Will's birthchart. Since they've been together, Linda has become uneasy about how Will "always gets what he wants." Linda wants to move to the West Coast; Will wants to stay in the East. Will lands a great job in the town where they live; his mother in the next county contracts a chronic disease, and Linda's job offer out west falls through. They abandon all thoughts of moving west. Then Linda wants to rent an old house in a quiet residential neighborhood north of town. Will promotes moving into a luxury condominium now and selling it in a few years. The house that Linda wants to rent is partially destroyed by a freak tornado, then Will wins a condo in a radio contest.

Beginning to appreciate that Linda might feel uneasy? That can happen when the composite chart resembles one partner's chart much more than the other's. When does that occur? There are no hard and fast rules, but keep the following guidelines in mind. When two or more signs in the composite's primal triad are the same as those in one person's chart, regardless of whether the Sun, the Moon or the Ascendant occupy those signs, that configuration constitutes a strong resemblance between the composite and that one person's chart. If a stellium in a particular house in one person's birthchart reappears in the same house in the composite chart, the two charts also resemble each other, although not so much as in the first case. If an individual's chart and the composite chart both lack any planets in one of the elements, there is a certain, fainter correspondence between them. In general, the more astrological configurations that the composite chart has in common with one of the couple's charts, and the more that the composite chart gives you the same feeling as one of the partner's charts, then the greater the resemblance between the two.

Such a partnership works like the Feudal System. There is a concentration of power in favor of the individual whose chart the composite resembles, as if life unfairly, arbitrarily gives one person every right and privilege, leaving nothing for the other person. The experiences that one person needs are precisely those that the relationship requires, and events tend to occur in such a way that what happens in the couple is what the "sovereign" wants, and the "serf" feels powerless.

A relationship with a Feudal System composite can be very touchy. The serf can accuse the sovereign of deliberately tyrannical behavior. Sadly, there may be truth in that accusation. Feudal System sovereigns rarely start out with the intention of controlling the partnership. However, the composite chart, the logic of the entity itself, favors the sovereign, and it takes a very conscious person not to abuse that power.

If you're the sovereign in such a couple, strive to become that conscious! Make every effort to consider your mate's point of view, to yield. Share your power. Such compromise creates positive outcomes: trust, openness, willing commitment and participation. Sovereigns can be benevolent when they recognize where their bread is buttered.

"Power corrupts, and absolute power corrupts absolutely," according to the proverb. But in the Feudal System composite, the sovereign does not have absolute power. The serf can always walk out. If you're the serf, remember that, but don't threaten it constantly, and don't give way to paranoia, subversion, and passive aggression. Assert yourself reasonably. Distinguish between the flow of events and your mate's premeditated actions. Aim for a democracy. And if you're positive that your mate will persist in taking advantage of the composite, claiming a mile when circumstances give him or her an inch, recognize that you are not trapped in the Feudal System. You can always leave.

We think that Duke Ellington and Billy Strayhorn's composite chart is an example of the Feudal System, and that Ellington and Strayhorn dealt with it well. Ellington was a third house Taurus with an eleventh house Moon-Saturn conjunction in Sagittarius, and Aquarius rising. Strayhorn was a second house Sagittarian with a tenth house Virgo Moon, and Scorpio rising. Ellington was poised, sophisticated, independent, curious, extremely observant, hard-working, a leader and a genius. Strayhorn was friendly, convivial, communicative, ambitious and devoted to excellence at his craft, but unassuming, and probably prey to some insecurities. His Scorpio Ascendant probably made him more direct and intense than Ellington's cooler Aquarian surface. Their composite was a second house Aquarian with a Sun-Venus conjunction, Mercury conjunct that Venus, a tenth house Libra Moon, and Sagittarius rising. Therefore, two signs out of the three in Ellington's natal chart, with its Sagittarian Moon and Aquarian Ascendant, were the same as in the composite chart, with its Aquarian Sun and Sagittarian Ascendant. That configuration indicates the Feudal System, with the composite resembling Ellington more than Strayhorn. This makes sense given the dynamics of their relationship. They confidently and prolifically (second house Sun) wrote (Sun-Mercury) and performed (Sun-Venus, and tenth house Libra Moon) works of musical genius together (Sun-Venus in Aquarius), often traveling to do so (Sagittarian Ascendant). Strayhorn held his own musically, yet blended in; Ellington was the band leader and the household word. However, Strayhorn is represented in their composite too, since he has a Sagittarian Sun, in the second house like the composite's Sun. Moreover, the interaspects between the two men would encourage Ellington to be a "good King:" his Moon-Saturn conjunction conjuncts Strayhorn's Venus, and his Sun conjuncts Strayhorn's seventh house cusp and opposes Strayhorn's Ascendant.

Democracy

Christine has a fourth house Scorpio Sun, a tenth house Aries Moon, and Cancer rising. Sam has an eighth house Taurus Sun, a ninth house Gemini Moon, and Libra rising. Their composite shows an eleventh house Cancer Sun, a ninth house Taurus Moon, and Virgo rising. Christine's Cancer Ascendant is represented in the composite chart by the composite Sun in Cancer. Sam's Taurus Sun is represented by the composite's Taurus Moon, and the composite's ninth house Moon echoes Sam's ninth house Moon. The composite's Virgo Ascendant is reminiscent of Christine's tenth house Moon—that is, both positions have something to do with meaningful work. Neither Christine's chart nor Sam's dominate this composite, and they both find common ground in it. We call this situation Democracy.

Democracy is easier to live with than either Culture Shock or the Feudal System. Its dangers, however, are identical to those of the other two patterns: components of each person's nature that are not supported in the composite chart may find that they have to struggle for recognition in the relationship. If that happens, Democracy can turn into the tyranny of the majority over the minority.

In our previous example, a composite chart with a peaceful Cancer/Taurus/Virgo blend doesn't contain much room for the expression of Christine's fiery Aries Moon, or Sam's Gemini Moon with its need for experience and stimulation. The couple must depend on their composite ninth-house Moon to pull them out of any rut that starts to form. The composite's Cancer Sun also has to carry the intensity of Christine's Scorpio Sun and Sam's eighth house Sun, without becoming hypersensitive and shutting down risky but essential lines of communication.

If you're in a Democracy, enjoy and make good use of the points of harmony revealed by your composite chart, without disenfranchising parts of you not directly represented by the composite. If those qualities still find room for expression somewhere in your lives and in the relationship, they are less likely to behave like anarchists sniping at the government.

Maria Shriver and Arnold Schwarzenegger's composite chart is a fair example of Democracy. He's a second house Leo with a Sun-Saturn-Pluto conjunction, a sixth house Capricorn Moon, and Cancer rising with Mercury and Venus in the first house. Schwarzenegger is a strong, self-willed, shrewd, charismatic, work-oriented, very determined and ambitious man with a lot of charm in that gentler Cancer Ascendant. She's a sixth house Scorpio with a Sun-Saturn conjunction, a fourth house Leo Moon, and Taurus rising. Shriver is intense, service-oriented, ambitious, persistent and proud, with deep connections to her roots, home and family. Their composite Sun-Venus conjunction, so often present in the charts of couples and close friends, is in hardworking Virgo and in the family-oriented fourth house.

They say they are both disciplinarians who want to raise their four children to be kind, loving and appreciative, and to give something back to society. Schwarzenegger and Shriver have been great supporters of one another's work. Some of that work has been media-oriented and some of it educationally-oriented, with composite Gemini rising. And some of it's been creative, with their fifth house composite Libra Moon-Neptune conjunction. Their composite fourth house Sun resonates with his Cancer Ascendant and her fourth house Moon. Their composite Virgo Sun resonates with their natal sixth house Moons and Sun-Saturn conjunctions. Their strong composite fifth house finds a parallel in his Leo Sun and her Leo Moon. Part of the challenge for them will be making enough time for fifth house courtship behavior and "down" time, given their busy lives.

These three composite chart patterns—Culture Shock, the Feudal System, and Democracy—are meant as guidelines to start you thinking about the possible patterns of relationship among individual birthcharts and the composites they form. Most situations probably resemble one pattern more than another, but few pure examples of any type exist. As you work with composites, you may well discover other patterns, too.

Regardless of what category the composite chart represents, we need to add one more dimension to our thinking in order to complete the picture. We must consider what aspects the composite's planets make to each individual's charts.

Aspects Between the Composite and the Birthcharts

The composite chart describes the entity of the relationship itself. "Entity" is a synonym for "ghost." Ghosts typically haunt people; people seldom haunt ghosts. When you consider the aspects between the composite chart and the birthcharts, concentrate on the effect that the entity of the couple, symbolized by their composite chart, has on the individual birthcharts. Aspects made by the composite to the birthcharts describe that effect. Aspects made by the birthcharts to the composite are not dismissable, but greater weight should be assigned to the composite chart's connections to the birthcharts. The composite "entity" haunts the couple more than they haunt it.

Rule one: When analyzing aspects between the composite and the two birthcharts, pay more attention to the composite's effect on the birthcharts than vice versa.

Once you've absorbed Rule One, you can understand these interaspects as you would any other. The difference is that the entity of the couple solarizes Joe's Moon or Jan's Sun, rather than an individual's doing so. If Joe stays with Jan, he can expect that their life together will bring the lunar side of his character into prominence (solarization). Meanwhile, Jan will experience the core of her identity (Sun) as flooded with feelings and images (lunarization) by her association with Joe.

Should you draw an interaspect diagram for *all* of the composite chart's planets and their impact on each birthchart? That's up to you. The human brain can only handle so much data without turning into spaghetti. If the thought of laboring to calculate all those interaspects makes you wish you had never heard of astrology, don't do it. We suggest running your eyes over all three charts, keeping alert for interaspects made by the composite's primal triad (Sun, Moon, and Ascendant), and Venus and Mars, at a minimum. The primal triad is the heart of the composite chart, while Venus and Mars say much about the couple's relating style as a couple. If you can deal with more information, take a look at interaspects made by the composite's Mercury and Saturn, which give clues about how each person experiences the level of communication in their partnership (composite Mercury), and the blockages they share or in which they collude (composite Saturn). Add more planets as you feel capable of understanding them without blowing your circuits.

Let's look at some examples. *The Changing Sky* describes Gauguin and Van Gogh's turbulent friendship, which did not improve Van Gogh's precarious mental state. Their composite Sun conjuncts Van Gogh's Saturn-Uranus conjunction, enhancing his sense of struggling against limits or being stymied in attempts at independence. Their composite Moon opposes Van Gogh's Pluto-Uranus conjunction, adding a lunar, emotional, irrational quality to Van Gogh's expression of these two outer planets. Among other things, Pluto can feel like a voice saying "Your life is a joke," and Uranus can feel like a voice saying "To hell with everything; break away." Van Gogh had other responses available than those he made, but his friendship with Gauguin made those voices louder.

Simone de Beauvoir and Jean-Paul Sartre both have Scorpio rising; so does their composite chart. Their style (Ascendant) as a couple is much the same as their individual self-presentations (Ascendants). Their lifelong association required no adjustment of their masks (Ascendant). Comparison of these three charts yields many aspects made by the composite to each birthchart, indicating a great impact made by the relationship on both of their lives.

Rosalynn Carter didn't think she'd be able to make political speeches but rose to the occasion while campaigning with her husband Jimmy. Their composite Sun conjuncts Rosalynn's Ascendant and her first-house Mars-Venus conjunction, bringing out the charming (Venus) warrior (Mars) in her mask (Ascendant). Their composite Mars falls on Rosalynn's third house Saturn, challenging (Mars) the communicative (third house) blockage (Saturn) that she felt.

Pete Townshend and Roger Daltrey's composite Sun falls on Townshend's Venus-Mars conjunction, stimulating Townshend's creative (Venus) drive (Mars). Their composite Venus falls on Daltrey's Sun; the music they created together Venusified Daltrey's retiring fourth house Piscean nature, made it more attractive and noticeable. It also opposes Townshend's twelfth house Moon, drawing on his lunar depths for their art.

We've defined what a composite chart is, and looked at some examples. Our next step is to discuss something vaster and more mysterious in Part Two: the souls' history together.

PART TWO: THE SOULS' HISTORY TOGETHER

CHAPTER FOUR: THE LUNAR NODES

"I feel as if I've known you before."
Haven't we all said those words? There's a formal feeling we typically get around total strangers, even congenial ones. And there is a loose and wide-open feeling we get with people we've loved for a long time.

The feelings are easier to tell apart than night and day.

But sometimes that logic breaks down. Sometimes we meet someone and immediately bypass five years of polite diplomatic negotiation. We are friends, instantly. A bizarre, inexplicable familiarity arises.

If our orientation is metaphysical, we might say, "Lisbon, in 1492—right?" Literally having known each other in a prior lifetime seems the most obvious and compelling explanation.

Even if we're not sure about reincarnation, the phenomenon itself remains and begs for understanding. However we choose to explain it, there it is.

In both volumes of *Skymates*, we use reincarnational language, but if you prefer to think in terms of some mysterious resonance between the strands of two people's DNA, that will work too, with a little translation. All we really need to acknowledge is the common truth of human experience: we all meet people whom we already seem to know better than logic can explain.

This strange familiarity that exists between souls takes a lot of forms. It's not always a warm feeling. We take instant dislikes to people who've given us no offense. We can feel threatened—or arrogantly superior. We can feel dismissive of someone, or that we would give them the shirts off our backs. We experience sexual attractions in circumstances ranging from inappropriate to truly peculiar. Some people scare us—and we have no idea why.

Clearly, these enigmatic attitudes do not always arise. But when they do, we recognize them. It is a common human experience, shared by almost everyone, but lying just across the border between our socially contracted consensual reality, and the actual truth of life as we truly encounter it.

That feeling, when we do experience it between ourselves and a stranger, is invariably reflected in one astrological symbol: *the composite South Node of the Moon.*

The Dragon's Tail

Halfway between your South Node and mine lies our composite South Node—it is calculated by midpoints, exactly as we would calculate the composite Mercury or Neptune. Like a planet, it falls in a house; it makes aspects, and it has a planetary ruler according to the sign in which it falls. Historically, it was given the poetic name, *the Dragon's Tail*. And it is always opposite the North Node, or *the Dragon's Head*.

Now, you and Napoleon have a composite South Node. It's a mathematical construction, so it exists between any two charts. This does not mean that you and Napoleon were kissing on the porch swing in a prior lifetime! This leads to our first fundamental principle:

Only take the South Node seriously if the relationship itself is serious.

If two people become sexually or romantically attracted to each other, even that is not a green light for reading the South Node. Maybe they remind each other of mom or dad, and something psychological is happening between them that doesn't really have anything to do with karma. Maybe their hormones are spiking that day. Maybe they're just lonely. Maybe convenience is colliding with opportunity. But if they stay together for a few consecutive weekends, *if the shock of sexual intimacy doesn't boot them out of each other's orbits,* it's a good bet that they have some kind of prior life link.

What kind of connection? Human relationships come in a lot of flavors. Lovers tend to assume that they've been lovers before, and often they are right—the exchange of sexual energy definitely sets karmic wheels turning. But, as we will see, many other kinds of connections may have existed previously between souls who share a bed in this lifetime—and, similarly, souls manifesting as parents and children, or as friends, in this lifetime may well have been Abelard and Heloise in a prior lifetime.

If we are sleeping together in this lifetime, learning that we were brothers, for example, in a prior life can feel quite weird, but it's all there in the South Node. Ditto for learning that we may have killed each other.

What Reincarnates?

All the planets have South Nodes, and they all make reference to the past. But it's the Moon's South Node we generally read. Why? There is actually a simple answer. What survives the trauma of death and rebirth is not our *factual* memory—not our "Mercury" memory, so to speak. It is our *emotional* memory: the Moon memory. We carry an underlying mood or attitude forward from the past, and only fragmentary knowledge at best of names, details, history. You can see and feel that underlying mood in the South Node of an individual birthchart, and you can see and feel it in the underlying spirit of a relationship.

Imagine a child grievously abused. She grows up with the trauma repressed—at a conscious level, she has no idea it happened. But everywhere she goes she carries an attitude of shame, fear, suspicion, and insecurity. It taints her relationships, her attitude toward her body, and her self-image. You can feel the mood surrounding her like a cloud. And yet in the Mercury sense, she "remembers nothing." But the Moon carries the memory intact, as perfect as a butterfly encased in glass. The heart's memory is stronger than death; the mind's memory is not.

That is precisely how the Moon's South Node works.

In all counseling work, there is an obvious case to be made for an upbeat, supportive, positive approach. But with the South Node, a negative bias permeates everything, and that's completely appropriate. This can be a bit of a stretch for astrologers with warm hearts, but here's the reasoning behind it: what we carry forward from the past—or at least what manifests through the symbols of the composite chart—is material which we, as a couple, need to work on resolving. The happier material probably does get through the after-death pipeline, but it doesn't seem to be reflected in the astrological symbolism. There is an efficiency here: the composite chart seems to tell us only what we need to know.

The composite South Node primarily represents unresolved wounds, tragedies, limitations and failures from the past which potentially interfere with our ability to fulfill our soul-contract together in this lifetime.

The South Node is always history. By definition, since evolution carries us forward, we were *less* evolved then. The couple is haunted by this part of their past, and vulnerable to repeating it. Even the South Node's "good stuff" feels tired and overly familiar. We already know it, so there's not a compelling need to learn it again.

Remember that the Moon's South Node is emotional and attitudinal. Ever tried to reason with a depressed friend? Every suggestion we make is greeted with a sense of foredoomed impossibility. Such a person believes what he or she says. They think they are being logical. What they don't see is that they aren't seeing "reality;" *they are only seeing their own consciousness*. It is, of course, that way with all of us: wherever we go, we meet our own minds. Thus, the emotions and attitudes implicit in the South Node tend to define a couple's reality, and to be mistaken for it.

Finding the Karmic Story

Any novel worth reading is full of made-up facts that come together to tell some great truth about life. Our aim in prising the karmic story out of the nodal structure is very similar. We do *not* expect to unearth specific, verifiable past-life facts: for that, go to a good psychic or hypnotic regressionist. What surfaces through nodal analysis is a *parable* that parallels the actual past-life realities. It tells the essential truth—Moon-fashion. It tells the emotional, psychological story. We take that information and flesh it out in a concrete, material tale that makes it come alive.

In our experience, because of the way the astrological symbols trigger intuition, often this "story" we create proves to be more than just a parable. Often it is echoed, in psychic readings, in prior-life dreams and in regressions, not to mention in real-life experience in this present lifetime. That's just part of the magic of astrology. But the core point is simply this: *the story doesn't have to be "factual" for it to be "true."* Even with no particular intuition, the technical procedures we explore in this chapter will produce powerful, evocative, and psychologically relevant results.

Maybe, for example, a couple were pioneers in the American West in a prior lifetime and were killed by beleaguered, desperate Navajo warriors. Maybe in our analysis of the composite South Node, we come up with a story describing them as immigrants crossing the Atlantic on a ship taken by hungry pirates. The facts are completely incorrect—but the *story* is still "true." Emotionally, it boils down to the same dynamics.

The South Node's Sign and House

The sign the South Node occupies tells us about the prior life *nature* of the couple and what their *soul-contract* was in the past. Just remember to tilt your interpretation a bit negatively, then think of the South Node's sign almost as you would a conventional Sun sign.

South Node in Aries? Together, they had a *warrior's* nature and energy—but you'll be looking at issue of stress and fear, along with the impact of violence received or violence offered.

South Node in Libra? Probably we're seeing a *partnership between equals*, a fair bet for a past-life marriage—but watch out for too much "politeness," indecision or concern with appearances: the Libran shadow.

The *house* that the South Node occupies tells us about the *physical scene of the couple's life together* in the karmic past—what they were actually doing, and also some insight into *the circumstances which compelled or constrained them.* South Node in the ninth house? Think about institutions of learning or religion. Consider travel or immigration. Eleventh house? Movements. Tribes. Large groups of people. The nearly irresistible force of mob psychology. Second house? Issues around money or the material basis of survival.

Next, put the house and the sign together. South Node in Libra and in the eleventh house? They were partners, but crippled by indecision and too much concern with what others thought of them (Libra)—probably in the context of a *compelling, but stultifyingly proper society* (eleventh house, modified in the Libran direction.)

Try switching to the South Node in Aries, while keeping it in the eleventh. They still knew each other, but now in a more belligerent, angry or adventurous (Arian) way. They were still operating in the context of a group, but now that group is not so polite. It takes on an edge of explosiveness and destructiveness—that's the eleventh house, now tilted in the Arian direction. It sounds like an army—that would, at least, be a great metaphor. For purposes of our parable, we can say that these two were *comrades-in-arms*, whatever the form of their present relationship.

Let the symbols of house and sign speak to each other, in other words. Let each one flavor and deepen the other one. That's how we build the foundation of the nodal analysis.

Run It Through The Filter

Linking the South Node's sign and house, as we just saw, begins to narrow the field where the karmic story will unfold, but it is still unsatisfyingly vague. We can bring all that to a much sharper focus. There are 144 possible combinations of sign and house, but a lot more than 144 possible human stories! Still, we've already made progress worth celebrating. We've winnowed the list down to less than one percent of all human archetypal possibilities—0.69% of them, to be precise.

But we can go much further toward precision. What follows is a series of technical procedures. They may seem a bit overwhelming—and yes, to succeed here, you do have to juggle a lot of balls at the same time. But there is one principle that overshadows everything and if you understand it, you will stay on top of the details. Every new "ball" we juggle actually makes the work of finding the story easier. Every technical dimension of the composite South Node—its sign, house, aspects, and planetary ruler—serves to *narrow our focus*. It adds information, of course—but *more importantly, it eliminates possibilities*. It filters the information.

We start with the infinite field of all possible stories. With each step, we winnow. In the end, what we have left is the essence of the karmic tale—*the thematic story-line,* not necessarily the facts—that links the two souls and brings them together again in this life.

We seek, through our twin processes of discovery and elimination, a story that is consistent with all the nodal information and assumes nothing else.

Planets Conjunct the South Node

When a planet is conjunct the South Node, it further defines the nature of the energy and circumstances of the couple in the past. Again, think of the South Node like the Sun. Work with this configuration as you would work with a planet conjunct a person's Sun—except continue to tilt the interpretation toward suboptimal expressions.

Remember that this negative bias, while it might feel counter-intuitive, is ultimately the most helpful tack to take. We humans are creatures of habit; we tend to repeat patterns of behavior, even when they are not helpful or when we've already "gotten the message." One very significant dimension of karma is really a fancy word for "habit." Couples are affected by it as much as or even more than individuals—and, given the soul's innate timelessness, that can be a habit from last year or from the last century.

Jupiter conjunct a composite South Node? Add elements of expansiveness and victory to the mix. Add a dollop of what the world would call "luck." And be alert to Jupiter's eternal shadows: all that glitters is not gold; pride goeth before a fall; be careful what you pray for, you might get it.

A little while ago, we considered an Arian South Node in the eleventh house, and brought up the metaphorical image of an army as a context for prior life experience. Armies have privates and cooks and latrine-cleaners. They have sergeants and generals. They have heroes and cowards. Half of the armies win and half of them lose—at least among the ones who actually fight. Many armies just sit there and don't do much at all. In other words, our "0.69% of human possibilities" still contains a vast array of options.

Add Jupiter to that Node though a conjunction, and the focus gets a lot crisper. These two souls were likely in positions of authority, glory and power. Very probably, they "won the war." Pin some medals on them. Quite certainly, life offered them the chance to become inflated and overextended, to overplay their hands, to play God. They got lucky. We can eliminate latrine-duty.

The Planetary Ruler of the South Node

If the composite South Node lies in Gemini, Mercury is its ruler. Wherever Mercury lies in the chart, we find another set of clues about the karmic story. If the South Node is in Taurus, we need to look for Venus. In Cancer, we pay closer attention to the Moon.

In essence, the planetary ruler of the South Node is an extension of the Node itself. It describes *another dimension* of the karmic story. It provides *another angle* on the tale. Often, it seems to correlate with a *pivotal chapter* in the karmic story.

If, for example, we see the South Node in the ninth house, but its ruler is in the twelfth, we might reason this way: in a prior life, this couple took a voyage (ninth house), *but the ship sank* (twelfth house: loss, trouble). There are many other possibilities, but that is certainly one of them!

In the example we are developing with the Arian South Node in the eleventh house conjunct Jupiter, let's now place Mars—the nodal ruler—in the eighth house, the traditional "house of death." Warriors kill and are killed; they see a lot of death. They are face to face, in general, with the taboo and the extreme. *What impact does it have on two people to have faced death together?* Or to have killed together? Answer that, and you've added another pivotal psychological dimension to your emerging nodal story.

Now, instead of the eighth house, try putting Mars in the fifth (play; creativity; pleasure). That's harder, simply because the connections between those happy subjects and war aren't so obvious. But warriors are under a lot of stress. Their level of tension demands release. What does a soldier do on leave? One answer is that he raises hell! The pent-up fires demand release, and they do so with pressing urgency and a vulnerability to extremes. How might a solider carrying that kind of inner pressure respond to victory? After arduous battle, how are the citizens of the "liberated" town treated? There's more than a single possible answer to that question, but since we're dealing with the South Node, let your mind range toward the darker possibilities.

Because of the nature of rulership, the *planet* that rules the South Node will always have the same basic tone as the *sign* of the Node. That means that the planet itself doesn't actually tell us much that we didn't already know. Where the Node ruler's usefulness comes in is through its placement in the chart. *Thus, the planetary ruler of the South Node essentially functions as a marker for another sign and house that have relevance to the karmic story.* Any aspects the South Node's ruler makes to other planets, especially conjunctions, also add detail and texture.

There is one specific case we'd like to highlight. With the South Node in Leo, the Sun is the ruler—and the very essence of the couple today is deeply imprinted with the mark of the past. All couples have karma, but for those two, it is particularly essential that we understand it. For the sake of their basic vitality, they need to be true to their composite Sun sign. Yet, in so doing, they run the danger of slipping into a lower, less conscious version of that sign because of the downward pull of ingrained karmic patterning. They are like dried-out alcoholics who need to sit soberly in a bar night after night.

The Nodes are like planets in that they can be prominent or obscure in a composite chart. As with planets, this prominence or obscurity corresponds to the relative gravity or modesty of impact of the underlying karmic issues upon the life of the couple.

One more point about the ruler of the South Node. What do we do with a Pisces South Node? The majority of modern astrologers would say that Neptune is its ruler. But traditionally, the answer was Jupiter. It's the same with Aquarius—Uranus and Saturn are both its ruler, depending on whom you ask. And Scorpio is shared—or fought over—by Pluto and Mars.

Our feeling is that in each case both planets have an obvious affinity for the sign in question. The word "rulership" is probably the real culprit, in that it sets us up to think that one planet should be "king." But it doesn't have to be that way: think of affinity, rather than hierarchy.

We suggest that with a South Node in Scorpio, Aquarius or Pisces, you recognize both rulerships. What's produced the best results for us is to start with Uranus, Neptune or Pluto, then let the traditional ruler add more detail.

Planets in Aspects to the South Node

All aspects to the South Node, other than the conjunction, refer to *forces that acted upon the couple* in the prior-life drama. They point to external realities, although they often have inward and subjective correlates as well. Very typically, these planets refer to *other people*—relationships that played some kind of shaping role on the main pair.

Squares and *oppositions* correspond with people or situations which were experienced as challenges, resistance or negativity. *Trines* and *sextiles* are linked to people and circumstances which were experienced as supportive—but given our suspicious bias in all nodal analysis, we need to be careful about being too glowing in our appraisal of the sextiles and trines. They might simply represent unambivalently good things: safe havens and "tea and sympathy" in otherwise difficult scenarios, but just as easily they can indicate ways in which we were supported in folly.

In our unfolding military karma example, let's imagine Venus in Leo in the second house, making a trine to the Aries South Node. Maybe our heroes had money (second house). Maybe they were good-looking (Venus in Leo). Good news? Historically, how many children of wealthy, ruling class families have been bamboozled by their tribe into accepting military rank? Has that always worked out well for them? And remember that fifth house Mars—how does "too much" money interact with a compulsive, tension-driven need to raise hell? The answer is, "supportively!"

With trines and sextiles, always be alert to ways in which the dyad could have been "supported" in folly or self-sabotage.

As we will soon learn, the most evocative aspects to the South Node, other than the conjunction, are squares and oppositions. These are powerful—and sufficiently distinct for us to treat them separately.

The so-called "minor aspects" can play a role in this kind of analysis too, but we tend to shy away from them, favoring a deeper look at the foundation above spreading ourselves too thinly over details. Very briefly:

Quincunxes suggest tensions, wild cards, situations or people that came in out of the blue and changed everything or required a lot of adjustment.

Sesquiquadrates suggest situations and relationships that tied us in knots, were intellectually confusing, and which smacked of "damned if we do, damned if we don't."

Semi-squares suggest chronic but tolerable vexations that took their toll by attrition. Think of mosquitos.

Quintiles suggest breaks in the action, temporary reprieves, "divine visitations," and creative interludes.

Planets in Opposition to the South Node

Any planet in this position would be more conventionally described as being "conjunct the North Node." We'll get to that! For our purposes here, we are concentrating on the South Node of the Moon, and so it's the opposition that draws our attention and focuses our understanding.

A planet opposing the South Node represents something or someone who blocked, repressed, defeated or tantalized the couple in the past. It either represents something insurmountable and irresolvable, or something unattainable. It symbolizes the brick wall of reality.

Jupiter opposing the South Node could indicate all the good things of life, just out of reach. Picture two Dickensian orphans, their bellies empty—and their noses pressed against the steamy glass of the elegant restaurant two nights before Christmas. Or imagine the King (Jupiter) has declared war, and the lovers are parted, never to see each other again, as one of them is conscripted into the army. They hate it. They didn't choose it. But how can you argue with the overwhelming might and authority of the King? His call-to-arms is the "brick wall of reality." You have no choice but to deal with it.

Those are two very different stories! Both are consistent with Jupiter opposing the South Node. *How can we know which story to tell?* We couldn't—if we blundered by starting our analysis with this aspect, or by interpreting it in a vacuum.

By the time we consider the South Node's aspects, we should have understood the framework of the story. We find places for the message of those aspects in the context of the basic elements already established.

Any tenth house planet opposite the South Node will correlate with figures or structures of social authority existing in tension with the needs or desires of the couple. A ninth house planet suggests conflict with religion or law, or perhaps enforced migration: refugee status. A fourth house planet links to the inescapable demands of family or clan; a fifth house one can aim our attention at the pressing, morally-unavoidable demands of children—or the labyrinth created by addictive or compulsive pleasure-seeking.

Always, with planets opposite the South Node, one reality is central: whatever the problem was, there was no way around it.

Planets Square the South Node

Any planet square the South Node is naturally square the North Node too. As with the opposition aspect just discussed, the aspectual link to the North Node is best treated as a separate issue. At this point, we're only concerned with the South Node—which is to say, with uncovering the karmic story.

A planet square the South Node represents a person, circumstance or issue that crossed, vexed, afflicted or otherwise undercut the couple's intentions or needs in the karmic past. It is therefore a past issue left unresolved, which presses again for resolution in the present life.

Neptune square the South Node? Explore a feeling of life slowly being leached from the couple. Perhaps Neptune was in the fourth, and correlated with an endlessly needy, insatiably demanding, ever-dependent family. "Mom moved in and began dying when she was sixty. Now she's ninety, still going strong and still dying—and if she doesn't die soon, it'll kill me."

Perhaps Neptune was in the fifth house or the twelfth, either one of which can correlate with escapist behavior. With Neptune square the Node from either of those houses, we could imagine a couple drinking themselves into oblivion, turning themselves into ghosts of what they might have been.

In these two Neptunian examples, recognize that *other options existed.* That manipulative mother could have be told to stand on her own two feet. Boundaries could have been set. People can break addictions. Neither of these better answers are easy ones, and it is possible that the higher possibility was simply not recognized at the time. But the key point is that squares (as distinct from oppositions) to the South Node often correlate with *vexatious situations in which our own blindness or error plays a large role.*

Blindness and error are part of life, and we all succumb to them. And always remember one of the cardinal insights into spiritual evolution: *you were even dumber in the past!* These lapses should not be greeted with guilt or shame, only with the recognition that we're wounded, that we run the risk of repeating the old pattern, and that now there are better choices.

Not all nodal squares represent our own errors—that's just a useful possibility to explore when framing the story. Some squares simply represent our frailty before the enormity of life. Squares tend to "blindside" us—thus, they often link to circumstances which we never saw coming. That's especially true with the edgier planets—Mars, Uranus or Pluto—squaring the Node. These all tend to leave the mark of *trauma* on the couple. Perhaps the Node is squared by an eighth house Uranus: a couple is in the middle of their process together when one of them is taken unexpectedly by death. Terrorists crash a jet into a building, and last night's fight is the last conversation we'll ever have in these bodies. How can we imagine the impact of such a sudden Uranian trauma? How long does it take to "get over" something like that—and what does that phrase even mean? From a metaphysical perspective, we would surely have some "unfinished business" with a soul ripped from our lives that way. There's one human story behind having composite Uranus square the South Node—and a glimpse at a composite chart some astrologer will face in a generation or two.

Projection

Those hungry orphan children we met a while ago, the ones with their noses against the glass of the fancy restaurant—what do they think of the rich people eating those fine lavish meals? The lover whose true love is forced by the King to leave her and fight a war—what is her attitude toward law and authority?

When we are hurt, taunted or blocked by another person, we tend to think ill of them. We put our noses in the air. We say, *"I would never in a million years be like that."* And God writes it down in a little black book.

We reject the things that harm us. We put them out of our hearts. In the language of the shrinks, we *project negatively* onto such entities. These projections are in fact rejections of part of what we ourselves are. Sooner or later in the journey, such projections must be withdrawn. And we hate that!

Planets square or opposed to the South Node often represent people we must learn to stop hating, judging and rejecting, or we'll reject parts of ourselves which we need if we're to continue our journey together.

Please note that this isn't a generic reference to the sweet virtues of forgiveness and acceptance. It's more concretely relevant than that. For example, with Jupiter on their composite North Node, perhaps a couple (those starving orphans in a prior life) needs to experience wealth and status in this lifetime. Perhaps they need to lose their adaptation to poverty, anonymity, or to just "getting by." Why? As we'll discover in a few pages, the Moon's North Node clarifies the answer, but maybe they have something important to do for their community in this lifetime—*and they can't do it without being in a position to hobnob with the ruling class.* Maybe they have a soul-contract to play Chopin duets together in this lifetime. Have you priced a grand piano lately?

For them to go forward, they must stop judging those whom they judged so vehemently in the past. It's not only about virtue; it is about the fierce logic of soul evolution.

As usual in spiritual matters, this withdrawal of projection actually has almost nothing to do with the people our previously orphaned partners are judging. It's really about themselves, and about a part of their own interior spectrum of possibilities which they are judging and rejecting.

If a hungry person steals our food, we don't reject the part of ourselves that wants to eat.

Pulling the Karmic Story Together

By the time you've considered all the pieces of the puzzle, you've got quite a lot of information, especially if there happen to be many planets aspecting the South Node. All the juggling can be overwhelming, but we encourage you to proceed anyway. Remember that every piece of the puzzle, while it adds details, also simplifies the picture. Just knowing the sign of the South Node gets the story down to about eight percent (one in twelve) of all human possibilities. Adding the South Node's house gets it under one percent. Progress! A planet conjunct that Node? Hooray! You've cut out ninety percent of the remaining possibilities. Every South Node has a planetary ruler—another ninety percent of your possible confusion evaporates! This is really the right way to think about the process, and not just because it's a little more encouraging. It's also sound methodology. What we are aiming to find, as we said earlier, is a story that is consistent with all the nodal information and assumes nothing else. Half of that is a process of discovery, but the other half is process of strategic elimination.

Every astrological symbol represents a very broad field of archetypal possibilities. The sixth house, for example, represents your health and your responsibilities—and your mentors, your daily routines, and your humility. And that's just the psychological material! The sixth also refers to your pets, your aunts, uncles, nieces and nephews, the tools in your toolbox, your sister's home, your children's finances . . . the list is overwhelming. And it should be, since we are dividing the universe into twelve huge boxes!

Visualize this archetypal field as a gigantic pizza pan full of icons or figures or characters or props, representing each of its elements. Warriors: high-ranking generals or lowly grunts? Orphans: hungry or adopted by loving parents? Kings: tyrannical or benevolent or dethroned? Lovers: blissfully fulfilled, or separated by overpowering circumstances?

Do the same with all the other archetypal fields pertinent to the nodal analysis. Now see where the pizza pans overlap. See where they have common ground. See which icons, figures, characters or props they either hold in common, or which ones daisy-chain together into a natural storyline, like a gun might suggest a murder, or a ship a voyage.

You've found it.

That's the chart within the chart.

That's your karmic story.

The Dragon's Head

The composite North Node of the Moon is opposite the South Node. Much of its meaning follows from that simple geometrical observation:

☺ It puts maximum tension on the South Node—it represents an unexplored, unknown possibility for the couple.

☺ It answers South Node questions and resolves South Node dilemmas.

☺ It represents the couple's evolutionary intention and soul-contract.

However:

☹ Due to the couple's inexperience with the North Node, they will likely be tentative, awkward and confused in that part of life, inclined toward "interesting and constructive errors."

☹ It has no intrinsic energy at all; it's nothing but an excellent suggestion.

Earlier, we looked at an invented example of a couple with their South Node in Aries and the eleventh house, conjunct Jupiter and ruled by a fifth house Mars. We posited a comradely background where they shared military experience, probably as officers selected from among the "good families."

Their North Node must lie in Libra and in the fifth house, since those placements lie opposite Aries and the eleventh. Thus, their soul-intentions are Libran: to deepen their partnership, but also to experience peace, grace, and serenity together. Libra is opposite Aries, as peace is opposite war and accord is opposite discord. We can easily see the evolutionary direction of their soul-contract. Serenity is opposite tension—and, after the stress of war, there is a profound need to find some tranquility.

Libra represents our *aesthetic functions*—our ability to respond to beauty and to appreciate the arts: these emerge as useful "yogas" for these two to practice together. In general, there is a feeling of moving out of the inherent roughness and rawness of war, and into a more civilized framework reflecting gentler aspects of the human tradition.

In this North Node, we see that *these two have made an agreement to calm down together; to heal from war.*

With the North Node in the fifth house, there is a hunger for shared creative self-expression—and we hit paydirt! Libra carries the archetype of the Artist. The fifth house urge to express oneself creatively links very directly to that archetype. Thus we recognize an elemental clause in their soul-contract: *to support each other in all creative work, and ideally to share that work.*

The fifth house is about *joy* and *pleasure*. After war, we need some! Something hardens in us under constant stress. Something grows stony when faced with chronic violence, ugliness, and fear. With the North Node in the fifth house, there is a soul-contract to *soften in each other's arms.* How? Art is one method, as we've already seen—a couple thrilling to a live performance of Beethoven's ninth symphony, tears in their eyes at the final choruses, reaching for each other's hands. Feel the opening of their shared heart? There's Libran fifth house energy.

Speaking of pleasure, remember that we learned that the South Node ruler, Mars, also lay in the fifth house, where it suggested a karmic vulnerability to potentially destructive hell-raising. As we guide this couple toward the higher ground, we have a tightrope to walk here: affirming their evolutionary need for pleasure, while cautioning them about damaging levels of dissipation. The key is to emphasize the healthiest fifth house expressions, rather than setting strictures on the less healthy ones.

The *courtship* dimensions of the fifth house suggest further methods for achieving this "post-traumatic" softening: how pleasant it is to bring each other roses! To light candles with dinner! To take time for a cup of tea and a conversation! Lovers do it. Why do we ever need to stop?

Children are another correlate of the fifth house. With a composite North Node there, especially in Libra, the traditional sign of marriage, it's easy to imagine that having children would be part of this couple's soul-contract. That's of course a very personal choice, and it's not the astrologer's business to advise anyone to make it. Having kids is consistent with that North Node, but it isn't the only possibility. It would be fair to say that part of their work together is finding the place in their relationship that's sufficiently *calm, settled, safe and stable* that they *could* choose to have kids.

And who would want to bring a child into a war-zone? In a nutshell, these two are learning that *the war is over.*

Planets Conjunct the North Node

If there is a planet on the North Node, we've already met it. That planet is the same one opposing the South Node in the earlier stage of our analysis. There, it represented something troublesome, insurmountable or unattainable. Now we see it linked positively to the couple's present evolutionary intentions. They are trying to integrate the higher elements of that planetary energy into themselves.

Working with a planet on the North Node is a good exercise in learning to see both the high and the low sides of all the planets. Saturn opposing the South Node? In the karmic past, there was some basic, insurmountable *lack*—a poverty in some sense—that stood between you and what you wanted. It was probably embodied in some person who represented laws and limitations—someone saying "thou shalt not" or "impossible!" Now, as a couple, you need to embrace that same Saturn energy, but move it into its higher manifestations. Together, you need *to internalize the kinds of present-tense self-denial that allow you to build a future which you can respect.* Saving for a house together. Putting each other through medical school. Raising healthy, sane kids. Staying together. And you thereby overcome an internalized karmic attitude of "coping" in a spirit of gloomy fatalism and acceptance of defeat.

Keep the South and North Nodes clearly distinguished in your thinking:

A planet opposing the South Node hurt you or stalled you in the past. Read it negatively. That same planet, conjunct the North Node, shows you the way forward. Read it positively.

The Planetary Ruler of the North Node

The planet that rules the sign of the Moon's North Node helps us get where we need to go. It supports the realization of the evolutionary intention implicit in that Node.

The planetary ruler of the North Node represents a useful tactic for fulfilling the soul-contract, or an important piece of the puzzle, or a helpful clue about how to get it right, or just the icing on the cake—a way to "make an A" in the North Node work.

The critical theoretical point here is that the North Node's ruler derives its meaning from the North Node itself. We have to understand the two of them *in that order* or we'll lose our focus.

Say that a sixth house Venus is the North Node ruler. The soul contract has to do with responsible (sixth house) relationships (Venus)—but that's not a very helpful observation, since all composite charts are about relationships in some form, and most of them benefit from responsibility.

Let the North Node itself bring clarity and focus to that interpretation. Maybe the composite North Node lies in the tenth house. This couple has a soul-contract to make a mark in their community. To succeed, they'll probably need to hire (sixth house) artistic, creative, socially skilled people whom they love (Venus) personally.

Now leave the North Node in Libra, but put it in the fifth house. To fulfill those evolutionary intentions (now having to do with shared creative expression), these two must find *artistic* (Venus) *mentors* (the sixth house).

The thinking behind this process can seem confusing until you remember the fundamental principle. Start with a thorough understanding of the North Node, then apply common sense in trying to imagine how its planetary ruler might help the cause. The context of the basic sign/house nodal structure determines the specific meaning of the nodal rulers.

Planets Square the North Node

A few pages back we saw that planets square the South Node represented something the couple *left unresolved* in the karmic past. Half the meaning of that same planet's squaring the North Node is implicit in that statement. To go forward, this leftover issue must be resolved.

In the words of Steven's partner in the two volumes of *Measuring the Night*, Jeffrey Wolf Green, such a planet represents a "skipped step." It haunts us, and the only way for us to advance is to go back and get it right. It's like driving in a strange city: miss a critical turn on the highway, and the only thing you can do is turn around and go back.

Maybe someone "solves" the problems in one relationship by escaping into another one—and we all know that isn't likely to work. Very probably, whatever you're not facing in the first relationship will emerge as a problem in the new relationship too.

We use the term "skipped steps," but the irony is that no one can really skip any steps at all. We can only defer them.

The energy of a planet square the nodal axis *hangs in the balance* between the past and the future. Easily, it can fall backwards and recreate the old South Node dilemma, but ideally it needs to move to a higher level and "serve the North Node."

A few pages back, we looked at Neptune squaring the South Node. One possibility we considered was that in the karmic past, the couple lost their evolutionary focus in an alcoholic haze. Another was that they allowed the life to be sucked out of them by a parasitic mother. Different stories—but in both cases we see the dark Neptune signature: the uncreative, unproductive, unintentional loss of self. Because of the square to the Nodes, that Neptunian energy is hanging in the balance. The couple needs to move it forward and higher. It won't go away! If they don't get it right, they'll get it wrong—again. This time, Neptune wants to flower as an avid, shared spiritual life, or as a deep engagement with the image-making processes we call art.

To look at the Nodes in an integrative manner, if this couple's North Node lies in the tenth house, this developing spiritual or artistic life needs to be reflected in their public, outward circumstances, perhaps in their professions. If, on the other hand, the Node lies in their fifth house, it suggests "art for art's sake." In the ninth or the twelfth houses, it would tilt more toward the spiritual and mystical dimensions of Neptune, and less toward the imaginative ones.

As always, our aim is to find the points of overlap, and let each symbol speak to all the others.

It is critical to remember that resolving the issues connected with the planet square the nodal axis is the *price of admission for going forward.* Until those issues are addressed, we are blocked—stuck, whether or not we know it, in the past.

The blockages and distortions implicit in the planet squaring the nodal axis must be released and clarified before the soul-contract can be fulfilled. Otherwise, the North Node is inaccessible

A Common Dilemma—and its Resolution

The key to everything we've seen in this chapter lies in understanding the natural tension of the opposition aspect between the North and South Nodes. Since opposite signs and opposite houses always represent different sides of the same coin, the Nodes partake of the same polarity.

Libran peace "cures" Arian stress—as Arian courage and forthrightness "cure" Libran mealy-mouthed indecision. Third house curiosity and open-mindedness cure ninth house dogmatism—as ninth house faith cures third house doubt and uncertainty. This "oppositional" thinking underlies all of nodal theory, not to mention much of the rest of astrology, Jungian psychology and Hermetic philosophy.

But sometimes the North Node and South Node seem to resemble each other, and confusion can arise. There are several examples of this phenomenon, and all of them are resolved in much the same way.

We might, for example, see a Gemini South Node in the ninth house. That puts the North Node in Sagittarius (the ninth sign), but in the third house—which has a natural resonance with the third sign, Gemini. So which way are we going?

We might see a Gemini South Node—but Mercury (which rules Gemini) is conjunct the North Node. The future looks a lot like the past!

We might see a Sagittarian North Node—with Jupiter ruling it from a conjunction with the Gemini South Node. The past looks too much like the future!

In all these cases, the answer is the same: keep a very clear distinction between the higher and lower expressions of the symbols. Always, the soul-contract is to go from lower to higher. Where past and future bear symbolic resemblance to each other, sort it out through the high-low distinction.

Gemini South Node? *Too much thinking or running around in circles, frantically but pointlessly, in the prior life.* Mercury on that Sagittarian North Node? *They are on a philosophical quest for a meaningful existential framework* (Sagittarius) in this life—but to succeed, they'll have to *think, study, maintain intellectual openness*, and be willing to discover surprising, even shocking, truths together—that's the higher expression of Mercury energy (or of Gemini energy, for that matter).

When the ruler of the North Node is conjunct the South Node, think along the lines we have just laid out: in the past, this couple "mastered" that planet's lower expression. Now they are trying to get to the higher ground, *so they can go back and re-do the past, getting it right this time.*

Conclusion

Coaxing the prior life story out of a composite chart (or a birthchart, for that matter) at this level of detail is a relatively new technique in astrology. It has its own emerging advocates, detractors, principles and procedures, but most of the basic brain-programs that allow us to do conventional astrological interpretation work well here too, once we've made a few translations.

Past lives can seem to be a vague area, one in which an astrologer could really "say anything" and no one would ever be the wiser. People ignorant of the actual techniques and values underlying this approach have sometimes leveled that charge. *The key here is that karmic patterns tend to repeat.* We may not be able to see the past, but we typically see the relevance of the prior-life story to the couple's *present* issues, often right down to details. We invite the couple to evaluate what we are saying—and to doubt it, if they so choose! It is in the present tense that evolutionary astrology can defend its claims and perspectives. We have never claimed otherwise.

In Part Three, you'll find a complete "cookbook" analysis of both the North and South Nodes in every sign and every house. It's a good launching pad to help you get down to that 0.69% level of precision we described earlier. Beyond that level, the possibilities become so multitudinous that no book could cover all conceivable combinations of symbols. That's where you need to think astrologically. If you are systematic about it, and if you remember to stop and think humanly about what the symbols are telling you, you'll find the story often leaps out of the chart.

In Chapter Seventeen, we present a complete, integrated analysis of the composite chart of a specific couple—F. Scott Fitzgerald and Zelda Fitzgerald. In those pages we spend quite a lot of time on their composite Nodes. Reading through that section a few times will help you know where to put your own feet when the time comes to find your own path through another couple's story.

Below, we've condensed the theoretical material of this chapter into outline form for you, before we move on to Part Three.

Strategies in the Synastric Analysis of the Composite South Node of The Moon

The most elemental information regarding the unresolved prior-life situation of the dyad derives from the *sign* and the *house* of the Moon's South Node.

1. The **sign** describes the prior *personality* and *energy* of the dyad, and its *evolutionary agenda* at the time.

2. The **house** describes the actual, existential *circumstances* in which the dyad encountered its experiences.

Almost equally revealing is the planetary ruler of the Moon's South Node. According to its sign and house, we discover:

1. Another *active, tactical, specific* dimension of the dyad's larger agenda, nature, and circumstances.

2. A *crucial crisis* or pivotal chapter in the novel of the dyad's prior-life story.

Hint: pay close attention to the darker, Shadow-side of the sign, house, and planetary ruler for clues about any challenging impacts on the present life.

A planet **conjunct** the Moon's South Node or its ruler significantly modifies, deepens, and develops what we've learned from the sign/house dynamic. It expands upon the intentions, nature, and evolutionary or existential strategies of the dyad. It refers to the *dyad itself,* in its own nature.

All other planetary aspects to the South Node tend to refer primarily to external realities: to circumstances and specific people existing in relation to the dyad in the prior life. (What follows can also be applied with some caution to planetary aspects to the ruler of the South Node.)

A planet **opposing** the South Node represents something or someone who *blocked* or *repressed* the fulfillment of the dyad's evolutionary intention. *It symbolizes the brick wall of reality.* It also represents something that felt far away or unattainable, and thus *longed for.*

A planet **square** the South Node has four dimensions:

1. People or issues that *crossed, vexed, or undercut* the dyad's evolutionary intent.

2. It is therefore issues *left unresolved* from the past, which press again in the present life.

3. Simultaneously, it is a *skipped step*, which must be faced and resolved in order for evolutionary progress to continue.

4. The planet now *hangs in the balance* between past and future—thus, we look for ways it can serve the North Node's intentions . . . or be swept into supporting the repetition of the South Node's patterning.

A planet **trine** or **sextile** the South Node represents people or circumstances which *supported* the dyad in a prior life.

Hint: always be alert to ways in which the dyad could have been "supported" in folly or self-sabotage.

PART THREE: THE COOKBOOK

CHAPTER FIVE: THE COMPOSITE SUN

Some couples are radiant, and their radiance is magnetic. They may not be theatrical or charismatic. As individuals, they may even be shy. Yet something draws us toward them: a certain warmth, a sense of the life-force shining from them, a *sunny* quality in the aura that emanates from them. They go through interpersonal complexities just like any other pair of human beings, and yet watching them one simply knows they will pull through. Their relationship is robust and resilient; its *recuperative powers* are self-evident. We naturally have faith in them. Their breaking up would surprise us, even in this age of epidemic instability in human commitments. In their communities, their love is like a lighthouse in the storm. Without planning it or intending it, they have come to be *role models* for other lovers, glowing with confidence, mutual support, and natural authority. We prize them. And, like circling planets, we orbit them like a solar hub.

One look, and we know that they have responded well and wisely to the logic of their composite Sun. The sheer vitality of their bond declares it.

Two sane, mature souls come together. Their values are sound. They've done their share of inner work. On paper, the relationship seems blessed and natural. And yet they simply run out of gas. Their bond unravels. Every relationship has its challenges—the "viruses" and "bacteria" of our unresolved psychological and karmic baggage as individuals, the natural friction between the natures of any two individuated adults. But in this case, it seems as if the *immune response* of the couple to those infestations has collapsed. Pettiness reigns. Both people are diminished. Their conflicts embarrass them, at least in the cold light of morning. Their erotic response to each other goes flat. A mood of grayness suffuses any room they occupy together. If we were to let the inner poet conjure images, they would be of wintry skies and bare trees, with a tepid sun sinking into a cold, dull sea.

Such is the result of a starving composite Sun.

In this second, sadder example, let's emphasize that each of these people may remain sane, strong and vital *as individuals*. It's the relationship itself that's experiencing an energy crisis, not necessarily the two people who compose it.

COMPOSITE SUN IN ARIES

Deep in the core of this relationship is a fire. It is fierce, hot, and unforgiving—and the one offense it can never forgive is to be starved for the fuel that keeps it alive. That fuel is the soul-food of Warriors: adventure, intensity, a sense of living passionately and close to the edge. To be true to themselves, a couple with the composite Sun in Aries must be fearless—or, more accurately, they must *never let fear make a decision for them.*

When in doubt, buy a sloop and set out for the Antipodes. That's the spirit, if not the letter, of the Aries soul-contract. Two people alone on a small vessel in the middle of the sea, a storm raging around them—it blows out the emotional cobwebs! There's a kind of purity and simplicity in the love between Warriors when they are *in extremis* and relying on each other. They're not arguing over word-choices at such a time. Faced with life and death, the little annoyances that drive people crazy in intimacy slip into their rightful perspective. For the couple with their composite Sun in Aries, it isn't actually necessary that they risk their necks so dramatically, but they do need the kind of stretching that comes from taking risks together. Traveling to places that frighten them a bit could be on the list—and for one couple that could mean driving five hundred miles to Peoria, while for another it might mean reaching the summit of Mount Kilimanjaro. Sports might figure positively in their life together. So could hiking, biking or hang-gliding.

All the imagery we've explored so far has been physical, but not all the Arian work is centered on the fears we have around keeping our bodies intact. There are also emotional and psychological fears, and facing those is actually closer to the heart of the evolutionary intention of this composite Sun. In fact, the more physical kinds of adventure simply support the development of the courage and the mutual trust that allows these two people to do their deeper inner work together.

Perhaps one of them is bothered by the other one's defensiveness in a certain area of their relationship. If he or she brings up that subject, there's going to be an emotional bloodbath—but if the subject is left unaddressed, then tensions and estrangement build toward the boiling point. "There's something we need to talk about . . . " Those are the fateful, necessary words, and it takes courage to speak them. That courage is the very essence of what it means to have the composite Sun in Aries.

If the couple goes ahead and deals with each other bravely, directly, and honestly, the fur will fly sometimes. The fights will be glorious. And the two Warriors will love each other more deeply and more respectfully over the years. If, on the other hand, they go down the coward's road, then the Arian energy devolves into pettiness and bickering, and a mood of endless, undefined *stress* in the relationship. It's critical to remember that, while intimate courage is really the key, its development must be supported by a rough-and-ready, adventurous attitude toward their life together in the world. That's the foundation. The higher ground is not only a lot more satisfying. It's also a lot more fun.

COMPOSITE SUN IN TAURUS

The logic of Taurus is the logic of the inner animal. Of all the signs, it is the one closest to the way of nature. The basic mood, needs and values of a couple with this composite Sun reflect our biological heritage as *creatures* on this earth: the desire to be safe, in familiar surroundings, comfortable, warm and well-fed. Walk into any home such a couple might share and you can feel it right away: put your feet up, settle into that supernaturally comfy sofa, and relax. But not before enjoying a long bear hug. This earthiness is disarming; you soon find yourself talking about how you really feel. And if you feel bad, you are soon comforted. Even a cup of tea in such a home seems to get you quickly back to basics.

Despite pervasive phallic mythology, most men don't really think of themselves as bulls. Very few women identify themselves with cattle. We've found, with Taurus, that it helps to expand our zoological horizons—we've learned to be open to leaving the bovine world behind and look for other animal-metaphors better suited to the realities of the couple. Incidentally, a couple with this composite Sun may very well find themselves literally attracting animals into their lives: cats, dogs, horses, and maybe more exotic species. Asking about their pets is often a terrific icebreaker. That's the exoteric reality. Be admitted into the secret world of such a relationship, and one often finds a fantasy life in which each member of the dyad plays an animal role: in privacy, they're snuggle bunnies, or proud lions, or mischievous, wild-eyed monkeys.

The maintenance of basic vitality in this relationship depends upon establishing stability and peace. The more rapidly psychodrama can be put aside, the better—so long as necessary struggles are not swept under the carpet in the name of the general *bonhomie*. All forms of non-verbal relating are helpful here: sex, of course. But also simple touch, and listening quietly to music together. Making a sacred ritual of sharing long, easy meals helps. So does having pets. And a garden, if possible, or at least potted plants. Paramount is time spent in nature together, far from the noise of the human world, to celebrate everything the wise animal inside us knows and values.

COMPOSITE SUN IN GEMINI

Imagine that you were born blind, and that a miraculous operation restores your sight. Suddenly the world is a dazzling riot of color and form. You see your spouse's face for the very first time. You know the names of all the objects in the room, but not which names belongs to which ones. Is that a rose, a teacup, a candelabra? Why are those flames dancing and shimmering in the fireplace? No one had ever told you that fire was in motion. And its colors! Which is yellow and which is orange and which is blue?

Presented with such an overwhelming new set of perceptions, what would you want to do? Explore every last inch of this fascinating world. Now stretch your imagination a bit further and pretend that *all* your senses, not just sight, had been restored. The hunger *to experience everything you possibly could* would become that much more powerful, wouldn't it?

A couple with the composite Sun in Gemini runs on much the same fuel. Feeding the core energy of this relationship requires what, to a more peaceful couple, can look like a serious case of cognitive overload. But for the composite Sun in Gemini couple, a fast-paced, colorful, almost bewildering diet of mesmerizing new experiences, ideas and conversations is absolutely essential. Accept a dinner invitation to such a couple's home, and you may walk into a living room where the wife is surfing the local library's online catalog while watching a music DVD. Meanwhile, the husband is taking a long distance call from Singapore on the kitchen phone and peering at stock quotes on his laptop. Two friends have resumed his interrupted dinner preparations from a recipe written entirely in Italian, which neither of them speaks. A third friend is trotting to and from the living room to ask the wife for help translating the recipe. A cell phone beeps, and there's a mad scramble to locate both it and its owner. The doorbell rings. Your host puts Singapore on hold to answer the door and falls on the visitor's neck with happy cries: it's a long-lost friend the couple hasn't seen for ten years and who's shown up unannounced with a magnum of Champagne—and a couple of trapeze artists he's representing and who need a place to sleep that night.

Overwhelmed? Intrigued? Ready for a freewheeling evening and hot competition to get a word in edgewise? So are the composite Sun in Gemini couple. These people do well to befriend and encourage one another's curiosity about this endlessly fascinating and mysterious universe. While they can have great fun debating how many angels can dance on the head of a pin, they should never be positive they've answered such questions. Why? Because certainty withers Geminian energy, while questions and puzzles nourish it. The writer Shirley Jackson once said, "Give the reader something to wonder about," and that's excellent advice for a composite Sun in Gemini. This couple should give one another lots to wonder about, and make their journey through the world far more interesting together than it would have been apart. Developing their skills in the various ways that we humans communicate, with one another and with anyone else, will always help them, as the curious seekers inside this pair well know.

COMPOSITE SUN IN CANCER

Cancer is the Crab—or the turtle! In either case, it's a creature with a wall of shell around its soft places, and that's really the point: Cancer represents the ultimate vulnerability, and also our natural skills at defending it against pain or attack.

Leaving aside physical trauma, what are the most painful experiences that can befall us? Quickly, most of us think of relationships breaking up: we all know how much that hurts. A very common answer to the question is "losing a child." That's so painful that most of us don't even want to think about it. Losing a friend, even losing an aged parent—these are the griefs of life. And every one of them is rooted in that ultimate human risk: *loving.*

With their composite Sun in Cancer, this couple is faced with a high-stakes evolutionary challenge: loving each other absolutely, committedly, and without any recourse at all to defenses against each other. The more deeply we love, the greater the potential hurt. With Cancer, the stakes go through the roof because this is the ancient sign of "home and hearth"—of bonded relationships. And that means relationships that, in principle, only death can unweave. There is No Exit.

It's almost a lost art. We live in a time of experimentation in terms of the meaning of love, commitment, home, and parenthood. Hardly anyone says "until death do us part" anymore. As a culture, we're currently enamored with individuality, personal growth, and freedom. That's not the Cancer way: radical commitment is the theme here. And that's like handing a crazy person a gun and then saying "please don't shoot me."

For the couple with the composite Sun in Cancer, the very core of their bond depends upon promises they keep. It thrives on words such as "forever" and "always" and "never." Those are the magic words that open the door to a tenderness, a security, and a faith almost beyond modern imagining.

This doesn't mean that all partners who happen to have their composite Sun in this sign should immediately commit to a lifetime together! Maybe that's not what their relationship is ultimately about. What it does mean is that, if two people with their composite Sun in Cancer hedge and vacillate about total commitment, the fire will go out of their connection. The Sun won't shine anymore. Such commitments are serious and profound, of course, and no one should rush into one. Courtship is necessary as trust gradually builds. But sooner or later, they arrive at that ancient Rubicon: they cross over into becoming a "home" together, or their vitality—and their sexuality together—quickly leaches away.

If they do cross the line, the couple with their composite Sun in Cancer will create a wonderfully nurturing *home* together. Friends will flock there, especially when those friends are feeling fried or frightened. Stray cats will mass at their door. If they choose to have children, those will be lucky, happy kids, rich in love. But everything hinges on their profoundly adult decision to make that homeward leap into absolute commitment.

It's funny how in the astrological literature Cancer is often represented as timid. That shows how far our culture has drifted away from understanding the fierceness and courage it takes to follow this path.

COMPOSITE SUN IN LEO

Children swinging as high as they can on playground swings will shriek, "Look at me!" And if mom and dad ignore them, you can feel the kids' empty sadness from fifty yards away. There is something in us all that wants to be seen and noticed, something that wants to leave an *impression* on the world. Astrologically, the sign Leo represents that drive. With composite Sun in Leo, the basic vitality of a couple depends on that kind of visibility. They've got to be seen.

We have to be careful to think deeply here. Try on this statement: "If no one pays attention to them, they don't exist." Sounds pretty pathological, huh? But no sign of the Zodiac is inherently crazy! The shallowness and lack of a solid center that our statement implies may describe Leo's shadow, but not its true nature. Imagine an artist without paintbrushes, or a fine pianist without a piano. The pain they feel is not pathological; it's perfectly natural. Dogs can be surgically modified so they can't bark, or cats so they can't meow. Just ask your heart how you feel about that. Something inside us knows it's simply wrong. It's a violation of the animal's nature. The creature will suffer sorrow, just like the painter and the pianist.

This couple needs to bark, meow, paint bright colors, and bang on the keys! They are true to themselves when they take up space and provide a little entertainment for those around them. This process can stretch in a healthy way from silly, simple earthy things all the way to the stars. At the simple end of the continuum, with composite Sun in Leo, a couple needs to dress up and go to a fancy restaurant from time to time. It's good for them to learn to dance. They need to experience themselves together as a *beautiful couple*—even if they're not "beautiful" in the conventional sense. Leo is the Lion, the "King of the Beasts." And everyone knows that Kings need castles. It's supportive to their well-being and their faith in their relationship that they would put a lot of energy into having a home that helps them feel proud, an expansive place where any guest immediately feels smarter and better-looking. This feeling of living life to the fullest, this generous feeling of expansiveness, celebration, and *joie de vivre* are the lifeblood of Leo, and a couple with their composite Sun there needs those feelings.

To say the same thing backwards, we must recognize the deadening effect on such a couple of a steady diet of practicality, sobriety and austerity. Not to say that they can't go down such a road—only that it will kill them.

Reaching higher, let's recognize that with the composite Sun in Leo, two people benefit enormously from a shared creative life. We can imagine, for example, that they would join a local theater group together. Performing on stage would provide a merry memory, a place in their mental scrapbook to which they could return year after year—and every time they did, they would feel a little boost in their sense of bondedness. To design a house—their castle—jointly is something sweet to their shared spirit. Supporting each other's individual creative efforts is part of the Leo process too. If one writes a poem, the other one takes it seriously and reads it carefully. And if one tells a joke, the other one laughs loud and hard—even if it's not very funny! Why? Because laughing is a big-hearted, generous act, and that's what fuels the love of this Leo couple.

COMPOSITE SUN IN VIRGO

Love is hard work, and Virgo thrives on it. With their composite Sun in this sign, these two people have taken on an evolutionary project. They've got a challenging task ahead of them. Notice how immediately these words make it sound as if they've made some kind of major cosmic error in meeting each other? That's not the point at all! The point is that Virgo is about rolling up our sleeves and getting on with it—whatever "it" may be, from cleaning the house to dealing with each other's unresolved psychological issues. Whoever said, "if it ain't broke, don't fix it" was not a Virgo. Remember that astrologically the Sun represents *vitality*. For this couple to feel alive together, they have to feel as if they are growing, changing, and pressing ever higher. Lazing on the beach—or in bed—is not taboo. In fact, they'll need it, given the effort that relationship demands. But always the centerpiece is their own evolution, and it doesn't matter if they use that kind of language or not. What matters is growth and improvement, step-by-step, over the years of their relationship.

Together, they develop an uncanny capacity to scope out whatever is wrong in their interpersonal dynamics. Generally, what they see is real. The trick is to keep perspective; always, the underlying risk is that they begin to niggle each other to death. Forgiveness has a role in love, as does silent forbearance. Humor is essential. Some issues can't be resolved today.

Put them in a comfortable box with nothing to do and a couple with their composite Sun in Virgo will quickly drive each other mad. The key here is to stay out of the box! And they can do that by honoring another fundamental dimension of Virgo: this is the Sign of the Servant. What that means is that part of the core soul-intention of this couple lies in making a difference in the lives of other people. They are naturally helpful—and people around them will be drawn to them as if by magnetism in times of need. Sometimes the needs are emotional, but often they're purely practical: Will you help us move house this weekend? What do you know about air conditioners? With their composite Sun in Virgo, these two have practically put out advertising as Helpers in their community, family, or "tribe." They actually benefit from this, and not just in terms of karmic "brownie points." Focusing on the needs of others helps balance their attention away from what otherwise could become an obsessive concern with themselves and their own issues—a concern which, while inherently healthy, can lead to a crash-and-burn scenario of emotional exhaustion, lost patience, and rampant tension.

Virgo is of course the Virgin—but fear not! There's no reason to expect that a couple will have sexual problems or undue primness just because their composite Sun lies in this sign. In fact, we have at least one reason to believe the opposite. Virgo is an Earth sign, and that means about what you would expect it to mean. It's earthy. Given half a chance, the physical side of love comes naturally to this couple. But again, like everywhere else, they need to find a balance between constantly improving that part of their life together and just simply enjoying it as it is without "helpful" comment.

COMPOSITE SUN IN LIBRA

Libra is the balance scale, and it represents the idea of two equal but opposite entities coming into equilibrium with each other. Thus, it is naturally the symbol of loving human relationship at its best—that is to say, a bond based upon harmony, mutual respect, and equality. With their composite Sun in Libra, our couple has a high ideal toward which to strive! They are definitely "going for the gold."

A graceful quality naturally radiates from these two. They look good together. They seem to "fit." Perhaps there's a kind of symmetry between them: they are similar types. Or perhaps it's more as if they complement and complete each other, with one of them a thinker and the other a feeler, or one practical and the other visionary. It can go either way—and in either case, from the outside perspective, there's a sense that they did well in finding each other. People tend to believe in their relationship, or even to hold it up as an ideal.

Whether our two individuals actually experience it that way is another question! They surely can, but as always it takes effort to make love work. The single most important existential vitamin for these two is *calm*.

Serenity. Everything healing and positive that sustains this relationship has its ultimate source in that sense of spacious, graceful timelessness. It's worth a thousand insights. By instinct, together they will move in that direction, attaining it perhaps through simply creating a visually beautiful home full of art, light, and music. They'll relax over their meals, and have a candle on the table on winter evenings. In lovemaking, they'll take time to be tender. In conversation, they'll hear each other out without inappropriate interruption or gratuitous crudity. Primness isn't the point; nothing as funky as two human beings in a bodily, intimate relationship can ever be "prim" for long! The point is more like never losing sight of human grace.

Simply to predict that our couple with the composite Sun in Libra will automatically behave so elegantly would be naive. Such balance is the true core of their relationship, the "divine plan" for them. The more they approximate it, the happier and more vital their bond will be. Conversely, we need to recognize that nothing will destroy their faith in their love faster than the jagged emotional edges of crassness or disrespect, or resorting to the familiar arsenal of emotional weapons of mass destruction. Paradoxically, we need to warn these two that avoiding natural conflict can actually worsen it when it finally breaks out. They need to be wary of false compromises—and by "false" we mean compromises that are actually grossly dissatisfying to one or both of them, and undertaken only out of fear of a serious row. Libra is all about "fairness," and that is of course a beautiful, necessary part of lasting love. But even fairness has a dark side when it drives these two into bland agreement—a calm before an inevitable storm. Let their motto be, "Love, honor, and negotiate!"

COMPOSITE SUN IN SCORPIO

Clearly, our ancestors were not trying to comfort us when they decided to name a sign of the zodiac after a scorpion! The spooky little stinging creature makes most of us shudder. We think about sudden, dreadful death, whatever we may know about the actual probabilities. Having their composite Sun in Scorpio isn't likely to sound very encouraging to our poor couple!

On the other hand, maybe they know enough about pop astrology to know that Scorpio is usually associated with sex, which might represent a more heartening perspective.

Death and sex. Fear and desire. The end of life and the very source of life. How come these two are so often associated? Unravel that mystery and you've begun to understand the sign of the scorpion—and to grasp what motivates this couple. Death is generally a taboo topic in social situations, quite unlike sex which tends to be the subject of a lot of playful banter. But once we stop joking about sex and start being honest about it, people often get pretty nervous. It's a very delicate topic, full of psychological undercurrents—just like death. People get nervous during honest conversations about sex, just as they get nervous about being honest in the face of such topics as ageing, disease, our fears, our shame. Astrologically, Scorpio simply refers to the *mechanism of honest self-awareness* in the human mind: our ability to delve into the things that make us feel scared or crazy. With their composite Sun in Scorpio, these two people will delve so deeply into each other's "stuff" that their relationship will often feel like psychotherapy. That, or it will be a living demonstration of their *need* for psychotherapy! Simply said, they are powerful triggers for each other. They "press each other's buttons." That can be a profoundly healing and energizing experience for them, or it can push them into shattering realms of intensity, draining drama, and unending heaviness. What makes the difference? Certainly a part of the answer lies in their individual willingness to face that degree of intimacy—it's not for everyone, nor should it be! People have a natural need for privacy and boundaries, and there is something about Scorpionic energy that runs right over those kinds of barriers. Thus, *respect* is essential here—and a wise corollary of respect, which is vigilance in making sure that neither partner "becomes the psychotherapist" while the other one gets cast as the madwoman or madman. We should add that a sense of humor is critical too—with Scorpionic material, we often find ourselves in situations where you either laugh or you cry. Both are necessary! Finally, and perhaps most importantly, trust is the foundation of everything for this couple. We can only be this psychologically naked with someone whom we know is not going to abandon us or betray us, who will never violate our confidentiality, and who has taken the same risks of self-disclosure as we have.

If any of these pieces are missing, these two people tend to slip into psychological warfare, moodiness, and sniping. But with all these pieces in place, our couple with the composite Sun in Scorpio can come to epitomize the modern, post-patriarchal model of healthy, committed intimacy: two souls, bound by a shared commitment to grow, and virtually unable to conceive of being closer to anyone else than they are to each other.

COMPOSITE SUN IN SAGITTARIUS

There is no sign of the Zodiac so oriented to sheer intensity of sensory experience as Sagittarius. With their composite Sun in this sign, these two people have signed up for a roller coaster ride. Regardless of their natures as individuals, there is something in the chemistry they share that attracts life's wild side. It's all a bit like Gandalf the Wizard knocking on the Hobbit's door—once the portal is opened, there is no turning back. Maybe they feel settled in a home and a community. Wheels turn, and before they know it they've been transferred to Ireland—or Patagonia! Maybe they've settled into certain values and philosophical perspectives—and they meet someone who glows in the dark with the fire and the power of some alternative path.

It really has to be this way. Sagittarius, to be fully alive, needs to be packing in the experience of ten lifetimes. Should life become too prosaic and predictable, something vital seeps out of this relationship. Boredom can kill it faster than any other toxin. Together, these two need change, freshness, and wonder. They need to stretch. They do tend to magnetize extremity into the life they share, but of course, Gandalf can knock and the Hobbit can choose not to open the door. In other words, they can potentially make a militant choice to value stability above their own natural course through life. If they do that, then we'll see chaos nagging at them all the time, eroding their peace—plus, a disturbing tendency toward one-dimensional dogmatism in their shared thinking. More tellingly, we will also see a kind of tiredness creeping into the relationship, as the life-force drains from them.

Ultimately, the feeling for this couple with their composite Sun in Sagittarius is one of being on a Quest. Together, they are endlessly seeking something. The actual nature of that something is elusive, but what it boils down to is a *meaningful* life. They will pursue it down cross-cultural roads, taking pieces of the puzzle from various different nations and mythologies. They will chase it through education in the broad sense—learning together, and talking about what they've learned, whether it's through books or classes or other sources. They'll perhaps be drawn to religion, and almost surely to philosophy. Always, the road stretches a little further before them—just one more horizon, and they'll be there.

COMPOSITE SUN IN CAPRICORN

One of the main things that gives angels their sense of humor about the human race is the way various virtues go in and out of style. Currently, the virtues we associate with Capricorn seem a bit *passé*. And that's sad, because they are precious ones: integrity, character, a sense of personal honor, dignity. They're preciously relevant in many areas of life, but perhaps nowhere so vividly as in a life-long vow of mutual care and defense between two people, whether they are sexual partners or comrades. When we find the composite Sun in Capricorn, the soul-stakes are very high. In the long run, whether or not they remain together, the dignity of these two human beings will depend very much on how honorably they treat each other during the course of their relationship.

The highest—and most challenging—prospect here is the idea of *marriage*. We go ahead and use that traditional term because of its innate gravity, although we welcome a future in which there's less emphasis on pieces of paper filed in courthouses and more upon a promise held sacred by two people and professed publicly in their community. If two people come together with their composite Sun in Capricorn, sooner or later they will face the serious issue of whether or not they choose to make that kind of vow to each other. If that is their higher destiny and they vacillate too long without answering it, vitality and energy quickly drain out of their relationship. Drifting in limbo is death for this archetype. Capricorn, more than any other sign, thrives upon Great Works—and in the context of a composite chart, that Great Work is by definition a long-haul, deeply committed relationship.

Of course just because the midpoint of two people's Suns happens to fall in Capricorn doesn't mean they must head for the wedding chapel or fail spiritually! Obviously, that would be silly and extreme. But it does mean that they need to handle their relationship in a way that makes them feel proud, no matter where it ends up. Honesty, tempered with gentleness and maturity, is essential. No prudery is intended here: even in the briefest of relationships, there can be respect and a feeling of decency—and a residual feeling of connectedness that neither person would ever deny or dishonor.

But one night stands and their like are not what Capricorn symbolizes. Its tastes and predilections run toward steeper mountains. And, if a couple chooses to scale such peaks, an alchemical process is triggered in each of their psyches. Soon that ancient Capricorn archetype, The Elder, begins to make its presence felt in the air around them. They come to *represent* the mountain in their community—something solid and consistent in this swirling world of endless change, a beacon to which people can turn when they are confused or feeling lost. After a while, their higher destiny together begins to reveal itself, at first not so much in their own minds, but rather in the minds of those who watch them, awed and inspired by the mighty thing they are doing together day by day.

Offering that gift to the people around them is the higher work these two have taken on. Once they've crossed the line into commitment, their successes give us all hope—and, conversely, if the stone of their failure strikes the waters of the community, concentric circles of hopelessness and despair spread far and wide. Fair? Not at all. But the Elder archetype is about giving a gift, not about demanding one—and for these two, that's where the path of energy, vitality, and purpose lies.

COMPOSITE SUN IN AQUARIUS

Couples have been trying to live together, one way or another, for a couple of million years. Long-term loving remains difficult despite all the experimentation and post-mortem discussion groups. Still, in those countless centuries, humanity has learned a few things:

Forgiveness is precious. Commitment is essential. Honesty must be tempered with tenderness. Passion changes over time. Children change everything. Beware of in-laws. Say five nice things for every hard one. And so on.

It's a precious legacy, handed down through the generations in the form of customs, folklore, and chicken soup wisdom. Flawed by sexism, undercut by sexual shaming, twisted by patriarchal perversity as it may be, these principles generally work better than flying blind—unless, that is, this couple's composite Sun lies in Aquarius! Then, we can count on the fact that there will be at least one relationship ideal, "obvious to everyone" which would be the kiss of death for these partners.

Their task is to figure out which one it is.

Perhaps they are meant to be totally, monogamously committed to each other—but not even *try* to live together under one roof. Maybe, once together, it becomes essential to the relationship that they quit their jobs and go raise llamas or ostriches. Maybe they're not supposed to have kids. The point is that the natural expression of this relationship involves breaking some "rule" that both partners were both trained to hold as obvious and natural. Once they see it, they feel liberated—and the bond between them can breathe and grow. Until they see it, they are haunted by an ill-defined sense of something being wrong. It's as if the music is written in the wrong key for their voices. All the harmonies are strained.

Going further, it's clear at this juncture of history that humanity is re-defining marriage, family, and intimacy. So far, we've mostly figured out what *doesn't* work. Love, sex and procreation aren't going to go away, but what will they look like in a hundred years? Here's part of the answer: assuming that this couple gets it right, some of the "weird" aspects of their relationship today will be perfectly normal in the future. Aquarius is always the cutting edge, always the place where Life is experimenting with new possibilities for the human future. That still leaves these partners without much guidance in the present tense! But it does underscore the wonderful gift they've signed up to give the next generation. Every deepening discussion they have and every creative solution they put together not only benefit them, but also echo down the corridors of time. How? Easy. People are watching them.

COMPOSITE SUN IN PISCES

Rare is the wedding or commitment ceremony that doesn't invoke the divine mysteries. Almost always, there is talk of God, souls, the Holy Spirit—the sacred dimension of life. Those perspectives may not be on our minds every minute of every day, but they always pop up when we think big questions about why two people might come together to share a life. Astrologically, Pisces represents the part of human consciousness that sends a tap root down into that bedrock. It is the archetype of the *Mystic*. With their composite Sun in this sign, the energy that animates this relationship depends totally upon these two people spending a lot of time tuned into that broader, deeper sense of themselves. They need meditative time together, and lots of it.

Who can walk into a room lit only by candles and not feel a change in attitude? Who can walk down the beach in the moonlight without being lifted into a new place? With their composite Sun in Pisces, these two people need regular doses of exactly that kind of magical experience. Some Piscean couples encounter it in "officially" spiritual settings—religious ceremonies, meditation groups, and so on. But that formality isn't necessary. Sometimes candles are enough.

Once we get over our discomfort, there's usually something ridiculous about other people's relationship spats. Everyone's "stuff" is hanging out, usually liberally spiced with self-righteousness and psychiatric interpretations of each other's behaviors and motivations. For all our talk about the spiritual dimensions of love, it's also clear that ego makes its presence felt when we vexatious, flawed human beings try to love. From the higher Piscean ground, ego looks pretty hilarious! Thus, a sign that these two people are centered and strong in their relationship is that they consistently "get the joke" about themselves. Lots of laughter is a very positive spiritual sign. Even in the midst of a passionate, angry exchange, it's not unusual for one member of a Piscean couple to suddenly get the giggles about it—and the giggles, after a moment, often prove contagious.

As always, every front has a back. Pisces can "transcend" itself right into oblivion—and it's usually a bleary oblivion of lassitude, resignation and escape. The composite Sun is the ego of a couple, and ego serves a good purpose in the cosmic scheme. It's the pro-active part of us that's in the driver's seat of the psyche, that goes and gets what we need, even if faced with resistance or censure. With their composite Sun in Pisces, what this couple needs is a regular diet of shared soul-time. They can call it yoga. They can call it moonlit nights in the desert. They can call it lying in a bed listening to music with the lights down low. Whatever they call it, they need it. Without it, their love withers on the vine. With it, they shine like a beacon of magic in their community.

COMPOSITE SUN IN THE FIRST HOUSE

An invisible gravitational field radiates from this couple. People are affected by them. The impact may be overt or covert, depending on other factors in the composite chart, but once you look for it, it is unmistakable. These partners are trend setters. If they're happy, when they walk into a crowded room, the jokes get funnier—even if their own mouths are closed.

If they're feeling low, the room gets quieter. If they're feeling sexy—well, make sure you're not serving martinis.

The paradox is that, despite the power and confidence that radiates from them as a couple, inwardly there is a feeling of uncertainty about this relationship. Are they "supposed" to be a couple or not? What is "God's position" on that one? God is mum, kind of like one of those enigmatic Buddhas with the inscrutable smile. Ultimately, there is no house as free as the first. There, human will reigns supreme. There's not much interference from any sense of destiny. For this relationship to work, it must be a conscious choice. They must burn bridges behind them and not look back. Should they? It's up to them. Not every dating couple that happens to have their composite Sun in the first house is supposed to spend life together. All we know for sure is that, sooner or later, they will come to a fork in the road. They'll choose this love, or they'll choose to leave it. *And it will need to be a totally adult decision*, without any figures of authority—worldly or divine—intervening.

A few lines back, we mentioned the gravitational field around these two. Whether they know it or not, they are leaders in their community. People are influenced by them, even model themselves on them. There are serious, far-reaching undercurrents here. If this couple breaks up, there's a spike in the local "divorce rate." If they remain committed and vibrant together, more people in their crowd are likely to take the plunge into serious coupling. First house energy is always about leadership, and with composite charts, it's about leadership in terms of the local attitude about committed love. If they choose to be together, they can light the way for many others to take that path. And if they choose not to be, that's all right—they can still model kind, sensitive, honorable endings. The world benefits from that too. But if they model catastrophe, prepare for a minor epidemic.

COMPOSITE SUN IN THE SECOND HOUSE

Self-confidence is always a big issue with the second house—and right away let's make it clear that this self-confidence isn't to be confused with the "hormonal courage" that arises naturally about ten seconds after a first kiss! With their composite Sun in the second house, these two people are working toward believing in themselves as a couple enough to trust the real-world, grown-up potential of their relationship.

There's an irony here, one familiar to every bright twenty-one-year-old who's read the words "experienced only" a few too many times in the want ads. For a couple truly to believe in itself, it really helps to have some miles on the relationship. To have survived a few storms. But no relationship starts out that way! At first, they must rely on faith—and hormones. With the composite Sun in the second house, the risk is simple to define: too much aversion to risk. And love is always a risk. The upshot is that this couple could fritter away their potential "making sure they were ready." They could delay escalations in the level of commitment for too long. They could hedge their bets with fugues in their heads along the lines of "maybe this relationship will work, but then if it doesn't, there's always . . . "

To exhort every couple with the composite Sun in the second house to promise themselves to each other immediately would be wrong and irresponsible. Not every relationship is *supposed* to last a lifetime! We only caution them that hesitation can take as costly a toll as haste—and add that they benefit a lot by giving themselves signals of the seriousness of the bond. They might, for example, plan to go on a cruise together *six months from now*. Or buy a little sailboat together to share. Such steps send deep signals down into the soul, announcing the expectation that the relationship has a future. That triggers two positive possibilities. The first is that they begin to believe more in themselves. The second is that, if the relationship really doesn't have the "legs" it needs for the long run, they scare themselves into seeing it. And better sooner than later!

COMPOSITE SUN IN THE THIRD HOUSE

You're driving in traffic through an urban landscape. A jaywalking pedestrian dashes out in front of you, knowing you'll slow down enough to avoid vehicular manslaughter—and betting his life that you see him. A light turns red: hit the brakes. A driver just ahead does something crazy. Adjust. Observe. React. Welcome to Chaos Theory. Welcome to the third house. With a composite Sun in this sector of the chart, the couple has signed up for a wild ride. However orderly they may be as individuals, however neat and controlled, so long as they remain together they'll be improvising decisions at the speed of light in the face of unpredictable reality. Together, they are a magnet for the unexpected and the improbable. And together, two halves of a greater whole, they have what it takes to enjoy the ride.

Navigating an automobile illustrates third house consciousness. But so does a rollicking conversation between two people engaged with a fascinating topic. One makes a statement. The other one half-agrees—and takes the topic in a new direction. Which prompts a creative leap in the first person. And a joke from person number two, which leads to a tangential remark, which swings back into the topic from an unexpected angle. And soon both people have learned something they never knew before—and said things they didn't know they knew!

Traveling, learning, talking: all these activities are likely to be central to the shared experience of a couple with a composite third house Sun. The word "media" figures prominently in their life together. As an entity, they are simply *curious*—and the maintenance of the basic vitality of their relationship depends upon indulging that need for endless fascination. Thus, boredom and predictability are anathema here. Hurling themselves headlong into the unexpected and the unknown is essential. An open mind and a willingness to improvise are needed tools. Language is absolutely pivotal here—a silent third house relationship is soon a dead one.

Are there actually patterns underlying apparent chaos? That's a hot topic in modern physics. From the perspective of a third house composite Sun, we can define one such pattern. Understanding it brings us to the evolutionary heart of this configuration. *Whatever this couple believes and expects, they'll draw the opposite to themselves.* It's as if the universe insists upon saying to them, "I am more complex than your conception of me."

COMPOSITE SUN IN THE FOURTH HOUSE

The stakes are beautifully high with a composite Sun in the fourth house. This is the classic "house of the home," and it refers to the Holy Grail of human intimacy: a truly bonded, stable relationship that provides a sense of "home" for both people involved. It is about radical commitment and a lifetime of mutual support. Its orientation is naturally domestic. It tends toward fertility—with this configuration, if you don't want kids, practice birth control diligently! There's a sense of permanence and stability, of a relationship "meant to be."

Sometimes a couple that has been together for decades will refer endearingly to each other in terms that baffle young lovers: "she's like an old familiar shoe," or "we hardly need to speak to each other anymore." Not the kinds of words on-screen lovers whisper to each other with the buildings blowing up behind them! Clearly, there are potential horrors in those sentiments. They reek of the blind, sexless boredom of a love that died long ago but never fell over. As a culture, we've gotten estranged from the beauty of the fourth house, which makes it a little harder for modern couples with this configuration to find their rhythm. Naturally, as this love matures, these two find themselves less oriented to the outer world: to appearances, to their careers, to the night life. They'll probably find their blood-families playing a big role in their life together. We mentioned the fertility of this configuration. Let's add that the nurturing energy here extends beyond children: friends-in-need will abound. Stray cats meow at the door. Something safe and calming radiates from these two, and anyone under stress will be drawn to them like a home-made meal after a month of fast food.

Once this relationship moves in the direction of commitment, the physical location of the home they choose to share is a big issue. The overriding principle is that they are very sensitive to their domestic scene, and pushing it up the list of priorities is a very positive move. Often, in practical terms, it comes down to spending more money for a place they love—and it's money well-spent. A cheaper place might allow them to vacation in Europe, but the daily drain of an uncomfortable home outweighs that. Furniture they love, maybe a little garden, some extra effort to keep the place cleaned up and attractive—all these are relationship-affirming moves. Above all, they need quiet time together in their "Hobbit-hole." Some couples prefer city life, and that's fine—one can have a comfortable, safe home there too. But the classic response to the fourth house Sun involves a strong sense of relationship with *the land itself.* Probably, sooner or later, this couple will discover their "true home," and it will be a piece of land that speaks to them from under their feet. If they can possibly buy a place, that's to the good. It's easy to visualize them planting an apple tree there—and eating apple pie fifty years later!

COMPOSITE SUN IN THE FIFTH HOUSE

How long can you fall in love? A month? A decade? A lifetime? For the couple with their composite Sun in this "house of love affairs," the basic vitality of their bond depends upon keeping that magic alive. There's room for realism here—this couple, like all others in history, will experience frustration and boredom with each other sometimes. That's only natural. But they compensate for it with the kind of attention that lovers pay each other. They need to compliment each other freely. Enormous benefits come to them from simply dressing up and going out to dinner at a nice restaurant. Ditto for showing up with flowers "for no reason." Some couples make a joke of never remembering their anniversary—not this one, at least if they're healthy! Like new lovers, *the myth of the relationship* needs to be fed. Taking each other for granted is toxic. Too many oblivious "yes, dears," and Eros seeps out of the connection. A fifth house relationship tends to be high maintenance. Balancing that, it's also highly energizing for both partners.

Shared creativity is pivotal to a couple with their composite Sun in the fifth. After they've cast off the magical hormonal training wheels of the early stages of sexual bonding, finding artistic outlets that engage them both is an enormous support for their faith in their connection. It can be as simple as reading each other's poetry—and a fifth house relationship will bring out the poet in both of them! It can be as elaborate as some kind of public performance. Maybe they play music together or co-author a book. Maybe they step on stage together in a community theater. Perhaps they hang a show of their photographs. In any case, there is something about the aliveness, immediacy and emotional risk of shared creative work that feeds them. It helps keep the nakedness of new love present for them, and that is the soul of the fifth house.

All through their life together, the couple with the composite Sun in the fifth house will experience something of a "revolving door" in terms of their friendships. This doesn't mean they'll have no life-long bonds with other people; they can and do. But it guarantees a pattern of people coming into their lives in very big, time-consuming ways—and then disappearing. This isn't necessarily painful. Often it happens naturally, as, for example, when a theater ensemble bonds deeply, then moves apart after the show is over.

Finding a right, healthy relationship with the human need for pleasure is another fifth house issue, and this couple will wrestle with it. At the obvious level, we need to say that they should beware of the insidious way addictions and compulsions can creep into the life they share. At the more subtle level, we do need to add that *a celebration of life* is essential to the fifth house—and thus to the evolutionary intentions of this couple. It comes down to ensuring that they are actually enhancing their joy rather than going down the sad road of some kind of escapism.

COMPOSITE SUN IN THE SIXTH HOUSE

In the standard lexicon of astrological interpretation, the sixth house is as sexy as a dish rag. The interpretations generally emphasize duties and responsibilities, "spiced" with daily routines. We'll do better than that below, but first let's pay the devil his due: with the composite Sun in the sixth, these two people will indeed attract more than their fair share of hard work. Likely, weighty responsibilities will find them. Perhaps it takes the form of familial duties: the elder parent who can't be abandoned and who can't care for himself or herself. The demanding or incapacitated child. There are some duties from which we simply cannot walk away and ever respect ourselves again. The sixth house represents that part of human reality.

If the responsibilities aren't so close to home, they probably take on a professional tone. There's a good chance this couple will find themselves sharing work somehow. Unbeknownst to them when they first meet, they are a natural team, custom-designed to do a job brilliantly well. Each has skills the other one lacks. Once the alchemical process of their bonding gets underway, it's as if the word magically goes out to the community. Very soon, circumstances are pulling them toward their natural service—which can provide a solid center of gravity for the relationship and a very real basis for believing in themselves. The work they share, even though it exacts a price from them, definitely pays more than money. And the clincher is that if they shirk the more public service, they'll surely manifest all this sixth house energy in the form of more dispiriting duties that descend upon them as "the luck of the draw."

Mentoring relationships are another big part of the sixth house. As this relationship matures, this couple will find themselves over and over again in the role of showing other couples the way. Sex comes naturally to human beings, but relationship is really an art. And like any other art, it can partly be learned—and taught. Destiny call our couple with the composite Sun in the sixth to both ends of that process. When they first meet, they need to keep their eyes open for their own teachers. A good bet is that this will be an older couple—or at least a couple who's been together a while—who offers critical support and insight to our heroes in their salad days. Later, they'll find younger couples knocking on their door, ostensibly asking to borrow a cup of sugar—and looking to learn the secret of sane, lasting love.

COMPOSITE SUN IN THE SEVENTH HOUSE

With the composite Sun here, this couple has enrolled in post-doctorate work in seventh-house relating skills. Developing and maintaining intimacy, trust, reciprocity and commitment is the territory here. As individuals, they may be profoundly independent, assertive, even suspicious or combative. Nonetheless, as a couple they must learn to share, to connect, to let down their guard with one another, and to compromise. Each person must assume that the partner's needs and feelings are just as important as his or her own, not more so and not less so.

Fortunately, given the nature of the seventh house Sun's composite terrain, these two people are often drawn to each other immediately. A spirit of friendship and camaraderie can swiftly arise · here, a sense of complementarity. Even if we don't fall in love, if we have a seventh house composite Sun, on some level we feel that we have business with this person. We want to throw our lot in with him or her. *Constant awareness of the other person* is a feature here; we are rarely indifferent to someone with whom we have a seventh house composite Sun. Such emotions are most conducive to the work of the seventh house.

Remember that this house, the traditional "house of marriage"—although the eighth may have just as good a claim to that title—is the house of that which is not the Self. The house of the Other. It has also been called the house of open enemies and the house of worthy opponents. How can all those names apply to this house? Sooner or later, conflict arises with someone who is not yourself, not your clone, not your twin. We've all learned that before we even left high school, yet there is such a powerful tendency, and possibly an unconscious tendency, for a couple with a seventh house composite Sun *to identify with each other* that the first conflicts can come as a shock, and may even feel like a betrayal. "You mean you don't want what I want? You, my other half? You, who complete me? How can that be?" If your seventh house composite Sun partner lets you down, you are so sensitized to him or her that you feel *profoundly* let down. What do you do then? Deal with the conflict, don't run from it. This composite Sun prefers harmony to wrangling—but it also must learn how to handle conflict in order to maintain the harmony it desires. Affirm the affection and connection between you, listen to one another without judging or blaming, find common ground, and work out a mutually agreeable compromise. Easier said than done, but that's the work of the seventh house, and with enough consciousness and good will on both sides, this couple is well suited to its accomplishment.

A potentially helpful factor is that these partners are a magnet for other people. They draw friends. Let's take it a step further: they *need* friends. It's possible to maintain a seventh house composite Sun and never see anyone outside the relationship, but it isn't easy. These people need to connect with others: with other couples, with other individuals. To share good times, to compare notes about relating, or just to blow off steam about one another to someone who loves both partners, has a sympathetic ear and can keep confidences. Minor annoyances accumulate in any bond. We are more sensitized to them if we have a seventh house composite Sun, because we are more sensitized to everything about our partner, for good or ill. He rarely wrings out a washcloth properly, and water keeps getting on the bathroom floor. She keeps hogging the counter space in the bathroom. Please understand that we are referring to *minor* annoyances, not relationship-damaging ones that require a discussion with the mate. These partners both need to take ten minutes and ventilate, separately, to their closest friends about these minor things. "I adore Jack, but . . . " At the end of the ten minutes, chances are they'll each be more able to put the little things in perspective and conclude, "But those are minor, and I'm glad I'm with him."

COMPOSITE SUN IN THE EIGHTH HOUSE

Why, ultimately, does sexuality exist? Arguments about the Darwinian advantages it gives us over amoebas are compelling—but that line practically demands a wisecrack. Many aspects of this universe serve more than a single purpose, and sex is doubtless one of them. Once we accept the metaphysical notion that our world is an incubator for the evolution of consciousness, the pieces of the puzzle fall into place. What promotes conscious evolution faster than sexuality? What, in other words, so confronts us with the realities—and the limitations—of our present consciousness? For the majority of us, the most compelling answer is usually lying in the bed next to us.

Nothing drives us deeper into our psychological selves than sexuality. And that is precisely what the eighth house represents astrologically. With their composite Sun in the eighth, these two people have taken on a Great Work. Together, they will evolve—or tear each other to shreds. Something in the chemistry between them triggers the emergence of whatever issues they least want to face—fear of abandonment, jealousy, possessiveness, insecurity, gender-anger. It all comes up. And it either gets healed or it dominates the relationship. Piece by piece, step by step, they go deeper and deeper. Whatever they uncover, there is of course more behind it. In the end, if they've succeeded and stayed together, then they face the ego's pluperfect challenge: death itself—and remember that in traditional astrology, the eighth is indeed the house of death. Two people who've loved each other for a big chunk of a lifetime sooner or later confront the prospect of one of their deaths. Imagine looking each other in the eye and dealing with that one in a spirit of stark naked emotional honesty! That's the composite Sun in the eighth house.

So who'd want to bother with having such a composite chart? Why would they? There are two answers. The first is soul-evolution itself: nothing we can possibly do on this earth so accelerates the growth of the human spirit. And if that sounds a little abstract for you, try this one: fabulous sex. When we are young and inexperienced, we often imagine that sexual energy sustains itself automatically, or at least that it will do so if we hook up with someone who looks like a movie star. Life soon enough disabuses us of that notion. It's not the bodies that sustain sexual heat between two individuals; it's their souls. Without soul-nakedness, give it six months or a year and we might as well be siblings sharing a bed. Enter the eighth house composite Sun: that soul-nakedness is the essence of the process these two have triggered between themselves. They'll pay a price in terms of psychological effort, humility, and sheer emotional exhaustion sometimes. And they'll get what they pay for in the form of intensity, sustainable passion, true closeness, and a sense of having hit the button on the evolutionary warp drive.

COMPOSITE SUN IN THE NINTH HOUSE

Get out the suitcases! With the composite Sun in the ninth house, these two are going to need them. The destiny they trigger as they come together will literally stretch their horizons. Even if they are homebodies by nature, circumstances will arise that press them to leave home—and more pivotally, to leave *the defining context of their familiar culture*. Maybe they'll simply travel a lot. Quite possibly, the life they share will lead them actually to move to another part of the country or perhaps to make their home overseas. Perhaps their families are of different ethnic, regional, or socioeconomic origins. It's all "travel" in the broad sense of the word.

There's more to the ninth house than travel. Anything that expands our horizons is part of it. With their composite Sun in the ninth house, if they're healthy and happy as a couple, you'll find these two sitting in the front row of lectures on new archaeological discoveries in the Yucatán. You'll overhear them at the next table in a restaurant talking about books they've read or new ideas they've encountered. Anything that stretches them feeds them. Together, they share an evolutionary intention to press beyond any limiting framework, be it cultural, philosophical or mental.

Traditionally, religion is a central ninth house theme. That may still be accurate today. Quite possibly, a couple with their composite Sun in the ninth will find themselves increasingly identified with a particular faith. It's also helpful to note that the ninth house embraces any kind of "lens" through which we look at life—religion can do that, but so can a philosophical perspective, such as liberal or conservative politics, entrepreneurialism, or even cynicism. They're all "religions" in the larger sense, and they can all potentially fit the driving ninth house need for a sense of *meaning* in life.

Life without something in which to believe may be empty, but we must also recognize that people create prisons for themselves with their own belief-systems. Here lies the shadow for the couple with the Sun in the ninth house. Their basic energy and vitality as a couple depend on a steady diet of anything that stretches them by evening beyond what they knew that morning. Once we've "come to understand the meaning of life," we've got life in a neat little box. The freshness goes out of our experience. Together, these partners are on a quest for meaning—but whatever they find, it's more than that. *To endlessly seek something they dare not find:* that is the destiny of our pair of gypsy-pilgrims. Think about it too hard and they'll blow some mental fuses. Live it every day, and they'll find their relationship invigorating, surprising, and never the same.

COMPOSITE SUN IN THE TENTH HOUSE

To think of the tenth house in terms of career is mainstream astrology today. And that's accurate enough. But just because a couple has their composite Sun in the tenth doesn't mean they'll be rich and famous, or even particularly ambitious. Those questions are more related to their individual birthcharts. To get to the true heart of what this configuration means, we have to go beyond the blinders of our present culture and grasp some of the deeper layers of this house. Then we have to put two and two together.

First, the tenth house represents the human need to play a meaningful role in one's community. That drive goes way beyond any fundamentally ego-driven need for money, status or power, but *it is not inconsistent with them.* That's a critical point: you can do something publicly in which you believe and simultaneously get paid, empowered and respected for it. And who would really want a job that paid *only* money? Ultimately, the tenth house has more to do with those loftier drives than it does with mere status. It's more about the dignity and self-clarity that comes from giving than it is about "getting ours."

Next, remember that the composite Sun is always, by definition, about a relationship. So, in understanding what it means to have the composite Sun in the tenth, we put these two factors together, and realize that the *couple as a unit* is destined to offer a gift to their community. Quite possibly, they'll work together as a professional team with each one contributing something unique and essential to the partnership. "Chicken soup" wisdom about relationships often cautions against adding the strains of a collegial, working relationship to the natural strains of intimacy. That's fair advice in general, but it does not apply in this case. For this couple, considerable vitality and confidence arises from being partnered in their "Monday through Friday" lives as well as in the bedroom. As their destiny together unfolds, this option of sharing their work will quite likely present itself as a possibility, and they should take it seriously.

Going further, we can count on any couple with their composite Sun in the tenth house playing a significant "tribal" role simply through the outward symbolism of their relationship. Regardless of their intention or even their awareness, people will be modeling themselves on these two. They'll be held up as a standard, and their style of intimacy—at least insofar as it can be observed casually—will impact the values and choices of other couples. Sexual bonds are probably the oldest human institution, but of course their stylistic mythology changes with each generation. With their composite Sun in the tenth, these two people are style-setters. In monkey-see, monkey-do fashion, if they "moon" on each other in public, others will follow. If they tend to process their disagreements openly, other people will do that too—and ditto if they err in the direction of keeping their dirty laundry private. If they part, there will be an epidemic of relationship endings around them. And if they love each other well and truly, they will have offered a sweet gift to this lonely, crazy world. Whether they know it or not, this couple is leaving deep footprints behind them.

COMPOSITE SUN IN THE ELEVENTH HOUSE

The eleventh house is about our images of the future. With the composite Sun there, a couple draws energy in the present-tense from pictures of where they may be in time. It's almost like borrowing money—you take it from the future and you use it today. Here's how it works:

A couple who have been dating for nine weeks agree to go on vacation together this summer—three months from now. They both walk away from the conversation happy and maybe a little shaky too. Even if they didn't discuss it explicitly, a lot more just passed between them than a decision about a trip to the beach. They've signed a contract to still be together a bit down the road. They've affirmed their shared faith, for now, in their connection. They've narrowed their options—and defined themselves as a couple.

In a new romance, a lot can happen in three months. Quite possibly, they'll be split up by then. There goes their deposit on that nice beach house!

A couple decides to marry or otherwise commit to each other "until death do us part." And it's exactly like the beach trip—in the same way that a nuclear bomb is just like a firecracker! It's all a question of scale. The principles are precisely the same. Such a commitment is energizing—and frightening. It can add dignity and meaning to two lives. It can literally increase one's longevity and boost one's immune response. It can "cash out" one's dreams with shared resources, financially and in terms of all the advantages of teamwork. And, if the relationship crashes and burns, it can take a big bite out of one's soul.

With the composite Sun in the eleventh, these two benefit a lot from thinking strategically. The most dangerous condition for them lies in reaching a kind of "comfort zone" of rudderless contentment. They are really much better off striving together toward shared goals: a big trip to South America, a house they might design and build together, deepening their yoga practice. Above all, there is a sense of moving endlessly toward a more perfect partnership. Not every couple with a composite Sun in this house is supposed to go down the long road of life together, and it would be wrong to interpret the configuration that way. Still, a long, directionless limbo of "dating" will quickly drain their batteries. The eleventh house sustains itself on progress and commitment—committing to the beach house this summer or committing to life together, as appropriate.

One more piece of the puzzle: the eleventh house is often related to "friends," although words such as "networking" or "teamwork" make the point more clearly. Bottom line, these two share destiny with a lot of other people. Many of the plans and goals that sustain them are not attainable except through some degree of cooperative effort. Perhaps they join a couples' group. Maybe they derive a lot of their identity from a religious affiliation—or from weekend contra dancing. Metaphysically, they are participants in a kind of "group soul," and what they have come to this world to do and experience together is inseparable from that larger framework.

COMPOSITE SUN IN THE TWELFTH HOUSE

Loss, trouble, secret enemies—the traditional litany describing the twelfth house would be quite dispiriting for any couple who found their composite Sun placed there. If they read on, they might finally run into the notion that this house has something to do with monasteries and convents. Once through giggling about what that insight boded for their sexual life, they'd probably be eager to forget about astrology entirely and head for the bedroom.

They'd have our blessing, too! Only we would encourage them to make sure to turn off the lights and light a candle or two before they lie down together. And when they were making love, we would encourage them to keep their eyes open at least part of the time. We would, in other words, encourage them to use their sexuality as a doorway into another world. With their composite Sun in the mystical twelfth house, *conscious sexuality is their monastery!*

What about all those grim predictions in the traditional books? They are not without foundation. We just need to keep perspective, and allow a little wiggle room for human freedom and human consciousness. Together, they have signed up for a high stakes path: in a nutshell, they grow spiritually, or they lose everything, including each other.

All through history, mystics have practiced intentionally *giving up their attachments* in order to get closer to the Divine. Whether we like it or not, many of us will have things we love ripped from us in the course of life—professional reversals, bereavements, the weakening of the physical body with time or disease. In response to these losses, some of us become bitter or depressed. Others turn to spirituality for solace. Many of us have witnessed the miracle of a person dying of cancer or AIDS who glows with the aura of a saint. Loss can be a doorway into spirituality.

Does this mean that our couple with the composite Sun in the twelfth house is destined to experience such losses? Not necessarily. If their relationship is truly used as an evolutionary vehicle—the actual agreement their souls made—then these losses are not necessary. It's only if they become forgetful that these "reminders" of the transitoriness of earthly life are triggered.

So how do they get it right? Much of it comes down to quiet time together. Candlelight helps. Keeping spirit in their bodily relationship is critical. They may be drawn to some shared spiritual practice. That would be of great benefit to them, even if they differ in terms of theology or religion. They must of course live in "reality," as we all do. But they can also create little pockets of peace together away from the noise and the shallowness, places where they can experience each other as consciousnesses passing briefly through this ghostly world of forms.

CHAPTER SIX: THE COMPOSITE MOON

"Happy together—unhappy together. Oh wouldn't that be fine?" So go the lyrics to the jazz song, "Rain or Shine." It's a rich, grown-up sentiment. Children want to be happy all the time and imagine that when they're not, something's wrong. As we mature—*if* we mature—we come to know that sadness is part of life too. We make peace with it. We console ourselves with the realization that sadness is the mirror in which we become aware of happiness. We learn that each has its own beauty. If we're fortunate enough to find a soulmate, more veils are lifted from the mystery. Happiness shared is happiness squared—and sorrow shared is one of love's sweetest faces.

This flow of sheer, shared feeling is the composite Moon's domain. If we could *average the mood of a relationship* over its duration, we'd see clearly into the heart of its Moon. This "averaging," by the way, wouldn't turn into gray neutrality. Instead, it would convey a uniquely personal style of shared response to joy and sadness—not to mention victory and loss, adventure, encounters with the unexpected, the challenges of hard work, and the very real challenges of simple relaxation. Each couple, just as each individual, responds to such stimuli in a particular way. Just think how an introvert and an extravert respond to the words, "There's someone you just *have* to meet."

Their composite lunar mood radiates from a couple as surely as one can feel the "sink" of a depressed person walking into a room, or the "lift" of a merry one. Nowhere is the lunar mood of a couple so visible as in the private spaces they create for themselves. The simplest illustration is the mood of a *home,* which leads to one of the main correlates of the composite Moon: *the domestic environment.* Not all couples live together, but when they do, the composite Moon gives tremendous insight into the nature and spirit of their home. More importantly, it prescribes certain stylistic necessities if the couple is going to weather the gold-plated intimate challenges of living under one roof. Even for two people who aren't trying to form a shared home, the composite Moon sheds a revealing light on their secret world—their private jokes, their intimate style when no one else is looking, the tone of their bond.

Life and love are battering experiences sometimes. How can a couple actually heal from a necessary conflict? Or an unnecessary one? How can warmth and trust and easiness be restored? How can two people escape from those silent, icy hell-worlds some lonely author of self-help books might label "good boundaries" or "respect for each other's differences"? How can simple monkey *looseness* remain alive? Mother Moon, in her infinite, forgiving humanity, holds the answers. To understand her message in a composite chart is to enlist kindness, humanity and humility to serve lasting love.

COMPOSITE MOON IN ARIES

This couple shares a warrior's heart. That's a prime Aries archetype. We could also invoke the pioneer, survivor or daredevil. However timid and retiring they may be as individuals, the happiness of their union is fed by adventures great and small. They need to prove themselves to themselves, develop their combined willpower, and face worthy adversaries. They thrive on challenges, testing their limits, and healthy competition—preferably with something outside the couple rather than with one another.

That last point is important. A composite Aries Moon couple whose idea of adventure is folding the laundry needs challenges just as much as a couple plotting to climb Mount Everest. Strange as it may sound, the lazier couple is taking a bigger risk with their love than the mountain-climbers! Warriors need battles, and all astrological energy manifests somehow. Whether it manifests well or poorly is up to us. Without something to push against in the outside world, without a consciously chosen "common enemy," a composite Aries Moon starts pushing against itself. Humor turns to sarcasm. Grudges become feuds. Bickering escalates into all-out vendettas.

Whether the common enemy is the mutual need to get into shape or to get home from that white water rafting trip in one piece, whether the shared challenge is buying a house or writing a play, this couple needs something to pursue together. They need combats and victories. When all that vibrant Aries energy is directed consciously and the heart of the relationship is fed, these two can not only have a lot of fun, they can experience a profound and growing loyalty to one another. Because they've faced foes together, each partner will know the mate is a good person to have at his or her back in a fight. For warriors, there isn't much higher praise.

On the domestic front, the home of our happy couple with a composite Aries Moon may be full of the "spoils of war"— or its weapons. A trophy from a doubles tennis tournament they won. Skis or bicycles on the wall. A pool table in the living room. The first dollar their business earned. Patience is not what Aries is about. Therefore, the home of a couple with this composite Moon is best designed to be dashed through at top speed, with frequently needed objects close at hand, a minimum of clutter to trip over, and few if any doodads to rearrange. It may not be the most relaxing home on the block, but a visit there can be most invigorating.

COMPOSITE MOON IN TAURUS

What nourishes the soul of the couple with their composite Moon in Taurus? Simple: a garden of earthly delights. Inside us all is a wise old mammal that's been around for a few million years—long enough to know exactly what it wants. The trick for this couple lies in listening to it.

We humans tie ourselves in knots. It's the dark side of that big, concept-generating brain inside our skulls. Most of us have been so busy "we didn't notice we were hungry." How smart does that look to the average raccoon? With the composite Moon in this sign, listening to the "inner raccoon" is the first step on the path to a lasting sense of well-being in the relationship.

You'll notice we said "raccoon" instead of "bull." That might raise a few astrological eyebrows. But Taurus isn't narrowly about bulls—it's about being true to our animal natures. Basically, to the couple with composite Moon in Taurus, we would say, "Pick your favorite animal and use it as the guiding image." In fact, if you've been together a while, you've probably already chosen it. It's there in the secret Moon-life you share together, the one you'd be embarrassed if anyone knew about, where you pretend to be "pooh-bears" or meow at each other like cats.

That's your totem animal, and it has messages for you. What it needs, you need. Some of those needs are about being in your "natural habitat" regularly, paddling a canoe or hiking the mountains. That animal describes how social or how solitary your needs are. It reveals how much time together you need. It will offer insight into whether this "creature" you are likes daylight or moonlight. It will tell you how much stimulus you need—or can stand. It will, in other words, guide you unerringly through the questions that really matter—the ones that relate to the needs of that ancient creature in the two of you, beneath the veneer of civilization and its neurotic complications.

COMPOSITE MOON IN GEMINI

The soul of this relationship is elfin: curious about everything, magical, whimsical, hard to define or pin down. Quick. Full of riddles. The more these two people are true to that spirit and mood, the happier they'll be. With composite Moon in Gemini, there's wisdom in lightness and folly in an overly serious attitude. Here, truth looms in the mirror of humor. Every idea, however brilliant, soon gives way to another—and these two love to follow the threads of free association through that labyrinth! Conversation, lively and fast, is a sign of fundamental health for this pair—and if conversation stops, something between them is sick with sorrow.

Always with the Moon, we are talking about a place within to which we must soften and open. It has a deep kinship with the "inner child," or, simply, with the heart. Thus it's easy—perilously easy—for the adult parts of us to ignore it. That's always the trick with the composite Moon: the couple needs to feel the message of that "still, small voice" within them. If they do, they've caught that slippery fish we call happiness. If they don't, however productive, efficient and well-adjusted they may be, some basic delight is missing between them. And that brings us right back to that ultimate Geminian barometer of health and well-being: talk. This relationship should be one long fascinating conversation.

To keep the conversation going, it helps to have something new to discuss. Thus, we recognize another elemental need for the couple with this composite Moon: *stimulus.* Surprise. Change. Wonder. When in doubt, they need to do something they've never done before. It can be as simple as going to a new restaurant, or as complex as taking a class that stretches their intellectual horizons. In saying this, we also define their nemesis: boredom. And boredom sneaks into relationships, hiding inside the Trojan horse of adult responsibility, reasonableness and practicality—each of which is mortally perilous to these two if operating at more than bare-bones necessity.

The natural domestic environment for a couple with composite Moon in Gemini is probably media-intensive, with conversation pieces everywhere. Shifting furniture and repainting walls regularly can encourage conversation, and it's a good bet they'll move house more often than the average couple.

COMPOSITE MOON IN CANCER

The Moon is the heart, and it's stronger in Cancer than it would be in any other sign. For a couple with the composite Moon there, the volume is through the roof on "Moon energy." That covers a lot of bases, all of them soulful.

First, this is a very emotional relationship: the love is deep and the bond very powerful. Cancer and the Moon both link to the human need for hearth and home. With their composite Moon here, these two doubtless felt an eerie degree of familiarity with each other right from their first meeting. It's as if there were a pre-existing pact of mutual defense and protection, as you would find in families. In terms of serious commitment and long-term intimacy, it would be hard to find a more solid foundation on which to build than a composite Cancer Moon.

Still, there is a moody quality to the connection. That's not a disease and we shouldn't overreact to it. All couples naturally go through ups and downs. The swings are just a little wider with these two. The one mood which we need to watch out for is a kind of quiet "clamming up." When the Crab withdraws into its shell, certain of its basic needs aren't being met. A big risk, with the Moon in this sign, is that rather than risk the expression of needs, the couple retreats into silence. Far better to say the needs out loud and thereby get them met. With Cancer they are very primal, almost exactly the same as the needs of a newborn infant: touch, attention, time, gentleness, a feeling of tenderness, a sense of safety. One person approaches the other in the midst of a chaotic day and says, "I need a hug." If you just let that image wash over you, you'll get a good handle on everything we expect in a healthy, mutually-nourishing Cancer Moon relationship.

In terms of the domestic environment, one of the absolute basics with the composite Moon here is that these two are simply very good at nesting: they can make a room, or a floor, or an entire home feel as cozy and safe as apple pie at Grandma's house. There's a nourishing energy around them—it's likely that at least one of them is a good cook, and probably when people visit they congregate in the kitchen. Friends going though hard times will be drawn to them like iron filings to a magnet. Ditto for stray kittens. And should they choose to go down this road together, they would make skilled, happy parents of some profoundly lucky kids.

COMPOSITE MOON IN LEO

The mood of this couple, with their composite Moon in the sign of the King of Beasts, is regal. A quality of *presence* radiates from them. And, as we say in the American South, "they clean up real nice." Translation: they look comfortable and natural in expensive evening clothes. You can almost picture them as extras in a James Bond flick—hanging around the glittery roulette wheel in Monaco, looking slightly bored, and tempted to return to the yacht. An exaggeration perhaps, but it fits the regal mood of Leo.

The composite Moon always speaks eloquently of the reigning needs of a couple—so do these two need a yacht? It wouldn't hurt! But mostly what we see here is that need to treat other with that kind of devotion, support, and attention—they need, in a nutshell, to spoil each other.

Someone is telling a joke. He or she is being a bit long-winded about it, but having fun in a good-natured way. That person's mate is watching. Two scenarios: in the first, the mate is looking heavenward, bored and embarrassed by the partner's performance. In the second, the mate is enjoying every second of it, hanging on every word, laughing out loud at the punch line, even if the joke wasn't very funny. Which style of response is most conducive in the long run to a feeling of warm, easy spontaneity between two people? Which one supports them in feeling sexy, being emotionally self-expressive, and feeling safe? *Which one makes them feel like a king or queen?* Easy questions—and they profile what it takes for a couple with a composite Leo Moon to establish the kind of mood in their relationship that allows them to go forward together comfortably and happily. They need to egg each other on, encourage each other, and celebrate one another. A new hairstyle, a new shirt? Instant recognition and positive commentary. Birthdays are never forgotten. Always, underlying whatever surface details, you sense the currents of unconditional support, and the evolutionary call: come out, wherever you are! Show me who you really are!

In their domestic life, we again see the mark of the sovereign. Not everyone can afford a castle, but that's not the point. Self-expression and applause are closer to the heart of the matter. Each partner's creative works are happily displayed—paintings, flower arrangements, musical instruments. Any signs of personal victory or success are welcomed upon the walls and bureaus. Five minutes in the house and you have a three-dimensional sense of who lives there: that's the castle!

COMPOSITE MOON IN VIRGO

With their composite Moon in Virgo, the mood of this couple can be serene, but they'll have to work on it to get there. Easily, the energy between them can slip into a harried game of catch-up, with the nervous feeling of catastrophe lurking around every bend in the road. That is not what the configuration is ultimately about, and certainly that is not their shared soul-intention. But without effort, that's where they wind up.

Throughout these pages, we emphasize higher ground and more positive perspectives. Not so here. Is that because this is a bad place to have the composite Moon? Not at all. We do it because the spirit of Virgo is one of effort. It thrives on challenge, and it breathes evolutionary change. Point these two at the mountaintop and stand back. They are wired for effort. Some people say, "If it ain't broke, don't fix it." For this couple it's more like, "If it's not growing, it's broken."

Meditate with us for a moment on the concept of *discontent*—an emotion never in short supply with the composite Moon in Virgo. At first glance, it's an unpleasant word. Go a little deeper and the flower opens. Built into discontent is a sense of higher, better possibilities. It is highly motivating, and correlates strongly with a drive toward improvement. That's the energy here, and for it to be a positive force for this couple, it should be harnessed and directed. When they're healthy, they cultivate a spirit of open dialog. Constructive, supportive criticism is welcome between them. They'll be willing to ask advice and to seek helpful counsel about their relationship. Together they'll express faith in the relationship and in each other and, *in the context of that love*, they fearlessly name the mountain that lies before them: they know the relationship will be better next year than it is today.

Where trouble can start is when that discontent turns into unsupportive pickiness. They can fuss over trifles, especially silly outward details—housecleaning, family responsibilities, money. That leads to an erosion of their shared belief in their relationship. A spirit of harried exhaustion enters the emotional equation. But it doesn't have to be that way. All they have to do is aim a little higher. A "perfect relationship" is probably an unattainable goal, but for these two, there is glory, joy and fire in reaching for it together, step by step, day by day.

COMPOSITE MOON IN LIBRA

An aura of *rightness* surrounds this couple. With their composite Moon in Libra, people around them feel a kind of "lock" in their relationship, as if they were meant to be together. Probably they look good as a couple. Their bodies, their attitudes, their styles—all seem to fuse harmoniously. It's easy to imagine them dancing. Waltzing in the moonlight.

Underlying the elegant surface, a composite Moon in Libra suggests an evolutionary challenge. As always, there are ways to get it right—and plenty of ways to misuse the tools and make messes. Libra, the Scales, is about balancing opposites. Light gives meaning to dark. Wet gives meaning to dry. Truth gives meaning to kindness. Similarly, these two people can give meaning to each other. *But only if they don't blur into each other.* Their individuality must remain intact. The inherent, natural tension of opposites must remain alive. "Wet" and "dry" aren't supposed to agree on "slightly damp!"

When this relationship is healthy, we see these two celebrating their differences. Discussions are spirited. When one wants to go to Yosemite and the other wants to go to Kitty Hawk, they don't settle on Omaha. They negotiate everything and *take turns* bending to each other's will. With the composite Moon in Libra, there's a risk they'll prioritize agreement over actually knowing each other. That misses the evolutionary point and would drain the soul out of their bond.

The tension between opposites is . . . well, *tense*, sometimes! How do they live with that? Libra harmonizes itself fundamentally though aesthetic experience. These two benefit enormously from time spent engaged with the arts. Attending concerts or dance performances. Walking through art galleries. Gazing at beautiful sunsets. It's profoundly helpful for them to share a creative outlet: designing a garden, forming a banjo and mandolin duet, or singing Motown tunes as they cruise down the highway. Earlier we mentioned waltzing in the moonlight. Dancing would be good for them, as each of their bodies viscerally learned the rhythms and moves of the other, and tweaked themselves into graceful harmony at that level.

Similarly, the natural home environment for a couple with composite Moon in Libra reflects this need for outward support for the inner condition of serenity. Art on the walls. A good stereo. At least one pretty room in the house, where keeping it lovely is viewed as a sacramental duty. With all these harmonizing behaviors in motion, and with a balanced, attractive domestic environment, the deeper, lasting, *more individualized* romance this composite Moon promises can blossom.

COMPOSITE MOON IN SCORPIO

When our astrological ancestors named a sign after a scorpion, they weren't aiming to soothe our nerves. With a composite Scorpio Moon, this couple faces daunting profundity together. They'll enter the depths like shamans, or the psychological depths will rise up in each of them and destroy the relationship. Stark statements perhaps, but they reflect reality.

Together, these two are well-armed for the task. With their composite Moon in the sign of the scorpion, there is a natural intensity to their bond. It's easy to imagine them getting spookily honest on their first date, talking about places inside themselves they'd never discussed with anyone before. That kind of honesty comes naturally—at first! Of course, Chapter Two is entitled "Oh My God, I Can't Believe We Talked About THAT!" Fears and insecurities arise. In reaction, closeness is punctuated with distance or aloofness—which of course creates a response in the partner. Soon, they need to talk deeply and honestly about that development too. And the whole relationship can potentially spiral down into exhaustion for both people. Should that reality emerge, then their mood turns into one of brooding caution and heaviness. In a nutshell, *these two can get deeper more quickly than they can handle!* They need humor and outward distractions. They need friends who can offer—or demonstrate—the one quality these two most lack: *perspective.*

Moon-energy is not naturally oriented to thinking. It's more about feelings, instincts, and reflexes. That's why we're emphasizing caution here. Together, these two human beings are wired to pick the locks on each other's deepest secrets and psychological wounds. That is almost the definition of intimacy. But human beings need boundaries too. They may need time before they can trust each other that much. All that can be blown away by the reflexive Scorpio Moon drive to delve into the depths.

Domestically, it's easy to visualize these two living in a haunted house or perhaps in a mysterious, moss-encrusted cave. Encoded in those silly images is a serious point: their penetrating soul-intentions are best supported by a home environment that triggers reactions of depth and seriousness in each of them. Bold paintings on the walls. Maybe Mexican Day of the Dead figures on the mantlepiece. A statue of Kali in the corner.

A shaman's rattle or drum on the coffee table. Sitting there together, they'll feel right at home.

COMPOSITE MOON IN SAGITTARIUS

This pair of human beings has a gypsy soul. If they're going to be happy together, they need what the proverbial gypsy needs: an open road, a flamenco guitar, and a rose in the teeth for good measure. In the old astrological paradigm, we might say to them, "I see travel in your stars." In the modern one, we'd rephrase it: "I see a *need* for travel in your stars." That minor distinction is actually hugely important in that it honors something dear to the Sagittarian heart: *freedom*—which includes the freedom to fail as well as the freedom to get it right. The point here is that travel—and more generally, the notion of life lived to the full—is completely optional. Claim it, and this couple is radiant. Watch network television every night, and they become dull and petty. It's their choice.

Their flight from dullness and pettiness is further enhanced by a shared process of ongoing education. Sagittarius is the *scholar* as well as the gypsy—although we must instantly affirm that this lunar need is about the joy and adventure of learning, not about pedantry or life lived strictly above the neck. Attending lectures together, reading books and talking about them, visiting a planetarium or a museum—all those activities feed the Sagittarian composite Moon. So might signing up for an afternoon of shooting each at other with paint guns! The point is, *when in doubt, do it.* Repetition is the venal sin here—and boredom the mortal one.

Underlying this kaleidoscopic hunger for experience is the most elemental Sagittarian drive: the urge *to understand life and find meaning in it.* These two will experience their relationship as one long philosophical conversation. They are very concerned with justice, and with questions of right and wrong.

The happiest domestic environment for such a pair reflects this basic Sagittarian expansiveness. Their home will likely fill up with artefacts from their various adventures—Nepalese icons crowding Celtic crosses and fulsome pagan goddesses. A kind of easy, slap-dash chaos pervades their natural environment. Good humor, intelligent curiosity and expansive good will fill the air. There are cartoons on the refrigerator and a pile of letters from virtuous non-profit organizations on the kitchen table.

COMPOSITE MOON IN CAPRICORN

When two seventeen-year-olds announce their engagement, we experience trepidations. We fear that there's an excellent chance they don't yet have the maturity to make a relationship work. Two seasoned souls in their thirties make the same announcement, and it feels natural and right. Of course we may be dead wrong about both relationships. Maturity, that ultimate Capricorn quality, is not rigidly related to how old we are. With their composite Moon in Capricorn, we can't guarantee that these two have the maturity to deal with the challenging realities of committed intimacy. But everything else being equal, a Capricorn Moon is about the best promise astrology can offer in that department.

By instinct, together these two people see reality with clarity. They add two and two and come up with four. One spin-off is that they'd probably make a good team in the business world, or in any endeavor where a sober ability to calculate odds is relevant. More to the point, in terms of their relationship there's a grounded attitude. They expect a lot of each other—but not too much. Little so inflates our hopes and expectations as much as fresh love. New lovers often imagine themselves to be "perfect for each other." And the rest of us roll our eyes, knowing that human beings are difficult creatures, full of contradictory needs and psychological razor blades. From the beginning, these two keep an instinctive grasp on *terra firma*. They understand that relationships must be built stone by stone, like fortresses. Capricorn likes vows—the mortar that binds love's stones together—and is good at keeping them. Not all bonds are meant to go the distance, but a couple with their composite Moon in Capricorn moves toward "resolution," not rapidly, but persistently and seriously—and "resolution" means either commitment or a clean finish.

Should they go down the long road together, these two need to recognize that there is potentially a down side to all this maturity. Their "inner child" needs breathing room too. Together, they must master the *discipline of relaxation*—knowing when to take a break, when to ask for a hug or reassurance, when to say "no" to yet another responsibility.

In their domestic environment, a couple with this composite Moon often finds comfort in everything old and enduring. In conjuring up their dream-home, we'd see a lot of stone, some perhaps carved long ago. If possible, they benefit from owning their own place—again, there's that Capricorn signature: a commitment to the future as enduring as a pyramid. Maybe we're all ultimately "renters" here in this transitory world, but Capricorn carries the dignity of commitment, kept promises, and the long haul.

COMPOSITE MOON IN AQUARIUS

You never know what they are going to do next. All you know is that it will be the last thing you imagined. With the composite Moon in Aquarius, these two aren't necessarily setting out to shock anyone—it just seems to happen as a side-effect of their listening to their shared heart. Their relationship has the "soul of a rebel." When they are true to themselves, they re-invent the rules. A "normal" life would be the kiss of death for these two. Their relationship is just not wired for it.

The Moon is always very sensitive to the nature and quality of the home environment. If two people with the composite Moon in Aquarius live together, one look at the space they share gives tremendous insight into the health of their bond. Basically, if you immediately get a sense of who they are as individuals from a single glance at their home, that means they are on the right track. On the other hand, if the place is fine but sort of "generic," their love may not be doomed, but they'd better start thinking for themselves as quickly as possible.

Interior decoration won't of course make or break a relationship. That's not the point. It's only a barometer of deeper Moon-issues. Every family and every subculture has its own sense of what constitutes an "appropriate" kind of home. There are acceptable colors, levels of neatness versus chaos, assumptions about the purpose of each room and so on. With a healthy response to the composite Moon in Aquarius, these two people aren't steamrollered into blindness by all that. They create a space that reflects who they are and what they like—and if others disapprove, no worries. *The creation of a highly individuated living space reflects a deeper commitment to creating a relationship that also follows its own natural rules.* And that of course is the deeper point. These two, for example, might need more time apart than most couples. They might choose to vacation separately or to have separate friendships. They'll tend not to make plans for each other. They'll support each other's right to have idiosyncrasies, even when family or community pressures arise. Probably, they'll behave in ways that are "inappropriate for their ages."

All that is the higher ground. If they slip into more conventional assumptions about intimacy, a kind of coldness sneaks into their relationship. They become sardonic and aloof, living in their heads.

But that's the garbage can. The real point is that, with the composite Moon in Aquarius, the older these two get, the weirder they'll become! And if their hearts are in the right place, they'll enjoy every minute of that process, even if their friends are marveling and scratching their heads.

COMPOSITE MOON IN PISCES

With the composite Moon in Pisces, together these two have the soul of a mystic. For their relationship to feel right and healthy to them, they need almost everything a typical mystic would need—we say "almost everything," because fortunately celibacy is not on the list!

Throughout history, mystics in all cultures have craved solitude: escape "from the madding crowd." It's the same with these two, except that they need to escape *together,* so it's not about individual solitude, it's about the renewing impact on them of quiet time spent alone together, relaxing in privacy. Mystics meditate, and that's a healthy practice for these two people as well. Naturally they can frame that process any way that feels good to them—they can call it prayer, or yoga, or contemplation, or just quiet time watching the evening fall. They can call it shared creative time. Anything is fine, so long as it includes a quiet awareness of each other combined with a sense of the "spaciousness" of consciousness. But without that magical silent time together, the soul seems to drain from their bond. And with it, they feel alive and connected to each other.

The paradox in Pisces is that, in common with all the signs, it represents an evolutionary need. Thus, certain experiences are essential to its well-being—and it takes a degree of ego-driven willpower to make anything happen in this world. But Pisces is ultimately about going beyond the ego. The bottom line is that poor Pisces can just sit there like a rabbit in the headlights, "transcending" its way into the life of a ghost. With the composite Moon in Pisces, these two people need to defend aggressively their need for quiet time and shared solitude. This relationship needs boundaries around it. Together, they need to conspire against their own vulnerability toward letting their relationship drift. And if drift it does, then it will probably be drifting on the currents of other people's demands and expectations.

A home environment conducive to contemplation is of great benefit to these two. Comfort, and an ability to create dim light, are essential. A feeling of well-defended, uncontested privacy is pivotally important. A piece of that might be as simple as having a telephone answering machine left on with the volume down, at least at certain times. Perhaps a trickling fountain in the home would help them. Almost certainly music would play a role in terms of creating the right atmosphere around the home. If their tastes run in this direction, religious or spiritual symbolism and iconography in various rooms of the house can contribute to the feeling. A hot tub wouldn't hurt. A mood of easy quiet, one that lets the distractions of the world slip away, is the point. There, these two can find the peace that sustains their happiness.

COMPOSITE MOON IN THE FIRST HOUSE

With the Moon about to rise in the composite chart, we are sure of two points. First, the Moon's general influence is very strong on these two people. Second, everybody around them will know that. Nothing in the first house is very good at hiding. By definition, it shines out into the world, forming a big part of a couple's outward style and affect.

Let's take these two pieces of the puzzle one at a time, starting with the sheer power of the lunar influence. There's a lot of "soul" in this relationship—and a lot of moodiness to go along with it. Feelings are central to all intimate human bonds, but they run at a higher voltage with these two. Add that feelings don't always make sense—that's not their job in the psyche. Instead, they directly reflect and monitor the condition of our hearts. Just think of a baby, which is a pretty good illustration of pure emotion unchecked by reason. Babies typically break out crying at the drop of a hat. Then it's our job to figure out what they need. Maybe they don't know themselves. Maybe they're crying for fundamental, immutable existential reasons. That's how the lunar energy works in a couple with their composite Moon in the first house. As individual adults, they've presumably learned how to restrain the impulse to burst into tears because they're a little bored in the grocery store. But the *relationship*—which is what the composite chart is all about—carries its emotional energy closer to the surface.

The key, then, is to make sure its needs are as well-met as possible at all times. The nature of those needs has a lot to do with the inner agenda of the *sign* the Moon occupies, so reading that section again is a good idea here.

All this could potentially sound as if having the composite Moon in the first house is a liability. That isn't really true. There's good news: feelings of emptiness or of having lost emotional contact with each other certainly are not going to sneak up on this couple. There's a very "present tense" spirit here; problems are not unwittingly swept under the carpet.

Anything in the first house shows. People can see it. Part of this is reflected in the fact that the heart of this relationship is fairly transparent to the world. If these two people are angry with each other, they won't hide it well—and when they are feeling love for each other, it's like a warm bath for everyone in the room.

Let's add that the Moon is a nurturing, caring energy. With it in their first house, these two individuals tend to draw out emotional needs in the people around them. The phone rings and a friend's voice says, "Hi. Mind if I drop over? I'm feeling a little blue and could use some company." With a dear friend, what follows may be a very soulful evening that leaves everyone feeling an ancient Moon-truth: that familiar, reliable love is the soul of life. With someone they don't know so well, it's more complicated. Maybe they help heal a relative stranger's heart, and that can be a good feeling. Or maybe the intrusive needs of others become a stumbling block in terms of these two meeting their own needs—in which case boundaries need to be set. But if they make the wrong judgement there, they'll soon know it. The big inner child they share will start bawling and whining until they figure out what's wrong—and fix it.

COMPOSITE MOON IN THE SECOND HOUSE

The Moon is always changing, and the same goes for whatever part of the composite chart it occupies: that area of life is usually in a state of fluctuation. With the second house, the main theme is the level of faith the couple has in their relationship. It tends to go up and down. One week, they're "born to be together." The next, they're questioning the fundamentals. Naturally, this can be a harrowing experience for all concerned. And that brings us to the next step, where we consider the evolutionary perspective. What are these two *learning*? What's the soul-intention behind the psychological phenomenon? In a nutshell, they are *proving themselves to themselves* as a couple. This is a relationship that is learning to believe in itself.

Immediately we hit a delicate point. How do we know that the relationship is actually supposed to last? We don't—and we shouldn't—assume it. It proves itself by passing through a series of initiations. If, after solid effort, any of the hurdles prove too high, probably the best bet is to release the connection.

All the hurdles are lunar in nature. The first one involves the fact that everyone's Moon is innately a bit ridiculous and silly. Think of the dumbest movie you love—and how embarrassed you might feel if a professional rival saw you gleefully imitating one of the characters in it. Think of your most irrational and extreme opinions. These are all lunar attitudes, and revealing them is the first hurdle. In a nutshell, it is a willingness to *risk embarrassment* with each other. To reveal the "inner child."

The second hurdle has to do with that classic, central dimension of the astrological Moon: *vulnerability*. Can these two show each other their "soft underbellies?" Can they cry in front of each other, or express personal insecurity or self-doubt? Can they let out their feelings? The third one involves each partner showing the fruits of his or her imagination—taking the great emotional risk of *being creative* in each other's presence.

The fourth lunar hurdle is about the *nesting instinct*. Deep down, almost everyone wants to find true love and a real home. Some people are afraid even to say it. If these two pass the first three initiations, in their own time they begin to become so entangled in other's emotional lives that a break-up would be devastating. Can they risk trusting that nesting instinct with each other? Can they "mate" like mourning doves—for life, trusting the ancient mammal-brain programs, and not looking back?

With each of these steps, the couple with the composite Moon in the second house gains confidence in their bond. If they get past those hurdles, they've created something precious—and a fifth hurdle arises. Unlike the others, this one is optional. It's about that ancient Moon-mystery: fertility. Children—and the vast commitment they represent. Not all couples want kids, or are in a position to have them. It may sound strange to some ears, but this fifth step can take another form: anything to which we are radically committed as nurturers—a pet, a piece of land, the needs of the destitute. The key is that, as with kids, the commitment is not temporary. It is total.

COMPOSITE MOON IN THE THIRD HOUSE

Together, these two people are magnets for what many would view as total chaos. Two comments: they're wired to handle it, and they like it that way! With their composite Moon in the third house, they've signed up for a wild ride. To call them "busy" is like calling an interplanetary rocket launch "complicated." As soon as they think they have everything settled, the rules seem to change. The life they share is a massive improvisation. A lot of that endless adjustment is, seemingly, circumstantial in origin. We say "seemingly" because underlying it is a synchronistic principle: something in their own psyches is calling that unsettled weather into manifestation. And underlying *that* is the core evolutionary intention of their souls, which in a nutshell, is to have plenty to discuss.

Plenty to discuss? The line may seem a bit anticlimactic. But it shouldn't be. Communication is a critical human function, and, astrologically, it's the heart of the third house. With their composite Moon there, these two are nurturing their capacity to speak to each other from their hearts. The most fundamental work here lies in verbally putting lunar material out on the table: emotional matters, human needs, insecurities, fears. But, with speech as with everything else, practice makes perfect. Establishing a free-flow of language is a necessary first step. Nothing hinders that intention more than being bored and having nothing to say. And nothing helps it more effectively than a constant diet of wonder and amazement. So, together, these two people create a tremendous feel of sheer *curiosity*. There is a restlessness in their relationship, something that goads them always to ask another question, see another perspective, take in another bit of information. Probably their life together is mobile. Often cars—or airplanes—are important to a couple with this configuration. They'll travel a lot. Many times, circumstances arise that require something like *commuting*—and it may not be for work. An elderly family member who lives three hours away, for example, may require attention every month or so—which affords them a monthly six-hour conversation. The key is that there is constant evolutionary pressure on them to deepen their capacity to listen to each other and to express themselves. Even when discussing light or abstract matters, their deeper skills are developing. And when it comes time for their hearts to use the miraculous bridge of language to link across the abyss of their separateness, they'll be ready.

COMPOSITE MOON IN THE FOURTH HOUSE

The fourth house is the house of home, hearth and roots. Those roots may be psychological—how our family of origin affected us. Perhaps they are ethnic or cultural roots. Or geographic roots. In every case, fourth house symbolism points "downward," toward the archetypal realm in all its profound inwardness and personal mystery. It's opposite the tenth house, which is the house of public identity. Thus, the fourth is the house of private identity—one's inner life, hidden life, home life. It refers to the whole matrix of the personal unconscious.

Note these two streams in fourth house symbolism: the inner life and the domestic life. When you're asleep and dreaming, your fourth house is active. When you're fixing a meal for beloved friends or family, your fourth house is active too.

The optimal psychological health and happiness of a couple with the composite Moon in the fourth house depends on their spending a lot of time simply hanging out at home. Maybe they're engaged in a shared hobby. Maybe they're gardening on a fine Saturday afternoon. They thrive on long quiet talks over dinner. Or cuddling up and listening to music.

The couple with a composite fourth house Moon needs a sense of shared roots. Some of that rootedness is strictly between them and involves no outsiders: a well-thought-out and well-cared-for home, with lots of comforts and privacy and perhaps an affectionate pet to warm up the space, is essential. It serves as a cocoon, an enfolding nest where it's easy for them to claim fourth house "down time," to float, to daydream. Sometimes the circles extends a bit more widely: those shared roots might include an intimate circle of friends *who feel like family.*

Kinship ties—relatives—used to be part and parcel of the fourth house. For many modern people, that's no longer the reality: we're mostly not so deeply involved with our cousins anymore. But for the couple with the composite Moon in the fourth, family issues—in joy or burdensome sorrow—may loom a little larger than they do for other people. Please understand that we are not talking about spending lots of time with both sets of in-laws no matter what, nor about trying to reconcile all differences. Some families are toxic and some differences are irreconcilable. But there is a need for a fourth house composite Moon couple *to understand* the family systems that helped form each partner. Many times there's a degree of involvement, and perhaps even love, that harks back to another era. And often, but not always, with this configuration there is a real drive to create a family of one's own, whatever form that family might take.

COMPOSITE MOON IN THE FIFTH HOUSE

How sweetly and unknowingly new lovers nurture each other's confidence and self-expression! Even a bad poem puts tears in the eyes. Dumb jokes evoke gales of laughter. A glimpse of naked flesh produces gasps and sighs. No wonder everyone loves falling in love! And the fifth house rules that merry process, start to finish. The last thing anyone wants to do is analyze it to death, but we need to endure that risk in order to understand how a couple with their composite Moon in the fifth house can keep the magic alive beyond the first six weekends of the relationship.

It comes down to confidence and self-expression. Those are the critical fifth house ingredients. Lovers support those qualities in each other essentially through one simple, effective device: *they pay attention to each other.* Whatever the other person does merits loving scrutiny and generous interpretation. And there is no reason why that kindness has to end. All that "has to end" is that it happens automatically. Freshness and that delicious strangeness naturally and inevitably wear off with the passage of time. Familiarity arises—and with it, potentially, blindness, numbness, and even contempt. And as soon as we see any of those in the eyes of our partner, something inside us loses its spontaneity. We no longer feel supported. In fact, we may no longer feel safe. And the fifth house processes stop cold.

For a couple with their composite Moon in the fifth house, such "maturation" of the relationship is fatal. Their evolutionary aim is to keep on falling in love—forever. That may sound unrealistic, and in some ways it is. But intention and skillful means are powerful tools here. These two can succeed, at least for four days out of every week. And that's enough.

How? One huge piece of the puzzle is that they need to find a playful creative outlet to share. Dancing together. Playing music. Maybe enjoying a sport at which they can develop their own personal styles. Such activities naturally invoke some of the energies of new love—easy laughter, a sense of freshness, emotional energies revealed, imagination expressed.

Another piece of the puzzle lies in this couple befriending other couples and individuals. Such new relationships trigger more freshness. Old stories can be told again. New surprises and possibilities arise. Likely, there will be something of a "revolving door" for these two in terms of friendships.

There may be lasting friendships as well, but there will almost certainly be a theme of people coming and going.

Children may play a role in the bond as well. With most of us, kids are an obvious possible correlate of loving, and fertility is probably a bit more likely with these two than with the general population. The key here, though, is the role of children in the relationship—think of them as little experts on childlike behavior, come to share the wealth!

COMPOSITE MOON IN THE SIXTH HOUSE

The sixth house is about work and responsibilities and both of them will proliferate for this couple. There's a fair chance that circumstances will arise that allow them to work together professionally somehow. If they do that, they'll probably find it satisfying. While there are inevitably additional strains on a relationship with that dimension, for these two the benefits outweigh the down side. Working together will make them feel closer and further deepen their involvement with each other. They've just got to be careful to set boundaries between their work and the rest of their lives, or work will surely eat the whole pie.

Another argument for working together, should that possibility arise, is that if they don't choose that path, then the sixth house energy will have to find another one. And of course it will: non-professional responsibilities will loom, and they'll be sufficiently extreme to stand out as notable. Maybe an elderly parent will need a home. Perhaps a child with special needs will enter the picture. Destiny—or karma—may call for those kinds of realities, and it would of course be wrong to think of them as evidence of some mistake. The bottom line is that the sixth house is about *service*, and this couple with their composite Moon there will called upon to serve. The path of service invariably involves some degree of self-sacrifice for the benefit of other beings. One of the world's best-kept secrets is how satisfying that can be!

Still, a couple with the composite Moon in the sixth does need to be vigilant about the insidiously draining effect upon their bond of getting completely lost in the efficiencies of daily routine. It's a natural part of the sixth house, but it can be like a river that overflows its bank. Learning how to say no, and how to set limits on how far they will go in terms of being the answer to everyone else's prayers, is a critical survival skill for these two.

As time goes by, they will attract other couples, probably younger than themselves, into their lives. Likely, no one will think to use the word "apprentices," but that's really what is happening: these two people, having loved each other well for a while, will begin to pass on the skill-set. When to fight—and when to shut up and forgive. The balance between kindness and truth. The role of humor. How to live with sexuality for the long run. Whether they start out knowing it or not, a couple with the composite Moon in the sixth are a link in a long chain of lovers, a chain that goes back further than they can imagine or remember. And if there are stable relationships in the future, it will be partly because of what they demonstrate. Of all the services they offer, this is arguably the kindest.

COMPOSITE MOON IN THE SEVENTH HOUSE

Having the composite Moon in the traditional house of marriage seems like "good planning" on the part of this couple. The Moon is all about the heart, so its presence there warms the atmosphere between these two, deepening the feelings of intimacy and shared vulnerability. The Moon is moody too, so there's a sense of having their emotions, both the sweet and the sour ones, close to the surface. Not much can be hidden in this relationship, and that's part of the true intimacy they share—which is of course not always simply about expressing feelings of romantic tenderness.

Going further, the Moon is connected to the most primal parts of the psyche: instincts, animal reflexes, non-verbal communication. Much will pass between these two that no outsider could decode, especially once the relationship has lasted a while. Another side to that coin is that the basic transactions of intimacy between them—the foundation of their bond, in other words—depend on their ability to get "underneath" the civilized parts of themselves. That means a touch or a glance can mean more than words. Sleeping together, literally, has tremendous significance. Without necessarily knowing it, they will become quite positively reactive to each other's natural physical odors, smiling when they sense one another that way—provided, at least, that the ever-volatile "mood" between them is in its positive phase!

There's another fundamental dimension to our understanding of the meaning of the composite Moon in the seventh house. As every neophyte astrologer knows, this is the house of relationships. But a composite chart is itself about relationship. Extending the logic rigorously leads us to an elemental insight: *the couple itself must have relationships.* Together, they have soulmates—people without whom they cannot reach a state of full self-actualization. These people, who may be individuals or other couples, have a strong "Moon-signature" in their natures. They themselves are sensitive, expressive of emotion, moody, and probably nurturing in disposition. If they are couples, the aura around them is that they are together permanently, that they have truly become a "family." There's a good chance they have children, or at minimum some profoundly fortunate pets. These people are not really "gurus" for our couple with the composite Moon in the seventh house. The bond is more balanced and mutual than that, more in the category of an even exchange equally helpful to all concerned. The critical point is that these two need to look into a mirror that only their lunar soulmates can provide. What they will see there allows them to fulfill the happy promise of the Moon in the house of marriage.

COMPOSITE MOON IN THE EIGHTH HOUSE

Almost everything connected with this house triggers strong emotions: sexuality, death, psychological depth and confrontation. Add the emotional Moon to the eighth house stew, and you begin to get the picture: with a composite Moon in the eighth, this couple has signed up for stormy weather. Let's add that they've also signed a reliable astrological contract for lasting passion.

When we're kids just out of puberty, we often imagine there are easy formulas for keeping passion alive: all you have to do is find somebody cute enough, and the heat will take care of itself. That illusion quickly collapses in the face of experience. How old are we before we've seen sexual desire evaporate like dew in the desert? All it takes is a few ugly betrayals, clueless remarks, or bitter, unresolved fights. We no longer even want to look our former beloved in the eye, let alone lie down together. Add the fact that all relationships encounter difficulties, and the picture is clear. The secret of lasting body heat lies in dealing skillfully, honestly, and immediately with the natural tensions of any relationship.

With their composite Moon in the eighth, nothing of a psychologically edgy nature is going to remain buried for very long between these two. Their relationship seems to have a defective repressive mechanism. That can be beautiful, in that it promotes truthfulness, transparency and a kind of "nakedness" between them. Naturally, it can also prove volatile. Jealousy, anger, possessiveness or insecurity—whatever they don't want to see in themselves—is quickly out in the open. One side effect is that eighth house Moon relationships tend to "resolve" rather rapidly: that is, move to greater depth or come to an abrupt end. That's good news, even in the less-pleasant scenarios. If a relationship is going to wind up on the rocks, do you want it to happen quickly, or five years down the road?

The only caution we'd offer is that for most of us it takes a while to digest a growth experience. If we have a successful one on Tuesday, we don't need another one on Wednesday. But the Moon is emotional, not rational. Hot material tends to keep coming up as long as the relationship lasts. Part of the price of continuing passion lies in enduring the scars it creates—that's a humble, realistic perspective in that it doesn't promise a magic bullet that will make the reality of the eighth house composite Moon disappear. There isn't such a bullet. But forgiveness, patience, commitment, and some humor go a long way in that direction. With an eye on those virtues, this couple can create the sort of bond that many of us would envy—at least looking at it from the outside.

COMPOSITE MOON IN THE NINTH HOUSE

Gazing into our crystal ball, we see Frequent Flyer miles and lots of bookcases in the future for these two. With their composite Moon in the ninth house, they'll pack the experience of five relationships into this one. Together, they're all about stretching beyond the constraints of the Known World—at least the world as they presently understand it. The mood of their bond is one of pilgrims on the road together, endlessly going further.

Happiness is, of course, an emotion. Being logical about it has serious limitations. Although reason can play a role, nobody ever becomes happy through purely logical means. Some people feel happy playing golf. Others, doing cross-stitch. To know what will make a person happy, you've got to suspend reason, *feel the Moon*, and do what it recommends without asking too many questions. That's as true of couples as it is of individuals. For the couple with the composite Moon in the ninth, the secret of happiness lies in recognizing that they need a far richer diet of change, newness, and fresh experience than most of us. When in doubt, move to Argentina!

It's tempting to say that they are "impractical," or at least that they need to be—and as always, let's affirm that the Moon only offers good suggestions, with no guarantee we'll heed them. There's no compelling astrological reason for us to assume that these two won't lead a boring life—only that the soul would go out of their relationship if they did. The charge of "impracticality" is an interesting one in other ways, however. What, ultimately, is "impractical" about using our brief moments in this uncertain, impermanent world in *an attempt to figure out why we're here?* Such broad, philosophical perspectives come readily to this couple. Many a night they'll stay up late talking about big ideas—or delightfully debating them. Principles are important to them. They may be drawn to religion or metaphysics. But always the rocket fuel that truly propels their joint quest is raw, undigested experience—and that brings us back to the notion of travel. The magic here is not simply the idea of seeing new places; it's more like internalizing the perspectives and values of different cultures. This triggers a kind of inner travel, to complement the pretty, exotic postcards.

One more notion: the Moon is very connected to home and domestic life. Putting it in the cross-cultural ninth house often suggests opportunities for these two to live abroad or to relocate to another part of the country. Very likely, that would be a positive, life-affirming step, at least for a while.

COMPOSITE MOON IN THE TENTH HOUSE

When two people fall in love, for a while their relationship is like a magical island, apart from the world. They are doing a complex and ancient ritual: the merging of souls. They are like two candle flames that come together as one, yet maintain their own natures at the same time. That's a beautiful, subtle process and, instinctively, we honor their need for privacy—for a while. But soon they're asked to rejoin the community, to contribute again to the larger reality we all share. That larger social reality is the tenth house's domain, and with the composite Moon there, public life will have a deep and fundamental impact upon this relationship.

There's a tendency in modern astrological practice to think of the tenth house in strictly career terms. That's an incomplete perspective, as we'll see, but it does provide a good launching pad. It's tough to put a bad day at the office behind us. Almost inevitably, the dark mood left in its sorry wake spills over onto the dinner table at home. And there's the other side of the equation: professional triumphs leave their happy fingerprint on our evenings as well. That's true of everyone, but it's simply a very compelling force in the life these two share. For good or ill, work casts a long emotional shadow over their home life. Their relationship's emotional quality is a barometer of their contentment about what they are doing with their lives.

Thus, finding the right work—and supporting each other in it—is a critical piece of the puzzle for our couple. In practical terms, this might manifest as a situation where one person's mental well-being has been sacrificed on the mighty altar of income—and the evolutionary challenge lies in generously supporting that person in finding a more satisfying profession even at the price of a pay cut.

Let's go beyond purely professional interpretations of the tenth house composite Moon. This house has a feeling of *mission* about it, and we don't always get paid for doing our missions. Together, these two have something significant to do for their community. Its impact will surely go beyond their personal relationships and actually touch the souls of people whom they probably don't even really know personally. The exact nature of that mission can't really be determined from the Moon, although knowing what *sign* the Moon is in will help narrow it down a bit. We do know that the Moon tends to be a nurturing, supporting, healing force—and that therefore their shared mission lies in those categories. Something out there *needs* these two and is depending upon them.

The Moon is also about our "nesting instinct," which is the capacity of some humans to commit to each other and form stable home-bases. Manifesting that reality is also part of their mission. Especially today, with so much evolution happening in terms of the meaning of family, the community needs a few guiding beacons in that department, whether they are traditional or wildly experimental. If these two choose to bond in that way and face love's challenges with enough wisdom and humility, they'll offer us that precious gift *just by being who they are together.*

COMPOSITE MOON IN THE ELEVENTH HOUSE

Two views of the eleventh house persist in traditional astrological writing: it is about friends, and it is about goals and aspirations. If we're careful, both perspectives teach us something about this pair.

The idea that a couple with the Moon in the eleventh will surely have lots of friends is generally true, but not always. More trustworthy by far is the notion that, in order to accomplish what they've set out to do together in life, they require *alliances* or *networking*. Some human activities can't happen in a social vacuum—basketball comes to mind, as does playing in a string quartet, or working for a corporation. None of those actions requires deep affection and shared intimate processes. In fact, many times it's cleaner and clearer to avoid emotional complexities there, and instead favor courtesy, diplomacy, and strategic silence—ancient social instincts that have allowed humanity to survive for a few million years.

Are those collective realities meaningful to this couple? That question brings us to the second traditional view of this house: *goals and aspirations.* Elemental to the psychological health and happiness of this pair is a shared dialog about their own values and broad intentions. Where do they want to go in life? What's ultimately important to them?

Say that the answers to those questions reflect spiritual values. Say that their shared values are basically traditional. Then perhaps they will be drawn to be active in a local church or temple—*and thus be involved with those group enterprises.* If their answers are political, perhaps they will become involved in political parties or causes. In both cases, we will see the core ideal: *the goals and aspirations should underlie, inform, and define the alliances.* That's the critical notion. The crowd depends on the goal, not the other way around.

If there are no such overriding goals, then the couple finds itself overextended in meaningless, emotionally draining social activity. They become involved with people with whom there's very little common ground. They may imagine that this vitiating social superficiality is the problem, but it's not. The real problem is their own lack of clear direction.

Notions of strategy and the long view permeate the eleventh house. A couple with the composite Moon there feels better when they are engaged in creating something big together. Thus, when healthy, there is naturally an emphasis upon projects, plans and great works. How could we manage to go live in Europe for a year? *And who might help us?* How can we live ecologically-responsible lives? *And where are the intentional communities that might be part of the solution?*

Many times, given the domestic associations of the Moon, there is a long-term goal involving the manifestation of a home—building a house together or sustaining the vision over many years that leads to "growing a family."

COMPOSITE MOON IN THE TWELFTH HOUSE

If you're in a relationship, here's a feeling you know well: the sheer relief that can arise when, after a day spent with acquaintances or distant cousins, you two finally retire to your bedroom. Hooray! Tension leaves your bodies. At last you can rest and relax. Comments you've been dying to make can finally be said. There's something wonderful about being alone with your partner. It meets a primal need in our psyches.

Multiply that need by a hundred, and you've gone a long way toward understanding a couple with the composite Moon in the twelfth house. Their happiness and well-being depend on having lots of time alone. They renew themselves through isolation.

As individuals, they may not be so reclusive. Possibly they're both extraverts. That's a question we can only answer with a look at their individual birthcharts, not at the composite. As always, the composite is about *the needs of the relationship*, not necessarily those of the individuals in the relationship. Whatever this pair's individual natures may be, we know for sure that because of their twelfth house composite Moon, too much social interaction, even happy interaction, drains their batteries.

Underlying the twelfth house composite Moon is the archetype of the *mystic*. This house refers to actions motivated by spirituality. Throughout history, mystics have backed away from the world and gone apart to meditate. Something akin to that happens automatically when these two withdraw. Even if they're not thinking in spiritual terms, the veil of the social ego naturally parts when they're alone. That may be mystical kindergarten, but it's a healthy first step.

Taking it further, it is profoundly healing for this couple to engage in more conscious, intentional mysticism—meditation, religious practice, yoga. Between that lofty stage and "kindergarten" are some other, less recognized steps: experiencing aesthetic rapture together, gazing silently at a perfect sunset, or riding the crest of the energy-wave coming off the stage at a concert. Or just sitting quietly in a dimly-lit room with no agenda other than being close and silently sensing each other.

Traditional astrologers takes a far bleaker view of the twelfth house, calling it the house of troubles. They might predict misfortune, and imply that these two should part before the ax falls. As tempting as it is to dismiss such fear-mongering, there may be a little bit of truth in it. Underlying all the points we've made about mystical withdrawal is an evolutionary intention these two share: to grow spiritually together. They can do it the easy, natural way, which is what we've described so far. Or they can wait until loss or catastrophe bends their knees and compels them to turn to the world beyond this one for help and solace. The stakes are obviously high, but the darker potentialities of this configuration are optional.

CHAPTER SEVEN: THE COMPOSITE ASCENDANT

Picture that rarest of miracles—a big, fancy, dress-up party full of strangers *that actually works!* Everyone is loose and having a good time. The band has found its groove, exuberance is in the air, and everyone is feeling three times more interesting than they were when they got out of bed that morning. Single people and couples are there, but since this is a book about composite charts, we'll concentrate on the latter.

Meet the Joneses—everyone else has. They're friendly, extraverted . . . maybe a little overbearing in the long run, but they're sincere and warm. Pleasant enough in modest doses.

Here's Joe and Bobby, a gay couple, radiating a mix of knockout elegance and sly good humor in their perfectly tailored Armani suits.

There's a couple we haven't met yet, and probably won't. They're quiet, and a little mysterious. Shy people? Spies from Kazakhstan? Oh—they're gone. Where did they go?

The pyrotechnical Joneses have Sagittarius rising in their composite chart. Whatever the intimate realities of their relationship may be, when they're observed in the world, their style has impact. They are colorful, theatrical, and in your face.

Joe's and Bobby's smooth and well-tailored composite chart shows a Libran Ascendant conjunct Venus, with Saturn deeper in their First House, just over the line into Scorpio.

That quiet couple who disappeared? Cancer rising, or maybe Scorpio—they were gone before we could find out.

Every partnership has a face it wears for the world. Secrecy or phoniness aren't the issues here—although the composite Ascendant is in charge of those tricks too, when circumstances demand them. Here's the point: at that party, none of those couples had any business revealing the true inner dynamics of their bond to the general public. In society, a certain amount of "editing" is appropriate, expected, appreciated—and lamented when absent. We all know the discomfort created by a couple bickering in a social situation. Unless we know people very well, we expect that any references to their sexuality will be brief, probably humorous, and not too graphic. Strictures such as these operate in every stratum of society, every culture and every epoch. Humans seem to appreciate a little distance among themselves. Intimacy, in other words, is a *gift* we bestow on a few trusted friends, not something we offer everyone indiscriminately.

The composite Ascendant is the buffer between the secret world of the couple and the general public. When two people are making a conscious and individuated response to their composite Ascendant, they generally function well in social situations. They seem comfortable together. They've "got their act together."

A weak response to the composite Ascendant tends to have the opposite impact: there's an awkwardness about the pair when they're seen in public. Often, the effect is that they don't seem right for each other—a statement which may not actually reflect the deeper realities of their relationship. Still, once a couple gets past the courtship phase, they must exist in society. And most couples who have been together for more than a few months come to appreciate the support and camaraderie of others. All that is infinitely more difficult if the composite Ascendant isn't working right.

Each composite Ascendant suggests a set of specific shared activities and attitudes which can contribute mightily to the ease of the bond. They help the couple dance together naturally and without excessive damage to their toes, figuratively—and literally too.

Our consideration of the composite Ascendant should expand to include the Ascendant's planetary ruler. Thus, if a couple has Cancer rising, the Moon is going to play an extra-important role in their chart. If they have Gemini or Virgo rising, play close attention to their composite Mercury. Read our basic interpretation of that planet in terms of its sign and house elsewhere in this "cookbook" section of *Skymates Volume Two: The Composite Chart.* Along with those layers of meaning, add that a high response to this Ascendant-ruling planet also enhances the smoothness of the relationship, helping the couple feel comfortable together in the world. A weak response undercuts them, leaving them feeling awkward and unnatural.

COMPOSITE ASCENDANT IN ARIES

Whatever inner lights illuminate the secret world of this couple, those lights blaze into the world through fire engine red filters. If the rest of the composite chart is passionate and intense, then stand back: together, these two are as unstoppable as a downhill freight train. Even if the rest of the composite chart is relatively mild, there is still a certain tingle in the air when they walk into the room. Together, they radiate confidence and pluck. One senses—wisely—that this team would make a better friend than enemy. What we are picking up here is not hostility; it's more like a simple potential for formidability. Imagine coming upon Arnold Schwarzenegger, stripped to the waist, armed to the teeth—and smiling at you with genuine warmth. That's the picture.

The deeper forging of this bond requires initiation by fire. Even though together these two are a powerful team, they still must be "blooded" if they are going to have full faith in themselves. They need to face challenges together, and learn to trust each other as comrades. All this may sound dreadfully militaristic, but these are the natural metaphors of Aries the Warrior.

In practice, with the composite Ascendant in Aries, the path may entail shared physical adventure. Maybe they learn to sail—and learn to count on each other's moves in forty knots of wind. Perhaps they take up scuba diving and explore a deep, jagged wreck together. Maybe they're milder people than that—and they drive a car across the country together or visit Peru, bonding in the heat of those adventures.

Not all Aries evolutionary work is so physical, although one cannot deal authentically with this sign without recognizing the psychic transformations triggered by having our bodies on the line. Still, together this couple may come into their natural poise and "centeredness" by fighting joint battles that offer no physical threat at all. They might, for example, take on a crusade against a rapacious land developer threatening to destroy a community or an environment. They might stand up to an intellectual or spiritual bully.

Becoming a "couple" is a uniquely human mystery, hard to understand or explain, let alone accomplish. Desire and affection between people are far easier to grasp. Always, with the composite Ascendant in Aries, the road to attaining that feeling of naturalness and smoothness is a little more challenging than it might be otherwise. Flowers and poetry—those sacraments of intimacy—are less effective here. So put them aside, and strap on those boots, sunglasses, and backpacks. Cupid is waiting out there, somewhere to the left of the rattlesnake.

Be sure to take a close look at Mars, the planetary ruler of Aries, in the composite chart. It will carry the story further, with a specific reference to areas where this passionate bonding-in-fire is especially suited to the realities of the couple.

COMPOSITE ASCENDANT IN TAURUS

Adam and Eve must have had it pretty easy in the Garden, at least until the unfortunate affair with the apple. Imagine having no worries about status or weight-loss or style! Imagine no one competing for your mate's attention, no deadlines and no bills! Imagine no family of origin and no in-laws! Everything would be gloriously simple: nothing but instinct and the present tense, with our natural goodness shining through. Even with the composite Ascendant in Taurus, getting back to the Garden is tough—but the more these two people succeed in re-creating it, the happier they will be.

Taurus thrives on naturalness. For this couple, a deepening sense of rightness seeps into the bones of their relationship when they stay in touch with their instinctual animal natures. They need a lot of silence together, for one thing. That doesn't mean they shouldn't talk; all couples need communication. But for these two, time spent without words can be eloquent. Similarly, they benefit from days spent alone together in the forest or desert or by the sea. They thrive on physical touch. Sharing food brings them closer together. It is comforting and affirming for them simply to be naked together—and if that leads to sex, so much the better! Venus, goddess of love, is the ruler of Taurus, and the sensual side of their relationship is profoundly important, and probably vigorous. Couples bond in primal ways through sexuality—and the more they try to understand that fact in a cerebral way, the less they know.

From the Taurean point of view, the human world is a shallow, pretentious place. People are always posing, trying to be seen as sexy or cool or important. Because of the silly insecurities created in us by "civilized" life, it's easy to be swept up in that game. With their composite Ascendant in Taurus, the entire basis of the relationship between these two depends on finding safe havens out of reach of all those games. They may live in a city and have high-powered careers. They may even be invited to hang with movie stars and have their smiling faces in *People* magazine. Fine—but it is still profoundly helpful for them to get away from that kind of environment, and to let simplicity, instinct, and nature wash over them from time to time. And it is desperately important that they get far enough away from those kinds of values inside themselves that they never lose sight of the joke of it all. How does all that glitter look to an eagle—or to a wise old Navajo?

Nature—an unpretentious naturalness—calms us. That serenity is a big part of the evolutionary aim of composite Ascendant in Taurus. One practical spin-off is that this couple benefits from a fairly steady life together: they need familiar friends and familiar places. Some degree of financial security helps calm them too, along with a cautious attitude toward risk, and toward change just for the sake of change.

Outwardly, these two probably look good together—that's part of the Venusian signature. They radiate a soothing quality of unpretentious naturalness. They seem to be silently telling everyone that it's fine for them to be exactly who they are, and that underneath our clothing, we are all perfectly naked.

Be sure to take a close look at Venus, the planetary ruler of Taurus, later in this section. It will carry the story further, with references to specific areas where this calming, centering Taurean work is particularly central to this couple's shared evolutionary intentions.

COMPOSITE ASCENDANT IN GEMINI

Will all of you who enjoy being bored out of your skulls in a relationship, please raise your hands?

Anyone who can count to zero has no trouble with the math here. Boredom, numbness and predictability are the great enemies of lasting love. No one likes them. But with composite Ascendant in Gemini, they are fatal. For this couple, keeping their life together *interesting* is absolutely pivotal. Instantly, we need to make a sharp distinction between "interesting" and *fast*. Gemini and fast are practically equatable. With this Ascendant, these two people constantly feel the tendency of their life together to accelerate into ever-increasing over-extension and existential clutter. This Geminian "zoom-factor" should never be confused with being interesting! We've all had days that were incredibly full—and incredibly forgettable. If there is a devil, this is where he will try to get to these two. They are not likely to spend much time sitting around with nothing to do, but they are vulnerable to starving themselves to death on a rich diet of cotton candy. The key here is simple: the antidote to boredom lies in exposing themselves to perceptions that they've never entertained before and which fill them with shared curiosity.

With their composite Ascendant in Gemini, this couple should take seriously the idea of attending classes and workshops together. It's easy to imagine them radiant, hanging out in a café after class with six people they've just met, talking about what they've learned. It's natural for people with this composite Ascendant to be drawn to the *media:* books, film, television, the Internet, magazines. That's fine and natural but again, they need to be careful: the Geminian need to be fascinated can be seduced by the kaleidoscopic flicker of content-free imagery. Is their intelligence being stretched and their curiosity truly fed? Do the media experiences leave them with anything new to talk about? Those are the critical questions. If the answers are positive, they are on the right track, and their poise and confidence as a couple will blossom. If they are negative, then the relationship, however busy, is not moving or evolving and will become increasingly vulnerable to foundering.

Conversation needs to rise to an art form here. Probably these two have plenty of wit—likely, they "perform" well together and are good at making other people laugh. Much of that depends on the quickness of their chemistry together. Between themselves, it's helpful to recognize that deep statements can at times also be simple ones—and serious truths can be drowned in too many words. Similarly, some emotional realities are paradoxical enough that it takes a paragraph to express them. An enthusiastic interruption can leave the speaker feeling unheard and the listener quite mistaken about what was being expressed. As they slow their speech, more interesting statements are put on the table, and the composite Ascendant is purring.

There's an animated, buzzing vibration around this couple. People are drawn to them because they seem to be fascinating, and probably fun. Because of their vivacity, strangers will underestimate their ages—and often imagine that their relationship is a relatively new one. Their aura of openness leads others to offer them unusual opportunities and experiences, and many times it's good for them to go for it. "When in doubt, do it" is a dangerous statement—but with the composite Ascendant in Gemini, it's generally a merry policy.

Be sure to take a close look at Mercury, the planetary ruler of Gemini, later in this section. It will carry these ideas further, with references to specific areas where this appetite for wonder is particularly central to their shared evolutionary intentions.

COMPOSITE ASCENDANT IN CANCER

Got the blues? Feel like you need a hug? Maybe a little tea and sympathy? Head straight for the home of your friends with their composite Ascendant in Cancer. If you do that, your instincts are sound: these two will take good care of you. But you may have to wait in line, because you're not the only one who can feel their warmth and comforting presence from ten miles away. It's not that they are so extroverted or social—they may in fact have been looking forward to a quiet evening of reading or watching a familiar old film together. It's just that anyone who gets near them feels a little better—not giggly or high. Nothing so wild. Think of the way you feel about three minutes after settling into a hot bath after a long, hard day. That's about it.

Maybe you're on our Cancer Ascendant couple's short list, and you've actually got a the key to their front door. They might be off visiting family on the other side of the country. No matter; if you need soothing, all you have to do is walk into their house and sit there for a while. When it comes to making a place comfortable, these two have a magical touch. Just settle into that sofa and put your feet up. In a few minutes, you'll be all right.

Everything about this couple radiates through the "stained glass" of the *Mother* archetype. Whatever the rest of their natures might be, their mask in the world exudes a consoling, reassuring, unassuming gentleness. The rest of us believe in them as a couple—and if they were to separate, it would feel as if something terribly wrong had happened.

That's beautiful and appealing—but any couple working with this composite Ascendant needs to be cautious about other people draining their own inner batteries, even with positive projections. For these two to feel centered, they have an absolute, non-negotiable need for time spent alone with each other. They need to be really careful about that Mother energy drawing an endless stream of needy people to their door. Their home life is very important to them. Passing quiet, easy hours together in their Hobbit hole is one of the most healing activities available to them. Trouble is, people they love may not allow them enough of that sustaining solace.

"Family" is absolutely central to the logic of Cancer—and we're putting the word in quotation marks because its meaning is so flexible nowadays. They may declare you to be "family," even though you are not related by blood or marriage. And once you are family to these two, you'll always have a place in their hearts. Their loyalty is unquestionable.

Here's the paradox: in order to thrive, the Cancer composite Ascendant needs committed human connections—but it must also learn to set solid boundaries. Otherwise, other people's dramas can so distract them from their own private intimate processes that something withers between them. They might lose those life-sustaining Cancer vitamins: a sense of safety, privacy, and sanctity in their domestic environment, a sense of control over its borders. They might lose that precious feeling of having enough time to stretch slowly out into sharing the nuances of their own complex emotions. With every escalation of commitment in outside relationships, both the prizes and the risks head north. This is deeply true with dear friends, especially when they are in need. With literal kinship—mothers and fathers, for example—learning to set clear boundaries can be pivotal. If these two take that ultimate Cancerian step and have children, then profound caution must be exercised that they don't completely sacrifice their natural right to withdraw into their own nourishing, sustaining secret world.

For more insight into how a couple with a Cancer composite Ascendant can take care of themselves, have a close look a few pages back at the position of the composite Moon, which rules their Ascendant.

COMPOSITE ASCENDANT IN LEO

Styles change. What's considered beautiful in one century might be a source of personal insecurity in another. The most obvious illustration is our varying enthusiasm for body fat: compare the *zaftig* reclining goddesses of the Renaissance with the more willowy feminine ideals of modern Hollywood. In classical Rome, a large, hooked nose on a man was seen as a sign of virility and authority. Nowadays, a man with such a proboscis is under social pressure to consider corrective surgery. It's worth spending a few pages lamenting the pointless hurt these styles create for people, but we'll spare you that. Instead, let's consider it from the angle of psychological *realpolitik*: being considered appealing is a real boost in the self-confidence department. If we feel attractive, we'll often take more self-expressive risks and be bolder about asking for what we want—and expecting to get it.

People who are naive about such matters imagine that one's allure is a fixed quantity. You are born with it, and that's that. They may try to pave over whatever tricks God played on them with cosmetics and clothing, but deep down they know the fearful truth. With a little more wisdom and experience, we recognize that the game is a lot more subtle: attitude, style, and a sense of theater go a long way to creating an aura of magnetism around a person. With their composite Ascendant in Leo, the fulfillment of the evolutionary intentions of this couple depend upon their playing this stylistic card. They may not need to be beautiful in the narrow sense of the word, but they do need to become *impressive.*

Why? Isn't that just a superficial concern? Yes, it is—and, in a sense, the composite Ascendant itself is superficial. So is your skin! For this couple to have the experiences they need in this world, this colorful Leo appearance is the ticket that gets them aboard the right train. There are two dimensions to that observation. The first is that impressive, appealing people can get through doors that would be barred to others. The second, and more important, consideration is that, if we *feel* impressive and appealing, we will often be more willing to take more creative risks. We are simply not as fearful of rejection.

Automatically, with the composite Ascendant in Leo, we tend to see a certain *flair* in this couple. Others may be more aware of it than they are. They are not necessarily loud or extroverted, but eyes turn to them as they enter the room. There is a certain "royal" dignity about them, as if they ought to "be somebody." With only modest exaggeration, we can imagine that we've dressed them expensively and sneaked them into the Academy Awards banquet. Movie people at other tables are whispering to each other, wondering who they are . . . "I've know I've seen them somewhere before. I just can't place them."

If this couple can learn to cultivate these qualities and to trust them, they can increasingly begin to take on *leadership* and *style-setting* roles in their communities. Their soul-intentions depend on doing that. These two would benefit by literally going on stage together—acting or presenting workshops. A great "yoga" for them is having a serious, creative professional photographer take their picture. Coaching each other about language, clothing, and physical posture is central. It's good that they remember the "joke" inherent in all such concerns—and recognize that the joke can be on them if they don't take it seriously!

For deeper perspectives on how the couple with the Leo composite Ascendant can take care of themselves, have a close look a few pages back at the position of their composite Sun, which rules their Ascendant.

COMPOSITE ASCENDANT IN VIRGO

Maybe your jeep has broken down in the Kalahari desert in South Africa. Good luck—you are eighty yards from the only gas station within five hundred miles! You walk up to the attendant and explain your plight. He's friendly, concerned, and—here's the bad luck—perfectly incompetent. He doesn't even have a telephone. He can't fix your car. He may have tears of compassion in his eyes. He may be the soul of good will. But he's about as useful to you as a runny nose on your wedding day.

Competence is a precious commodity—and with their composite Ascendant in Virgo, this couple radiates it. There is something grounded about their appearance. People tend to trust them quickly, and generally that trust is well placed. One look, and we instinctively take them seriously. We may not even know them, but we are instantly sure that they are *good at something*. They radiate skillfulness, earthy reasonableness, and an undefined proficiency.

Our assumptions are probably accurate—a couple with this composite Ascendant, given a bit of time together, soon develops into a *team*. Sometimes the complementarity of their skills is evident right from the starting line: they may even have met through their professional lives. Other times, they are attracted to each other for more typical romantic and psychological reasons. But, as the wheels turn, they come to recognize that their skills lock together like a jigsaw puzzle.

In any case, we all quickly sense that these two could be useful to us. Wearing the mask of the "servant," they seem to invite requests for assistance and advice—even when they might actually prefer that we left them alone! Even people who normally wouldn't be intrusive feel a kind of permission to approach them. Mercury—the planet of communication—rules Virgo, and therefore it's quite evident in their style: together, these two are verbal, even if they are more quiet as individuals. The chemistry between them seems to bring out language skills. Since most social interaction is verbal, this communicativeness also contributes to their "availability."

The "servant" role is simply a reality here. There isn't much these two can do about it, even if they don't like it. Where freedom enters the equations is in the *determination of the nature of the service* they will render. With the composite Ascendant in Virgo, their soul-intention pivots on finding the *right work* to offer their community—and the right work is something that gives them joy and a sense of meaning as well as benefitting others. They will be happy if they succeed in finding it—and, if they don't, they will be under constant pressure to accept duties that return nothing to them.

Naturally, it is not unusual to see couples with this composite Ascendant drawn to the idea of actually finding a profession they can share. In many ways, that is the ideal. But work is not always something we get paid to do—or at least that is not our sole source of support. The real issue, from the evolutionary perspective, is finding the nature of that *shared talent* where their joys and their skills fit together in a way that makes the whole greater than the sum of the parts. Then they experience the fulfillment and the dignity of offering that shared talent as a gift to the people around them.

Be sure to take a close look at Mercury, the planetary ruler of Virgo, later in this section. It will carry these ideas further, with references to specific areas where we might locate this precious skill.

COMPOSITE ASCENDANT IN LIBRA

Some people view themselves as the most fascinating topics in the world. In the standard joke, they say, "Well, enough about me—what do *you* think of me?" Naturally, we find such behavior off-putting. We don't feel any sense of connection with such individuals. On the other hand, when someone finds *us* fascinating, we generally take that to be a sign of their good taste and their wisdom in matters of character! We open up to them, often imagining that we have a lot in common—that our values are similar, that we vote for the same people, and so on. That may be an illusion, but it's not an unpleasant one. The world could use more of it, and if there were more couples with the composite Ascendant in Libra, we would enjoy a lot more simple graciousness, sensitivity and support as we went about our lives. We would all feel more *interesting* and *appealing,* and some of the usual social chill in anonymous human interactions would thaw. With these two, once their relationship gets established, it is as if everything inside them takes on an appealing glow of bridge-building empathy as it shines out into the community.

The orientation in Libra is toward the *other person*—that's a critical piece of our understanding. It's not that they put themselves forward in an extroverted or assertive way, it's more that they draw *us* out. With these two, we don't have the feeling of being seduced or manipulated, or even necessarily entertained. When we walk away from them, we are not blown away. We're not in love with them. We just *like* them and feel a certain *simpatico* between us.

Furthermore, they have learned more about us than we have about them—and half of what we feel we know about them is probably incorrect. They didn't lie or intentionally deceive us. It's just that their orientation was more toward outreach and connection than it was about self-revelation. For them, the real content of the interaction was not actually personal information; it was the quality of the interaction itself.

With the composite Ascendant in Libra, a big part of the soul-intention of this couple revolves around the awareness-triggering impact of other people—and other couples—upon them. They are taking in a lot of data about relationships in general, digesting it, and turning it into wisdom in the context of their own bond. Thus, people who serve well as bad examples are as useful to them as people who serve as good ones. To that end, Spirit has given them the capacity to have the string quartet over for dinner one night and Hell's Angels over the next. And they will learn from both!

If life were infinitely long, this strategy would be instructive for them. But life isn't—and that leads us to the realization that these two benefit a lot from learning to do some careful selection in terms of who lies at the other end of the bridges they excel at building. To get some insight into the optimal answers to that question, have a careful look at the location by sign and by house of their composite Venus a few pages ahead. Venus rules Libra, and thus is the ruler of their composite Ascendant. People who are described by the higher possibilities of that Venus placement are their true allies—and people who represent lower expressions of it can weave tangled webs for them. With the latter type, these two need to run away politely! And with the former, they benefit from cultivating real trust and, comparing notes, moving into the deeper waters together.

COMPOSITE ASCENDANT IN SCORPIO

Everyone's got a few embarrassing memories. Some of them are just silly, like when we put salt in our coffee, thinking it was sugar, on the day we met our new in-laws. Once we feel comfortable with other people, we often revel in sharing those kind of tales. Everyone laughs, and we all feel closer and more human. But other memories and inner realities are less comfortable, and we tend to keep them private. We might have had second thoughts about a relationship to which we've committed, or doubts about whether we should have had children. Most of us have a few sexual stories we'd prefer didn't get into the *National Enquirer.* Legal, moral and ethical lines get crossed. We carry these secrets inside ourselves, and find the thought of being "discovered" so unnerving that we don't even want to think about it—until we encounter a couple with their composite Ascendant in Scorpio. Then, unaccountably, we hear ourselves saying, "I've never told anyone this before, but . . . "

There is a disarming aura of intensity around this couple. Once we get near them, the usual superficialities of social life fall away. Frivolous posturing and banal conversation—the staple ingredients of civilized existence—feel unnatural to us. We want to get down into the meat of things. Their sexuality is usually very up front—you can feel it between them, even though they are probably not talking about it. You sense the psychological depth in their bond right away. Something about their chemistry brings out confession in other people. They seem to demand truth, and they do that without ever actually asking for it. You simply know that they would see through any false front you put up as easily as we see through the lie of the child caught with a hand in the cookie jar.

Humor has a part in all this. We humans have always made jokes of the things that are most frightening and personal to us: death, sexuality, ageing, and so on. With their composite Ascendant in Scorpio, these two are probably pretty *funny* once you get to know them. But even their humor just seems to pull us into their gravitational field more deeply.

At the evolutionary level, this couple is moving through a developmental stage involving a kind of "talking cure" healing process that is happening between them. The key is to recognize that this process requires *outside input of a taboo nature.* They need honest information from others. Without it, they can't keep perspective on their own psychological intensity. How much saner we all might be if we didn't have to face so much of life in silence! But conventional wisdom demands that we avoid unpleasant subjects in social situations—you don't ask Grandpa if he's in his Viagra years yet. With their composite Ascendant in Scorpio, this couple has reached a passage in which shared truth is everything. To that end, their outward style is practically advertising for it.

Be sure to take a close look at the position of Pluto, the planetary ruler of Scorpio, in their composite chart. It will carry the story further, with references to specific areas where this goose-bump level of emotional honesty is especially suited to the realities of the couple.

COMPOSITE ASCENDANT IN SAGITTARIUS

Sagittarius, in some astrological writing, is viewed as "idealistic but impractical." That viewpoint breaks down when we demand a definition of "practicality." For many people, the word boils down to staying safe and making money, but what's really so practical about that? We have our brief, uncertain lives in this world, and no one gets out alive. Any truly practical response to living has got to face those facts—and in facing them, we immediately recognize the practicality of philosophy! Why are we here? What is really important in our lives? No way we can lead "practical" lives without having some working hypotheses regarding those issues. These are Sagittarian questions, and with their composite Ascendant in that sign, this couple is wrestling with them. A quality of high-minded principle radiates from them, as does a quality of *seeking* and an openness to exploration.

Let's continue to be ruthlessly practical. If the purpose of life lies partly in trying to *determine* the purpose of life before the bell rings, what kinds of methods make sense? Let's start with a popular one that makes no sense at all: cautiously take up a defensive position in life. Establish safe, boring relationships, pursue safe, boring careers, make sound investments, and hope fervently that you'll live forever. Here's a wiser approach: *hurl yourself into living*. Gather wide experience. Entertain exotic perspectives. Then engage the intuition, and decide where to place your precious faith. With their composite Ascendant in Sagittarius, that latter method is the one that fulfills the soul-contract of this couple. They have made a deal to take chances together, even if that means they'll sometimes make mistakes—in fact, even their mistakes will prove quite instructive to them.

Together, these two wear the mask of the gypsy. There's something dashing and colorful in their style. They are ready for adventure—and adventure makes them feel more centered and confident as a couple. Traveling benefits them enormously. It blows out the mental cobwebs and gives them a broader perspective. They gain a kind of legitimacy in their own eyes when they can tell people that they are just back from living in Argentina for a year, or that they are off to India to study yoga.

Immediately, a natural objection arises: not every couple with the composite Ascendant in Sagittarius is wealthy. That kind of questing life may be appealing, but there are bills to pay and so on. This leads us right into the deepest layers of the soul-contract that binds these two: together, they are learning about *faith*. And faith is meaningless without risk. To have faith is to be willing to recognize that a certain course is the right one, and then to trust God to provide the means and the methods. Pay close attention at this point to the position, by sign and house, of their composite Jupiter. That's the ruler of their Ascendant, and it will pinpoint certain areas where this openness to risk is most pivotal for them. We've used traveling as an illustration, and it's often quite relevant to couples with this Ascendant. But there are other areas of life where faith and risk are catalysts for evolution. Their Jupiter will point the way to them.

COMPOSITE ASCENDANT IN CAPRICORN

Confusion is part of life. We all arrive at existential crossroads, knowing that the success or failure of our lives depends on our making the right choices. And we stand there, clueless. Should we commit to this relationship? Move to Idaho? Quit this safe job and accept that exciting, insecure one? Have a baby?

Blundering is costly, and yet usually at these crossroads the voices in our heads are arguing. Is that wisdom talking—or just fear? Is this true love—or an infatuation I'll be paying some psychotherapist to explain before too long?

In traditional cultures, faced with these kinds of dilemmas, we knew what to do: go have a talk with an *elder.* That didn't just mean someone who was old—plenty of people become old without becoming elders. Elders have *digested* their experience and turned it to a tempered, nuanced understanding of life. At every level, from the psychological to the purely practical, they simply *know things.* And we trust them and naturally turn to them.

With their composite Ascendant in Capricorn, this couple already plays the role of elders in their community. That statement has nothing to do with their chronological age: there are "elders" who are twenty years old. The point is that a quality of grounded wisdom radiates from this couple. People sense that they are valuable fountains of knowledge. They'll turn to them for opinions and perspectives on everything from what car to buy to the most perplexing relationship dilemmas. And, nine times out of ten, the advice these two offer is sound, solid, and helpful.

The soul-contract they've signed involves gathering a set of experiences that allow the elder archetype they carry to develop and blossom. While couples can play that kind of supporting, sobering, counseling role for others at any age, years in the world do deepen it. With their composite Ascendant in Capricorn, these two carry the seed-intention of literally growing old together, becoming one of those gray-haired couples who immediately make us think of wizards—which, incidentally, is another Capricorn archetype. As they evolve together, we begin to see a wintry strength in them. They carry not only understanding, but also integrity, character, and a steely determination to look the reality of life straight in the eye.

How can they accomplish this aim? We learn about life essentially by living it. For this couple, there are many mountains to climb. Some astrologers think of Capricorn as an unfortunate sign. There's no such thing, but Capricorn does refer to challenges and difficulty—and to the positive qualities of character that arise in us if we rise to them. With their composite Ascendant in Capricorn, they achieve their right orientation to life by daring to push themselves toward the limits of excellence. They thrive on *vows,* starting with a sober commitment to work through their own relationship, aiming to "grow" it over time. They may benefit from having children: another "great work." Accepting a larger sense of mission in their community is another evolutionary tactic for them. Perhaps they open a no-kill animal shelter, help establish a spiritual institution, or lead an environmental crusade. Always, the key is the realization that an elder is tempered and forged by challenges.

A close consideration of the position of Saturn, the planetary ruler of Capricorn, will typically offer a lot of specific insight about the nature of these great works, and the concrete arenas in which they are taking place. It is particularly imperative that this couple rise to those missions, because it is through them that they come into the full power and authority of their "wizardhood."

COMPOSITE ASCENDANT IN AQUARIUS

These two stand out in a crowd, not necessarily because they're trying to call attention to themselves, but simply because they just don't seem to fit in. Even when they're sitting still, you can tell that they walk to the beat of a different drummer.

Sometimes these zany, out-of-synch Aquarian qualities show up in obvious, external ways: she's taller than he is; he's younger than she is. They are married, but have no rings and no kids—or they are living together, but not married. They're gay; they're of different races. Those distinctions are outward, and run counter to mainstream customs. Far more importantly, a *socially-transformative* energy radiates from a couple wearing the mask of Aquarius, the Rebel, the Non-conformist and the Exile. Their very existence is helping to change the world.

Upon first meeting, these two can come across like amiable but detached extra-terrestrials. They may or not be friendly, but they are definitely "not from around here." Why do they live in a planned community when they barely socialize with anyone in it? Why is there an observatory on their roof? They never send any Christmas cards. Good grief, is that a pet *iguana* living in their art gallery? Gosh, they're hard to understand—but fascinating.

And if they've done their work on themselves, they won't mind a bit that you're having trouble figuring them out. "You like us? Great. You think we're weird? That's *interesting*." A couple with this composite Ascendant needs to develop a thick skin, because they have to get past any needs they might have as individuals for social approval. The creation of their bond involves learning to think for themselves, and making their own decisions about how they will—and will not—structure their relationship.

That may sound easy, but it often involves puzzling or disappointing others. Sometimes, poignantly, it involves hurting them. Maybe they leave the religions of their childhoods. Maybe they move from the town where their families have lived for eight generations. Maybe they choose not to have children, or adopt an interracial child. Whatever the rules, sooner or later you hear the sound of some of them being broken.

Which ones? Give careful consideration to Uranus, the planetary ruler of Aquarius, in the composite chart. It will carry the story further, with a specific reference to an area where this mutual declaration of independence is especially relevant to the evolutionary realities of this couple.

COMPOSITE ASCENDANT IN PISCES

There is a fine line between taking ourselves too seriously and not taking ourselves seriously enough. On one hand, we have self-absorbed egotism. On the other, drifting—a very *cosmic* and humorous drifting perhaps, but it's still not leading anywhere. With their composite Ascendant in Pisces, this couple needs to be wary of the second pitfall. This isn't because they are weak. It's because of a strength they have, but which they necessarily know how to handle. When these two came together, the chemistry between them was mystical—or perhaps we should say psychedelic. Suddenly, they were having uncanny psychic experiences together. Suddenly, they were bigger than the world, or above it, or outside it. They were looking at the rest of us the way the angels do—with love, but also a shake of the head at our ridiculous vanities and our silly posturing. Together, these two get the joke of life. One manifestation of that is simply their fantastic sense of humor. Another is a vulnerability to just *watching* life as it happens to them, without claiming the specific experiences that actually are the intentions of their souls.

What are those experiences? Pisces is the archetype of the mystic, and we can answer our question simply by considering what mystics want. Immediately, we might think of mountaintops or wildernesses for meditation. We might think of lofty spiritual teachers or candle-lit cathedrals. The key is the realization that none of those consciousness-invoking situations or experiences are likely to just materialize in front of two people sitting at home watching television! They've got to go seek such experiences actively, and that requires effort. It demands *some ego-energy and some focus*—and that means choice, intention, a willingness to act. It also implies an openness to displeasing others when they have alternative plans for us. With their composite Ascendant in Pisces, the fulfillment of the soul-contract between these two depends upon their *behaving outwardly* like mystics: meditating or praying together, seeking inspiring teachers, visiting sacred places.

Always, they can act. To Pisces, all the world is a stage. They can play a lot of different roles together, and understand the arbitrariness of all of them. That skill allows them to move easily through varying social environments. It's easy to imagine them as spies, playing their parts with flawless grace, all the while watching and studying everyone around them. Where the risks come into the equations is when we imagine their functioning as "spies" in a life they have created—and never leave. Their understanding of the grand joke doesn't make them any less a part of it.

The alternative? Actively to engage in the exploration of consciousness together! Their "religion" is their own business. Maybe they are Hindus, or Shamans, or Jungians—or Jehovah's Witnesses. No matter. What matters is that they actually work the methods together as a couple, using them to open doors into higher states of consciousness. To get more specific insight into certain mystical experiences which are pivotal to their journey, be particularly alert to the position of Neptune in their composite chart. It rules their Pisces Ascendant and thus gives some very concrete suggestions about the path that works for them.

(Please note: there is no "Composite Ascendant in the Houses" section here, because the Ascendant itself is the cusp of the first house.)

CHAPTER EIGHT: THE COMPOSITE MERCURY

Mercury may not be one of the officially romantic planets, but almost everyone understands that effective communication—Mercury's territory—is one of lasting love's essential ingredients. Chemistry and electricity are amazing phenomena: a couple destined to spend decades together might meet for the first time and instantly recognize their connection. That's real and authentic. But if they're going to stay truly connected through the inevitable negotiations that adult love entails, they have to be able to speak their hearts, hear each other well, and convey that hearing back to each other effectively. Eloquence isn't the point—under certain circumstances, it can be intimidating, bombastic and repressive. Nor is the point even so narrow as the concept of speech, although speech is absolutely central to Mercury. We communicate receptivity sometimes with our silences. We communicate concern or compassion with an eloquent, well-timed touch. In intimacy, much communication occurs wordlessly through the mysteries of our eyes and the soul-contact, or lack of it, that they signal. Mercury's place in the composite chart teaches us about those exchanges too.

Furthermore, not all communication described by composite Mercury involves serious transmissions about The Relationship. What human bond could thrive without humor? Or without shared interests outside itself? Those are Mercury territories as well, and must be fed in accord with the nature of the planet's position in the composite chart.

Each couple must find its own natural communicative style. Some people convey deep, intimate data to each other in single sentences. Or in jokes. Some successful relationships average ten thousand words a night, some a hundred. There are compassionate, effective communication styles that may sound like argument or attack to the outside observer—and ones with real teeth that may sound wimpy. In every case, the discovery of the communicative style that works is a make-it-or-break-it issue. And in every case, we can learn a lot about that style with a glance at the composite Mercury.

COMPOSITE MERCURY IN ARIES

Aries wants challenges, adventures and victories. It seeks courage and admires heroics. It wants potency and penetration, to be dynamic, to make an impact. It likes brinkmanship and winning. This doesn't mean couples with this composite Mercury are always fighting, nor always discussing sports. But verbal sparks can fly here, and these two should establish good conflict resolution skills. Their natural communicative style is blunt, forthright and goal-oriented, like two hunters tackling the same mastodon.

This pair can enjoy healthy debate and relish a spirited sort of verbal one-up-manship. They may tease each other mercilessly, to the point where acquaintances who don't know them well may gasp at the risks they're taking, and fear they're headed for blows or the divorce courts. Think of two warriors bantering in a tavern: swapping stories, bragging, calling each other names and trading friendly insults, all in ways of which Miss Manners would not approve. But woe betide anyone who threatens either of them; they'll promptly join forces against the enemy.

The need here is to share challenges in Mercury's realm, and be brave enough to communicate about potentially explosive topics. A key to working with this composite Mercury is having the courage (Aries) to deal with both major anger and minor irritations *quickly,* rather than letting them fester and explode, or be displaced onto a substitute issue. If this couple has a spectacular fight over what color to paint the bathroom, the paint is not what's really at stake. Another strategy is sharing a Mercurial challenge: enroll in a class together, collaborate on the Sunday crossword puzzle, or invent silly limericks during long car trips. Equally helpful, if there are no unresolved tensions brewing between these partners, might be outlets where they can deliberately compete against each other in a harmless, low-key way: a Scrabble tournament or a poker game. If their individual Mercuries are in softer-spoken or more affiliative signs, this composite Mercury's taste for mixing it up can take some adjustment, but it can also bring plenty of spice into both of their lives.

COMPOSITE MERCURY IN TAURUS

The God of Speech in the most non-verbal of the signs! What could that mean? For starters, non-verbal does not mean uncommunicative. It's just that the essence of Taurus has little to do with human speech. This sign is about reconnecting to our instinctive sides, our animal natures, our primate selves. Once upon a time in human prehistory, we had not yet developed a spoken language. Did we still communicate? Certainly, and a couple with composite Mercury in Taurus dimly remembers how. Of course spoken language is important with this composite Mercury sign, but more than speech is important here: a hug, a sigh, a meal, a backrub. Body language matters as well. A relaxed posture, feet on the coffee table, and an arm laid invitingly along the back of the sofa convey a whole different message to Mercury in Taurus than the message sent by someone hunched over a computer keyboard amid half a dozen empty coffee cups.

This couple does well to take time to process things at a pace that's comfortable for them. "Back to basics" might well be their motto: back to what's most important not only to their sophisticated twenty-first century selves, but also to their inner primates. It might be easier to talk over an issue, simplify it and get at the heart of it while they're taking a walk, for example, or having a picnic by a lake, or cuddled up in their hammock, than it is in one of their offices after work. Concrete examples help, too. As the proverb says, "Actions speak louder than words." They may spend their evenings discussing the mysterious landscape of the human body, or natural history, or their garden, or cooking or working with clay. Music and dance can also be great facilitators and topics of conversation, and shared silences can be most eloquent.

The need here is for communication to be uncomplicated, free of hidden nuances or veiled complexities, and to happen at more levels than just verbally. That way, each partner can almost *sense* what the other one is thinking or feeling, in much the same way that some cats or dogs will sense when their owners are upset, and come to offer comfort. Living with composite Mercury in Taurus involves letting go of some of our constant internal chatter and tuning in to our instinctive side, to how the ancient prehistoric primate within us experiences the world. Individuals who are more mentally or intellectually oriented may find this mode of perception quite a stretch, but one that can truly sensitize them to their partners.

COMPOSITE MERCURY IN GEMINI

The endpoint of Gemini is pure perception, non-judgmental and all-encompassing. Ideally, Gemini is about sheer observation with no judgments, every synapse wide open and the whole nervous system firing. Gemini is, potentially, geared to notice *everything*. The flow and nuances of a conversation. The traffic in the street. The single longer hair in the partner's left eyebrow. What the cat's investigating in the garden outside the window. And, potentially, Gemini is geared *to weigh all those*

In real life, just to maintain our sanity, we don't do this. Instead we practice selective attention: we attend to the conversation more than to the hum of the refrigerator. But a couple with composite Mercury in Gemini can find it hard to practice selective attention. So stand back—a conversation between these partners can resemble a racquetball game at about Warp Ten. It moves fast. It keeps both partners active and engaged. It makes a lot of interesting ricochets. And it may rebound all over the place without arriving at any particular destination, unless the couple strives to keep it on the topic or topics they most need to discuss. If they've set out to have a freewheeling conversation with no particular goal, this verbal racquetball can be great fun. Indeed, life will be more interesting for this couple, and their bond will deepen, if they can spend time in this form of conversation. But it can be frustrating if they're trying to work out a serious difference. Perhaps they should agree to let each other know when they need to stay on a particular topic, and to gently remind one another if they stray off course. In this case, having their individual Mercuries in more orderly signs can be a plus.

COMPOSITE MERCURY IN CANCER

What does a planet in Cancer want? Tenderness. Safety. Belonging. A sheltering nest in which to do inner work and examine the heart. To become mistress of the inner world of Feeling. For a couple with composite Mercury in Cancer, profound subjectivity and heightened imagination color the communicative process and the sharing of ideas and information. Like a rare and delicate flower, this process opens with warmth, proper nurturing and light, and it closes under any hint of harshness or adverse conditions.

A conversation between this couple, when they are both feeling secure enough to connect deeply, will be full of feeling and optimally used to convey feelings. What kind? Whatever's appropriate to the situation, be it love, humor, sorrow or fancy—the waters of imagination run very deep in Cancer. A full current of emotion should flow between this couple, a sense that all their feelings, pleasant, unpleasant and in between, can be safely shared.

What happens if these partners don't feel safe enough with one another to communicate? They will clam up, at least about whatever it is that scares them, which is probably what they most need to discuss. And when a Cancerian planet has raised the drawbridge, that drawbridge is locked tight, and no battering ram in the universe can force it down.

To break the impasse, reassurances are needed. This couple should be careful that, within reason, they don't make something or someone else more important than one another's feelings. They must take care not to disregard each other's sensitivities and vulnerabilities. No one can promise never to hurt someone; sometimes our actions are hurtful, regardless of our intent. But we can sincerely try not to hurt each other. We can resist the urge to be sarcastic, or to hit below the belt. And we can avoid behavior that we know will hurt the partner, *simply because we know that it does.*

The safer that this couple feels with one another, the more the communication between them will blossom. Individuals whose natures are more blunt and fireproof may take time to adapt to a composite Mercury's need for this level of gentleness with one another, but the results are well worth it. Outsiders won't be allowed to witness some of this couple's best conversations, where they take the most risks with each other, and are tender and funny and passionate and whimsical and outrageous and insightful by turns, because outsiders have not been admitted to that level of intimate trust with its rich rewards.

COMPOSITE MERCURY IN LEO

Leo is about saying "yes" to life, about trusting life enough to love it, to create for it, to perform for it. Like Leo's ruler, the Sun, a planet in Leo needs to shine, to give out warm, radiant energy. At its best, it's like a good and generous king or queen, who recognizes and encourages the finest knights, and brings order and plenty to the land. Or it's like a consummate performer, who takes in applause and gives that energy back a hundredfold.

A couple with this composite Mercury should exchange mutual admiration with style and verve. Like a duet, each partner should contribute to the dialog. Conversations between them are best conducted with flair, humor, and healthy doses of praise and acceptance. Imagine a pair of stand-up comics, jamming away, or poets at an open mike reading. The more they make each other laugh, the better they'll communicate. As Henry Miller wrote, "Always merry and bright."

But life is not always merry and bright, and sometimes we have to discuss painful topics, which are not the easiest ones for this composite Mercury to handle. Yet, paradoxically, the more playfully this couple has learned to converse, the more they'll be able to trust one another to venture into darker subjects. Leo is not about the denial of anything negative; it's about being able to cope with sorrow while consciously maintaining a fundamentally optimistic approach to life. How can these two do that? By trusting Spirit, trusting each other, and finding lots of reasons to laugh together. A shared creative and performing outlet would be a big plus. This composite Mercury placement can be taxing for more introverted or serious individuals, but it can also help the depths in such people be more easily articulated.

COMPOSITE MERCURY IN VIRGO

The sign of the master craftsperson, the critic, the analyst and the perfectionist. But the goal of a Virgo planet is not so much to become perfect as to become *whole*, to become fully realized, to reach its highest potential. How? By humility and painstaking self-assessment—recognition of where we need to grow is a prerequisite of growth. By determined, step-by-step self-improvement. By an ongoing focus on the continuing development of expertise in some personally meaningful work or skill.

Therefore, a couple with composite Mercury in Virgo should cultivate the craft of detailed, careful, practical nuts-and-bolts communication, with no Is undotted and no Ts uncrossed, like an exceptionally well-written instruction manual. Conversation is a tool, used to sharpen their relating skills, and the more skillfully they wield that tool, the better. This takes practice, a lot of hours logged in at the exchange of ideas and information. It takes an honest appraisal of where and why they are not communicating as well as they could. It takes objective and pragmatic steps to correct those glitches.

This composite Mercury sign can be trying for individuals who are more geared to see the whole forest than every single tree in it, and they can get frustrated at what feels like having to belabor points. The shadow side of Virgo is a tendency to criticize, and these partners will be sensitive to one another's criticism or anything that smacks of it. Therefore, they must accept one another, and how each of them naturally communicates, as they are. That doesn't mean there's not room for improvement. But the focus should be on what and how to improve in order to deepen the bond between them, not to correct every verbal misstep in detail. For example, suppose he consistently makes a particular grammatical error. That error is a little and, for the relationship, essentially an unimportant thing, however much it may annoy her. It's not the same level of communicative glitch as, say, consistently forgetting to write down dates on their calendar, or always losing flight information. It's better to let little errors go, rather than to berate one another for them. Of course, if he has his Ph.D. oral exams tomorrow, it might be wise to mention the grammatical error. *Gently.* There's a big difference between correcting a mistake and correcting a person. One can be helpful; the other is invalidating and dismissive. Similarly, in the case of the calendar and the flight dates, don't say, "I can't believe how careless you are about our schedules." It's more helpful to ask, "What do you think would make it easier for both of us to write that stuff down? Should we move the calendar right by the phone and attach a pen to it?"

COMPOSITE MERCURY IN LIBRA

Libra's goal is harmony. Reciprocity. Homeostasis. Reconciliation of opposites, mutually agreeable compromise. Yet, by definition, a system that is striving to attain harmony doesn't start out in equilibrium. As if they were perched on opposite ends of a see-saw, a composite Mercury in Libra couple is always trying to keep their communication fair, equitable and in balance.

This doesn't mean that each partner has to say exactly as many sentences as the other one over the course of any given evening, or write just as many love letters—although at times the Libran obsession with "fairness" can look that way. It means that the quantity and the quality of this couple's communication should flow evenly in both directions: mind to mind, heart to heart. If one partner is conveying only ideas when the other partner is conveying only emotions, that is not reciprocity. Above all, each partner should feel both fully heard by the other, and responded to in kind.

The need here is to be well met and fully partnered in the communicative realm. A satisfying conversation between a happy couple with composite Mercury in Libra can feel like dancing: two steps forward, two steps back, whirl and pause and begin again, all in a graceful rhythm. Or it can feel like fencing: thrust and parry, feint and counter, give ground and gain it. Sometimes one of them may take the devil's advocate position purely to keep the ball rolling. If you've seen the movie *My Dinner with André,* you've had a demonstration of something like a composite Mercury in Libra in action! The subjects of this couple's conversations and their shared interests can be equally Libran: cultural topics, books, music, architecture, design, dance, the arts in general. Evenings spent wrapped up in long discussions with mutual friends can be a pleasure as well.

Charming, elegant gestures that affirm and maintain the couple's connection and invite communication help here, too: flowers, tickets to a concert, the gift of an interesting book, a spontaneous surprise. Doing a good job with this composite Mercury involves always being graciously ready to listen to the other person's point to view, to accept, explore and even enjoy the fact that one's mate's perceptions, thoughts and ideas are not the same as one's own. People whose individual charts display a tendency to want to be right all the time may find this difficult, but this couple needs to agree that they will disagree sometimes, and *vive la différence!*

COMPOSITE MERCURY IN SCORPIO

Mercury in Scorpio. A cross between a can opener and a laser beam.

Scorpio's endpoint is *making the unconscious conscious.* It seeks depth. It likes intensity. Scorpio probes inward, detecting layer after layer of previously hidden or unacknowledged material. Scorpio is driven to explore the traditionally taboo areas of life: sexuality, death and dying, the deep unconscious and the occult.

Conversations between a couple with this composite Mercury are not for the faint at heart. Always, they must be willing to go further, deeper. Their defense mechanisms are weakened by this placement, and their appetite for soul-revealing truths and gut-level honesty is increased. Polite, face-saving fictions should have no foothold here. No topic should be taboo. This couple feels in their bones that communication between them doesn't involve just their present, rational selves. It also involves their shadow sides, their damaged, wounded, crazy sides, their inner children of the past, their internalized parental voices and their projections onto one another. Sound like a crowded conference table? It is. But anything more shallow wouldn't be deep enough to hold their interest.

This doesn't mean that every conversation should be a therapy session, nor that this couple should be needlessly confrontive with one another. Just as a skilled therapist doesn't overwhelm clients with insights for which they are not ready, so should these partners treat each other with respect and consideration as well as honesty. Their life together will lead them into fascinating but charged psychological and intellectual ground—not terrain in which to tread carelessly. If one of them asks for a time out, the partner should grant it—as long as it truly is a time out and not an attempt at permanent evasion of an issue that needs processing.

This composite Mercury placement can be harrowing for more defensive or private souls. Also, those who already have a lot of Scorpionic energy may need to remember to lighten up once in a while, and that "sometimes a cigar is just a cigar."

COMPOSITE MERCURY IN SAGITTARIUS

Sagittarius wants perspective and relishes new experiences. It sees the big picture. It wants to act ethically, and yearns to find the meaning of life. Consequentially, it often knows how many angels are dancing on the head of that pin, what their names are, and what they all had for breakfast.

If a couple with composite Mercury in Sagittarius agrees about those angels, great. If they disagree but enjoy the debate, and widen each other's intellectual horizons thereby, that's a good use of this energy. But if they disagree and attach moral failings to one another's disagreement, they're in trouble. Tolerance and respect for varying points of view is crucial here.

So is making sure there's always something interesting to discuss and something new to experience together. In that respect, this composite Mercury sign is not unlike Mercury in Gemini. We're reminded of a couple we met at a conference at the Association for Research and Enlightenment, an institution centered around the work of the late psychic, Edgar Cayce. Why were they there? They were on their honeymoon! Another couple might have gotten a Eurail pass with this composite Mercury, or become spokespersons for a cause they both believed in.

Intuition—the intuitive function assigns *meaning* to symbols, data and events—is Sagittarius's strong point, rather than logic or observation. There is a distinct tendency to assign meaning to every experience, rather than treating the experience as an objective bit of data. In extreme cases, composite Mercury in Sagittarius can be so busy figuring out what that power failure during one of their wonderful far-ranging conversations *meant* that they overlook the fact that they forgot to pay the electric bill. Some innate chicken-soup common sense in their individual charts can go a long way toward reducing this tendency.

COMPOSITE MERCURY IN CAPRICORN

This is the chess player's or architect's Mercury, a Mercury that likes long-term projects which involve structure, organization, planning and consistent effort, and which produce measurable results. Writing a novel. Learning an instrument. Mastering calculus. Installing a computer system. Capricorn's tools are pragmatism, resourcefulness, self-discipline and reserve. Its goals are efficiency, integrity and the accomplishment of a Great Work or Works. For a couple with this composite Mercury, one of those Great Works is communicating as well and effectively as they possibly can.

Not every conversation these partners have will be about wiring diagrams, although this composite Mercury is often interested in how things work—signal chains, telescopes, economics, politics or birthcharts. The point is more to figure out what methods and techniques of communication work best for them: structure, not just content. Perhaps they need to learn how to fight fairly and constructively. Perhaps one of them needs to learn not to interrupt, or to avoid serious topics first thing in the morning. Maybe it takes years to discover the triggers of their more foolish arguments: if she feels that he thinks she's stupid; if he feels that he's not being heard. But once those triggers are determined, a way of dealing with them will be hammered out and put to work, and the number of their spats will decline. Always, the concrete is better than the abstract here, and it's best if these partners don't simply assume that they've been understood or that they've agreed on something. Instead, they talk it out, write it down, pin it to the bulletin board, and save those emails.

Shared intellectual projects can build bonds here, whether it's crossword puzzles or genealogy or a live action role playing game with the local science fiction fans. Individuals who are more emotionally expressive and subjective may find this composite Mercury's caution and lack of demonstrativeness a bit frustrating. Because of the natural reserve of Capricorn, these partners may be more cautious than they should be about revealing their feelings to one another, but learning how to do so can be part of the Great Work of improving their communication.

COMPOSITE MERCURY IN AQUARIUS

The goal of Aquarius is individuation. Independence of mind, heart, will and spirit. Radical authenticity. Being completely oneself. "You like me?

Delightful! You don't like me? Interesting! I wonder why I press your buzzers?" This rebellious sign is interested in whatever is unique. Aquarius has an ability to spot previously overlooked truths, to see that the Emperor is wearing no clothes—and how the needs for approval and belonging make people alter their behavior in a thousand ways great and small. It's hard to describe the optimal communication style of a couple with their composite Mercury in this sign, other than to say it will be original. What works best for them may not work at all for any other couple on this planet.

Conversations may include but not be limited to the space program, Ripley's Believe It or Not, every progressive topic under the Sun, biotechnology, paleoanthropology, chaos theory, speculative fiction, holographic art: you name it. This sign is said to rule aviation, astrology and computers—actually, Aquarius seems to be at least temporarily assigned the rulership of whatever is new and cutting edge *in that era*. A potential gift with this Mercury sign may be the ability to spot where each partner is not being true to himself or herself, and to communicate that perception. "I know that's what everyone in your family thinks, but what do *you* think?" These partners can thrive on humorously challenging each other's *idées fixes,* as well as society's consensus views. "Why not eat the frosting before the cake? Why get a degree in this subject when you're already earning a great living at it?" This couple needs to start with the premise that half of what they've been taught about the world is wrong, and then work on figuring out which half. *They must learn to think for themselves.* That applies to how they communicate, too. Conduct their important relationship conversations by letters? Have every dinner together in silence? Refuse to have a telephone? Send emails in code? If it works for them, why not?

Doing their best with this composite Mercury involves deep tolerance and respect for each other's individuality. That means a live and let live attitude about one another's differing points of view, theories and learning styles. It means being willing to try different ways to communicate and to pursue radical new ideas. It also means that neither partner tries to convert the other to his or her own point of view. No one's a final authority; no one's a censor. For people who tend to have a proselytizing attitude about their own opinions, this can be a challenging placement for Mercury.

COMPOSITE MERCURY IN PISCES

Pisces is always about surrendering. It's always about that part of human consciousness that is in closest touch with the multi-dimensional vastness of both the mind and the cosmos. Because of that contact with the infinite, Pisces can never be bound to the logic of this world. As Einstein, himself a Piscean, proved a century ago, time and space are illusions—just artifacts of our limited senses. Not every couple with their composite Mercury in Pisces spends their evenings discussing theoretical physics—more likely it will be poetry, film, music, transpersonal psychology, or mythology. But when they put their heads together, the communicative processes that arise naturally between them are not always bound to the space-time logic of our "reasonable" human world. That's fine. The place where their intelligences meet and make contact can work splendidly for them, once they learn to follow its n-dimensional threads.

Watch a happy couple who've lived with this composite Mercury for a few years, and you'll see an amazing demonstration of poetic mental dexterity. One of them makes a colorful point—and the point immediately seems to disappear, unremarked. No worry—it's gone through a worm-hole and will emerge ten minutes or ten days later, unscathed . . . whereupon the second person picks it up, turns it into a metaphor that saves an idea she first hatched between them two weeks earlier, like one trapeze artist catching another in mid-air. But wait a minute—how did she know back then what he hadn't said yet, and that he was going to say it? Don't ask.

Making this composite Mercury fly gracefully requires a lot of playfulness. It requires suspension of the ego's *need to be right*, its need for linearity and reason, and its need "to know what's happening." It requires that lots of information be stored in a thoroughly random-access part of both people's minds. It requires intelligence tempered by soul, poetry, and a respect for life's mysteries. It thrives on our ability to laugh at what we can't understand—and an appreciation of the way laughter itself can feel like a form of understanding. It loves quiet time, meditation, and the immense data-sets that can be conveyed between two people's eyes with a moment's glance. It's probably most challenging when each of the individual's natal Mercuries are more orderly by nature—a classic "Culture Shock" interpretive situation. That's one reason we opened this section with a reference to surrendering!

COMPOSITE MERCURY IN THE FIRST HOUSE

A planet in the composite first house is immediately evident to those around the couple; it becomes part of the couple's persona in the world. The first impression they will make—and should make—is Mercurial. They should strike others as an articulate, witty, communicative, curious and observant couple, as raconteurs who are most likely to be asked to a Trivial Pursuit tournament or a lecture series. But the first house is more than the couple's persona; it also represents a sort of astrological behavioral modification suggestion. If these partners consciously, intentionally assume the role of that first house Mercury and act upon it, both in their outer lives and with one another, they will strengthen their bond, help it grow, and feel more at ease together in the world around them.

An astrologer whose name we don't remember once said that the Ascendant is the pathway you need to walk in order to help the Sun be its most radiant self, that the Sun is who you are, and the Ascendant is the road you need to take to get there. By that logic, this couple has a Mercurial path to walk, with one deliberate step after another. What does that mean? That maintaining good communication is essential. There are more modes of communicating than just the verbal one, but stony silences in any mode are anathema for these partners. They must exchange ideas and information, draw one another out and provoke each other's curiosity. This is a natural process early in a relationship, when we are fascinated by each other, want every detail of one another's biographies, and haven't heard all of each other's stories yet. In new love, we don't run out of things to talk about—and neither should this couple. They should make every effort to provide themselves with a steady diet of new topics of conversation: travel, classes, books, intellectual adventures and all manner of fascinating new experiences. The down side of this configuration is that they may overextend themselves into sheer exhaustion. The point is not to be hyperactive, which is trying for anyone, and particularly for individuals whose birthcharts suggest a need for quiet time. The point is more to promise each other that their life together will never be boring, and to keep that promise.

COMPOSITE MERCURY IN THE SECOND HOUSE

In a birthchart, the second house represents resources, self-esteem and finances. In a composite chart, the second house represents the couple's belief in itself as a couple (the relationship's self-esteem or self-confidence), qualities they should cultivate to enhance that belief in themselves (the relationship's resources), and their attitude towards money.

What could Mercury there mean? That these partners should learn to value a shared life of the mind, treasure all the forms of communication between them, and strive to enhance its quality. This doesn't mean that they both have to have Ph.D.s. Few things will make them more positive about their relationship than really good communication: long deep talks, sharing books and theories, sharing jokes, exchanging love letters, camping out in each other's email "in" boxes, and all the other ways that human beings converse with one another. The reverse is also true: if they're not talking, they'll feel as if something's wrong, and start to doubt the relationship. Lose the easy give and take of their ongoing dialogue with one another, and they'll lose faith in their bond. "Give and take" is the operant term here—if only one person is talking, that's not communication; that's a monologue or a lecture.

As for their finances, it's perhaps easiest to illustrate the attitude that this couple should *avoid:* when the economy tanked in the early years of the twenty-first century, a lot of people not only didn't read their 401K or brokerage statements—they didn't even open the envelopes. Willful ignorance is precisely the wrong approach to this couple's money. They need to stay aware of all the details of their financial situation, however painful those details may be. They should not only open those statements, but also get a basic financial education. That may mean reading books, taking a minicourse in personal finance at the local community college, or asking their banker or broker plenty of questions.

COMPOSITE MERCURY IN THE THIRD HOUSE

Composite Mercury is in its own house here, and that makes its influence stronger. Here is a couple who probably won't have any trouble talking, to one another or to anyone else. Their challenges may lie more in learning how to truly converse, not just jabber.

Certainly the potential is there for an unusually high quality (as well as quantity) of communication. It's important to use the promise of this composite Mercury to attain that high quality, rather than fritter its potential away in aimless chatter. How? Each partner should listen at least as much as he or she speaks, and listen attentively, rather than merely silently planning what he or she will say next. If one of them doesn't feel truly heard or understood, he or she should say so.

A powerful Mercury can mean not only a lot of communication, but also a whole lot of impulses of all kinds traveling along the nervous system. These two make each other's synapses work overtime. When they are together, each of them is more alert to his or her surroundings, more observant, perceptive, curious and restless. Also, each of them can be more wired, excitable or distractable as their nervous systems go into hyperdrive. For example, each of them may have a more pronounced startle reflex in the other's presence. Therefore, feeding that stimuli-hungry Mercury is only part of the equation. The other part is learning to relax, which means that sometimes that composite Mercury needs a rest. They might try turning off the computer and the stereo, hanging up the phone, putting down the magazines and taking a long rambling walk without any conversation at all, for a refreshing change.

COMPOSITE MERCURY IN THE FOURTH HOUSE

The natal fourth house of an individual shows her experience of her home, her hearth, her family of origin and her family now. It shows her roots—cultural, ethnic, geographic, socioeconomic, psychological, etc.—and her psychological or psychic inheritance from those roots. It reveals her attitude toward her hearth or family as an adult, and what kind of home environment suits her best. It also says something about the most deeply rooted part of her psyche, her own personal myth.

Much the same logic can be applied to a composite chart's fourth house. It reflects the home and hearth that the couple creates together. It also shows the couple's personal myth of the relationship's beginnings. What does that mean? Imagine that Joan's personal mythology of her relationship with Bob was that it was a fated, once-in-a-lifetime event, love at first sight, with her immediate recognition of her feelings. But imagine that Bob's personal mythology of the relationship was that they were good friends for a long time, and gradually he became attracted to her on a deeper level. Joan may continue to wonder why Bob is so slow to "get" the depth and truth and inevitability of their union, while Bob may wonder why Joan isn't equally grateful that their relationship was built on a good solid foundation of friendship first.

Planets in the composite fourth house suggest an alternate, "third party" view of a couple's early days, one they might be wise to hold in common. With composite Mercury here, they might think of themselves as having had great mental rapport early on, with each partner admiring the other one's intelligence or curiosity. They might tell friends how boring their lives had become before they met one another, and how fascinating they still find each other.

With composite Mercury in the fourth house, this couple needs a hearth that is Mercurial. There's a bookstore in our area of North Carolina called "Books Do Furnish A Room." Shared bookcases can certainly be a feature of this composite Mercury placement, and so can computers, photography equipment, or a collection of antique typewriters or chess sets. What's important here is *shared interests* (Mercury), and this couple's hearth should reflect those shared interests and their ongoing delight in exploring them together. If this couple owned that store we just mentioned, they might well have named it "Conversation Pieces Do Furnish A Room."

COMPOSITE MERCURY IN THE FIFTH HOUSE

In the birthchart, the fifth house is the house of creative self-expression and performance, romance and the beginnings of relationships, children, and pleasures. In a composite chart, it carries the same meanings for the couple, with some nuances. The composite fifth house shows energy that the couple needs to feel in order to experience a renewal of romance and of courtship behavior. It shows what sort of creative or performing outlet they may share. It can reveal their attitude towards children, and it shows what they simply enjoy, how they have fun together. That last part is important! Joy and pleasure are a fundamental part of any bond—we need positive, affirming reasons to stay together, as well as reasons that have more to do with responsibility and integrity. How to put great big smiles back on the faces of a couple who've been together a long time? Look at their composite fifth house.

With Mercury here, this is a couple who finds joy on the Mercury wavelength. Using their brains, feeding their curiosity, debating. Swapping books and stories. Joining the local chapter of Mensa. Taking classes together, or teaching them. Reading poetry together, or writing it. Checking out the local comedy club or lecture series. They might design their own website, start a book group, or try out for a play. A puzzle in progress, a chess set or a telescope might have a permanent place in a corner of their living room. They need a steady diet of interesting things to learn, discuss, experience and wonder about. Nothing will kill romantic feelings between them faster than too much boredom or routine. If they have children, activities like the ones listed above will help them enjoy parenting, too, along with family memberships in the local natural history or science museums.

COMPOSITE MERCURY IN THE SIXTH HOUSE

What does the sixth house signify in the birthchart? Skills. Meaningful work. Job description (as opposed to job title, which is the tenth house). Responsibilities. Apprenticeship. Mentoring and being mentored. In the composite chart, it represents all of the above *for the couple, for the relationship.* Shared responsibilities, shared work, shared mentors, and/or apprentices.

Not all couples work together in the same business, but all couples do have some shared responsibilities: their home, their vehicles, their bills. Children more properly belong to the fifth house, and the fourth house of family has something to do with them, too, but the responsibilities involved in raising them belong to the sixth house. Couples have their own attitude toward sixth house chores, and preferences for how to go about doing them. And while not all couples coach Little League baseball, many of them may unofficially mentor their nieces and nephews, or the teenage babysitter from down the street. Similarly, the partners themselves may have mentors. His great-aunt. Her grandmother. The older couple from church.

Imagine for a moment that these partners live in a large extended community where every couple chips in some time at various tasks for the common good. What would be the skills with which our couple could serve their community? Mercury skills. Perhaps they work on the community website. Perhaps they teach others to do so. Maybe they write the community newsletter or do the books or the mailing list. None of these chores are the couple's profession—the tenth house—but they are all skills with which they can serve, and at which they enjoy being competent.

Now imagine that our large extended community is a medieval village, and that our couple shares a trade or craft there. Their craft would be Mercurial: making paper, being scribes, telling stories, binding books. Young people who wanted to learn such a trade would apprentice themselves to this couple. Crafts for which one becomes an apprentice, in the sense of the word at the time, are few and far between these days. Yet we may still see the phenomenon of these partners helping the neighborhood teenagers with their homework, or loaning them books, or showing them how to express themselves more clearly. This couple has "Mercury chops" that they can share. When it comes to their own mentors, they'd do well to connect to people whose intelligence and curiosity they admire.

As for their own home, they have a responsibility to learn to communicate well. Also, it's not so much that communication itself is a chore, but that communication *about* chores is important. Who gets the car inspected? Who does the laundry; who takes out the trash? Perhaps they could make a list of duties and divide them, or trade them back and forth from week to week. Discussing what will work best is the key here, rather than falling into rigid habits or unquestioned assumptions.

COMPOSITE MERCURY IN THE SEVENTH HOUSE

The seventh house is traditionally the part of the chart that describes intimate relationships. That's still quite valid. But all composite charts, by definition, are about relationships. There is no symbol anywhere in one of them that *isn't* of a "seventh house nature," so to speak. Thus, when we observe a planet in the seventh house of a composite chart, we must overcome the reflex to think of it narrowly as "describing the relationship," even though it does that to some extent. Instead, we must think about the *relationships of the relationship*—the friends, soulmates, rivals, partners, and so forth who help the couple fulfill their evolutionary intentions.

With Mercury in the composite seventh house, these external partners play a crucial role in the primary relationship. Elemental to our understanding of any seventh house planet in any human astrological context is the fact that we cannot do what we came here to do without the help of the people it describes. For the couple with this configuration, there is a need for *information about relating* that comes to them from sources outside themselves. Left to their own devices, they are left clueless—perhaps not completely so, but with some critical piece of the puzzle missing, like a murder mystery with page 178 torn out. Who are these role models and exemplars? Who brings them these clues? The individuals or couples who do so bear the classic Mercury signatures. They are recognizable by their curiosity and probably by their intelligence. They read or are engaged deeply with media. They're quick and verbally fluent. They may be younger than the couple forming the composite chart—or at least have qualities that might be characterized as "youthful." And (somewhat scurrilously from an older person's perspective) that basically means open-mindedness, energy, a willingness to learn.

What is the nature of the gift these soulmates bring to the couple? Many times there are strictly practical dimensions to it. Imagine two people for whom it is essential, for slippery karmic reasons, to visit St. Jean Pied de Port in southwest France together. In this life, they've never even heard of the place. They meet someone who's just been there, hiking the old pilgrim road. Excitement is conveyed; books and photos change hands. The next year, they make the trip.

Other times, what passes from the Mercurial outsider to the couple in question models a *particular style of communication* that, in the end, works miracles for them. A way of saying heavy things humorously, for example. Or a way of listening reflectively. One of the sweet miracles of the seventh house is that this precious Mercury learning often happens quite unconsciously and easily, in the same manner that we often find ourselves picking up the expressions and gestures of friends with whom we spend a lot of time.

It's a gift. It's precious and it's free. With Mercury in the composite seventh house, the trick lies simply in remembering to make time in our lives and space in our hearts for the person making the delivery.

COMPOSITE MERCURY IN THE EIGHTH HOUSE

House of the instincts. House of taboos. Sexuality, death, the deep unconscious, the occult, the afterlife, the Other World and the shaman's journeys there: all are ruled by the Eighth House. Sex is part but not all of an eighth house bond. A sexual relationship with depth and tenderness that lasts more than a few months tends to head into eighth house territory, and each partner's shadow issues are raised. Trust issues? Fear of abandonment? Given enough time in the eighth house, such insecurities come to light; such childhood wounds become painfully evident. This is one reason why some people leave a relationship that has become in any way problematic. How to work through these dynamics? In an eighth house relationship, *healthy catharsis* happens. A difficult but necessary conversation that clears the air, a fight without which closeness wouldn't have been maintained, a gritty year in therapy. Is it pleasant? No. Is it necessary? Yes—if the couple wants to maintain an intense and honest relationship.

In the birthchart, this house shows what energies the person must possess, and seek in others, in order to maintain an eighth house bond. In the composite chart, this house shows what energies must be kept alive and healthy *in the relationship* in order to maintain an eighth house connection.

A couple with composite Mercury in the eighth house must be willing to keep the lines of communication open. The silent treatment should be verboten here. Certainly we communicate in more ways than just verbally, but with the God of Speech in the House of Passion, an ongoing exchange of ideas is essential. Too angry to fight fairly right now? Then write letters, or send email. Neither partner should be a stranger to what the other one is thinking, and neither should consistently dominate the conversations.

What topics should be discussed? Eighth house ones! A steady and unchanging diet of superficial chatter won't work here. That doesn't mean this couple should never tell each other jokes and never take in a mindless brain-candy sort of movie. But they need to be willing to risk addressing deep, gut-wrenchingly honest, and potentially embarrassingly self-revealing subjects when necessary. Their worst fears. The nightmare that woke one of them up screaming last night. The other partner's insecurities about the mate's office friendship that seems to be heating up. Difficult in-laws. What they really need in bed. In short, their shadows need to have a voice in the relationship. If they're wondering what that means, they could try reading Robert Johnson's book *Owning Your Own Shadow*, for starters.

If this couple feels as if they could, judiciously, say *anything* to each other, then they're on the right track.

COMPOSITE MERCURY IN THE NINTH HOUSE

In the birthchart, the ninth house is the house of the Quest. What is the Holy Grail or the North Star for this person? What can make his life the most meaningful? What does she believe in? How can he avoid narrow-mindedness and insularity? How can she broaden her horizons? In the composite chart, this house answers the same questions for the couple.

With composite Mercury here, a shared life of the mind is almost a "religion" for this couple. Not that they should literally worship the God of Speech! But without a shared commitment to an interesting life, they may start to wonder why they're together and what their relationship is all about. Ideally, they should resolve to keep nurturing each other's curiosity. If each of them feels that the relationship challenges them to grow more than they would grow if they weren't together, they're on the right track. Shared interests in travel might come into play here, or in literature. Or in computers, languages, biophysics, medieval cosmologies or paleoanthropology—the sky's the limit. This couple needs to communicate about the various ways they seek to understand the world. Quantum physics explains life differently than sociobiology does, and neither world view is right or wrong; they are merely different.

Our friend Marion Phillips, a blues poet, has a line that we love: "I want to be able to talk to myself without arguing about reality." But these partners need to enjoy debating with each other about reality. If they disagree, that should make such conversations all the more interesting.

COMPOSITE MERCURY IN THE TENTH HOUSE

In the individual birthchart, the tenth house refers to public identity, reputation, and mission in the world—one's "cosmic job description." In a composite chart, the tenth house follows much the same logic. It is the *couple's* public identity, what others have heard about them. It is their public image, their reputation as a team, the niche they fill in their community.

Follow a couple around for a week. Spy on them. Track their comings and goings in the world. Interview their neighbors and colleagues and distant acquaintances about them, never talking directly either to the couple or to their closest friends. At the end of that week, you'll have a pretty good picture of their composite tenth house. You'll see what is "widely known" and assumed about them by others.

With a composite tenth house Mercury, you might have heard:

"They do the children's story hour at the library."

"They run the local Toastmasters."

"A writers' group meets at their house every two weeks."

"Oh, those two? They teach a journal-writing course at the senior center."

You might also have heard, "Don't strike up a conversation with them if there's somewhere you have to be in a hurry! They'll talk your ears off." If they've gone down a darker Mercury road, you might hear them characterized as "the two biggest gossips I've ever met."

This couple *symbolizes Mercury energy* together in the larger community. Maybe they're paid for it; maybe it's volunteer work. Perhaps it's a mutual hobby to which they are devoted. Maybe they're known for throwing parties where people stay up simply talking until dawn. Given Mercury's classic association with youthful energy, maybe the neighborhood teenagers hang out at this couple's house.

Another face of Mercury is that of the messenger. A couple with this planet in their composite tenth house is like a lightning rod for new information, hunches and suppositions. They may be the first ones in their community to get excited about a new idea sweeping through the Zeitgeist, and to share that idea with others. They may be the first household on their block to get broadband Internet access. They may be the ones who help their less computer-literate neighbors sort through the cyber-maze. Or they may be the first to learn about the proposal to install a toxic waste dump entirely too close to their community for comfort, and circulate flyers to the neighbors.

In any case, a couple with composite Mercury in the tenth house has a Mercurial gift to share. Their ability to process ideas and information, to teach and learn, to read and write, to tell stories and listen to them, needs an outlet and an audience in the outside world.

COMPOSITE MERCURY IN THE ELEVENTH HOUSE

In the birthchart, the eleventh house represents plans and dreams for the future, and the people who can be helpful in fulfilling those plans. The composite eleventh house symbolizes the goals and plans of the relationship, and the allies who can help them meet those goals.

What does this couple want to have accomplished by the time they're in their fifties? Their sixties? Their seventies, eighties and nineties? With Mercury in the eleventh house, some of those goals will be mental, some intellectual and some experiential. Ideally, they should strive to have an interesting life, to learn everything they want to learn, and to keep on learning.

Perhaps they want to write a book together, or to learn Swahili before they visit Africa. Maybe they want to start a school, or teach seminars, or buy a recreational vehicle and tour the U.S. when they retire. They would be wise to live near a college or a university, to keep feeding that hunger for intriguing experiences and a colorful life. Long range planning for these dreams will require ongoing attention, logic and an ability to handle details: all Mercury traits.

Their natural allies are fellow Mercurial folk: quick-witted, curious, lively, articulate, and devoted to using whatever intelligence they possess to explore the world and discuss it with their fellow human beings. Such people don't necessarily always make decisions based on the most logical or rational thing to do, although such a mental approach to life may be a feature of their characters. They are rather likely to make decisions based on what would be the most *interesting* thing to do.

A word to the wise here: couples with composite Mercury in the eleventh house will require stimulating experiences for quite a long time. Therefore, since poor health and limited finances can restrict one's options, it's wise for such couples to have a goal of keeping their minds, bodies and finances in reasonably good shape.

COMPOSITE MERCURY IN THE TWELFTH HOUSE

In the birthchart, the twelfth house is the house of mysticism, a house that might also be called The Temple or The Veil. The twelfth house is where we recognize that the totality of our being is something far more vast and mysterious than what CNN or the local Department of Motor Vehicles might consider us. We recognize that we have an inner life, a soul, a spirit. Planets in this house function like our inner gurus, our guides and teachers. Sometimes a guru helps us evolve by providing us with mystical, numinous experiences, and sometimes a guru helps us evolve by rubbing our noses in the facts that we have an ego, and that we can trip over that ego in embarrassing ways.

In the composite chart, the twelfth house represents the visionary, transcendent function *of the relationship.* Couples don't have a shared soul, but couples can and do have opportunities to learn metaphysical lessons and grow spiritually. With composite Mercury in the twelfth house, such opportunities come to the relationship on a Mercurial wavelength.

Imagine that this couple's guru is Mercury. What sort of advice would he or she have? "Use your heads" would probably be high on the list. Blind faith is not a good option here. These partners must apply their intellects to the process of growing in spirit. What does that mean? Discussing that process, both with one another and with others. Studying about it, perhaps on their own, perhaps with a group. Deciding that it is not rational (Mercury) for them to operate in a world where they don't seek to grow in spirit.

If Mercury pulls the rug out from under their egos, what form might that take? Rationalizations. Nervousness. Taking such a stubbornly "logical" approach to everything that they choke the heart out of the relationship. There's a line from a song by Thomas Dolby: "She blinded me with Science." In the case of a couple with a less than optimal response to composite Mercury in the twelfth house, that line might read: "They bludgeoned each other with Reason."

CHAPTER NINE: THE COMPOSITE VENUS

Newly in love, we're quick to forgive. Even the worst faults of our partner glow appealingly in the compassionate light of humor, charity, and good will. Later, of course, we'll probably appoint ourselves that person's judge, jury, critic, personal coach, long-suffering spiritual advisor and criminal psychologist. Going through that stuff is part of love too. But we long for those Edenic days when love was all easy surrender. We long for those days when the elixir of Venus ran through our veins like thin, sweet syrup.

If love were all Venusian magic, if the planetary gods of war and boundaries and fierce truth never made themselves felt, then we'd be living in a fool's paradise. Love would take us nowhere; it would have no evolutionary purpose. There would be no wild ocean crashing and smashing our jagged stones into roundness. Love, after a while, would bore us.

For these reasons, it is imperative in modern evolutionary astrology to see *every* planet as a god or goddess of love, not just Venus. We love with our human wholeness, not just with this single symbol. So what purpose does Venus serve in the composite chart? We go back to that simple, innocent longing inside us—that hunger to be held in someone's heart without any second thoughts, to be understood, forgiven, and viewed always in the light of our inherent goodness, positive intentions and innocence. And our parallel longing to offer those same supportive sentiments to another. That charitable territory—and the healing it can create—are elemental to our understanding of the composite Venus. When it is prominent in the composite chart, that level of kindness and affection is generally prominent in the relationship too.

Unsurprisingly, one of the most reliable patterns in a survey of composite charts is to see the presence of a "big" Venus in long-lasting romances and friendships. Perhaps it rules the Ascendant. Maybe it's in Libra or Taurus, where it's extra-strong through rulership. Very commonly, you'll find Venus conjunct the Sun—that observation, in fact, is one of those potential "statistical proofs" of astrology that's just waiting for someone to come along and run the numbers.

Long-lasting desire and passion are connected to a prominent composite Venus, but softer language conveys the actual feeling more effectively—fondness, tenderness, simply *liking* each other. Courtesy too—both within the relationship and toward other human beings, which creates an aura of magnetism around the couple in whose composite chart the planet is shining brightly.

Wherever the composite Venus lies, it offers insights into *how to keep the magic alive*. It teaches us about the care and feeding of that precious romantic spark, so sweet in and of itself—but so invaluable in terms of helping a couple recover from hurt, failure and mutual disappointment.

To see Venus playing a central role in a composite chart is an encouraging indication, but we must recognize the pivotal role of consciousness and intention here too. A big Venus can sweep too much truth under the carpet, leading to a crushing debt of unresolved issues in a relationship. And even a modest Venus, with proper attention and care in terms of its development, can be made radiant. How? Read on.

COMPOSITE VENUS IN ARIES

The Goddess of Love in the sign of the Warrior! Venus is about reconciliation, compromise and harmony, while Aries is about the development of will, spirit and courage. Think of Aries as the Pioneer, the Daredevil, the Survivor. Venus prefers mellowness, but Aries thrives on challenges and needs an active, dynamic, exciting environment.

Such environments are often stressful. Is stress always a negative thing? Not necessarily. It all depends on *how we subjectively experience that stress*.

Imagine you're swimming. You've been swimming a long time. Reach, pull, breathe to one side. Reach, pull, breathe to the other side. The world has dwindled to the water and your movement through it. You're kicking slowly, to conserve your strength, but you're still swimming as fast as you can. You don't know how much longer you can keep up this speed. Another swimming figure looms behind you. It draws closer. Soon it will be level with you. Determination fills you: you *will* stay ahead, no matter how tired you are. Tapping into some deep and unimagined reserves, you swim faster.

Now think about the paragraph you just read in two different ways.

In the first scenario, you love to swim; you're participating at a swim meet, and the trophy's at stake.

In the second scenario, you've survived a shipwreck only to be chased by a shark.

In both scenes, you are exerting willpower and effort. You are releasing adrenalin. You are facing a challenge, and you feel tremendously alive and fully present in those moments. Which scene would you rather be in? Not a difficult question, right?

Now imagine a third scenario: the approaching swimmer is your partner in a relay race, and you're putting on that extra burst of speed to help your team get ahead.

This composite Venus sign is not for the faint-hearted. There can be a lot of spark and sass and freewheeling verbal by-play, both in and out of bed. A couple with composite Venus in Aries has a deep capacity for shared adventure. More than with any other composite Venus sign, these two can support each other's strength and risk-taking abilities. They can encourage each other to victories and accomplishments that neither of them might have achieved alone. They can "guard each other's backs" with fierce, unquestioned loyalty and devotion.

And, if they don't have challenges to share, if this couple tries to avoid all conflicts and challenges and jousting matches large and small, they can turn into sharks and attack one another from sheer pent-up Arian energy, even if their individual charts are mild as a balmy midsummer's evening. Either that, or they can be unwitting magnets for "shark attacks" from outside the relationship: a never-ending stream of petty annoyances and major hassles alike.

How to fan the Venusian flame within this couple? Recognize that they need to meet their need for brinkmanship in a conscious, intentional way, to choose deliberately just how their adrenalin will be released, rather than letting life choose for them. They should learn to deal with conflicts quickly, constructively and in proportion to the importance of the issue, rather than just blindly nuking one another. On the positive side, if their thirst for adventure is met in a conscious, intentional way, these two can experience a depth of devotion to one another and an ability to rely on each other that, at its best, can assume almost the mythic proportions of the Knights of the Round Table.

COMPOSITE VENUS IN TAURUS

Since Venus rules Taurus, this placement assumes extra prominence in the composite chart. This sign has a great need for simplicity, stability, peace, honesty and naturalness. Taurus is learning to be comfortable in the body and on the planet, to reclaim the physical, instinctual side of life. Like a member of an "uncivilized" indigenous culture, Taurus needs to live as much as possible according to the rhythms of nature. Sensuality is a strong factor here; this sign needs to touch and to be touched with unselfconscious earthiness. If Taurus were a pair of cats, they would be big, fluffy, affectionate, lazy, easy-going and comfort-seeking lap cats, quick to lounge on their owner's knee, clean their plates, sun their bellies on the lawn, wash each other's ears, or curl up together for a nap in the most comfy spot in the house.

A couple with composite Venus in Taurus needs just as cozy, cuddly, instinctual, uncomplicated and unembarrassed an existence together as that pair of lap cats. They can help one another truly relax, remind each other of what's most important in life, and get down to the bare bones essentials of existence in a human body. "Don't sweat the small stuff," is the motto here.

But, unlike the popular saying, it isn't all small stuff. Relationships make our deepest and most shadowy wounds surface. Relationships involve negotiations and compromises, and some conflicts *must* be processed if the relationship is to remain vital and alive. The ability to let little things go is one of the great blessings of a composite Venus in Taurus. But the need for serenity here is so great that this couple runs the risk of avoiding even necessary and constructive conflicts, of trying to ignore the mountains as well as the molehills. If those mountains are left unacknowledged, they can turn into the Continental Divide. The need for security here is so great that this couple may smother themselves with retirement plans, predictability, and perpetual defensiveness about any sort of risk or change.

To keep this composite Venus sign healthy, this couple needs to understand that disagreements are part of the natural order too—even that pair of lap cats has been known to clout each other on the nose from time to time—and that it's realistic and reasonable to learn to process important conflicts. These partners also need a big daily dose of pure Taurus food: affection, comfort, and sensory pleasures. Music nourishes Taurus. So does the outdoors. So do friendly pets, good meals and quiet time together. Psychoanalyzing one another's every facial expression and passing remark will kill this relationship. So will drama-mongering friends or relatives, a lifestyle that's too fast-paced, an overly phony, stilted or artificial environment, and too much time spent overriding or denying the needs of the body.

At its best, a composite Venus in Taurus can make each partner feel as if their relationship is something they can trust the way they trust gravity, something "fixed and constant as the Northern Star," a timeless source of comfort and peace. They can love with the mind, the heart, the body, the limbic system, the reptile brain, the ancient inner Cro Magnon man and woman. There is no endless questioning and chivvying of the relationship, only a deepening appreciation, bordering on reverence, for it.

COMPOSITE VENUS IN GEMINI

Put on your thinking caps and your hiking boots and stay alert, folks. If you feed a composite Venus in Gemini, it will keep you busier and demand faster reflexes than a game of racquetball played with a Superball, while wearing jet-propelled sneakers on your feet. This is the sign of the Observer, the Perceiver, the Journalist, the Communicator. Gemini energy needs a colorful, variegated, fast-paced life, and an attitude of perpetual curiosity and wonder. For Gemini, life is not about finding the Answer; it is about asking ever more intriguing questions. A couple with composite Venus in Gemini needs as fascinating a life as they can possibly lead together. When healthy, this composite Venus sign can help make the partners' lives far more interesting together than they would be apart. All the synapses are firing here. No other composite Venus sign beats Gemini for the capacity for communication and sheer mental stimulation in a relationship. Nor does this occur purely on an intellectual level: Gemini needs fascinating experiences just as much as fascinating thoughts.

What are the risks here? Overextension, so fast a pace that both partners do a 360 degree spin, then crash and burn. Endless chatter. Flightiness. A tendency to rationalize issues or emotions rather than dealing with them.

How to avoid such scenarios? Communication is everything, and communication is a two-way street. This couple's potential for mental rapport and good communication is almost limitless, a great strength that should be promoted. Each partner should listen as well as he or she talks, and talk as well as he or she listens. They should strive to communicate what they're feeling as well as what they're thinking. If it's too hard to conduct a charged conversation without interrupting each other, then they might write each other letters—and write each other letters when they're happy, too. They may find they are more eloquent with one another in mediums other than speech, so they do well to learn to communicate in as many ways as possible.

The encouragement of each other's interests can be another great boon to this relationship, and those interests may evolve into new ones shared as a couple. Lesley is a director with a passion for the history of the theatre. Jack may not be equally drawn to it, but he can ask why Lesley finds it so compelling. If his own interest is in fine woodworking, perhaps Lesley can tell him something about the sixteenth century stage, and ask him how those stages were built differently than they are today. Maybe they'll construct a miniature replica of the Globe Theatre together, or a set of marionettes for puppet shows. Perhaps they'll get so interested in the Commedia del Arte that they vacation in Italy next summer. In Rome they are smitten with love for Italian food, and when they return, they attend gourmet cooking classes. Soon they're designing kitchens together. Next thing their friends know, they've opened a dinner theatre that's a big hit. He does the sets, she directs, and they both supervise the cooking. All because they supported each other's interests!

What would have happened instead, if, when Jack met Lesley, he dismissed her as a pointy-headed intellectual, and if Lesley decided that Jack was as dull as his T square and saw? If neither one of them had talked to each other and drawn each other out, if neither one of them had made an effort to listen? Probably nothing, right? No connection, no spark. In an already established relationship with Venus in Gemini, preconceived opinions of one another and failure to communicate will kill the relationship about as fast as boredom will.

A healthy Venus in Gemini leads to a couple who are never bored, individually or together. There's always something to wonder about, something to explore, something to talk about, something to do. They can—and should—keep surprising one another on into their nineties.

COMPOSITE VENUS IN CANCER

The combination of Venus and Cancer is full of tensions and contradictions. Venus is about connection with others, but Cancer turns inward, toward the interior life. Cancer the Crab, Cancer the Healer, Cancer the Sensitive. It is perhaps the most introspective of the signs. A deep exploration of the inner world of feeling is Cancer's primary goal. Certainly it is the most emotionally and psychologically sensitive of the signs, and accompanying that sensitivity is a profound vulnerability.

Therefore, if they're brave enough to overcome their own self-protective reflexes, a couple with composite Venus in Cancer has a capacity for an infinitely nurturing and supportive tenderness with one another, for carrying balm into the most hidden and wounded places in one another's psyches. Yet if they don't make that journey into one another's inner lives *on tiptoe*, they also have a correspondingly heightened capacity to hurt one another. Even a few emotional body-blows will make this couple so hesitant to risk further injury that they will raise the drawbridge between them just when it most needs to be lowered.

Let's emphasize here that, with composite Venus in Cancer, this heightened need for caution and gentleness may not be apparent in the personalities of the *individuals*. They might both be very robust, lay-it-on-the-line types. That's always the trick with understanding composite charts in general: what's good for the entity formed by the pair often operates quite independently of what might seem best for the two personalities.

How best to protect and encourage that marvelous mutual susceptibility and desire to care for one another? *Both partners must continue to feel safe enough to reveal themselves to one another.* The magic depends on respecting each other's vulnerabilities, and practicing more gentleness than we would use to tend a frightened baby bird.

A big part of feeling safe includes maintaining the Cancerian "shell" of the relationship: the partners don't, for example, indiscriminately discuss each other's darkest secrets with people outside of their bond. It depends upon proceeding slowly, and stopping instantly whenever either mate needs a time out. Reciprocity is vital, so that one partner is not constantly opening his or her heart and getting support, while the other nods wisely, speaks soothingly and receives nothing in return. The compassionate sharing of *all* of one's feelings, sublime and ridiculous, clear and murky, welcome and turbulent, and without fear of hurtful repercussions, is the Holy Grail here.

When this composite Venus sign is being expressed in a healthy way, each partner feels that no one else has ever been so supportive of him or her, so kind, so understanding, forgiving, sympathetic and tender. The relationship feels like a giant safety net, always there, always ready to break the pratfalls and cushion the inevitable bumps and bruises of life together and life in the world.

COMPOSITE VENUS IN LEO

A match made in heaven. The love of my life. Soulmates. To some people, romantic expressions such as those are hype—inflated, sappy goofiness. To others, they are statements of fact, at least of subjective facts. Let's not try to settle such questions, and instead think about the psychological impact upon a relationship of a couple using such language to describe their connection. Raising the relationship to *mythic status* that way sets a high standard, but it also frames the relationship in bigger-than-life terms. The bond is infused with preciousness and specialness. And that is essence of composite Venus in Leo—the couple must believe extravagantly in itself. Leo is the sign of royalty and Venus is the goddess of love. Put the two symbols together, and you are looking at the "Aristocracy of Romance." It represents nothing less than the best there is.

Temper all this with a dose of reality. Even with composite Venus in Leo, these are two flesh and blood human beings. Maybe they have a terrific relationship. Maybe not. But given the realities of life, they of course trouble and vex each other from time to time. They'll surely fall short of that Leo "gold standard" on a regular basis. The key is that if they believe in themselves in a big way, they'll have what it takes to get through those difficult moments. With composite Venus in Leo, faith in their specialness is everything. If they don't believe that it is cosmically right for them to be together, their bond won't last. If it's not the "romance of the century," the spirit goes out of their connection.

How does a couple with composite Venus in Leo maintain that kind of magic, given life's realities? There are several secrets. Near the top of the list is that they need to celebrate their relationship at every opportunity. Most couples have an anniversary of some sort—a wedding date, the day they first met, whatever it might be. These two need at least half a dozen of them! And they need to remember them, and use those dates as an excuse to dress up and go out. They need to act as if they're falling in love, paying each other that deeper kind of attention new lovers naturally offer. Even when they are alone together, it's beneficial for them to pay attention to presenting themselves attractively to each other—and complimenting each other on appearance, style, sexual glories, and other gifts. Poetry and flowers help, as do respectful language and attention. Everything that supports the idea that *this relationship is precious* plays a pivotal role in the formula.

Being seen publicly as an attractive couple is useful for composite Venus in Leo too. Obviously, the core of love between them in their own secret world is the key. But an enviable public image is helpful. Leo is a performer, and performers need applause. We can imagine this couple dancing at a party. They're looking good and moving well together, as if their bodies have a God-given harmony. People look at them a bit wistfully, like orphans gazing at the mansion on the hill—and our heroes know it! The aim isn't to make others feel badly about themselves or their relationships. It is simply the natural function of the Leo-as-Royalty dimension of the archetype: to be seen, to be held as an ideal or a standard against which others measure themselves. They've got to believe that themselves, and if they can get a few others to believe it too, that's a huge support.

COMPOSITE VENUS IN VIRGO

Perfection is an impossible standard in love or elsewhere. Still, with their composite Venus in Virgo, this couple needs to make constant progress in that direction. They'll never arrive at that particular North Star, but like a sailor at sea, they'll benefit a lot from knowing where it lies. The vitality of this configuration depends on constant evolution, constant growth, constant improvement. No matter how wonderful—or how dreadful—the relationship feels at any given moment, the key to maintaining the romantic bond between these two people lies in pressing endlessly toward perfection. Facing seemingly insurmountable issues, they'll be fine—so long as they are both slogging away at them. And doing very well together, apart from a few niggling, minor grievances, they'll quickly be in trouble if they let those grievances slide. Some people say, "If it ain't broken, don't fix it." But with composite Venus in Virgo, it's more like, "If it ain't growing, it's broken."

A high maintenance relationship? Yes indeed. Does that make it a bad one? That really depends on the values of the two people involved. Individuals with a lot of evolutionary momentum will find this kind of relationship stimulating. Lazier ones will find it exhausting and crazy-making. And in either case, worrying the relationship to death is a threat. Fear of trusting and surrendering can masquerade as yet another "serious talk" about the impact upon the relationship of one person's tendency to overcook the vegetables.

Life's details are Virgo's domain. With composite Venus there, this couple needs to handle them efficaciously. Much of that comes down taking their clearly-defined responsibilities to the relationship seriously. In other words, if it has been agreed that one of them does the dishes while the other one does the grocery shopping, then there had better be food in the refrigerator and no "science projects" growing in the sink! With Venus in Virgo, love is expressed partly through responsibility. All the tenderness in the world evaporates when love can't "walk its talk."

Clear agreements about the nature of each person's responsibilities toward the other are pivotal. Always, the dark side of Virgo lies in evolutionary intensity mutating into discontent and criticism. Anyone can commit to making sure the refrigerator is full—but no one can commit to making sure that anyone else's *soul* is full. A feeling of emptiness in either person, *if misinterpreted as the other one's "fault,"* can translate into argument, slights and pickiness. Making sure that *reasonable* expectations are defined—and discussed—is effective medicine here.

COMPOSITE VENUS IN LIBRA

Venus is the planet of love and is said to rule Libra, so on the face of it the omens are auspicious for a couple with their composite Venus in this sign. Certainly, having a strong Venus in a composite chart is a helpful indicator. It correlates with feelings of warmth, affection, and tenderness between two people, with an outward aura of being a "plausible" couple—others will believe in their relationship and take it seriously, and that's a useful support for anyone. To go deeper in our understanding, we need to get past the simpleminded astrological ideas of "good" and "bad," and instead understand the actual nature of the Venusian energy that binds these two together.

Libra is all about *harmony*, and a meditation upon the joys and challenges of that word is our key here. Everyone loves the notion of harmony in a relationship, but it's an elusive condition, especially as people individuate. The more we know ourselves, the more unique we become—and the longer the odds grow against our ever finding anyone exactly like ourselves. That's basically a good thing, but it does make harmony a lot more slippery. Positively, there are two pieces of the puzzle here. First, these two need to make a concerted effort to see to it that their differences are negotiated in a fair way. The slightest feeling of inequity in either of them can undercut their Venusian feelings toward each other, which means an erosion of their sexual and romantic responses to each other. Second, where there are "irreconcilable differences" between them, they need to do a kind of alchemical transformation of their attitude. They need to *turn the potential of polarization into a sense of complementarity.* What that means is that they must find a way to appreciate that differences can make them stronger, not weaker, as couple. Maybe one of them is extraverted while the other is introverted. Obviously, that could trigger a lot of mutual vexation. But it can also be framed as something helpful. Life requires both introverted and extraverted skills. As they learn to appreciate each other's differences and depend on them, they've graduated to the Libran Ph.D. program!

Given that people are different and ultimate harmony is an impossibility, this alchemical transformation of attitude is critical to the couple with composite Venus in Libra. Otherwise, they'll "make nice" until their differences fester into an underlying loss of faith in their romance.

Let's add that composite Venus in Libra suggests a refined, aesthetic energy radiating from this couple. Together, they'll likely be drawn to artistic pleasures—performances, galleries, perhaps shared creativity. Given time, paintings will hang in their home. Fresh flowers will catch the sun on their kitchen table. And the accord they create between themselves will shine out from them into the social world in the form of grace, mutual respect, and palpable affection.

COMPOSITE VENUS IN SCORPIO

The sign of the scorpion—even without interpretation, the words invoke a mood of mystery and danger, of taboo and occult peril. What is sweet Venus doing in a place like that? The old astrologers asked that same question and came up with the notion that there was something wrong with having Venus in Scorpio. They said Venus was "in detriment" there—and tended to correlate the configuration with trouble in love: storminess, conflict, and secret affairs. That indeed accurately portrays the darker potentials of this composite placement. But, as usual, it leaves out the higher ground.

Scorpio is fundamentally an astrological reference to *honesty*. And in intimacy, where our hearts are so terribly vulnerable, honesty is a very dangerous transaction. To understand composite Venus in Scorpio, it is imperative that we not veer off into glib clichés and truisms about the virtues of always "telling the truth." We must recognize that honesty can trigger truly primitive reactions in both lovers—just think for five seconds about the kinds of explosive sexual jealousy, possessiveness and fear that attractions outside a primary relationship can create.

The key here is that, for two people with their composite Venus in Scorpio, the magic depends on that kind of searing, naked psychological contact. The process is painful, volcanic, and exhausting, yet essential for them. When healthy and functional, given a little time, these two human beings will know in their hearts that they've never been known so well or seen so clearly, warts and all, by anyone else on the planet. They will be able to say to each other, in a spirit of gratitude, humility, and wonder, "No one else could have hung in there with me the way you did. No one else could have gone the distance."

To support this kind of love, people with composite Venus in Scorpio always need a lot of time alone together. They must have clear agreements about the boundaries between their relationship and the rest of the world—truths said in the bedroom go no further, under pain of death . . . or at least of a scorpion's sting. Sex is of course important for any couple, but it takes on truly alchemical proportions with composite Venus in this sign. It's the core ritual; it's the glue that binds them together, and which defines their separation from the world. For this reason, sexual fidelity is particularly pivotal with these two—as is, paradoxically, a willingness to be honest, open and accepting regarding each other's feelings of attraction outside the relationship.

COMPOSITE VENUS IN SAGITTARIUS

Freedom—that's the essence of Sagittarius. And love is hard on freedom. Thus, the combination of Venus and Sagittarius has often been correlated with instability in intimate relationships. The traditional idea is that they begin with a bang and peter out, leaving a lot of idealistic, great-sounding talk in their wake. That's a decent description of the Sagittarian garbage can, but how about the higher ground?

Sagittarius is, above all, about principles and ideals. With their composite Venus in that sign, these two people need to make sure right from the beginning that they are in philosophical accord about the "rules" of human bonding. For one thing, the romantic, erotic dimensions of their relationship simply thrive on such talk. A sure sign that their bond is healthy is that they stay up too late on a work night talking enthusiastically about life's big themes. Little will destroy their connection more effectively than serious differences, at the level of principle, over the ground rules of intimacy. And many of the most pivotal discussions they'll hold will revolve around finding their own unique way of resolving the tension between love and freedom.

If one of them tends to work long hours, that takes away something from the relationship. Does he or she have a right to make that choice? Maybe one of them enjoys loud music. Who is to say that he or she has no right to enjoy that release? At 8:00 PM? What about at 1:00 AM? Maybe one loudly espouses Buddhist philosophy in front of the other one's conservative Presbyterian parents—inappropriate behavior, or an expression of one's natural right to freedom of thought? None of these questions have obvious, clear answers, but all of them represent the sorts of issues that need to be unraveled *at the level of principle* for this relationship to prosper.

Sexuality is often the single most pressing area of debate for couples with their composite Venus in Sagittarius. In addition to one's partner, there are usually lots of thoroughly beguiling people with whom intimacy could be rewarding. Nonetheless, humans have generally found that commitment is a very helpful support to lasting intimacy, so let's assume that our couple has agreed upon the principle of an exclusive sexual bond with each other. Beyond that, there's a lot of territory that needs to be explored *at the level of their shared beliefs and principles.* How acceptable is flirtation to both partners? What about non-sexual intimacy with other people, especially ones who are attractive? Again, these are not questions with single answers. The point is only that, with composite Venus in Sagittarius, these questions need to be discussed. Ideally, they are considered early in the relationship before commitments are even made.

Let's add that some of the pressure for Sagittarian freedom in this couple needs to be met through shared adventures. They benefit enormously from traveling together. Ditto for taking classes together, meeting other couples, especially exotic ones, and generally avoiding the stultifying "normalcy" that so often arises once a couple settles down together.

COMPOSITE VENUS IN CAPRICORN

A nineteenth century woman is asked why she has chosen to become engaged to a certain gentleman. She responds, "I have come to admire his sterling moral character."

Hearing a line like that today is like looking at the skeleton of a prehistoric creature. The words sound quaint and antiquated. People don't speak or think that way any longer. "Psychology" has replaced "character," and sometimes it seems as if money, physical appearance, and social status are about to replace psychology! But Capricorn represents the *idea of character*. It is about integrity, virtue, and the ability to resist temptation. Add one eternal truth, and we are on the road to grasping the meaning of composite Venus in Capricorn: whether morality is in style or out of style, *relationships test our characters*. And if we flunk the test, the relationship either dies or becomes diseased.

With their composite Venus in Capricorn, the well-being of this couple depends upon their not failing each other. They need to "walk their talk" together, trying to behave like two honorable adults. When they hurt each other, as they of course will, they need to accept that reality humbly and apologize for it. Perfect, flawless behavior is an unreachable goal, but honesty and endless *striving* toward integrity are not. For these two, their erotic and romantic vitality depend on that effort.

Wait a minute! Honesty and integrity are great, but are they really *sexy*? At first, this Capricornish principle might seem unrealistic. Probably, that perspective is accurate in the early stages of relationship. Then, what turns us on is generally a more primordial kind of stimuli. But Capricorn is always about commitments over time. It's about the long haul. And nothing kills sex faster over the time frame of months and years than *a loss of respect* for each other. And what do we respect in another person? Beauty? Money? Not really. We respect character.

With composite Venus in Capricorn, issues about *vows* come up compellingly and dramatically. Ultimately, these are vows of commitment to the relationship itself. While no one should rush into such promises, without them romance withers. Capricorn is never about "one day at a time." It's about forever and always. And there are little vows too—like promising to meet your partner on a certain street corner at 7:00 o'clock. If you show up at 7:15, apologize! Why? Not because fifteen minutes matters, but because your word matters.

All of this focus on virtue can cast a dark shadow. With composite Venus in Capricorn, while we'll stand by all we've written, these two also need to remember to loosen up and cut each other some slack. It's important that they make time for play. After working so hard to ground their relationship on lasting psychological bedrock, it would be sad if they forgot to enjoy it.

COMPOSITE VENUS IN AQUARIUS

Who makes the rules of love? Probably a few come straight from God, such as the principle that cruelty and insensitivity aren't ultimately very good aphrodisiacs. But most of love's "rules" are human fabrications. For centuries, people assumed that women should obey their husbands, for example. Not too many people in the western world view that as a relevant notion nowadays.

What about the idea that making a home together is the ultimate and highest expression of a sexual partnership? That's still a widely-held perspective—but is it true? Can't we make a case that people are more authentically open to each other at the emotional level if they don't have to see each other's faces day in and day out? What about the idea that two people need to be within a decade or so of being the same age? Who says that? God? Or the idea that children are the natural desire and expression of any heterosexual union? Or that couples are "naturally" formed of just two people? Or that long-distance relationships don't work? Or that sex is essential to a marriage? Or that sex naturally becomes less exciting with the passage of time?

With composite Venus in Aquarius, it's not that this couple needs to throw all those cultural assumptions out the window. Many of them will very probably in fact have deep relevance to them. The point is only that they need to question cultural assumptions and make sure that the answers they accept are actually the result of their own independent processes of thought and dialog. Why? Because at least a few of those social assumptions about relationships just won't work for these two people. If they accept that indoctrination without question, their bond will be forced in unnatural directions. Erotic joy will leach out of their time together, and *for no reason except an unconscious desire to play by the life-eating rules they learned from their parents and peers!* In a nutshell, these two people have to re-invent the rules of intimacy. Their relationship needs to be their own creation. The more they succeed in that intimate individuation process, the happier they will be—and the stranger they will look to the neighbors!

COMPOSITE VENUS IN PISCES

Pisces is the mystical sign, and with composite Venus there, this relationship must contain a *consciously spiritual* dimension. However hot the connection feels at first, in the long run if their souls aren't touching, soon enough their hearts and their physical bodies follow suit.

So what do we mean by a consciously spiritual dimension? It's potentially a slippery concept, so let's start out by saying what we *don't* mean by the term. It has nothing to do with sharing a religious affiliation—the world is full of sincere Buddhist couples, or Jewish or Christian ones who never experience each other spiritually, in spite of their theological agreements. Similarly, it's not about holding a common philosophy. Ultimately, it's not even about both people believing in God. What it comes down to is that they take the time to see each other's souls. They may not even use the word "soul." That's all right. The words don't matter. But there is an eternal place that lovers can go. When they are there, they have the feeling of looking *into* each other rather than *at* each other. They are no longer objects. They are no longer even personalities. There is a feeling of melting and surrendering, and a feeling of the grip this three-dimensional world has on them becoming a little looser. For some reason, it's easier to get there in dim light—candles, moonlight, firelight. For some reason, eye contact provides an easy doorway into that spiritual space. No one can force it or do it on schedule. It cannot be rushed. It's not an idea or something to understand—it is an experience or a perception. And if it is shared consciously, for a couple with their composite Venus in Pisces, it is like life-giving magic. Their faith in their bond is fed by it. Their sexual life roars. Their troubles and vexations with each other slip into the background scenery—and in the foreground there is a sex-sustaining, love-feeding feeling of extraordinary, undeniable *specialness* to their connection.

Meditation classes may help them. So will sitting quietly on a deck in the falling light of evening. Even though Pisces isn't ultimately about religion, shared religious practice may help them too—provided it's more than ritual. Mostly, what this couple needs is unstructured, unthreatened private time. With that and a little attention to each other, these processes launch themselves rather automatically. That makes it sound easy. But the key here is realizing that Pisces, in common with the rest of the signs, has a potential dark side. Mystics tend to give things up—even things they need. A composite Venus in Pisces may go hang itself on a cross, pointlessly. That life-giving quiet time together may be sacrificed—because the acquaintances of some acquaintances are in town and need a free bed tonight. Mom might call two minutes after the candles are lit. With composite Venus in Pisces, these two need to learn to surrender *to each other*—not to surrender their relationship to the demands of the outer world.

COMPOSITE VENUS IN THE FIRST HOUSE

Any planet in the composite first house is in the spotlight. It shines forth into the world vividly in their social behavior, and it plays a big role in the inner life of the couple too. Having Venus strongly placed in a composite chart is always an encouraging sign for a relationship. This is the goddess of love, after all—and if loving each other is the point, then it's good to see this planet making a bold statement in the chart. Still, as in all things astrological, there are evolutionary challenges here as well.

Above all, the first house is about *choices.* We have freedom to respond creatively to any placement of the composite Venus, but nowhere is taking personal responsibility so critical as in the first house. These two must *choose to love*—and to follow the spiritual path of lovers. When we first meet someone to whom we are attracted, that's hardly a challenge! But as time passes and familiarity breeds numbness, staying on that road becomes an act of will. What comes naturally at first must be locked in intentionally, and maintained with the same vigilance that a parachutist might bring to maintaining his parachute. Falling out of love might not be quite as bad as falling out of the sky, but it's best to avoid both experiences—especially for these two, with the stakes so high and something so precious held between them.

New lovers bring a quality of deep attention to each other. They are interested in each other. They don't interrupt each other or assume that they already know what the other one will say. In every move they make, they convey mutual respect, along with fascination, tenderness, and support. When they know they are going to see each other, they prepare—they make themselves attractive, taking care with their clothing and with the state of their physical bodies. For the couple with composite Venus in the first house, the aim lies in willfully, consciously continuing those behaviors—*choosing* to remain in love, instead of imagining that lasting love is a bit of random luck the gods give some people and withhold from others. To *behave* like lovers is the key, even when anger, disappointment, and frustration are in the air.

Outwardly, these two have a Venusian air about them. They look good together, regardless of how attractive they are as separate individuals. Probably, they are attractive socially too—people want to invite them to parties. They just seem well-suited to each other, and a kind of warm magnetic field surrounds them. If they were to break up, their friends would be surprised. Mostly, this appeal is a good thing—those social expectations actually support their deeper evolutionary work: having others believe in them helps them believe in themselves. But carrying the flag as the wonder-couple has its debits too: these two need to be careful of social over-extension, and even more careful of becoming so emotionally identified with the role of the happy couple that their muckier psychological selves creep up on them unawares.

COMPOSITE VENUS IN THE SECOND HOUSE

With the possible exceptions of bed and dinner, are we ever truly ready for anything? Who in the history of the world has ever been "ready" for marriage, or for the birth of their first child, or for their big professional promotion? It's an inescapable fact that when we start something new, we are significantly ignorant of it. That's just the nature of beginnings. Inevitably, we make mistakes—and hopefully we learn from them. Part of us understands this principle, and feels a well-founded, characteristic *insecurity* when we start something new or escalate a responsibility or a commitment. That self-questioning part of us, astrologically, is called the second house. With composite Venus there, these natural doubts and trepidations are exaggerated in this couple. The danger for them is that they may simply not *believe in* their own relationship sufficiently to invest in it, trust it and grow it. One classic illustration of the down side of this configuration would be the couple who date for ten years, but never quite get up the nerve to take the next step.

Traditionally, the second house is correlated with money and movable possessions. A better word might be "resources." If we have enough resources of the appropriate sort, our insecurities in life are lessened—just think, for example, of how you react to your car making disconcerting noises when you have plenty of money in the bank, versus when you are feeling poor. The key, with composite Venus in the second house, is for this couple *to acquire the resources that allow them to believe in their love.* What might those resources be? Sometimes they are *relationship skills* which can be acquired through seeking counsel: a good psychotherapist who models communication skills, or dear friends who've been together in intimacy for ten years and are willing to offer insight and support. Many times a *public ritual of commitment* makes a real difference—there can be a kind of pride and dignity connected with being married, which might be the needed confidence-booster.

While it is a misleading to think of the second house in narrowly materialistic terms, it does have a natural linkage to physical objects and our psychological relationship with them. Thus, the exchange of rings can be profoundly important for a couple with a second house composite Venus. Or an exchange of flowers! Knowing that each partner is carrying a photograph of the other one can make a difference. As a relationship escalates into the "living under one roof" stage, issues around financial trust and interdependency become pressingly central—potentially problematic, but also potentially healing. What might appear overtly to be a disagreement over money is typically an issue around trust. Going deeper, that issue of trust often is not actually a question of whether each partner trusts the other; instead it is about whether, together, they trust their relationship.

In the end, with composite Venus in the second house, a couple can *prove themselves to themselves.* As they gain faith in their love through the ancient device of betting on themselves and burning bridges behind them, they build trust, adult interdependency, and faith from the ground up—and may, in the end, prove far more resilient than their love-at-first-sight cousins.

COMPOSITE VENUS IN THE THIRD HOUSE

Knowing the right words to say is one of life's sweeter skills. Rabbits and foxes don't worry much about it, but for we humans, *how* we say something is often even more important than what we say. Language is the glue that holds social reality together. With their composite Venus in the third house, this couple is probably well-spoken together. Their metaphors are complementary. Their rhythms of speech, their senses of humor, their vocabularies flow together in an appealing and harmonious way. Together, they're a great team when it comes to composing letters in emotionally-trying circumstances—letters of sympathy and condolence to grieving people, for example. They can function effectively as *mediators*, should they find themselves in situations of conflict involving families or organizations in which they are members. Given half a chance, they could probably write poetry together.

Within the deeper evolutionary logic of the relationship, composite Venus in the third house emphasizes the pressing need to *communicate gracefully* with each other. At a simple level, there is a certain ambience of dignity that arises when two people living in intimacy strive to practice some degree of courtesy and politeness with each other. "Please" and "thank you" are part of it. Saying "excuse me" instead of nudging each other out of the way. Knocking on the door if a partner has closed himself or herself in a room. Stiffness and formality are far from the point—180 degrees opposite the point, actually. The aim is to be *comfortable* together in that most fractious of circumstances: deep and unrelenting intimacy. Anyone who has shared life with another person for more than a few months understands how near the surface the Shadow comes after a while. The slightest flaws in another's character are magnified out of all proportion. Lapses that wouldn't call for a second thought were a friend to be guilty of them become grounds for assassination. The sheer mutual *abrasiveness* of two humans in close proximity is the great enemy of sympathy, sweetness, and romance. Courtesy—and its crown jewel, the careful use of language—are the best hedges against that kind of erosion. With their composite Venus in the third house, these two need to practice those skills.

Sooner or later, every couple must bash their way through frank negotiations regarding some dimension of their relationship. Even in purely practical matters—financial decisions, for example—differences between people can fuel strong emotions, especially if one of them feels insecure in his or her knowledge. And of course every human pairing will quickly encounter the eternal dilemmas: each other's families, attractions to other people, and so on. Inevitably, such imbroglios are hooked into their unresolved psychological issues, defense mechanisms and blind spots. A history of courtesy, gentleness, and respectful listening go a long way toward getting such talks off on a good foot, and those tactful, diplomatic qualities are pivotal when it comes to keeping them on track. As the saying goes, "war is the failure of diplomacy." That's true in intimacy as much as it's true on a geopolitical scale. With their composite Venus in the third house, this couple has what it takes to avoid those painful private wars that can kill even a deep love. To fulfill their evolutionary intentions together, they also need to practice those skills actively.

COMPOSITE VENUS IN THE FOURTH HOUSE

Peel away the layers of the onion, and right in the center you find the fourth house. Physically, it's beneath our feet—where the Sun is around midnight. Similarly, it refers to energies that lie deep down in the core of what we are. With their composite Venus in the fourth house, peel away the surface, and the underlying feeling with these two people is *love*. Of course, like anyone else, they'll get angry with each other, question the relationship, maybe even part ways—but their love won't go away. It's too fundamental for that to happen, whatever other emotions get into the stew. Love is in their bones. Composite Venus in this house is one of the most basic foundation stones of lasting warmth, intimacy, and commitment.

Traditionally, the fourth house correlates with home. With their composite Venus there, these two are very drawn to the domestic environment. Even early in their relationship, we'll see each of them expressing interest in where—and how—the other one lives. It's common to see such a couple, two weeks after they've met, deciding to skip the restaurant and spend the evening at one of their homes eating pizza and watching a movie, cuddled on the sofa as if they've known each other a long time. This pleasant feeling of *domestic naturalness* is one of the cornerstones of their bond.

As their relationship develops, these two quickly feel a pull toward creating a home. Venus is seductive, and so some hesitation about moving too rapidly into that kind of entanglement is appropriate. Still, if the rest of the relationship is reasonably harmonious, the gravitational pull toward sharing a domestic environment is strong, and well-supported astrologically. Once they've decided to take that step, some critical choices loom. With their composite Venus in the fourth house, these people need a beautiful place to live. For what it's worth, they'll probably be lucky in terms of finding such a place, but most of what we're considering here lies in the realm of choices they can control themselves. Large piles of money are of course a great advantage here, as elsewhere in life. But there are many expensive living spaces that have little beauty in any sense—and many inexpensive ones that do. Sunlight streaming through a *clean* kitchen window, glistening on the funky wine-bottle vase and catching the red veins in a rose's petals: that kind of loveliness feeds a fourth house Venus, even in a ghetto. Whatever their finances, having art on the walls, a place sufficiently orderly to convey a feeling of peace and ease, a music collection that actually gets played—all these are pieces of the Venus puzzle. All of them support this couple's evolutionary aims. The intent is to create a gracious, serene incubator in which their love can grow in dignity, humor and mutual appreciation. For these two, the aesthetics of their physical domestic environment, for better or worse, set the tone of their romance. A quiet place to live breeds quiet in their hearts. Lovely paintings on the wall support erotic appreciation of each other's charms. Music on the stereo encourages harmonious conversations and negotiations. The home is a metaphor for the heart.

COMPOSITE VENUS IN THE FIFTH HOUSE

These two people shine when they're together. They seem bigger than life. They may not be flamboyant or even extroverted, but there is a certain subtle magnetism that radiates from them. And it is infectious. They walk into the room, and everyone feels a little more elegant, a bit more witty, and a lot better-looking. The fifth house relates strongly to the notion that all the world's a stage. It is the most theatrical part of the chart. With their composite Venus there, these two naturally *express* their Venusian energy—their attractiveness and grace. They put it forward. That's just part of the chemistry they trigger in each other.

Traditionally, one of the meanings of the fifth house is "love affairs." Part of the evolutionary intention of this couple is to keep their relationship feeling as much like a love affair as they can, given the realities of ongoing intimacy. Obviously, the sweet bubble of romantic illusion bursts sooner or later—but that doesn't have to put an end to reading poetry to each other, surprising each other with flowers, or enjoying oysters and champagne in candlelight!

"Love affairs," astrologically, are not always sexual relationships—in the fifth house sense, they actually refer to any kind of emotionally close human connection, so long as it doesn't last very long. With their composite Venus in this house, this couple's destiny includes a bit of a revolving door in terms of the people and couples they befriend. There's no reason they can't have lasting relationships with friends—that's another issue entirely. Metaphysically, this configuration tells us that, together, they're finishing up a lot of "business" with other souls—and when the business is finished, those people tend to move on, making way for others.

Creativity is central to the logic of the fifth house. Together, these two have a tremendous potential for expressing themselves artistically. If they were to play music together or perform theatrically together on stage, they'd cast a spell over the audience. Depending on the rest of the composite chart, maybe their creativity is drawn in other, less "arty" directions. Maybe they take up landscaping or gardening. Perhaps they decorate their home in a uniquely self-expressive way. And the fifth house is also simply about the human need for pleasure: creating a beautiful, tasty dinner for a few friends and laughing together until the wee hours is an art, too!

Children are joint creative products as well—and classically the fifth house is the house of children. Not all couples are in a position to have kids even if they want them, and certainly it would be narrow to read the house strictly in parental terms. Still, if there is a desire to have children on the part of these two people, likely they will get their wish—and probably their offspring will grow up to become their good friends.

COMPOSITE VENUS IN THE SIXTH HOUSE

Put two naïve children, male and female, alone on a desert island. Come back in a century or two, and you'll probably be greeted by a crowd. Sex is basically instinctual. Even given no "advanced training," people tend to figure out the elements of the operation. But for how long will that sex be *good?* And what about the relationship? For how long will those two people *care* for each other? How long will they *want* each other? Those are harder questions. Sexual instincts and reflexes may be part of our hard-wiring as members of *homo sapiens,* but making love last is an art. And like most arts, its skills can be learned, remembered, and passed down to the next generation. With their composite Venus in the sixth house, this couple is part of such a *lineage of lovers.* To fulfill what they've come together to accomplish, they must seek instruction and guidance from people more advanced on love's path than themselves. If they succeed in that and their own love lasts, they will feel the call to return the favor to others.

Early in this relationship, these two people benefit from putting their "radar" out there. What they are seeking are happy, stable couples. And such couples will be there, waiting—that's the law of synchronicity in action. We can go further: let's say our couple with composite Venus in the sixth house are passionate, independent types, doubtful about whether they're cut out for a committed relationship. *Then the mentors they should seek are similarly passionate and independent.* What our couple faces, these mentors have already faced. That is the whole point. They've been down that road, made mistakes and learned from them. Both our sixth house Venus couple and these mentors will feel drawn toward each other. They'll enjoy each other's company. Nobody really even needs to understand that anything important is passing between them.

For the couple with their composite Venus in the sixth house, humility enters the equations at this point. They need to accept a simple fact, one that should entail no humiliation at all: love is difficult! No one would try to perform brain surgery without some training, and making love last is probably even harder—if you doubt that, just ask your friendly local brain surgeon. They need healthy relationship behaviors *modeled* for them by lovers who've gone down that road before them. They also need to ask direct questions whenever mere watching isn't enough. Probably the relationship these mentors have with each other will be Venusian in tone. That means they'll be romantic types, attentive and probably sexy with each other. They'll flirt with each other even if they are ninety years old. And there's a good chance they'll be artistic in disposition, if not literally artists of some sort.

Once our couple with composite Venus in the sixth house has found these teachers, and hung out with them for a while, something deep, precious, and ancient is transferred directly from the teachers into our couple's cells—and as our lovers mature, one of their own profoundest joys will lie in passing on that cherished flame.

COMPOSITE VENUS IN THE SEVENTH HOUSE

The Goddess of Love in the House of Marriage—with their composite Venus in the seventh house, these two people are off to a good start! There's really no simpler way to spell L-O-V-E astrologically. At least initially, the building blocks of a lasting connection abound for them. They simply *like* each other a lot.

To appreciate their natural affection most clearly, view it against this backdrop: when two human beings come together, they almost always have to take a while getting comfortable with each other. Even if the attraction between them is compelling, they simply still don't know each other very well. There's a little bit of awkwardness and politeness at first—and, more often than not, various tensions, frictions and misunderstandings quickly arise, especially if the strangers have moved precipitously into the emotional cauldron of love and sexuality. With these two, those pitfalls are not so deep: the "fairy dust" is strong enough to bridge that gap between just having met and actually becoming intimately familiar with each other.

The easy linking of the two personalities is fundamentally a precious thing, and lots of people who stay together happily for decades have composite Venus in the seventh house. With that positive thought in mind, let's keep perspective: nothing astrological can guarantee a relationship working. There's nothing that lacks a potential dark side—and nothing so sour it can't be made to work! The risk with composite Venus in the seventh house lies in disillusionment. The level of trust, commitment and vulnerability can escalate very rapidly here. That's fine, but when the Shadow makes itself felt, it can feel like a shocking betrayal. The rose-colored glasses can shatter, leaving pain and anger. For these two people, there needs to be a lot of emphasis, especially early in their romance, on keeping their dialogue honest. That honesty is not simply about refraining from lies—it's about actively searching for truth. It's about warning each other, in advance, about the minefields that lie ahead.

As the traditional "House of Marriage," the seventh house is always about relationships. With a composite chart, we need to be careful in our thinking, and make sure we include a piece of the puzzle that even astrologers often miss. *This relationship has relationships!* These two people—together—have soul-mates. These soul-mates may be other individuals or other couples. They're not teachers. They're more like friends or co-counselors. The critical point is that our couple cannot succeed without the perspective, support, and help they get from these other people. Most of the time, it boils down to that ancient reality: couples benefit from the support of other couples. Just like artists, athletes, and stamp-collectors are helped by their peers, so are lovers. With composite Venus in the seventh house, this couple is supported in maintaining faith in their path together by their friends—and the universe will be generous with them in that department!

COMPOSITE VENUS IN THE EIGHTH HOUSE

People sometimes try to think of sex as a biological need, like our need for food. But nobody has yet died from a lack of sex! Others try to spiritualize it and make it something almost otherworldly. That's closer to the spirit of *Skymates*, but let's stay grounded: sex is very down-to-earth and physical too. Like eating, it links us very directly and undeniably with our heritage as *creatures* on this planet. Birds do it and bees do it . . . et cetera. The point is that sexuality is probably the single most complex dimension of human experience in that it requires the integration of almost every aspect of our humanity: body, mind, emotions, language, soul, rhythm, surrender, force. If any piece is chronically left out, we feel that something is missing. We come away from sex feeling hungry, and probably sad or angry.

Astrologically, the eighth house describes the deepest elements of our sexuality. Any planet there gives us a lot of insight into what part of the psyche absolutely must be engaged if we are going to be able to sustain any kind of sexual response in a relationship. With their composite Venus in the eighth house, maintaining a romantic feeling is central for this couple. Without it, sex, however orgasmic or gymnastic, would collapse. Sex can exist without love. That's not always a pretty sight, but it's a common enough situation in the adult world. Not for these two, though.

These romantic, sexual feelings abound automatically at the beginning of a partnership with this composite Venus. From the beginning, these two make love, rather than other activities that might superficially resemble it. Tenderness and sweetness and care flow like a tide between them, washing the shores of the two alien continents, bringing them closer together. Once sexuality is expressed, the bonding process is kick-started. Caution and mistrust are bypassed. The mating bond, with all its instinctual needs and fears, gets established quickly. This is a beautiful thing—but it requires a lot of care and feeding. Always, the stability of this connection depends on satisfying the Goddess of Love, and not unduly offending her. She likes to see people treat each other as lovers, which means never taking each other for granted or behaving dismissively or crassly. Venus wants people to seduce each other from time to time—even if they've shared a bed for thirty years. She wants music playing and candles burning. She's fine about earthy language—Aphrodite isn't prim!—but she never tolerates anyone being objectified. She knows that the most erogenous zone of our multidimensional "bodies" is the soul.

In a nutshell, with composite Venus in the eighth house, these two have been given a priceless gift from the gods and goddesses. Their task is to take care of it!

COMPOSITE VENUS IN THE NINTH HOUSE

One traditional association for this house is "long journeys over water." In times gone by, a long journey over water was an adventuresome undertaking. It would carry you into a new culture, with a different language, customs and expectations. Such journeys were not taken lightly. Often, one went in search of something: a better life; safety from repression; education; financial fortune.

These same goals still underlie the ninth house: a need to experience *newness*, to break up stale old routines, to step outside of the more ordinary and mundane aspects of daily life. The motifs of the *quest* and the *pilgrimage* figure prominently here. And these are not merely outer journeys. In fantasy literature, a group of characters may go on a quest and accomplish an outer goal—in *The Lord of the Rings,* Frodo throws the Ring into the cracks of Mount Doom; Samwise meets the Elves—but they also make some discoveries about themselves and their inner lives. Frodo discovers his own courage, Sam his capacity for loyalty. In parallel fashion, this house also has to do with one's philosophy of life, what makes life most meaningful, one's personal Holy Grail.

To keep their love alive, a couple with composite Venus in the ninth house needs to be wary of sameness and predictability settling into their relationship. If there are *never* any mornings when they wake up not knowing what will happen to them the rest of that day, their love may grow flat. The too-vanilla flavor of their life together gets translated into boredom with one another.

Such a couple also needs to honor one another's belief systems, religion, politics and world views—that's ninth house territory too. Sharing perspectives about these topics is a relationship-enhancing plus. If there are honest differences in these areas, the partners need to accept and respect them, rather than embark on a campaign to proselytize one another.

How to maintain the romantic Venusian magic? Such a couple thrives on shared journeys—literally traveling together. Whether it's a trip to Fiji or just to the nearest campground, they're sure to discover something important about the relationship and about one another on the way. But inward journeys matter too: they might attend a marriage enrichment seminar or a dream workshop together. So do journeys of the mind, such as attending a course on ancient Sumerian culture or classical Pompeii. Last but not least are intuitive journeys which seek to understand and interpret reality rather than just explore it. Depending on their theological predilections, these two might relish a Tibetan Buddhist lecture series, or church-hopping every weekend. Above all, they need *newness:* to share new places, new experiences, and ideas they've never thought about before. With composite Venus in the ninth house, constantly changing perspectives keep love refreshed and alive.

COMPOSITE VENUS IN THE TENTH HOUSE

"Career" is the usual meaning of the tenth house, and maybe these two will share their professional destinies as well as their personal ones. Most couples don't actually work together, though. We'll have to spread our nets a little more widely to be sure we catch the meaning of their composite Venus. The tenth house correlates with our social role. It's connected with questions of reputation, status and public image every bit as much as it is linked to work. As this relationship develops, increasingly we'll see this couple drawn toward playing a Venusian role in their community.

At the simplest level, a Venusian role involves embodying the collective mythologies of beauty and love. People who really don't know these two will probably tend to think that they have a great relationship. This doesn't mean that the opposite is necessarily true! But the curious part is that people who hold this high opinion of them don't really know them—they're just making an assumption. Based on what? In essence, it's on how the couple looks to them. They just seem right together. More deeply, they seem to reflect the ideal values of a certain stratum of the community—and here's a place where the angels start laughing! If our couple with composite Venus in the tenth house is in Hollywood, they probably look chic. If they're young and fashionable, they probably look cool. Republican golfers? Respectable. Hippies? Hip. Conservative Christians? Decent. New Agers? Sensitive. Feminists? Egalitarian. Each subculture has a set of ideals about love; whatever subculture these two are part of, they've got the credentials.

This task of carrying the ideals of the group is actually serious. At the deepest level, with composite Venus in the tenth house, these two have taken on a serious mission: that of helping their community restore and maintain its faith in the possibility of human love and commitment. They didn't ask for this job, either—it was assigned to them!

On a more concrete level, we may see this couple drawn to the arts together. Perhaps they perform together somehow, or are simply often seen together at concerts and gallery openings. Given time, if they choose to live together, their home will probably blossom into a showplace. It's easy to imagine paintings hanging on the walls and a piano gracing the living room. We'll very likely also see them playing a *counseling* role among their friends—they are the ones to whom people turn when their own relationships are shaky. That counseling role, by the way, is often the practical way in which they accomplish their mission in the community.

If they do work together professionally, they'll be happiest and most successful in a Venusian profession. It could be counseling, or at least something that involves their people skills. It's also easy to see them teaming up in a role that involves *aesthetic* decisions: art and creativity, decoration, or design.

COMPOSITE VENUS IN THE ELEVENTH HOUSE

Every couple pays lip service to the idea of prioritizing the relationship. But in practical terms, the subtle work of keeping a bond fresh and alive often gets sidetracked by daily distractions: social activities, domestic responsibilities, paying the bills. With composite Venus in the eleventh house, these two need to keep clear perspective. This house refers to *strategy*—taking the long view. They need to decide what is truly important in the context of years and decades together.

Love may blossom out of a clear blue sky, but maintaining and growing a relationship never happens automatically. It's the product of a systematic set of choices. To be sound, those choices must always be guided by a set of values and a sense of priorities. If their love is going to last, these two need to act as if making it last were an important consideration. What feeds their bond? Do they need to make sure they have a long vacation, far away from family, every year? Are evenings alone together at home more important than keeping up with a wide circle of friends? Or the opposite? Should they systematically scrimp so they can afford a big, comfortable house—or should they live simply and save their money for a trip to South America? There aren't any universal right answers to these kinds of questions, but they illustrate the core meaning of a healthy composite Venus in the eleventh house: strategic, long range thinking about what deepens and supports their love for each other. Their life together shouldn't "just happen to them." It needs to be something they create jointly and consciously: an incubator for love.

Anything in the Eleventh House tends to gain power and momentum as time passes. With Venus in this position, there are excellent prospects for the long-term growth and deepening of this relationship. But that blossoming in turn depends upon the two of them visualizing a happy future together. They benefit from trying to see themselves as two old people together, holding hands. That's not just about positive thinking, either. More centrally, it's about knowing what they want, agreeing to it, and working methodically toward building it. With every intention that they realize, with every successful manifestation of their determination, their love grows richer.

"Friends" are a traditional meaning of the eleventh house, although the word can be a little slippery. This house is not really about intimacy so much as teamwork, networking, and collective enterprises. Probably, this couple finds itself engaged with a fair amount of social activity. Many times that public focus arises out of their values and interests more than out of simple extraversion. Maybe they become involved in an astrological society or a religious organization. Maybe it's a dart-throwing league! Maybe it's just a big social circle. With Venus's natural orientation toward aesthetics, these two may find themselves engaged in group activity linked to the arts, or surrounded by creative friends. Likely, these associations are pleasant—that's in the nature of Venus too. But these two also need to keep their eye on the prize: social over-extension can drain and divert them unless it's helping them fulfill their long-term intentions.

COMPOSITE VENUS IN THE TWELFTH HOUSE

Falling in love, many couples describe their relationship as "spiritual." That lofty notion has been widely institutionalized in marriage and commitment ceremonies all over the world: most of them employ language that makes reference to God. But even when those words are heartfelt, the reality for most couples is that their relationship isn't truly about spirituality.

For most, it quickly becomes centered on the mundane foundations of psychology, practicality, and partnership. And many a bond does just fine on that basis. But not for these two! With their composite Venus in the twelfth house, their romantic and sexual feelings toward each other are very dependent upon the constant renewal of their shared spirituality. It's as if Aphrodite were their guru, offering rewards and punishments according to their behavior.

Is sex spiritual? In many of the older religious traditions, the answer was a resounding No. Sex was for procreation only. It should not be enjoyed, lest the souls become entangled in corruption. Many of us have begun to look upon those kinds of attitudes with suspicion, although they continue to thrive in certain quarters. The opposite notion—that sex is sacred—is more attractive and real to most of us nowadays. But even there, we need to stay grounded. The sexual reality for most couples is probably more emotional and playful than "spiritual."

Before we go any further, let's define exactly what we mean by "spiritual" in this context. It's simple: keeping a sense of the other person's soul in the forefront of your own consciousness right through the point of orgasm. That's it. Much of it has to do with the nature of the eye contact between the lovers. A lot of it is connected with tolerating the incredible sense of psychological nakedness that deep love-making creates. Why do people often close their eyes in sexual situations? Why is fantasy about other lovers so common? So much of this has to do with our fear of that undefended, wide-open vulnerability. With their composite Venus in the twelfth house, these two people need to conquer that fear. They need to use sexual energy in a conscious way. They need to see Spirit in each other's eyes.

To accomplish these mystical aims, this couple needs a big dose of the same thing mystics all over the world crave: time alone, away from the "madding crowd" and the distractions of everyday life. If they don't defend that territory, we'll see the darker face of the twelfth house: they'll fall into a pattern of escapism together—television, baby talk, alcohol, drugs. To avoid that, it is imperative that they develop the custom of withdrawing into their secret world: door locked, answering machine turned on, and supplies in the refrigerator. Shared meditation practice can be helpful—but we need to remember always that for them, sex *is* a meditation. Their individual religions, practices or spiritual philosophies are not the point: since this is the *composite* Venus, the only issue that matters here is what they do together, as a couple. And the less public that magic is, the deeper it will become.

CHAPTER TEN: THE COMPOSITE MARS

Here's a dirty little astronomical secret: Mars, the fabled "red planet," is actually more the color of a dusty old terra cotta garden pot. One look and you can see it—the right description would be "orange," not "red." Yet everyone—even the most rigorously cerebral of planetary astronomers—persists in calling it red. Why?

Well, we're all astrologers, whether we know it or not. And Mars *feels* red to us, despite the contrary evidence of our senses. Red: the color of passion. The color of heat and blood. The color that underlies the skin of our faces when we feel rage, sexual fire, the physical extremes of athletic extension or the ragged edges of adventure. Among the old astrologers, Mars got a bum rap. It was called "the lesser malefic," and equated with conflict and trouble. Those associations are valid, but let's make sure we preserve the glories of the "red" planet too. Who would want to live a life without any passion?

As we've seen, the principles of the composite chart apply to all kinds of human interactions, not just sexual ones. But in this book, we're focusing primarily on the realities of committed physical relationships. And Mars, the god of war, is also the god of sex. Earlier, we recognized that Venus, the goddess of love, didn't actually tell us everything we needed to know about love—the rest of the composite chart filled out the three-dimensional human picture. Sex is similarly complex; Mars hasn't cornered the market on the subject. Like Venus, it simply provides a kind of focused window through which we can enter a big terrain. Every couple knows that sometimes the term "love-making" is quite apt; sex can be a tender expression of affection and surrender. But most couples also understand that sexual love has another face: something primordial and wild needs to be released between them from time to time too. That's the territory of Mars, and its condition in the composite chart gives us a lot of insight into how to maintain that precious spark.

Teens, with the fires of puberty's biochemical onslaught burning in their veins, have little way of understanding how fragile a jewel physical passion between adults can be. "Common sense" marriage-mythology often assumes that romantic hunger is a passing phase. But the composite Mars may disagree! And in doing so, it carries us directly into the more traditional domain of the war god: anger.

Anger: the world's worst aphrodisiac. Nothing kills the ability to feel sexual impulses toward another human being faster than unprocessed rage. And rage comes from hurt. And, in love, hurt is inevitable. Thus, *the ability to express anger and to resolve it is the absolute epicenter of sustainable sexuality.* Where Mars lies in the composite chart, we get insights into the most effective conflict resolution skills for the couple. We may also learn something about certain "hot button" areas where conflict is probable—and where the price of the damage can be crushing, if the issues are not addressed skillfully and directly.

COMPOSITE MARS IN ARIES

How would Warriors or Daredevils make love? With Mars in its own sign, the natural erotic style of this couple is forthright, immediate, and full of vitality and fervor. Even if their individual Mars signatures are those of milder folk, this couple thrives on a level of heat, adventurousness and directness that may seem blunt at times. If this sounds off-putting, remember that Aries is the sign of the Hero, too, and that each partner can view the other as a prize to be won and treasured and protected. They may enjoy a renewed courtship ritual of "wooing" one another, pressing their suits with ardent expectations. Love should be an Event engaging one's total attention, a Triumph not taken for granted.

An evolutionary intent here is to claim the mate, to dare to love, not wanting anything to stand in their way. Perhaps they take an occasional weekend alone together, defend that time vigorously, and woe betide anyone who suggests other plans.

Again, think of warriors: shared challenges and adventures build this bond. They may tease each other mercilessly, but leap to one another's defense if anyone else ventures a jest or a criticism. And, like warriors, they may growl at each other a lot, too. More than with perhaps any other composite Mars sign but Scorpio, unprocessed anger will weaken their erotic bond. But not all anger requires a therapist to mediate—some of our spats come from just being two animals sharing the same territory, much the way two cats in the same home will sometimes get on one another's nerves and cuff each other. Once these partners have understood that they need to blow off everyday steam and process petty annoyances quickly, rather than letting them fester, they may even enjoy sparring with one another in a way that might puzzle or alarm their more soft-spoken friends. Of course, major issues need to be dealt with too, and the sooner the better. Bear in mind that one hair-trigger dynamic here can be any perceived disloyalty on the part of the partner. An evolutionary intent is to learn that the expression of anger can be a safe, healthy and relationship-building process—shunning such expression can eat away at the passionate heart of their connection.

COMPOSITE MARS IN TAURUS

Some people would rather talk about sex than actually experience it. Before we go one word further, let's quickly say that with composite Mars in Taurus, the odds are long against that being the issue with these two! Taurus is the most physical and sensual of the signs. Typically, a couple with the red planet in this position will have an earthy, natural, and accepting attitude toward the appetites of the body.

Still, talking about sex can be profoundly interesting. Doubtless, it will still be a major topic of conversation centuries from now, on star ships exploring the arms of our galaxy. Nothing so reveals our humanity, and no other human interaction is half as complex or multi-dimensional. Sex is physical, of course. But it's also deeply psychological. And if it's going to last, it had better be spiritual too. It's about generosity—and about need. In taking, we give. In giving, we take. It brings out the best and the worst in all of us. Nothing else makes so crazy, or so sane. No wonder we tie ourselves in knots about it!

The evolutionary intention behind a couple with composite Mars in Taurus lies in either avoiding those knots or in untangling them. Together, they share a soul-hunger to return to a primordial sexual simplicity. To say they "shouldn't talk about sex" would be going too far—but they need to recognize that too much talking or thinking can get them in trouble. There are deep, wordless wisdoms in the cells of our bodies. For composite Mars in Taurus, these silent wisdoms are the true teachers.

And what do they teach? Simple things, easily forgotten by people who've gnarled their instincts in webs of theory, chatter, "sophistication," and unnatural cultural stimuli. Things like this: how beautiful we are naked. How lovely our varied bodies can be. How much we need simple touch. How much more comfortable it is to share a bed with someone you know and trust. How long it takes to learn one another's bodies, and how delicious it is to be with someone who's taken the time to know yours. How vulnerable sex makes us. How rare and precious is true, sustainable passion between people. How elegantly we age, and how our sense of beauty changes with the passing years. How easily sex can put us back in synch with a partner. How readily the lack of it can exaggerate our reaction to petty annoyances.

With composite Mars in Taurus, this couple is trying to return to these body-wisdoms. The enemies of their sexuality lurk in the seductive disguises of civilization. One of these enemies is "Puritanism." By that, we mean the cultural repression and shaming of the body, anything that makes the body the enemy of God or family. This couple should beware of any belief system that discourages the unabashed expression of the body's heat. Those belief systems obviously include certain religious perspectives, but let's quickly add three modern "religions" to our list: The First Church of Thinness! The Holy Temple of Youth! The High Tabernacle of Rich and Famous!

Another force the couple with composite Mars in Taurus needs to resist is the distorted hyper-sexualization created by the media, advertising, and entertainment industries—the distortions that enter our sexual imaginations whenever we are, for example, staring wide-eyed at sexy movie stars on a screen. What messages are we internalizing then? Are we saying that, with composite Mars in Taurus, a couple should avoid the movies? Heaven forbid! The issue lies in self-awareness—when we resort to fantasy life for the fulfillment of intimate needs, we've moved away from sensual, immediate Taurean reality. A little self-scrutiny can quickly reveal whether our self-confidence or our bond with our partner has been diminished.

Let's add the "psychology industry" to the list too: insight can be precious but if we aren't careful, we can drown instinct in insight. Taurus benefits more from simply trusting instinct than from all the in-depth analyses in the world.

For these two, taking time away from all those "civilized" influences and returning to the Garden is the heart of what keeps them yearning for each other.

COMPOSITE MARS IN GEMINI

With this composite Mars, the mind is the first and most important of the erogenous zones. Sweet nothings are important here. So is an open-minded, accepting, endless curiosity about one another. If the act of love is viewed as, among other things, an ongoing, fascinating, funny and discussion-worthy experiment, so much the better.

Gemini when healthy is youthful, active, quick, verbal, inquisitive, perceptive and restless. It likes stimulation. Regardless of how placid these partners are as individuals, this composite Mars prefers activity to stillness, variety to boredom, questions to answers. This couple may exchange jokes, cards, email, text messages, phone calls, faxes, and concert and theatre tickets. Keeping each other interested can involve keeping each other guessing, in and out of bed. But a key to this composite Mars sign is communication with content. Learning each other's erogenous zones is part of it. So is not judging one another—within the context of loving rather than hurtful or distasteful behavior, there is no "right" and "wrong" way to make love. It's essential to make sure that communication works both ways, rather than getting stuck in the roles of lecturer and listener. Indeed, not getting stuck in any kind of rut is paramount here.

One evolutionary intent is to avoid the sort of stultifying routines that deaden lovers' responses to one another or blind them to each other's infinite mystery. Another is to communicate about a variety of forms of loving, without passing judgment on them or on each other. Perhaps this couple is undoing the effects of having been brainwashed, religiously or sociologically or in some other way, about there being one and only one appropriate type of love.

If tension builds up between this couple and isn't resolved, conversations can quickly turn into disagreements. What should have been friendly debates can take on a bitter or cutting edge, particularly deadly because this couple is so articulate. Nervous chatter about nothing, verbal sniping or, worse yet, stony silences may replace honest dialogue. If they find they can't talk about the weather without arguing, it's high time they addressed the genuine conflicts between them.

COMPOSITE MARS IN CANCER

"Try a little tenderness," advises an old soul song. When this composite Mars is working well, these partners understand that advice very well indeed.

Even if their individual birthcharts say more about Stormy Passion, the natural expression of this couple's sexuality is warm, nurturing, giving, and caring, with a marked sweetness. They may seem to fuss over each other: "Are you comfortable? Are you happy? Are you warm enough?" The underlying message is, "Have all your needs been met? Let me take care of you. Are you hurting? Let me heal you." Cancer is the sign of the Sensitive, and few partners can be so exquisitely tuned in to each other. Few can so well build a protective "nest" from their relationship. A fundamental evolutionary intention is to treat each other kindly and provide a safe and nurturing environment for the development of a very tender sexuality.

Yet that very sensitivity can be a double-edged sword. If one partner is getting all the nurturing, with the other one having tacit permission to behave in less than fully adult ways, the reciprocity that every relationship needs will suffer. Also, sooner or later, "baby" may rebel against "Mommy," and they'll both get hurt and angry.

Cancer is also the sign of the Crab, but it could as well have been called the Turtle or the Clam. If they feel hurt or angry, these partners need to guard against clamming up or retreating into their shells. If tension builds up and isn't resolved, they may sulk, become passive-aggressive or clingy, or come up with a barrage of irrational complaints that are smokescreens for the real issues.

All that glorious tenderness won't unfold and blossom *unless they both feel safe.* Their very Cancerian attunement to each other may make them more hypersensitive together than either might have been with someone else. Is that good news or bad news? Neither, but there are wise and unwise ways to deal with that heightened mutual susceptibility. Each partner must respect the other's sensitivity, rather than coddle it. They should tread lightly in potentially charged topics, rather than totally avoiding them. Saying "I don't feel safe enough to talk about that right now" is a better bet than "I won't talk about that." If pain has been caused, sincere apologies are in order—and so are acceptance and forgiveness.

COMPOSITE MARS IN LEO

Some couples enjoy getting dressed up. Others don't. Which side of that line we fall on isn't the essence of composite Mars in Leo, but it's a doorway. Making an effort to look our best is, among other things, a celebration of our sexuality. Unless we've been terribly mistreated, we generally appreciate being noticed that way. We like to feel attractive, and to elicit an interested response from others. Sexuality, in the broadest sense of the word, underlies the whole fashion industry. And from the perspective of a healthy composite Mars in Leo, let's add one more word: Hallelujah!

Leo, at its best, is loose and unabashed. It celebrates itself. With Mars in this sign, the natural expression of a couple's sexuality has those uninhibited qualities. In public, they present themselves, if not flamboyantly, at least in ways that suggest self-confidence and an appreciation of their physicality. They support and encourage those more theatrical qualities in each other. They probably buy each other clothing. Maybe they enjoy shopping together; certainly they compliment each other, express attraction to each other, flirt with each other, and offer reflective comments on each other's "best colors" and so forth. One gets the sense that each one is *proud* to have "caught" the other. In private, the same logic is extended: sexual confidence, and even bravado, are supported, appreciated, and rewarded in the time-honored way.

If any of this sounds silly or superficial, think again: there's likely no more fundamental source of rage than suppressed sexuality. With composite Mars in Leo, speaking positively, we recognize that the encouragement and enhancement of the couple's erotic self-actualization is a basic evolutionary intention and that, if effective, it purges the relationship of an elemental barrier between these souls: anger. One result of this reality is that any perceived suppression of each other's sexuality tends to be greeted initially with exaggerated rage or hurt. If suppression persists, the rage and hurt tend to morph into iciness, pettiness and defensiveness.

Cutting to the bottom line, the defining moments for a couple with composite Mars in Leo relate to how they handle one basic issue: learning one another's sexual needs, preferences and styles. People have differing levels of appreciation for graphic language. They like different ways of kissing. Some want more frequent sex than others. Dealing honestly with such questions is of course imperative for all couples. But with composite

Mars in Leo, that honesty must be informed by diplomacy, a non-judgmental attitude, and complimentary, encouraging, and appreciative language.

COMPOSITE MARS IN VIRGO

The evolutionary intent for this couple is to experience and express their sexuality as it is: to be whole, not perfect. Their shared physical love should be conducted with mutual acceptance, a recognition that healthy people have natural sexual instincts—Virgo is an Earth sign—and an attempt to attune themselves to those instincts without shame, criticism or performance issues.

On the other hand, with composite Mars in the sign of the craftsperson, this couple is well aware that lovemaking is, among other things, both an art and a skill, and they can share a desire to improve at it. Lovers become "better" as they become more attuned to each other over time and with attentive practice. The natural fastidiousness of Virgo should be taken into account, which means avoiding crudeness or vulgarity, even if both partners' birthcharts suggest proclivities for mud wrestling and roller derbies. Different tastes and different drives should be discussed—Mercury rules Virgo—in an atmosphere of positive and nonjudgmental mutual regard and support. If Virgo's innate sense of detail, ability to spot where improvement could happen, and desire to be helpful are all used sensitively, rather than allowed to run amok, the outcome can be fortuitous indeed. Comments and requests should be offered—and accepted—as suggestions or what-ifs, not demands or complaints.

Above all, potentially hurtful critiques should be avoided. Sexuality is an area where everyone's ego is fragile, sometimes far more fragile than we think, until the damage has been done.

If unresolved tensions build up in this relationship, a pattern of criticism, sexual and otherwise, can arise. Nitpicking over details. ("If your trouser hems were longer, your legs wouldn't look as short.") Pointless "observations" that are actually subtle digs. ("Your head moves a lot when you sing.") Disparaging of one another's hobbies. ("I can't understand why anyone would be interested in that.") Invalidation of each other's efforts. ("Do I have to be responsible for that, too?") The accumulated meaning is "You're not okay. You're never good enough." Give this dynamic some time, and the criticism can become overt, sarcastic, hostile and incredibly wounding. Either or both partners may start to feel that they can't do anything right. This pattern can be particularly painful for people with low self-esteem, who are more likely to take it to heart than to shrug it off, at least at first.

How to keep the relationship from self-destructing? Avoid unsolicited advice. Whenever possible, be supportive rather than critical. Praise rather than blame. And when issues do need to be discussed, keep it gentle, focus on the issue at hand, and on improving or changing the behavior or the relationship, not the partner. With that accomplished, this couple has a potentially vast reserve of attentive, detailed, growth-oriented mutual support, and that's a treasure.

COMPOSITE MARS IN LIBRA

With this placement, no matter how wild or earthy either partner may be as an individual, their shared physical love is best conducted as a highly civilized art. Graciousness is essential. Style cannot be neglected. Courtesy matters. So can flowers, candlelight, music, cologne, poetry, scented oil, lingerie, jacuzzis. And clean sheets and clean fingernails. Don't roll your eyes! With composite Mars in the sign of the Artist, the aesthetic component of lovemaking, and unhesitating recourse to anything that heightens that aesthetic component, are vitally important. The need here is to make the act of physical love as full of Beauty as possible. With that need satisfied, the full expression of composite Mars in the sign of the Lover becomes possible.

Libra always centers on *awareness of the other person as a separate being with needs that are not the same as one's own.* Therefore, the inevitable differences in this couple's erotic styles need to explored, and mutually agreeable compromises worked out. All of that negotiation needs to be done with as much elegance, civilized pleasure, and sophistication as the couple might use in choosing among several five star restaurants. Furthermore, erotic styles evolve over time, and what worked yesterday or last year may not work next week. Maintaining the Libran balance between these partner's needs should be treated as a work-of-art-in-progress.

This couple's evolutionary intent is to achieve a harmonious give-and-take in the erotic expression of their love, and to avoid crassness, crudity or selfishness with each other. If that goal is attained, they will have learned a great deal about how to handle intimate conflict outside of the bedroom, too. Therefore, any attempt to suppress, minimize or ignore differences in their sexuality can provoke rage or hurt in one or both partners, seemingly all out of proportion to the seriousness of the offense. If the tiff isn't dealt with promptly, fairly and honestly, this couple may retreat into icy formality. They may even go through the outer forms of sophisticated lovemaking, but without the empathic aim of truly trying to please one another. If this dynamic degenerates into something approaching "*I* like to do this, so we'll do it whether *you* like it or not," then this couple is in trouble. How to break the logjam? With a healthy influx of Libran energy: listen openly and sensitively to one another, then treat each other with romance, courtesy and focused empathy, and bring as much sheer beauty into the experience as possible.

COMPOSITE MARS IN SCORPIO

With composite Mars here, this couple's natural style of love-making is intense, passionate, revealing and full of profound closeness. This is a potentially white-hot placement for Mars, not just physically but also emotionally and psychologically. The evolutionary intent is to establish and maintain a bond that is searingly honest and transformatively deep for both partners.

Healthy catharsis is the goal here. Probing and revelatory conversation. Previously untold secrets may be traded, dreams and nightmares shared, fantasies and needs unveiled. There can be prolonged eye contact—and soul contact. Absolute frankness is desired. A sense of extreme closeness is deemed absolutely necessary. There are expectations of a willingness to keep forging an ever stronger bond, one that gets past the surface, past the defenses, under the skin and straight to the gut. These partners are lovers who don't hide from one another—who perhaps can't hide—and who are naked in every sense of the word.

Are you thinking that sounds like scary stuff? You're right, even if the individual charts also show an elevated appetite for intimacy. This couple has broadband access to each other's shadows, to each other's damaged, wounded, underdeveloped sides, and knowledge is power, sometimes dangerous power. Yet that access goes hand in hand with the passion here: you don't get one without the other.

In the early stages of the relationship, while the hormonal fog is still thick, this degree of closeness can seem like manna from heaven. Confession feels good for the soul. Being so fully seen and met and partnered feels like absolution, not just recognition. But as time goes on and the couple knows one another better and better, it's entirely understandable that one or both of them could get nervous about this level of intimacy. "When I think of all the crappy things she knows about me, I cringe. *Why* did I tell her *that*? And at this rate, what else might I tell her? Who might she be talking to about all this? Uh oh."

In short, it's hard to maintain this type of physical or emotional intensity all the time. Sometimes these partners need a breather, and that need should not be interpreted as shallowness, indifference or betrayal, any more than sleeping every night should be interpreted as running away from living.

Imagine that your longtime psychoanalyst got absolutely furious at you and was unprofessional enough both to attack you and to use his or her extensive knowledge of you to do so. How badly could that hurt? The potential for hurt is even greater here, because sexuality is involved here. If this couple's natural expression of sexuality is thwarted or suppressed, they may go through some devastating fights, precisely because they know each other's underbellies so well. Each partner knows exactly where to twist the knife. They should refrain from using their mental maps of each other's weak spots as weapons. They should respect the seal of the emotional confessional that their relationship promotes, and not betray each other's secrets or confidences. If they seem to be having obsessive arguments about a non-issue, they should try to address what's really bothering them—chances are it isn't the color of the carpet.

COMPOSITE MARS IN SAGITTARIUS

Here we have the God of War in the sign of the Gypsy, the Scholar, the Philosopher and the Pilgrim. Sagittarius hungers for new experiences. It likes freedom and dislikes restrictions. Yet it reaches its highest expression when it chooses to operate ethically and not to transgress natural laws—which is its evolutionary intent.

Partners with composite Mars here need to express their sexuality robustly and enthusiastically. There is probably an appetite for variety and experimentation. Humor is appreciated, along with frankness and unabashed zeal. Physical love is an adventure. Anything that adds some spark of freshness and innovation is valued—new clothing, trips out of town, or even a weekend in a fine hotel in their own town. This couple doesn't have to memorize the Kama Sutra, but they are happiest if they feel that there are still unexplored erotic possibilities between them. Furthermore, if they're bored with their lives in other ways, that boredom may start to creep into the bedroom. Leading as interesting a life together as possible—something new to experience, something new to talk about—can only make them more alive to one another and therefore help the natural expression of their sexuality.

This composite Mars placement may be difficult for more retiring souls. Yet what works *for the couple* is a freewheeling, saucy openness, a celebration of Eros in their relationship, in their lives and in the world. Insecure partners may need some extra reassurance, since the warmth and looseness that this couple inspires in one another may be taken for flirtatiousness or even come-ons by others.

It's vital for these partners to feel that each one understands and honors the ethical parameters of their relationship. If something feels ethically wrong in their behavior with one another or with others, the spark between them can go out pretty quickly. Yet if either partner feels squelched or censored in a fearful, prudish kind of way, then rage can build up and eroticism fade. Conflict may be handled in a more and more self-righteous way, moral aspersions cast, and holier-than-thou claims wielded like weapons. Therefore, it's important that those ethical parameters be something that *the couple has worked out together and freely chosen*, rather than something imposed from without, or imposed by one partner upon the other.

COMPOSITE MARS IN CAPRICORN

Capricorn is about a Great Work. With composite Mars in this sign, part of the Great Work is sustaining and maintaining the erotic heat between these partners. We forget who first joked, "A Capricorn is a repressed Scorpio," but there was definitely a kernel of truth in that one-liner. Capricorn is an

Earth sign and there's plenty of heat here; it's just expressed with more reserve.

The evolutionary intentions here are to behave with integrity and self-restraint, and to accomplish something significant together, to create some sort of "structure" in the world that's indicative of this couple's inner values and hard work—Capricorn rules manifestation on the physical plane.

To that end, this composite Mars sign probably operates better within the context of a commitment. This couple needs to make promises, to trust them—and to keep them. Those promises might consist of showing up on time, getting the bills paid, sharing the upbringing of a child, living within their means, or exchanging marriage vows. Whatever the promises are, they should be honored. To paraphrase the psychologist M. Scott Peck, "Love is responsible actions sustained over time." Shared projects feed the relationship too. Only then, with such a track record behind them, can these partners *trust* one another enough to tap into the earthy core of potential eroticism between them. That mutual trust has to be earned, but the rewards are worth it. There is deep sensuality here. Combined with surprising flashes of Capricorn whimsy and humor—where do we get our words "capricious" and "Saturnalia"?—it can be a heady mix.

Yet Capricorn is not the most emotionally expressive of the signs. Rather than making assumptions or trying to read cues, these partners may need to learn *to ask one another directly* such questions as "Are you just tired, or are you angry at me?" or "Do you want to have sex with me, but maybe just not right now?" Otherwise they may feel hurt or rejected when that wasn't the partner's intention at all. Such erroneous assumptions can cause a lot of damage and, in a vicious circle, make it still harder to ask questions and express feelings. Another trigger for hurt and anger is either partner's failure to fulfill his or her responsibilities, or a lack of respect. Such issues need to be talked about, or one or both partners may retreat behind an icy wall of Capricornishly correct behavior, "doing right by each other," and honoring the mere forms of the relationship and not its spirit.

COMPOSITE MARS IN AQUARIUS

The God of War in the house of the Rebel! This composite Mars placement doesn't necessarily refer to on-the-fringes sexual experimentation. It does mean that this couple needs to ignore all of the how-to articles in women's (and men's!) magazines about keeping sex steamy. Reading them might be amusing, but taking them as guidelines won't work here.

Every culture has its sexual icons, from Jean Harlow to Twiggy to Farah Fawcett to J-Lo, from Rudolph Valentino to Sean Connery to Harrison Ford to Johnny Depp. Those are individual icons, but we have relationship icons too, and they vary not only from generation to generation but within a generation. Napoleon and Josephine. Bonnie and Clyde. Lucy and Desi. John and Yoko. Ronald and Nancy. Courtney and Kurt. Antonio and Melanie. Brad and Jennifer. Not all of those couples are still together, or still alive, and not all of those relationships were happy ones, yet their stories have all influenced the popular culture of their heydays, and its contemporary mythology and "rules" about relating.

We have lots of rules. Can you spot (only!) some of them in the examples below? The man should be older than the woman. Money mates with beauty. Beauty mates with power. Bubbly, air-headed women are forgiven anything if they're attractive enough. Live fast, die young and leave a good-looking corpse. Women must have children. Some relationships are doomed no matter what. Tragic figures are romantic. Here are the conditions for a storybook romance. Here is how passionate lovers behave. Men are redeemed by good women. All you need is love.

Unless we live on desert islands with no TV, movies, radio or magazines, it's hard for modern Westerners to avoid such influences. Human beings are creatures of habit, and the less individuated we are, the more we unquestioningly tend to imitate the patterns we see all around us.

And blind imitation of those iconic patterns or of any other relationship "rules" is the kiss of death for the healthy sexuality of a couple with composite Mars in Aquarius. The evolutionary intent here is to encourage the couple's physicality *to be exactly what it truly is*, avoiding surrender to social pressure. Forget the Kinsey or the Hite reports. These two are making it up as they go along. Getting past societal and parental influences is one step. Getting past their own preconceived notions, or beliefs left over from past relationships, is another one. It's hard to describe the natural physical expression of such a couple, because when, where and how often they "should" have sex, what does and does not turn them on, even the importance of sex itself in the relationship, should all be entirely of their own conscious choosing.

The more these two allow themselves to be affected by outside influences, the more they can feel as if they're merely going through the motions and not truly participating. One or both of them may then become reflexively contrary. "You say yes, I'll say no. You say black, I'll say white." One or both of them may simply withdraw, physically and/or emotionally, or anger and resentment may be shown by acting out in sudden and unexpected ways.

COMPOSITE MARS IN PISCES

Pisces is the sign of mysticism, of visionary and transcendent experiences, of merging with something larger than the mere ego. What is that larger something? Spirit. The relationship. One's country. One's religion. The universe. The soul. Art, music, creativity. This couple should not "transcend" sex, but sex between them could be a high and transcendent experience.

In our book, *Skymates: Love, Sex and Evolutionary Astrology*, we quoted Rodney Collin from his book, *The Theory of Celestial Influence*:

> The key to the understanding of sex is the knowledge that sexual energy is the finest and subtlest naturally produced by the human organism. This sexual energy can be turned to any purpose, can express itself on any level. It contains the potentiality of the highest forms of creation, and it also contains the possibility of destroying a man, and wrecking him, physically, morally and emotionally. It can combine with his most bestial side, with criminal impulses of cruelty, hatred, and fear, or it can combine with his most refined aspirations and keenest sensibilities. And in either case it will immensely heighten the tendency to which it becomes attached . . .

For no composite Mars sign are Collins's words more true than for composite Mars in Pisces.

At best, there can be great sweetness, generosity and mutual soul-honoring here. This couple's natural physicality is expressed, however passionately, with sensitivity and with a sense of a flowing interchange of emotions, of merging on more than just a physical level. Shared interests in spirituality are helpful but not necessary.

Anything that helps make the act of love an otherworldly as well as a sensual experience is appreciated: soft light, candles, music, a warm fire, satin sheets, bubble baths, and the ringer on the phone turned off. Although this may be bewildering for more earthy individuals, crudeness is the opposite of an aphrodisiac for this couple.

Darker possibilities are available here, too. When Pisces doesn't step beyond the boundaries of the self in meditative or mystical ways, it can turn to less healthy ways to reach that altered or otherworldly state. This couple may need to be careful not to get too dependent upon champagne as an aid to eroticism, for example. Such substances may seem to enhance things at first, but if used in excess they can often blunt reactions later, besides carrying dangers of their own. Moreover, sex itself could potentially used as a way to avoid conflict, or to avoid facing various realities that the couple needs to face and work through together.

A late, great North Carolina band, The Red Clay Ramblers, did a song called "I Was Making Love, But You Were Only Fucking." If either of these partners gets a similar feeling about the relationship, resentment will start to build. If left unresolved, that resentment could show up as avoidance of intimacy, denial that there's anything wrong, various forms of numbing oneself, co-dependence, or passive aggression: getting "sick," being late, breaking promises, "forgetting" things, etc.

COMPOSITE MARS IN THE FIRST HOUSE

Anything in the first house is in the spotlight. It looms large in the relationship, and everyone around sees it vividly too. For these two, with their composite Mars in the First, we are talking about the "god of war," so stand back! The bond promises to be colorful and intense. Conflictual? Yes, very probably. Passionate? Again, likely yes. And the interaction of those ideas—conflict and passion—is the crux of the matter. With Mars this strong, you can't have one without the other.

No one in his right mind enjoys intimate conflict. It's painful and awful, unless we are sadists or masochists. But the alternative, given the inescapable fact that lasting intimacy is challenging, is to bottle up the tensions. That may work in terms of suppressing the *expression* of conflict, but it really solves nothing. Resentments build up. Armed truces and painful *détentes* are emotionally costly. Armed and fortified borders begin to exist between the two—and all of these unfortunate images are warning signs for a couple with their composite Mars in the first house! They could go down that road. It's not their doom, but it is the lower possibility. Before we attend to the higher ground, let's take one more step. Armed and fortified borders—imagine two people *in bed* with that kind of energy between them. Sexy? Of course not. Unresolved, unexpressed conflict kills passion. That is an elemental principle with the planet Mars. And these two have it strongly in their chemistry.

So what about that higher ground? The prize is passion that lasts. And the road there is one of *conscious, honest, fair conflict.* It is essential that these two recognize that "war" is part of love, as two jagged human stones are gradually smashed into smoothness in the tireless, battering waves of intimacy. There must be no taboo on anger here.

And it helps if there's also been a "Geneva convention!" These two must agree on the methods and rules of conflict. Can one person veto discussing a conflict for an evening if he or she is feeling too tired to do good a job of it? Can we agree that conundrums with my parents are my territory, and conundrums with your parents are your territory? Are there particular words we both agree not to use? None of these questions necessarily have obvious answers. The couple must figure out what works for them, to create a framework within which their battles can unfold with minimum mutual destruction, and maximum potential for positive, acceptable resolution.

With Mars energy so strong for these two, it is beneficial if sometimes they arrange to be pitted together against some external threat that is bigger than either one of them. Maybe they take up sailing, and depend on each other in the face of the primal might of wind and wave. Maybe they go to Italy and face figuring out the subways of Milan. The point is that not all this Mars force needs to be aimed at each other. Together, these two are a team. The "warrior archetype" is powerful with them. It's good for them to be on the same side sometimes. That keeps the other processes in perspective, and forges a deep mutual respect and interdependency.

COMPOSITE MARS IN THE SECOND HOUSE

Here's a very simple traditional reading of composite Mars in the second house: conflict and trouble over money. Of course common sense and universal human experience do suggest that financial disagreements and stresses are a common source of intimate friction, so the interpretation is a plausible one. On top of that, sometimes as fate or karma would have it, we observe couples with this configuration running into nasty "random" issues with domestic finances: job losses, accidents, fires, even theft. Such eventualities can indeed lead to trouble between these two as they attempt to survive the adversity.

But we also see conflicts over money that are less directly linked to "real world" challenges, and more reflective of dynamics within the relationship: trouble over the perception that one person is paying less than his or her fair share, for example. Or petty, dispiriting scenes over who paid for dinner last time.

Cutting to the chase, with Mars the issue is always the appropriate expression of force—courage, entrepreneurial spirit, and energy. Imagine a couple with this configuration struggling to "make ends meet" after the birth of a child. Should he give up his costly poker night with his buddies? Or should she not attend her expensive art class? Perhaps they are fighting over who will get the short end of the stick—when up above their guardian angels are saying *just go make some more money!* A shared underlying commitment to a fear-based view of survival, and hence of finance, is the evolutionary issue here. These two need to develop confidence, force, and focus as a couple, and money is the school house for that work. An exaggerated love of money—simple materialism—isn't the point, of course. That helps no one. But they have a right to survive and to thrive. As they awaken their shared Mars energy, these two can really forge themselves into a team, setting goals and attaining them. If they were a Paleolithic couple, they might have been born into a famine generated by climate change. They could try to live on lichen and moss—or they could bravely get up and go where the mastodons had gone. Nowadays, our "mastodons" are a little more abstract. They take the form of the money that buys us food, shelter, and certain material joys.

These two need to "go hunting" together.

COMPOSITE MARS IN THE THIRD HOUSE

The God of War in the house of speech! What does that phrase conjure up for you? Lively conversations? Heated words, stinging repartee, ruffled feathers, flying crockery? Well, all of the above may be possible. Even more so than most couples, this one needs to learn to *fight fair*. Keep in mind, as you read the paragraphs below, that speech is only one of the many ways we communicate, and that the following concepts can also be applied to this couple's tones of voice, facial expressions, body language, eye contact, letters and email.

For sexual heat to remain in this bond, as many lines of communication need to be kept open as possible. Attaining that goal depends largely on *how* those things are said. Honestly, yes. Directly, yes. Forthrightly, yes. With the aims of communicating erotic and non-erotic needs, and of expressing pleasure and displeasure, yes. All of those processes will help keep passion alive. But communicating sarcastically? With mockery, grandstanding, or teasing? Dangerous—because they're too good at it! *Words have power in this relationship.* Immense power, as if they were spells. Power to thrill and arouse, to infuse new energy into this bond, to clear the air—and power to wound.

Remember, also, that this is the house of perception, the house of questions, the house of wonder. If this couple is bored with their lives, individually or together, they may mistake that boredom for having tired of one another. Therefore, attention paid to maintaining an interesting, fast-paced life is attention well spent.

Yet "interesting" may also mean "stressful." Where Mars lives, stress is frequently a fellow tenant. Communication, the life of the mind, and a full and colorful life can be joyous things, but Mars may draw a bit too much third house activity to this couple for comfort, particularly if they are milder individuals. Their schedules may fill to bursting, leaving them pleading for an unstructured night off together. They need to be Martial enough to *claim* such a night, not merely long for it! Computers may break down, phone and Internet lines be subject to annoying and inexplicable interference, the mail fall prey to mysterious delivery problems, and cars malfunction as if possessed by minor demons. Such hassles can become trigger points for conflicts and flare-ups. ("You're driving both of us crazy! Can we just slow down?") If these conflicts are allowed to fester, both partners will be too tired and irritable to maintain a healthy sexual connection. If handled with humor, frequent double-checking of details, and the twin resolutions not to overextend themselves and not to schedule engagements for one another without asking first, then the resolution of such conflicts can draw them closer together and teach them more about good boundaries, verbal and otherwise.

COMPOSITE MARS IN THE FOURTH HOUSE

There is a deep core of passionate heat in this couple. With composite Mars in the fourth house, the fires can burn for a lifetime. But to do so, they need the right incubator: a safe place. A Hobbit-hole. A home. In modern astrological practice, there is a tendency to ignore something that was profoundly obvious to our forebears in the field: that the fourth house is ultimately the most relationship-oriented of the twelve houses. We still often call it the "house of the home," but then we tend to think of mere buildings, relating fourth house issues to questions of geographical moves and interior design. This view misses that most proverbial of observations: a house is not a home. A home is, above all, a set of relationships characterized by stability, loyalty, permanence, and an unquestioning pledge of mutual aid and assistance. And for the couple with composite Mars in the fourth, the full blossoming of their sexuality can only occur in that particular hothouse.

And "hot" it will be—in every sense. Where Mars lies, stress tends to follow. Home, ideally, is a place where one can relax. But with Mars in the fourth, the couple tends to magnetize hassles into their home. They may have more than their fair share of simple mechanical or existential misfortune there—burst pipes, leaky roofs, evil landlords, noisy or scary neighbors. Maybe they work at home, with all the demonology that entails. Perhaps they have to fight a protracted battle to get the kind of place they want and need. There may be knotty issues around different lifestyle needs. Any or all of these kinds of problems are likely to be epicenters of anger in the coupling process. Handled well, they bring the two people closer. Handled poorly, and we see the classic dark Mars scenario: a repression of sexual response within the relationship, followed inevitably by the fire and ice of rage.

Of all the potential stressors connected with home life for a couple with composite Mars in the fourth house, number one is typically that classic fourth house correlate: the family of origin. Demanding parents or in-laws can become a sore point, and that remains true regardless of whether their demands are groundless, insensitive and self-indulgent ("Thou shalt come to our house *every* Sunday for dinner"), or real ("I am penniless, sick, and have nowhere else to turn"). Digging deeper, the core anger-triggering issue here lies in the *unresolved parental projections* of either or both of the lovers with this configuration. The tendency to confuse one's partner with one's parent is of course one of the shibboleths of modern psychology. In this case, we look specifically at Mars-energy in that regard: unexpressed, unresolved anger at a parent, or repressed childhood hurt as a result of inappropriate anger or violence on the part of a parent.

As always with Mars, handling these questions poorly kills sex. And handling them well preserves and intensifies it.

COMPOSITE MARS IN THE FIFTH HOUSE

There's fire in the chemistry these two generate together. It needs to be released. If it backs up between them, it will only generate tension that quickly explodes into the sort of conflict that has the dramatic visuals of World War Three and the content of a scuffle in a kindergarten playground. Far better to release this energy in more enjoyable ways.

Mars loves the kinds of release that make us all sweaty and red in the face. Does that bring any creative possibilities to mind? We thought so. Sexuality promises to be a renewing, sustaining force in this relationship. Approaching lovemaking with imagination and daring is crucial: those qualities are intrinsic to any positive response to the fifth house. It's helpful to remember that one of the oldest associations with this house is "love affairs" or simply "courtship." So what is sex like between new lovers? The word "enthusiastic" comes quickly to mind. And most of us, upon reflection, realize that a big part of the enthusiasm comes from the sheer newness and freshness of the relationship. So, with composite Mars in the fifth house, newness and freshness become key concepts here. For these two, even after long years together, it helps channel this Mars fire for them to seize sexual opportunities as new lovers would: opportunities might arise to have sex out of doors, for example.

The fifth house isn't all about sex. We just can't get it right without a right relationship to Eros, that's all. With that kind of verve and spontaneity in place, the couple can move forward into two more areas of significance for them. One is sports. The other is shared creativity.

"Sports" must be defined broadly here: basically we are again back to anything that gets them all sweaty and red in the face. It doesn't have to be competitive, although tennis will do it. So could kayaking or hiking together. Or dancing—which leads us to think of the other fifth house pillar: shared creativity. A couple dancing together is engaged in an activity with many of the attributes of a sport, but they are also expressing something primal about who they are together as bodies and as souls. We can stretch our imaginations outward and see these two people drumming together—or nervously awaiting their cues to go on stage in a dramatic performance.

The fifth is often called the house of children, and some astrologers would predict trouble through kids here because of the association of Mars with conflict. That could be the case, but here's a creative way to frame it: if these two have trouble releasing their own "inner children" as we have been describing above, then they'll surely have trouble with real-life kids too. Fortunately, the formula works the other way too: if they make peace with their own bumptious, rambunctious, noisy, playful, hell-raising inner children, they'll get along fine with any children who come into the world through them or who fall into the orbit of their care.

COMPOSITE MARS IN THE SIXTH HOUSE

Stressful work and stressful responsibilities wear people down. Given a long run of that kind of pressure, two individuals will tend to get snappish, even cold and brutal. With composite Mars in the sixth house, there is a tendency for this couple to attract that kind of pressure into their lives, especially as their relationship develops over time. Given long exposure, it could even have an adverse impact upon their physical health.

This is about as far as the fortune-telling astrologer would go: there is a tendency to think of Mars as "bad," and to relate the sixth house to our duties. From the evolutionary perspective, the prospects are far less gloomy. There, Mars is always a *challenge to our fierceness*. Can you two growl? Can you set boundaries—and, more to the point, can you defend them? Where Mars lies, you will be Hunter or you will be Prey. Take your pick, but it will surely be one or the other.

So, we ask this couple: to whom have you given the right to set the agenda of your responsibilities? And why? You probably must work—but you don't need to sacrifice your health or your relationship on that altar. An impossible, soul-eating job? There are other jobs. Find one. Or set boundaries at work and courageously let the chips fall where they may. Demanding families? Once again, Just Say No. Life is hard sometimes, and ethical imperatives do bind us. But with composite Mars in the sixth house, without these fair and honorable boundaries your relationship will be devoured.

How can you learn to do this gracefully? One answer lies in a largely forgotten dimension of sixth house symbolism: *mentors.* Typically these are people sufficiently older than yourselves that you notice the age difference. They may not be inherently wiser than you, but experience has tempered their intelligence into an understanding greater than yours. You can profit from their mistakes—and they'll be happy to put those mistakes to that good use. How do you recognize these mentors? They'll have a strong Mars-signature in their energy and behavior: something appealing to you, but edgy and penetrating. You sense immediately that it won't work for you to behave foolishly around them. They will call you on it. And if you don't like that, they shrug their shoulders and walk away.

Taking it a step further, let's recognize that intimate conflict can be handled skillfully. There are techniques that work better than others. These mentors may help you two come to terms with how to handle your own more heated negotiations. For example, the mentors may teach you, through demonstration and example, that conflict is fine—nothing to worry too much about! And then they might show you how it goes better if you keep it specific: "It bothers me that you left your underpants on the bedroom floor again," rather than, "You are always such a pig!"

Seek these Teachers. Your composite chart promises that they exist. As this relationship moves into greater seriousness, you will encounter them. And eventually, you two will pass the gift they offer you on to others.

COMPOSITE MARS IN THE SEVENTH HOUSE

The God of War in the House of Marriage? Yikes! It sounds pretty grim—but Fear Not. For one thing, the seventh house always refers to "other people." In your personal birthchart, it signifies your partner or your close friends. But here we are talking about a *composite* Mars in the seventh house, and in the composite chart, the seventh refers to relationships that you have as a couple. It is these relationships, not necessarily your own, that are characterized by Mars energy.

That probably feels a little better than thinking of your own primary bond as doomed to endless war, but it is still daunting to think of a promise of ongoing conflict with others. Here we come to the heart of the matter: conflict with others is a real possibility, but there is higher ground too. Wherever Mars lies in a composite chart, the couple must practice the "yoga" of fierceness. Boundaries must be set—and defended. It is highly probable that early in the relationship you will encounter people—possibly couples—who seem hellbent on sabotaging your trust for each other or your faith in your relationship. These may be individuals whom you have trusted in the past. But there is something about you two together that pushes their buttons. The challenge here is to stand up to them, proudly and confidently. They can accept your love for each other and respect it, or they can kiss you goodbye. It's their call. And something steely and loyal is forged between the two of you in that encounter.

On a more simply positive note, with Mars in the seventh house the right friendships must be established to support the primary bond. These will be with Martial people. That means honest, direct folks, people who don't mince words with you, but upon whom you can count when the fur starts flying. If they are other couples, they'll probably tend to be rather frank with you about their sexuality and about their conflicts. You'll sense deep loyalty to each other, but no undue respect—they'll tease and challenge each other, much in the fashion of warriors with a flagon or three of ale under their belts.

In the seventh house, we are always learning something that we really need to know, but that we can only learn from others. The couple with composite Mars in their seventh house is learning something about the right channeling of heat, passion, anger, and friction within the context of an ongoing bond of radical, die-with-your-boots-on commitment: we trust slowly and we choose our friends carefully, testing their honesty and their loyalty.

But once chosen, we don't look back.

COMPOSITE MARS IN THE EIGHTH HOUSE

Any fool can fall in love, but it takes a lot of courage to stay there! Eternally, everything seems rosy at love's outset—and just as eternally, everything tends to get very complicated within about six weeks. Nothing is so effective as love at bringing our scariest, most emotionally-charged issues bubbling up to the surface. The eighth house is traditional astrology's house of death—and the title gets us in the right mood! Something always has to die here, and usually it's connected with our pride, our defenses, or our attachments. With their composite Mars—the war god—in the eighth house, this couple has signed up to face their fears, individually and together. They bring those fears out in each other.

At first, it doesn't feel that way. The universe really wants this relationship to come into being, so it uses one of its most effective and cunning tricks to accomplish that end: steam rises in the space between these two! It fills the atmosphere. There is a deep feeling of *wanting* each other. And of course, provided the usual existential green lights are reasonably in place, the majority of us find that kind of juice quite magnetic. In we rush.

That's not necessarily a mistake. But beneath the initial pulse of passion there lurks the war god. There is a wall of fire here. Its mortar is anger. And its bricks are every hurt, every insult, every shaming word that either of them has ever endured. Whatever gender attracts us, there is an excellent chance we've been wounded grievously by one of its representatives. These damaging experiences don't evaporate, even after we've stopped planning grisly passages into the Next World for our former beloved. They lurk inside us, waiting for the right trigger. And that trigger is typically not simply sexual energy—it is *mating* energy. We can be turned on erotically or romantically by a fairly large number of people, but with how many could we actually, potentially, form a life-long bond? It's a rare experience, and a precious one. But once we have approached that borderline, our deeper unresolved tensions and fears make themselves felt. And with composite Mars in the eighth house, these tensions and fears have teeth.

The low road here is a familiar story: a relationship that begins in a blaze of passion—and flames out before the VISA bill arrives for that first fancy French dinner.

To follow the higher road, these two must think like warriors. Strategically. Patiently. And courageously. Like warriors, they need to be able to trust each other—loyalty is central here, and thus some degree of commitment must arise early in this process. A minimum bet is a *commitment to honesty*, demonstrated and made believable by emotional risks in that department. As they see this kind of emotional courage in each other, that wonderful initial passion sees a City of Gold on the far horizon: a passion that survives the years. But it lies on the other side of a dark valley, populated with all the monsters that have been hiding under the bed for each of them.

COMPOSITE MARS IN THE NINTH HOUSE

Stretching the horizons: that's the ninth house in a nutshell. We can do it literally by traveling. We can do it mentally, through learning and education. We can do it by letting our hearts and intuitions reach outward in an attempt to feel the meaning of life in our bones. And above all we can do it by simply opening ourselves up to new experience in every way.

Now put Mars into the equation: the war god isn't necessarily as bloody-minded as his name implies, but he does like a certain edge on those new experiences. Not just "travel," but adventure. Not just "education," but a brave commitment to pioneering radical and controversial new thoughts. Not just some safe armchair philosophy, but a robust belief in the virtue of diving into everything head first. For this couple, with their composite Mars in the ninth house, those are the formulas for a healthy thrust of passion in the life they share.

Picture them emerging from the mountains after a four-day hike. They've experienced some dangers. They've comforted each other with touch when they both thought there was a bear outside the tent. They've come through heroically for each other, in other words. And the soul of the bond is deeper for it.

Not everyone is physically or mentally equipped for an adventure as physical as that one. Each couple must adjust the metaphor to their own reality, but always the core remains: something grows stronger in these two when they test the limits of their shared courage.

At a more intellectual level, composite Mars in the ninth house loves to explore controversial beliefs and bodies of knowledge—astrology is an excellent example! There is a distinct potential in this couple of actually moving such a body of knowledge forward—pioneering a new technique or theory.

A "warrior religion" arises naturally between these two—and that doesn't mean they are likely to start practicing human sacrifice in their backyard. By "religion" we mean a set of values by which they guide their lives and interpret their experience. Warriors admire courage, loyalty, and taking personal responsibility for one's actions and one's fate. Such an attitude *toward the relationship* is natural and appropriate for this couple: they can make it what they want it to be. They can be brave enough to keep it honest. They can show the courage it takes to ask for what they need and say what they see. They can fear the ragged edges of anger, but never let that fear silence them. And they can commit to defending each other with a do-or-die fierceness.

COMPOSITE MARS IN THE TENTH HOUSE

Something precious needs protection, and it's up to this couple to take care of it. That's their mission in this world. As befits the nature of Mars, that mission is *warrior-work*. They are likely to make enemies in the process. Furthermore, with their composite Mars in the tenth house, this battle promises to be public. The community will witness it. Before we start sounding like this relationship is based on the script of an Arnold Schwarzenegger film, let's add a few subtleties: some battles are fought quietly, just by holding the space for some truth or principle. Some weapons don't explode or have sharp bloody edges; words are a good example. And there are no enemies we have to hate. It is enough simply to defeat them.

Not everyone is comfortable with this kind of language, even after we extract some of the canine teeth from our language. But Mars is part of life, and thus competition is intrinsic to the way of nature—even if we would prefer to avoid it.

Perhaps these two bring an astrological lecturer to their town. Before they know it, they've upset a group of Fundamentalists. Maybe they become involved in an attempt to establish a greenbelt around their community—and incidentally protect a few innocent birds and squirrels. Suddenly, some housing developers are up in arms. We could imagine them starting a yoga studio—and finding, to their surprise and dismay, that they've made enemies of the people who run another yoga studio a couple of miles away. Competition wasn't their goal, but it's the perception—and, arguably, the reality, even if they are not specifically *motivated* to compete. Perhaps they become involved in a soccer league so their kids can get some healthy exercise, and it turns out that some of the other parents are treating the games like a World War.

In none of these situations did our couple ask for trouble! But sometimes trouble finds them, and sometimes walking away is not the best answer: the principles involved are in fact worth a little adrenalin and lost sleep. And whenever that is the case, we're back to square one: it is because there is something at stake that is under attack and worth protecting.

Not every couple with a composite planet in the tenth house actually winds up working professionally together, but it is a distinct possibility. Together, these two are simply a terrific team. Pressure may not "comfort" them, but it does bring out the steel in their bond. As a unit, they complement each other's skills and can be effective joint competitors in any area that excites and stimulates them both.

One side effect of having composite Mars in the tenth house is fairly obvious from all we've said so far: not everyone will feel positively toward these two. They'll come to be identified publicly with a rather distinct "position," and that position will certainly have its detractors. Spiritually, their inner challenge is to avoid hatred—and to make sure that the position they are defending reflects their deepest values. And outwardly, their challenge is to win. The issue is bigger than they are.

COMPOSITE MARS IN THE ELEVENTH HOUSE

Like Merlin the Wizard ageing backwards, the sexual passion in this relationship gathers momentum over time. That's if they play their cards right! Most of us naturally assume the opposite: that we're hottest at the beginning, then settle down into a more mellow expression of body heat. But sex is a tremendous mystery and deeply affected by human individuality, even at the physical level. Speaking strictly of the body, we can recognize that there's always a learning curve with a new lover—and a "teaching curve" too. Over time, people can learn what works erotically for each other. They can also learn the deeper levels of physical trust that allow sex, even in its most "gymnastic" expressions, to blossom. That is part of what is going on with these two people—again, if they play their cards right.

So how might they play them wrong? Repressed, contained frustration with another human being is a terrible aphrodisiac. When we are angry with someone, we usually don't want them even touching us. With their composite Mars in the eleventh house, the risk is that these kinds of tensions just build and build, with a catastrophic impact upon, among other things, their sex lives. The key then lies in working skillfully with anger and frustration as soon as they arise, finding reasonable accommodations and compromises, and making sure that every inevitable episode of vexation has a net effect of deepening their trust in each other. That's a tall order, and they don't have to nail it every time! But that is really the key. Either way, that Mars energy is going to grow between them—that's the nature of the eleventh house. Will it be sex or will it be rage? That's the big question, and they answer it a little bit with every passing day.

Naturally, in the darker scenarios, there is a significant chance that the relationship simply blows up before too many seasons have gone by. And if they are getting it wrong, that is probably a blessing for them—not to mention for the neighbors.

In the happier, higher scenario, we can add another piece to the puzzle. Sex pervades life, but sexual expression is different between post-pubescent kids kissing at a birthday party and two seventy-year-olds who've just met and are exploring a relationship. With composite Mars in the eleventh house, there is something about the natural sexual chemistry between these two people that improves with age. Their needs, styles, and appetites between the sheets all tend to converge over time, creating unexpected delights in their later years . . . assuming, of course, that they do their early work around the dance of anger.

COMPOSITE MARS IN THE TWELFTH HOUSE

Many a traditional astrologer would cast a nervous glance at Mars in the twelfth house, viewing it as portending secret enemies, surprise attacks, and injury. That view is unnecessarily grim, although we will integrate it—optionally!—into our evolutionary perspective before we are done. The key here is the realization that edgy, extreme experiences often strip us down to the bones, spiritually speaking. A near-miss in an automobile, for example, can lead a person to think profound thoughts about the ultimate direction and purpose of life. Illness has often brought new, more vigorous existential engagement to someone who survives it. The familiar cliché about there being "no atheists in foxholes" summarizes the point quite succinctly: when the chips are down, we turn to the eternal.

With their composite Mars in the twelfth house, these two people have signed up for a fierce path. Any planet in that house operates much like a guru—whether we like it or not. And Mars is a demanding one, especially if we resist it. That is the critical point: this couple can voluntarily go out and meet the extreme edges, or those edges can come and find them. Volunteering is not only the higher ground; it is also a lot more pleasant. What might that look like? Always, it is about taking chances *based on faith*. Imagine these two people camping on a mountaintop. It's late at night. They are isolated. Various carnivorous beasts lurk in the shadows—and overhead the stars have never looked so transcendentally glorious. They lie on their backs, holding each other, content to know this might be their last night on earth. That phrase is perhaps too dramatic, but it makes the point. The edge of fear, the sense of our smallness and fragility, the brevity of our physical lives in this vast, hard universe—all these forces come together in the perfection of that moment.

And their war-god guru gazes down upon them, respectfully and satisfied.

Of course if they decided they would rather spend their vacation safely in front of the television set, that's when the house catches fire! That's when thieves strike.

The point here is not all about magic moments on mountaintops, although that imagery is quite appropriate. Let's also recognize that there are chances based on faith that we take in the framework of the relationship itself: the scary interpersonal subject we bring up, the confession we make for the sake of keeping the relationship honest, the sexual fantasy or need we overcome embarrassment and fear to express. Those spooky paths can lead us to other kinds of mountaintops as well—and, as we have seen, mountaintops are the safest place in the world for these two souls.

CHAPTER ELEVEN: THE COMPOSITE JUPITER

Jupiter, in the astrological literature, is commonly related to beliefs and to the idea of religion. That's valid, but we have to be careful with the notion or it can mislead us. In the core of the planet's spirit is a quality of sheer exuberance: an enthusiasm for life, and an appetite for it. The terms "beliefs" and "religion" convey a kind of heady, cerebral dryness, like a set of reasoned position papers on the questions of life. And that's not Jupiter! It may be related indirectly to those kinds of attitudes, processes and views. But the direct relationship is with the *emotions* they trigger in us, at least if the attitudes and views are the products of authentic experience. Those emotions are profoundly life-affirming. They are happy. They make us want to clap our hands, laugh until the tears run down and then laugh some more. Jupiter is the part of us that *believes in life*. It's more about the *feeling* we call "faith" than it is about the *intellectual views* we call our "beliefs."

In intimacy, the composite Jupiter has everything to do with the capacity of the couple to have *faith in their union*. It carries the feeling that there is a cosmic, transcendent or theological reason for our being together. And that feeling is absolutely precious when it comes to weathering the hard times love sometimes presents. The simplest illustration would be a traditional marriage between two conventional people, performed under religious auspices—they believe that marriage is a sacrament, that God has brought them together, and that it would be a grievous violation of the laws of the universe for them to fail each other. We might question their belief-system, but that's not the point. The point is the sheer power of those beliefs in terms of keeping their union intact. *And the key is that under Jupiter we see the evolutionary need for an external, transcendent framework which gives meaning and support to the process of loving.*

Where do we find it? How can two people locate such a powerful foundation for this simple faith in their partnership? We look to the position of the composite Jupiter for the answer. In this area of their lives together, the couple must look for signs, omens and miracles. They must expect them. And here's the fun part: they must prime the pump by behaving in a way that is "pleasing unto Lord Jupiter." And, happily, that means blowing it out sometimes. That means investing in themselves. It means taking risks, being wise fools, celebrating. *The great yoga of faith is a willingness to be alive*, to embrace our appetites, and never to settle for anything less than the best. "Let's go to France this summer. We'll pay for it somehow . . . "

Paradoxically, where the composite Jupiter lies is often an area where the couple is vulnerable to short-changing themselves. Under the banners of "realism," "common sense," and "humility," they may fail to sit at Jupiter's feasting table. They may fail to see the possibilities that lie before them. Underlying this self-limiting behavior is a karmic wound—and hence the evolutionary perspective on the configuration. In a prior life together, there was an adaptation to limitation and lack in terms of the sign and house composite Jupiter occupies. A great dose of grayness was swallowed.

And now, the time has come to eat a rainbow.

COMPOSITE JUPITER IN ARIES

Aries is the cosmic Warrior. It is about courage and fire and the kinds of virtues that are forged in flames. With their composite Jupiter in this sign, the bond between these two people grows deeper and stronger when they stand their ground for each other in stressful situations. Like soldiers who have risked their lives for each other, the loyalty that links them can be fierce and lifelong. Iron needs fire in order to become steel, and that is the principle that gives these two faith in their relationship.

At a mechanical level of interpretation, we can safely predict adventures for this couple. Perhaps they share interest in a physical sport. Maybe they play tennis. It is easy to imagine them mountaineering or flying a plane. We can picture them in a sports car, top down and taking a curve with a certain *élan*—and perhaps discussing that interest in speed a few moments later with a traffic cop!

At a more evolutionary and open level of interpretation, it is better to *suggest* those kinds of vigorous activity. These two need adventure. They need edge. Why? Because in order to have faith in their bond, they need to come through for each other. Each one needs to see the other in warrior-glory. That isn't about violence; it's about honor, courage, and steady nerves. The more they take risks together and learn to count on each other, the deeper their love grows.

Not all these shared risks are physical. Composite Jupiter in Aries also manifests positively when one of them takes an emotional risk with the other. In any relationship, there are subjects people are afraid to bring up. Should one take such a risk, it's very helpful if the other partner takes a moment simply to say "Thank you for your courage," before responding to the content. Warriors may be profoundly loyal to each other, willing even to die for each other. But they also need to express respect and dignity toward each other, or their swords will be drawn. And that is the essence of composite Jupiter in Aries—this fire needs to be directed into forging the bond between them, or the relationship will start to look like one of those explosion-a-minute movies they make for pubescent boys.

COMPOSITE JUPITER IN TAURUS

We humans complicate relationships enormously. We have therapists and books and astrological techniques, all to help us do something that penguins and mourning doves do without much apparent intellectual challenge! All the complexities of our psychological lives aside, there is ultimately something very simple about intimacy. And that simplicity is the heart of Taurus. With their composite Jupiter there, this couple's ability to have faith in their love depends upon tapping into it.

Let's boil human sexual love down to its bones. First, there are three items on the sexual menu: celibacy, endless dating, or trying to make a relationship work. Any permanent takers for choices one or two? We didn't think so. That leaves choice three. So how do we do it? Choose someone who "smells right"—you've got to trust your instincts. Be kind to each other. Accept each others' imperfections. Make love. Go ahead and entangle your lives. Fight when you need to, and always forgive each other. Share a home once you've danced around each other successfully for a year or so. It's chicken-soup simple.

Well, if it were *really* that simple, we wouldn't be writing these words! But for this couple with their composite Jupiter in Taurus, the more they can take that grounded, instinctual attitude toward their bond, the deeper their faith in it grows. They need to feel that animal-instinct of rightness about their relationship. How can they maximize that? Always, the answer lies in simple things. It is enormously beneficial for them to make time to just hold each other: touch is elemental to Taurus, as is the simple, physical comfort of familiar intimacy. Eating long, slow delicious meals together helps. So does spending time in nature, away from the mental complications of urban life. One of the wisest moves they can make is to invite animal-friends into their relationship: they need cats or dogs or horses to help keep them aware of what is really, ultimately important. Their home needs to reflect these Taurean values too. Expensive luxuries may be part of it: a hot tub, a king-size bed, a sensual sofa upon which to flop. But spending money isn't the issue; most of us can actually relax a lot more naturally and effectively at home than in an expensive hotel. And with composite Jupiter in Taurus, that relaxation is the heart of the process. In calm, in simplicity, in naturalness, their love shines through.

COMPOSITE JUPITER IN GEMINI

Good communication skills are the foundation of any healthy relationship. That insight isn't going to win any prizes, of course! Everyone with an IQ above the price of dinner for two has said it a million times. Gemini is the sign of language, and so with their composite Jupiter there, it's easy for us to roll out clichés about the importance of talking everything out. With these two people, that's a truth—and maybe a "truer truth" for them than for couples in general. But it's still beside the point. The real point is that a witty, fascinating meeting of two intelligences is the heart of what gives them faith in their bond. To believe in themselves as a couple, they need laughter and verbal play. And they are probably good at it! They also need to *interest* each other consistently. If one of them has a wild idea, it's a delight to get it on the table. Even if it's completely wrongheaded, just the sheer zaniness and novelty can trigger speculation, new insight, lively exchanges—the soul of composite Jupiter in Gemini. It follows that each of them feeds their relationship when they independently feed their own minds. One of them may have a nose in a book or magazine and not be saying anything. That's just gathering grist for the mill. Give it a little while and that new information will be drawing interest in the endless dialog.

Gemini is easily bored. With composite Jupiter in Gemini, there is a risk of the relationship feeling predictable and stultifying, given the reality that after a while two people have heard each other's stories a few times. What gets our merry couple through that challenge is not patient, stoic endurance—it's the quest for more amazement and wonder. When in doubt, they need to attend a lecture together. Or go to a new restaurant. Or plan a trip to somewhere they've never been. Or look through a telescope. *Life* is not inherently boring. Relationships get boring because people do—and a sad truth is that people in relationships often settle into predictable, dull patterns that single people wisely avoid. If these two let that happen, they're risking losing touch with the basis of believing in themselves as a couple.

One final note: with composite Jupiter in Gemini, our two heroes need to be very wary of television, the Internet, and similar media. Certainly, they can be wonderful sources of stimulating ideas, and thus they flow naturally into everything this configuration needs and wants. The danger is the way those kinds of media can be isolating and soporific; the key here is mental engagement *with each other*—not just private sensory stimuli.

COMPOSITE JUPITER IN CANCER

Go to the movies and there's plenty of sex. But when was the last time you saw a juicy kissing scene between two people who'd known each other longer than a week or two? We romanticize the process of falling in love, but as a culture we seem to ignore it beyond the horizon of a brief affair. That's sad, because there is potentially a lot more love—and, actually, even better sex—a little further down the road, if we survive its many potholes! Celebrating this idea is the heart of understanding what sustains a couple with their composite Jupiter in Cancer.

Cancer is about home and hearth. It's about the deep, sweet familiarity that can arise between two people who've truly gone beyond courtship into the more profound territory of being bonded to each other. It's about a nurturing feeling of comfort that those two movie-lovers might glimpse after a year or two, if they survive the bumps. With composite Jupiter in Cancer, these two can draw tremendous faith in their love from experiencing that kind of commitment.

It can't be rushed. When we see this configuration in the charts of new lovers, we know that the stakes are high. There is nothing casual about this relationship—or, better said, if it is casual it will also be brief. And that's fine. In either case, they should savor the processes of getting to know each other and of coming to trust and appreciate each other. Passion is fast, but Cancer-bonding is patient and slow. The first time they sit quietly together, comfortable and connected despite having nothing to say, they've passed the first hurdle.

After a while, with composite Jupiter in Cancer, finding a *home* together will become pivotally important. It need not be fancy or expensive, but it does need to be a safe, nurturing kind of Hobbit-hole. Ideally, it will have the kind of kitchen that naturally draws people to congregate there. And the bedroom needs soft light and a sense of being separate from the buzzing world. Once this archetypal Cancerian reality starts to take hold, these two will increasingly feel the joy and freedom that come with safety and security in a relationship. Within that context, sexuality can blossom into the kind of natural tenderness and comfort they never show in the movies.

Given a little while, another Cancer territory will open up for our heroes, one that can further cement their ability to feel the rightness of their bond: nurturing others. Children are a natural expression of this energy, but we can also see their urge to care for other beings manifesting with a lucky menagerie of pets they gather—or broken-hearted friends sipping tea in that famous, mellow, consoling kitchen of theirs.

COMPOSITE JUPITER IN LEO

Leo is a performer. Even if it's shy, it needs some applause. Jupiter is about a couple having faith in themselves as a unit and simply feeling happy about being in the relationship. With composite Jupiter in Leo, we add two and two and realize that this couple needs to *strut* a bit. They need other people to believe in them. They need to look good to their community and they need to hear about it.

All this could make these two sound incredibly shallow! Why isn't their own faith in themselves sufficient? To answer that question, we really need to get past our cultural obsession with steely-eyed self-sufficiency. Watch a musician or a comedian blossom on stage when the audience is enthusiastic. Or watch a lover light up in your own bed when you've helped him or her feel beautiful and appreciated. None of us are really islands, whatever our pretenses. A movie couple may thrive on an attitude of "you and me against the world." But that feeling isn't really very likely to last in reality. If all our friends believe we're dating a dork, it takes a toll.

But what if everyone we love and trust believes that we've found a match made in heaven? That we've found the person with whom we are *supposed* to be? How precious that is! And this brings us right to the heart of composite Jupiter in Leo: these two benefit enormously from being seen in a supportive way. Part of the energy that sustains them must arise from outside their relationship, in the hearts and minds of their community.

How can they invoke that kind of support? Start by asking yourself what qualities might distinguish a "lucky couple." Those are the answers. They are kind and attentive to each other in public, always treating each other with respect and affection. They compliment each other. They often behave as if they've just met and are falling in love: they dress up. They are seen engaged in private conversation in restaurants. They attend cultural events together. They hold hands. They dance. Their relationship progresses through the natural escalation of commitment and life-sharing that unfolds as people love more deeply.

Any of those behaviors can be faked, of course. But why? Should a couple with composite Jupiter in Leo come to a place where it's just bad theater, they should probably part. But if those kinds of emotions are sincere, they need to recognize that expressing them publicly produces an outpouring of energy from their community—and, like a rocket booster, that energy can carry them into deeper joy, pleasure, and faith.

COMPOSITE JUPITER IN VIRGO

People in stable relationships live longer, healthier lives than singles do. Why? Some of it is probably simply a greater level of happiness. And love is very high on everyone's list of reasons to live. Most of us have discovered that it's harder to get motivated to prepare a healthy meal if we're eating alone. That probably has something to do with it too. No matter what the nature of our composite chart, these observations reflect reality. But for this couple with their composite Jupiter in Virgo, they take on great force. Virgo is linked to all the routines that help us maintain our well-being. For these two, a lot of joy and faith in their bond comes from fully appreciating *how much better their bodies feel* as a result of their love.

Noticing the better physical feeling is only the first step. With their composite Jupiter in Virgo, these two benefit enormously from actively pursuing a healthier style of living: to commit to eating a more conscious diet, to exercising together, to reducing stress. And to supporting each other in those regimens: we all know it's easier, for example, to exercise consistently if we have a buddy helping us remember to do it. Such changes bring many unintended, indirect gifts in terms of enlisting the partners' bodies in the belief that this relationship is good for them.

Even physical health is partly the result of mental and spiritual attitudes. Many are the magnificent gym-rats who are as insane as drunken Senators! In the long run, mental health counts too—for our daily well-being as well as our longevity. People in relationships generally report greater levels of happiness than do single people, but most of us can affirm that love has also brought us our worst moments too. There's nothing more dispiriting than a bad relationship. With their composite Jupiter in Virgo, these two need to practice good "relationship hygiene" along with their improved physical habits. What are the *routines* that support a thriving relationship? For each couple, the answers are probably somewhat different, but we can offer a few guidelines. Everyone is too busy nowadays; that takes a toll on love. An example of a healthy relationship routine is to establish a regular hour or two of intimate time—the answering machine is on, the time is sacred and special and protected. Anniversaries are remembered and celebrated. Certain restaurants or vacation spots are visited regularly, and woven into the mythology of the bond. Sex is rarely allowed to become perfunctory; time is taken so it can sustain the relationship rather than simply providing the release of a physical tension. Shared quiet, meditative time, perhaps within the context of a spiritual practice, is integrated into the weekly or daily cycle of events.

As these healthy mental habits synergize the life-affirming physical advantages of intimacy, the joy and meaning of this relationship enters the cells and synapses of this couple. Their composite Jupiter in Virgo is offering its merry gift.

COMPOSITE JUPITER IN LIBRA

Here are some joyful Libran concepts: soulmates, a marriage made in heaven, two people who are *supposed to* be together. And the all-time classic: "they lived happily ever after." Try them on. Try to do it innocently, without cynicism, without looking for any tricks. Sometimes love works out *great* for people. Sometimes it's the sweetest thing in the world.

For the couple with composite Jupiter in Libra, the evolutionary challenge lies in believing that those happy notions can have direct relevance to them. *They need to make a myth of their love.* And then they need to do their best to live that myth. To modern ears, this might sound dangerously unrealistic. We all know nowadays how hard love can be, how many broken hearts there are in this lonely world. For the couple with this configuration, there is room for all those painful truths. They can be annoyed and frustrated with each other; they can fail and disappoint each other. But everything painful is interpreted in the context of this overriding faith in the goodness and rightness of their love.

It's a tall order, but composite Jupiter in Libra supplies a method for getting it right. That method is centered on an exuberant, extravagant claiming of *all things Libran* in the relationship. One of the core principles in this sign is *aesthetic* and *artistic* experience. Let's start with that. The ballet is coming to town. It's expensive of course—so let's get front row seats! And, sweetie, you've got some beautiful clothes, but why don't you surprise me by wearing something new and special that night? Money is no object—why do you think God made the VISA card?

The last few lines sound fun, but slightly silly. And yet they represent a very pure distillation of Jupiter's over-the-top embracing of life in the context of the natural Libran attraction to all things civilized, elegant, and lovely. What might it mean to a couple to have an evening exactly as described? Might it not profoundly enhance their sense that there is something magical and special about their love, that it has roots in a higher world than this mundane one? Just watch them reach for each other's hands as the ballerina pirouettes across center stage.

Extending our imagery, we recognize the importance of the couple's prioritizing the beauty of their home—and that has as much to do with getting rid of yesterday's newspaper as it does with spending serious money on decorating or art. We see the pivotal role played by that other bulwark of Libran consciousness: *courtesy*. Intimacy always has its rough edges, but two people can still treat each other with at least the same dignity and respect they would afford a stranger. A "please," a "thank you," and an "excuse me" don't make a relationship stiff or uptight. They just make it civilized.

All these methods we've described draw their significance from the larger meaning of the Libran composite Jupiter: they enhance and support the notion that this precious love is higher than the world. And that feeds back directly into faith and happiness.

COMPOSITE JUPITER IN SCORPIO

Scorpio, in any relationship context, is always about the exchange of strong energies. With Jupiter there in the composite chart, for these two people such exchanges are the soul of their faith in themselves as a couple. So what exactly do we mean by "strong energies?"

Right at the top of list is sexual heat. Very likely, these two are blessed in that department. Adults enjoy sex: that's a fairly reliable principle. But for some couples it comes more naturally than for others. Certain people "fit" better than others—physically, but also in terms of erotic tastes and styles. Often the initial burst of passion that characterizes the beginning of most relationships obscures underlying dysfunctions and incompatibilities. What we are looking at here, everything else being equal, is a solid foundation for *lasting passion*. And if two people still *want* each other after a year or more has passed, they've got something precious: a basis for a fire that won't fade. It's far easier for such a couple to believe viscerally in the innate rightness of their connection than it is for a couple who've lost that lovin' feeling, however committed they may be to each other in principle.

There are strong energies other than sex, and they are part of the composite Jupiter in Scorpio picture too. It's fine when people "officially" love each other, but there's something very intense and real about looking straight into a partner's eyes and saying the words. In some ways, it's even hotter if no words are said at all—just stark naked humanity staring back at you.

Relationships always stir up darker layers of the psychic stew, and facing that material is part of having composite Jupiter in Scorpio as well. Only masochists like to fight, but accepting that conflict is part of intimacy is only realistic. Having this configuration doesn't suggest that these two people enjoy bashing each other! But it does suggest that they can take a very legitimate and healthy pride in their ability to be honest with each other, and to face the dark together. In the short run, those Scorpio skills are about having faith in the bond—but in the long run, they're also about joy and happiness, since nothing leaches those qualities out of a relationship faster than harbored resentments.

All of these processes, from sex to deep levels of psychic communion, require time, privacy, and peace. The more these two lovers with their composite Jupiter in Scorpio provide themselves with those three treasures, the more primordial their bond will grow. Given time, they will be as inseparable as a pair of mourning doves: mated, down to their cells, at the instinctual level.

COMPOSITE JUPITER IN SAGITTARIUS

Jupiter, in the old traditions, was a fortunate planet. Sagittarius was its favorite sign. So the combination was a lucky one. We can say deeper things than that about our couple with their composite Jupiter in Sagittarius, but simple luck is a real phenomenon. We'd be remiss if we didn't suggest that these two should enter contests! Their composite Jupiter supports their winning more often than chance would imply. And "contests" are really just a metaphor for other gambles life offers—many of them with far better odds than the typical lottery. For example, we might imagine these two deciding that they are tired of living in Arkansas and that they want to try their luck in a big city. Their friends are full of baleful predictions—within a month, they'll be living behind a smelly dumpster drinking cheap wine out of paper bags. And in fact, as a result of their bold geographic gamble, they wind up prosperous, glamorous and happy.

Behind this silly image is a basic principle of the universe: *life rewards faith.* And that is essence of Jupiter in Sagittarius. This is the part of the Infinite that doesn't want any of us to lead ordinary lives. With their composite Jupiter in this sign, for these two to maintain faith in their bond, they need to stretch beyond the confines of the predictable and the safe. They need bigness in their experience—and it's theirs by divine right, if they are bold enough to reach for it.

One way to prime the pump is travel. Nothing pleases Sagittarius like a place it's never seen before. It's the part of us that loves to see the sun rising over the open highway. Should these two fall into a bare patch on love's road, it would be helpful for them to plan a trip. Just to get away from their familiar scene will help them break free of their familiar patterns of conflict or frustration with each other. Returning from a trip, especially one that takes us out of our own country, we feel a little more dashing and colorful. We stand taller and our eyes are brighter. We feel more confident that strangers will find us interesting. We've done something unusual; that gives us points in the social calculus. For this couple, those attitudes translate into more faith that their relationship is something special. And that is the essence of Jupiter's gift: faith in their bond.

Having composite Jupiter in Sagittarius generally correlates with a rather philosophical spirit in a relationship. We have to be careful with that word, though—it doesn't mean they watch the world from an ivory tower. What it does suggest is that they are inclined to think together at the level of principle: to have serious discussions about what is right and what is wrong. There is also a compelling desire to learn. By the time they're old, they will know a lot of things that don't make them money. And that too is part of the river of joy that flows into the ocean of their love.

COMPOSITE JUPITER IN CAPRICORN

Partners who've loved each deeply for thirty years meet their youngest child's fiancé. The young couple is well-matched, but both of them are a little breathless about their relationship. They are certain their marriage will be perfect. They are the luckiest people in the world. Before them lies a future out of a fairytale—bright, flowing and untroubled. The older couple smiles a lot—a bit mysteriously from the perspective of the younger duo. Having been down the road of life, the older partners have a clearer sense of the nature of love's alchemy. They know it is far harder than the young ones imagine, and better too.

A couple with their composite Jupiter in Capricorn, whatever their age, has a lot of common ground with the older couple. There is something *tempered* and *mature* about this bond. It's as if, right from the beginning, they can see themselves with some of the wisdom that thirty years of love can create. Right from their first meeting, they've got their eyes on the long term perspective.

When we meet someone new and the chemistry feels right, we want to break out in song. We can't wait to see each other. It's a thoroughly wonderful condition. But imagine our older couple celebrating their thirtieth anniversary together—and add to the equations the idea that they still truly love each other and aren't staying together for dull reasons of a social or practical nature. What do they feel? A lot of emotions, but the one toward which we want to direct your attention now is *pride*. It is an *accomplishment* to make love work for that long. That's why we say "congratulations" at such a time. With their composite Jupiter in Capricorn, these two people draw faith in their relationship from those sorts of feelings. Thus, anniversaries are particularly important to them. It would be a waste not to celebrate them seriously.

Long before there are any anniversaries, couples go through formal stages of escalation in their level of commitment: Capricorn soul-food! An agreement to be exclusively committed to each other. An engagement, in some form. Buying a home together. Starting a family. In all cases, again the social custom is to offer our congratulations—and that's because the couple has navigated another milestone. For Capricorn, such milestones are the basis of dignity and self-respect.

Thus, for this couple, the basis of lasting faith in their bond lies in endlessly building it. The bigger their collection of milestones, the more they will believe in themselves and the more precious their bond will feel to them.

COMPOSITE JUPITER IN AQUARIUS

There's a rebel pride in breaking the rules. That's the soul of a composite Jupiter in Aquarius. For this couple, the road before them is one less-traveled. They need to celebrate everything that distinguishes them from other people's expectations. Cultures always have scripts for couples. After a certain amount of time, commitment or breakup is expected. Heterosexual marriages are expected to produce children. Monogamy, financial planning, relations with the in-laws—it's all down pat in the unwritten cultural rulebook. Different subgroups frame the details in their own unique way—what is expected of a couple in the Young Republicans club is not exactly the same as what's expected among rock music's night people. But the principle stands: relationships are not nearly the private, personal business we pretend they are. They are a cultural transaction, governed by custom.

For a couple with the composite Jupiter in Aquarius, those rules are made to be broken. The hook is that to break them you have to recognize them. And that's not always easy, since they've been with us about as long as gravity has. We've internalized those assumptions, so the real battle is within the individuals, and only later does it manifest as an outward battle against those who might judge them as "weird."

For these two people, the basis of their dignity and faith in themselves as a unit depends on their exercising a kind of creativity few people even imagine. If it's a man and a woman, maybe the woman works and man is a house-husband. Maybe they blow off solid careers in order to go live in the south of France for a year. Maybe they've got a sensory deprivation tank in their house. Maybe they commit to handling all their arguments by email, never speaking face to face in anger. Maybe they paint their living room chartreuse.

Quirks? Yes indeed! But they are *symbolic* quirks that defend their elemental right to navigate the eternal questions of intimacy in their own unique way.

Most couples sooner or later celebrate their commitment to each other. It may be a marriage ceremony in the legal sense, or it may be less formal. In any case, it's an ancient social instinct—to stand before the community and speak the words of a vow. For a couple with composite Jupiter in Aquarius, a very effective barometer of their psychological health as a couple is just how "weird" that ceremony is! The point isn't simply to shock people—that's easy to do, and doesn't really take much individuality. The point is that they've made this most primal expression of their love for each other something uniquely their own. That would be a most excellent omen for their future happiness.

COMPOSITE JUPITER IN PISCES

Unless we're Marxists or existentialists, marriages and commitment ceremonies generally involve prayer, meditation and references to the Divinity. It's an old, almost universal, human instinct. No matter what our cultural orientation, something inside us all senses that we need cosmic help if we are going to make a success of such a difficult undertaking. We also sense that beneath the practical, procreative and sexual dimensions of human love, something deeper is going on: two *souls* have entered into an evolutionary contract with each other. These are mysterious parts of life: the open secret that everyone knows and no one can really say—although we pay various kinds of priests to take a stab at phrasing it for us. With their composite Jupiter in Pisces, this couple has an inside track regarding those soul-sustaining points of contact with the next dimension. Their ability to believe in themselves hinges upon their using those contacts.

They've almost surely had experiences of psychic communication—maybe one of them sits bolt upright in the bed at the moment the other one has an automobile accident on the other side of the country. Or, more simply, one brings up the idea of going to a certain movie two seconds after the same thought enters the other one's head.

Probably, right at the beginning of their time together, there were omens—visitations from the angelic realm. What we mean by that is the idea that miracles of "chance" seemed to conspire to bring them together. The universe bent over backwards to introduce them. Eerie parallels have existed in their lives. Everything seemed to be pointing to the idea that they had some kind of soul-business together.

Those early miracles are a gift from the angels. The deeper point is that those miracles don't have to stop, but sustaining them requires some effort and openness on both of their parts. After the grace that comes at the beginning of their bond, they've got to work at being receptive. Some of that lies in being in the right places. Even if they have no formal religious feelings, how beautiful it is for these two people to sit quietly in a cathedral together! How much it feeds their souls to stand alone together in a canyon that was sacred to Native Americans a thousand years before the Europeans came. How sweet it is for them to say a simple grace before a meal. As they cultivate this welcome to the Divinity, they experience a deeper sense of the spiritual basis of their intimacy.

And that is the essence of composite Jupiter in Pisces: the basis of their believing in themselves as a couple lies in their believing that their souls are in communion and that some Higher Power is engaged with their process of loving each other.

COMPOSITE JUPITER IN THE FIRST HOUSE

There is a magnetic, happy energy around these two. When they RSVP their regrets about a party, the hosts are crestfallen—they know the party isn't going to be as much fun as they'd hoped it would be. It's not necessarily that this couple is always on an extraverted roll; whether they are shy or ebullient is really more a question about their individual birthcharts. But, quiet or loud, with their composite Jupiter in the first house, an expansive, generous energy radiates from them. People feel affirmed and accepted. They feel looser simply because these two are present, as if anything they are likely to do is going to be fine.

Furthermore, this positive vibration extends to people's interpretations of the couple's own relationship: unless they're screaming bloody-minded murder at each other and covered in bruises, the community around them tends to imagine that they are a happy couple, and that they don't have any problems. One result is that they are likely to be drawn into leadership positions, either overtly, or covertly as tone-setters for a group. This generous interpretation of their relationship can actually isolate them from support. Carrying a tribal ideal can render the people behind it invisible—just as we might feel sorry for a beleaguered movie star signing autographs, surrounded by fans.

None of this is meant to imply that these two have *more* than their fair share of intimate issues—only that the people who can really see them with insight and compassion are particularly rare and precious to them. Calling any of this "good luck" seems a bit one-dimensional from the human perspective, even though that is the traditional reading of this position for

Jupiter. And indeed, a trip to Las Vegas might prove lucrative for them! The traditional reading is not entirely wrong, just not very deep.

Going into the deeper waters of the evolutionary perspective, Jupiter always asks us, "Why not the best?" The challenge for this couple with their composite Jupiter in the first house lies in living up to their own legend. Mere appearances are insufficient. The aim here is really to live the ideal of an enviable, delightful intimate bond. The rest of their composite chart will describe the psychological and spiritual challenges they must face and meet in order to get there. Jupiter simply invites them to settle for nothing less—to ask each other, not for the impossible, but for *the best they have to offer*. To press constantly toward the higher ground. Paradoxically, to use hope—and hope's constant companion, discontent—as a goad toward constant improvement. On that path, they'll have plenty of "luck." The right teachers appear at the right moments, money is available when it is needed, and so on—but only if they are actually on that path.

If they are going to receive, they have to ask.

COMPOSITE JUPITER IN THE SECOND HOUSE

A simple reading of composite Jupiter in the traditional house of money suggests prosperity. Often that's an accurate prediction, provided we're careful not to go over the top with the idea. It doesn't guarantee a Lifestyle of the Rich and Famous, but it does imply that, together, these two are an effective money-making team. If they set their minds to it, they can create abundance—and not all of their success in the pocketbook department comes from hard work and sound planning, although those are probably necessary ingredients. But the universe seems eager to provide "matching funds" as well. Most people would read that as simple luck. They'll tend to buy the right stocks. The value of their house will double overnight. Obscure relatives die and leave them automobiles.

Underlying these merry outward predictions is an evolutionary drama. The real meaning of the second house is self-confidence. Having a few dollars in our wallets definitely helps us feel more capable of dealing with life, but money is actually only a small part of it. The real issues are more psychological. Above all, with their composite Jupiter in the second house, these two are learning *to believe in their relationship.* For the bond to work—and for that money-magic to start flowing—they've got to trust one core idea: that *they are good together.*

What if they aren't? That's a fair question. Lots of people become attracted to each other for perfectly honorable reasons and later learn that the deeper harmonies just aren't there. There's no shame in that. Having Jupiter in the second house doesn't promise a good relationship. It only tells us that for the bond to prosper, it must trust itself, invest in itself, and take some risks.

Jupiter loves bigness. It loves extravagance. It is attracted to bold moves, gambles and bright dreams. On a positive track, the manifestations of composite Jupiter in the second might start early: for their first night out together, these two hit a very expensive restaurant. Subliminally, they are sending their inner selves a strong message: this relationship is significant; it's *worth money*; it's important. As the wheels turn, perhaps they take a fancy vacation and put it on a VISA card. It's not irresponsible; they just realized that they needed the message: trust this bond. Feed it, support it. Later, we might find them hitting a bumpy patch in their courtship. They decide to go into couples therapy. Why? Because they believe the relationship is worth it!

So often these two find themselves facing that basic second house equation: in our modern world, money and self-esteem are completely entangled. If they doubt themselves, they'll probably create poverty for themselves—even if they have money in the bank. That poverty will be not only financial. Conversely, if they invest in themselves, the money flows, and their faith in themselves as a couple grows.

COMPOSITE JUPITER IN THE THIRD HOUSE

Listening to these two play off each other verbally is better than the movies. They trigger word-play in each other, bringing out humor and a contagious energy of fun. They are probably cuter and funnier than they know. It's not all about jokes, although they are probably skilled at making people laugh. Together, they're able to encourage and inspire, and not only to get ideas across, but also to *generate enthusiasm* for those ideas. They can, in other words, be very convincing. They could write political speeches or be evangelists—or sell used cars to Mahi-Mahi off the Hawaiian coast.

Jupiter brings a gift from the gods, and in the third house it's at least partly the gift of gab. Since we're talking about a composite chart, we need to remember that this quality arises between these two people. Individually, they may or may not have much of it themselves—obviously, if the potential is in their individual makeups as well, stand back. But even if these two are relatively silent or inarticulate as separate people, when they get together, they have something to say and an ability to say it well. Tweaking this concept a bit, let's recognize that some people who can speak in complete sentences and know a lot of impressive vocabulary are actually boring and unconvincing, while an actor like Robert DeNiro can say "huh" and make it persuasive and eloquent. There is a slippery art to effective communication, and these two bring it out in each other.

Just making people laugh is a gift to us all in this harried world. But with their composite Jupiter in the third, this couple can go further than that. It's easy to imagine them team-teaching, for example. Maybe one writes a letter to the editor about some issue that concerns them both deeply. The other one edits the letter—and the result is ten times more effective.

Within the secret world of the relationship, communication skills are their ace in the hole. Being able to speak and listen to each other effectively is one of the fundamental keys to helping a bond thrive. Again, that is not always about grandstanding eloquence—the art here is more subtle, and it's at least half about knowing when to say nothing and simply listen. These two have an instinct for those rhythms with each other. If they develop them consciously, they become a treasure.

The only caution here is that, with their composite Jupiter in the third house, this couple needs to recognize that fancy, complicated or comedic words can become a barrier between souls if overdone. We can hide behind endless talk. Or we can express our souls through it. That is their choice.

COMPOSITE JUPITER IN THE FOURTH HOUSE

Home and hearth—that's fourth house territory. With composite Jupiter there, the traditional view promises good fortune for those two people in that department. Some astrologers might predict something as a simple as a "nice house." That prophecy often proves accurate with this configuration. There is a definite tendency for a couple to luck out wherever Jupiter lies in their composite chart, and these two can almost count on fortune smiling on them in the real estate department. They attract good deals on desirable places to live. If they ever buy a place, they'll likely find themselves in that happy paradox: if they sold it, they could make lots of money—but they love it too much to sell it.

The fourth house goes way beyond real estate, however. A happy home is more than an attractive building. Home is a feeling created by familiarity, commitment and stability shared by creatures who love each other. Domestic life promises to unfold sweetly for these two. Whatever else is happening in their relationship, they probably have the blessing of simply being able to live together well. Even early in the relationship, a "family" feeling arises naturally between them. They seem to know each other more broadly and subtly than their time together would seem to allow.

These good feelings can be fed and supported. First, we recognize that, for most of us, the budget is full of tough trade-offs. If we want to take an international trip every year or two, maybe that's possible—but only if we live more cheaply between journeys. For these two, *prioritizing their home* is always a good choice. They should go ahead and spend the money on a place they really love, even if that means tighter constraints in other areas. For them, this is a smart compromise. It pays off in joy. Similarly, they might tighten their belts for a few years, trying to amass a pile of money so they can buy their dream house. Again, that's a wise choice. It might not be that for every couple, but for them, it definitely is the right use of resources.

One of the natural joys of domestic life, for many of us, is children. Kids may be a reality for these two and bring them lots of happiness—but not all relationships are suited for children. That's fine—then they need a couple of cats! Or dogs or horses or kinkajous. The point is that these two **deepen** their joy together and their faith in their bond when they are nurturing other beings in their home: that's basic to the fourth house alchemy.

Jupiter nurtures people in less formal ways too. We envision parties here: their house full of dear friends, with laughter and food and music playing, and everyone feeling as if they are eating at the table of the King—and, archetypally, they are.

COMPOSITE JUPITER IN THE FIFTH HOUSE

What if two people agree to fall in love forever? Not to *be* in love forever, although that's part of it. Really to *fall* in love forever . . . endless falling. An endless beginning. The idea sounds hopelessly unrealistic, but if any two people can pull it off, it's these two. With their composite Jupiter in the traditional house of love affairs, there is a feeling of celebration, discovery, and freshness about this relationship. The expansive, buoyant, hopeful energy of Jupiter is a heady catalyst for the playful, erotic spirit of the fifth house. Put the two together, and it spells F-U-N.

Notice how lightweight that statement seems? But fun is a profoundly serious need. Most of us have been in relationships, or phases in relationships, where nothing looks better to us than our partner's walking out the door. Most of us have known times when relationship equaled pain and vexation. Down that road, we reach a place where we don't hope for anything or expect anything. Our hearts become closed and defended. Why? Because pain has outweighed joy and pleasure by too wide a margin.

Press this reasoning in the other direction, and you reach the heart of a fifth house composite Jupiter. Say we have plenty of fun, joy and pleasure in a relationship. What are its effects? We open like flowers. We expect joy, so we drop our defenses. These two have the ability to stay in that Edenic state longer than most of us, and, even better, return to it at will.

New lovers feel this openness deeply. Some of it may be illusion—hormones and clear vision are opposites much of the time. But in that glorious, trusting innocence, we also *bond* with each other. There's a happy, easy feeling of "sweet surrender." Souls touch more deeply, without the frightened ego getting in the way, setting conditions and planning escape routes. This is the foundation upon which mature love must be built.

The evolutionary task these two people have taken on, with composite Jupiter in the fifth house, is to practice the discipline of creating, exploring, and exploiting that pleasure-bond. How? By continuing to do what nearly every couple does automatically for the first few weeks: pay attention to each other, express interest in each other, open up their own hearts and share. The process is helped along by simple sweet nothings—bringing each other flowers, remembering birthdays and anniversaries, eating dinner by candlelight, saying "I love you." Perhaps above all it is helped by remembering that sex is a gift to celebrated, not a right to be claimed or a bodily function to be serviced.

This wonderful, warm pattern is available to these two. If they commit consciously to sustaining it, they'll bridge across love's darker challenges with a lot more ease than most of us.

What if they don't? What's the dark side of composite Jupiter in the Fifth House? If they don't find that joy in each other, they'll try to make up the deficit in other ways, some of which may be destructive, such as the abuse of food or mind-altering substances—or just plain dumb, such as spending a lifetime keeping an eye on their TV to make sure it doesn't run away.

COMPOSITE JUPITER IN THE SIXTH HOUSE

Jupiter is playful and expansive, and the sixth house is about duties and responsibilities. Right away, we know that we are talking about a difficult pair of energies to combine. When we think of work, we don't automatically free-associate to fun and games. Start by recognizing that in the sixth house, we're looking at everything we "have" to do. The daily grind of making a living is part of it, but so is the rest of the life-sustaining daily grind: shopping, cooking, keeping the house in a sufficiently hygienic state to be consistent with longevity, and so on. Call it all work.

So, *can* work be pleasurable? Of course. With their composite Jupiter in the sixth house, that is the task that lies before this couple: making their duties as much fun as possible. The stakes are high because, should they fail, expansive Jupiter will fill them with a burdened feeling that this relationship is turning into a forced labor camp, with duties proliferating and joy eroding.

Sometimes we find kinds of work that are inherently rewarding, usually because we happen to be interested in them and are good at them. Perhaps one person enjoys cooking. Rather than "dividing the cooking responsibilities fairly," let that be his or her task then—and the partner can do the gardening or the shopping, if he or she gets some pleasure from those activities. Maybe they both dread housecleaning, so they team up to do it, put on some rock 'n' roll, and reward themselves with a fancy dinner in town. Much of it comes down to responding creatively to the fact that, while our daily duties aren't ever going to make our socks go up and down, with a little imagination and forethought, two people can adapt to them in merrier ways.

Always with the sixth house, we need to be on the lookout for mentors—people, usually a little older than ourselves, who have gone further down the road we're traveling and can maybe teach us a few hard-won tricks. With their composite Jupiter there, these two are likely to find other couples who've come up with low-impact ways of sharing the practical side of life. How to recognize these mentors? By their smiles.

COMPOSITE JUPITER IN THE SEVENTH HOUSE

At first glance we might get quite merry contemplating this configuration—don't worry, we're not going to say that the opposite is true! We're looking at "lucky" Jupiter in the house of relationships. Who could ask for more? But remember that the composite chart *itself* is about the relationship—the whole chart, not just the seventh house. In this context, the seventh house means the relationships that this couple has with other people. In simple terms, they'll probably be fortunate there, and that positive support will feed back helpfully into their own connection.

Think about the psychology of a wedding ceremony. In a nutshell, we get everyone we know and love together, then bribe them with champagne and free food in order to get them to express belief in us as a couple, and to offer signs of encouragement and faith in us. It's perhaps a cynical view, but it's not far off the mark psychologically. And it's a sweet process when we open our hearts to it. Relationships are scary and difficult. How wonderful it is to have some encouragement! How valuable it is to have people who believe in us! That is what Jupiter is about: faith, encouragement, affirmation. With their composite Jupiter in the seventh house, these two need friends who give them that boost. In evolutionary terms, this is the part of the chart that tells us about the people whose input, support and help we simply must have. They see things we don't see. They have skills we lack. This couple has such friends. Their task is to enjoy them and be vulnerable to them.

Perhaps an opportunity to take a lucrative job in a distant city arises. Is it worth leaving the friendships they have deepened and cultivated over the years in their own community? This is a serious question. Most of us are under a lot of time pressure nowadays. What happens if, in order to conserve time, these two decide to spend less time with the people they love? Very soon, their faith in their own relationship could begin to dwindle.

Who are these dear souls? Some may be individuals. Some may be other couples. All radiate warmth and an attitude of unconditional support for the bond that this couple is trying to maintain. They smile and laugh easily. Consistent with the nature of Jupiter, many of these people will have manifested considerable success. Perhaps they have money. Perhaps they have respect or name recognition in their communities. Very probably, they are successful in that deeper sense: they are happy people. They have a good relationship with life. And it's catching.

COMPOSITE JUPITER IN THE EIGHTH HOUSE

Given modern western society's social customs, most adults have had sexual contact with at least a few people. It's safe to say that not all of those relationships worked out in the long run. No need even to lament that fact. Exploration, breadth of experience, spreading our wings a bit in youth or in the aftermath of a major break-up are significant rites of passage for most of us. That kind of sexual expression has a place in life, but has almost nothing to do with eighth house realities. Here, we go for the gold—deep, instinctually-based bonding with another person. Mating. Nothing less.

A couple with composite Jupiter in the eighth has some aces in the hole in that department. There is an excellent chance that they're blessed, at least initially, with a robust physical enthusiasm for each other. They carry a kind of affirmation of looseness, of ease in the body and, particularly in bed, of a natural appetite to receive what each would most naturally give. There's an undercurrent of good humor to their lovemaking—not a joking attitude, but a smiling appreciation of the convergence of the sublime and the ridiculous in human sexuality. All this comes together to produce a powerful support for the mating and bonding processes.

Where are the challenges? They lie in actually using this merry tool for its evolutionary purpose, which is to build an epochal sexual bond—to feast in a hall of those pagan gods and goddesses whom many prim modern people mistake for pornography.

The method with composite Jupiter always lies in investing extravagantly in the relationship—giving it what it wants, regardless of cost or practicality. With Jupiter in the eighth, we might start by asking ourselves, "What do lovers want?" The answer generally boils down to rather simple requirements: privacy; a safe, comfortable place to be together; and above all, *time*. For lovers, hours go by as if they were minutes. That's almost a cliché, because it's such a universal experience. For the couple with composite Jupiter in the eighth, it's imperative to claim enough time together. That might mean taking a weekend away from their responsibilities and heading to a romantic bed and breakfast. It will certainly mean hiding behind the answering machine without hesitation. If they have children, those kids will learn that when mommy and daddy's bedroom door is closed and Armageddon begins, they should knock softly and wait. Supporting sexual joy, by the way, is rather obviously a big part of all these prescriptions, but let's emphasize that this eighth house bonding is bigger than intercourse itself. Sleeping together is part of it. Lying in a bed just holding each other is another part. With Jupiter in the composite eighth house, this couple has a treasure available to them in all those areas. The trick lies in believing in it—and in themselves—enough to claim it.

COMPOSITE JUPITER IN THE NINTH HOUSE

People fall in love and, after jumping successfully through courtship's hoops, settle down together. The phrase "settle down" is familiar, and so is the reality it represents: *you used to see them dancing, now you see them at Wal-Mart.* Once as sexy as movie stars, now they're as sexy as dishrags.

Have they perhaps "settled" for too little? It's a risk—there's something comforting about a solid relationship . . . maybe too comforting! People go to sleep, get conservative, lose their edge. These aren't laws of the universe, but they are very real pitfalls. With their composite Jupiter in the ninth house, we have two comments for this couple. First, the good news: they have excellent immunity to this "fall-in-love-and-die" syndrome. Second, to keep their relationship cooking, they'd better exercise that immunity actively.

A fortune-teller might say, "I see them traveling." The ninth house is reliably correlated with travel and adventure, so the prophecy is probably accurate. We prefer to say, "We *suggest* that they travel, that travel might be to Peru, or to the new Peruvian restaurant in town." Another fortune-teller might predict they'll take classes together. That's a fine idea—although we would equally recommend reading books or seeing documentaries that stretch their minds, *and then discussing them.* The education doesn't have to be formal or official; it just has to be endless, ongoing and fascinating.

Traditionally, the ninth house is about religion. It's quite possible that "church," in some sense of the word, will play an important, positive role in their lives. More broadly, the ninth house is really about our whole perspective on life: our values, our philosophy, the moral stars that guide us through the complex negotiations and trade-offs that life entails. For these two, the optimal attitude is one of optimism, hope, and a sense of possibility. That positive, confident view seeps into the foundations of their idea of themselves as a couple: they're together for a *meaningful purpose*; it is *right* that they are a couple, and with faith they can conquer any obstacles that their egos, their personal processes, or their wounds might ever conjure up.

COMPOSITE JUPITER IN THE TENTH HOUSE

Success! Money! Power! Cool friends! Be the envy of everyone—everyone, that is, with insufficient imagination to recognize that these things don't necessarily spell happiness. Nor, we hasten to add, do they necessarily spell misery. There are sad people in limousines and happy people in ghettos. With their composite Jupiter in the tenth house, this couple is dynamic. If they build their relationship on a sufficiently solid foundation that it lasts for a while, they are very likely to experience what will be perceived to be an improvement in their material circumstances and social status. Together, they trigger a potential for climbing the hierarchical ladder of their culture or subculture. Being invited to join the most exclusive country club? Yes—if that reflects the pinnacle of the culture *with which they are identified*. Given a different set of circumstances and values, this composite Jupiter could just easily correlate with "hanging out with the band" or even "sitting at the cool table in the high school cafeteria."

We're using dumb examples here to make a point—one of the dumbest things about our human species is our tendency to overvalue a trivial concern such as status. With their composite Jupiter in the tenth house, these two will surely climb. The trick is to choose a mountain whose top they admire.

Underlying the concept of social ascent is a fundamental evolutionary perspective: together, these two have a mission of a Jupiter nature in their community. First, it involves *leadership* in some form—Jupiter is, after all, the king of the gods. Second, some fanfare—status, social connections with powerful people, influence—is probably necessary for the execution of the mission. They must be *noticed*, in other words. Third, the work has the effect of giving hope, inspiration, and encouragement to people who need it. In some sense these two are *coaches* or *role models*. And fourth, they have to believe in themselves as a couple to attract this mission and be worthy of it. How? The answer lies in the rest of their composite chart.

COMPOSITE JUPITER IN THE ELEVENTH HOUSE

Over time, loves smooths us out. It teaches us humility. It puts sweetness in our hearts. We learn ways to see around our blind spots. We study forgiveness and generosity. We learn about each other's ragged edges, coming to understand the fear behind the anger, the pain behind the coldness. It follows that a relationship can become better and more precious over time. And that's the very phenomenon often reported at fiftieth wedding anniversaries. With composite Jupiter in the future-oriented eleventh house, this rosy scenario is available to this pair. Any planet in this house looms larger as time passes, and Jupiter correlates with joy, faith and gratitude. We say confidently that if this relationship lasts, it will improve. The word "if" looms large in that sentence! We add that not every couple really should stay together—most of us "see" a lot more people than we ever "marry," whatever that word means to us. That's part of life's journey. The futuristic aspects of the eleventh house really don't have much direct meaning until a bond has been seasoned for a while, except in one way. They give us hope. It is so helpful for these two to look to a brighter tomorrow, to have faith that they can get there, and that the prize is worth the effort. Without those Jupiter-feelings here and now, there won't *be* a tomorrow for them.

At a very concrete level, with their composite Jupiter in the eleventh, these two support their faith in themselves by *making plans.* Perhaps they've started with a summer romance. It's helpful to talk about going skiing together this winter. Perhaps they're a young couple, fully committed and sharing a rented home. They feed something primal in their bond by designing their dream house, even if owning it is pure fantasy at this point. The point is that positive images of the future help them attain that future. Supporting this is a special skill they have as a team, even if they lack it as individuals: *they are good at strategy.* They are good at making dreams come true. They have that magic about them.

Many astrologers call the eleventh the "house of friends," and would predict that these two would have lots of them. It's a fair guess. Generally couples with this configuration have busy social lives. Friendships and a sense of community are naturally desirable states, but there's room for higher and lower possibilities. A busy social life can be a joy or a distraction. Much depends upon this couple's becoming clear about the nature of their own goals and aspirations, then choosing to network with a "crowd" that shares those goals or otherwise supports them. If they want to be in a committed relationship, we would be nervous to note that all their friends are single. If they envision a childless future, they benefit from time spent with other couples who have made that choice.

COMPOSITE JUPITER IN THE TWELFTH HOUSE

Angels watch over these two. They will get concrete demonstrations of that seemingly flaky proposition. They survive a near-miss in an automobile, for example—one that should have killed them, but left them without a scratch (not to mention more faith in angels!). They take a risky job offer that works beautifully for them—six months before their safe, secure job is outsourced to New Delhi. They'll miraculously miss a tornado by a hundred feet. Caution, sense or wisdom have nothing to do with their salvation. All we can say is "Thank God." Or thank the guardian angels.

These gifts, these interventions from the spirit realm, are reminders, little wake-up calls offered to remind this couple that the world we grasp with our intellects is only a small part of something much larger, more purposeful, and a thousand times more astonishing. With composite Jupiter in the twelfth, these two are ready to stretch further into that expanded vision. Together, they are closer to God than either of them is as an individual. Their souls are like two elements in an achromatic lens—two different kinds of glass married together in a way that focuses more clearly than either could without the corrective properties of the other. The lens is trained on the mysterious, multi-dimensional fabric underlying our three-dimensional world.

If they heed the reminders, if they really listen to the call of the angels, would they become religious? That's certainly a possibility, but we shouldn't count on it. They might use different metaphors than the ones heard in churches. Certainly they'd spend more time alone together. Almost surely we would see evidence in their home of candles, oil lamps, or other sources of soft light. If we knew what we were seeing, we would very likely recognize objects there with spiritual or magical significance: the rock picked up on that magical hike through a sacred canyon, the cup that once held the Dalai Lama's tea. Most centrally, we would feel an aura of something spiritual around them—a certain peace, a feeling of transcendence.

There is one more kind of angelic intervention we can see with this configuration: the *blessing of loss*. Viewed simply, these phenomena often appear to be simple misfortunes, perhaps tragedies. Given time, they turn out to be the yeast in some very precious bread. Try this sentence: "Losing that (fill in the blank) was the best thing that ever happened to me." It's almost as if those angels not only loved us, but also that they're smarter than we are!

CHAPTER TWELVE: THE COMPOSITE SATURN

Singer Robbie Robertson says, "We grow up so slowly and grow old so fast." Just ten little words, but they hold a lot of truth. Kids use the phrase "when I grow up" all the time. So do forty-year-olds. The forty-year-olds are smiling, though. They understand something the kids miss—being "grown up" is an ever-receding Shangri-La, always near, never truly attained. Most of us will do a whole lot of "growing up" on our death-beds.

In traditional astrology, Saturn is generally represented in geriatric form: Father Time or the Wise Old Crone. That's good imagery, provided we recognize the inner meaning of the message. Saturn governs the endless process of *maturation*—an ongoing integration into our consciousness *of reality as it actually is.* A lot of that actual reality is hard to accept: how fragile our lives are; how quickly they pass; how rare is the finish that is worthy of the start. To the immature, those are depressing words. A mature perspective is more likely to view life as all the more poignant and precious for its transitoriness. Plastic flowers last longer than roses from the garden, but which would you rather have on your table?

Every relationship, just like every individual, evolves over time. Sometimes that's beautiful news, while other times it's a catastrophe. The principle fits a relationship that's more than a few months old as tightly as it fits people one at a time. In the old days, we would honor a couple simply because they had stayed together for fifty years. Nowadays, we may still say the words, but we're likely to value a relationship more for its loving qualities than for its mere longevity. Love is not an endurance contest. We all know that time can bring out the worst in two people as easily as it can bring out the best. Maybe more easily.

Where Saturn lies in the composite chart, the couple is challenged to mature. And the stakes are very high. If their response to Saturn is weak, we'll see the planet operating like a virus that gradually poisons everything warm, forgiving or kind in the bond. If the couple's response is strong, we'll see them moving ahead with dignity and grace, progressing toward a calm, realistic, patient *acceptance* of each other.

Where Saturn lies in the composite chart, the two people are faced with the challenge of a *Great Work.* Together, they are asked to climb a mountain. It may be a joint project unfolding over years, such as raising a family or building a business. It may involve some perceived misfortune to which they can potentially rise with strength and integrity. In every case, if they face Saturn's questions with discipline and commitment, their relationship moves a step forward toward the kind of love only true Elders know.

COMPOSITE SATURN IN ARIES

The world is full of things that can hurt us or eat us. Nature is inherently a very competitive place, often without much evidence of mercy. If we lack fierceness and tenacity, we can be blown to bits. Happily, there are gentler aspects to existence, but Aries represents that fiery potential in all beings which allows us to stand our ground and claim our right to live. With their composite Saturn in Aries, this couple is learning the discipline of courage.

Imagine two people on a sailboat fifteen miles out into the ocean. An unforecast storm has come up and the vessel is pitching wildly, threatening to founder. Inwardly, both of them would like to curl up and wish fervently for a change in the weather. But of course if they do that, they'll be in serious trouble. They've got to steel themselves to fight the storm. There are procedures to follow—reduce sail, fix their position, plot a course that minimizes their peril. A few hours later, it's all over. They've survived. Each one did what needed to be done. Neither one failed the other. They look at each other with renewed respect. Each knows the other one behaved honorably and bravely under pressure. They don't even need to discuss it; any words would seem trivial. Welcome to composite Saturn in Aries. Together, the inner warrior (Aries) in the heart of this relationship has taken a giant step of maturation (Saturn).

Not all Saturn in Aries work unfolds under such dramatic physical circumstances. Sometimes the battles are more psychological. A married couple may be very involved with the husband's family, under pressure to spend every Sunday afternoon with the parents. The wife and the husband's father have different political views. He's dogmatic and tyrannical, constantly baiting the woman. Maybe the wife complains privately to her husband about the situation—and he denies its existence! Maybe neither of them ever mentions it, electing just to "cope." The anger grows like a cancer between them. The unspoken, righteous defense never happens—and the couple remains children under the thumb of an oppressive father. Their unexpressed (Saturn) fury (Aries) manifests in petty bickering, depression, and underlying tension.

There's the dark side of composite Saturn in Aries: the miserable fruit of colluding in cowardice. Perhaps that's the end of the story. But perhaps one day the couple awakens. They agree to stand together and face down that ferocious father, claiming their right to their dignity—and their right to his respect. They let him know that, if he wants their love, he'll need to be worthy of it. And they let the chips fall where they may.

Like our couple on the sailboat, these two now look at each other with renewed respect, each knowing that the other behaved honorably and bravely under pressure. Imagine the dignity and wisdom in a couple who've walked the higher ground for twenty years. Now imagine the downcast mood of shame and futility of the couple heading back for more abuse on yet another interminable Sunday afternoon with that kitchen table tyrant. In those two images, you see the evolutionary intention and the karmic shadow of composite Saturn in Aries.

COMPOSITE SATURN IN TAURUS

Peace. Serenity of spirit. A grounded feeling of being at ease in our skins. The comforts of simplicity. Security. These are the evolutionary goals of Taurus. With their composite Saturn there, the great work of this couple's life lies in creating that mood in their relationship.

What brings us a feeling of security? In our modern culture, it is difficult to avoid immediately jumping from "security" to "*financial* security," so let's be realistic and start there. If you are having a bad month money-wise and your car starts making ominous noises, what do you do? Turn up the radio? But that fear still lingers subliminally. You don't feel peaceful or secure, and all the philosophy in the world isn't going to calm you.

Taurus always calls us back to the wisdom of the "inner animal." Animals don't care about money, and neither would we—except for the fact that money buys a lot of stuff that our inner animals need in order to feel safe: food, shelter, comfort. For our couple with composite Saturn in Taurus, rational financial behavior is in fact a significant part of their evolutionary strategy. Without it, anxiety naturally arises and poses a big obstacle to their maturational process.

With that said, let's accept the fact that the world is full of wealthy, anxious people. Taking care of the financial aspects of life is only one piece of the Taurean puzzle. If that's all our couple does, probably they'll be more anxious rather than less so—no matter how much money they have, something bad can always come along and take it away. That fact will prey on them, unless they bolster their financial planning with some other wisdoms from that "inner animal."

One piece of the puzzle has to do with the joy of *simplicity*: we are probably a lot more peaceful inside if we have a modest home with a modest mortgage than we would be in a palace we can barely afford. Even moving to a new home shakes up the inner animal. It would often prefer the low stress of familiar surroundings. With composite Saturn in Taurus, these two are learning to be cautious about creating the stress of unnecessary change in their lives. This doesn't mean they should avoid anything new—boredom is stressful too. But they do benefit from valuing the calming impact of old friends, a favorite restaurant, and life's other comfortable rituals.

Food is worth attention here too. Little gives us such a deep sense of well-being as sitting with dear friends and enjoying a good meal—and there's not much that pulls in the opposite direction faster than wolfing down caffeinated, sugary, industrial faux-food at a drive-through.

Of all the changes we might experience, one of the most stressful is a relationship's breaking up. Even the thought of it raises the blood pressure. Starting over and meeting new people may be exciting, but from the Taurean and Saturnian perspectives, it's simply unsettling: just think of the *horror* of dating, and you're getting into the Saturn-in-Taurus mood! Thus, for this couple, there is an evolutionary thrust toward radical commitment to each other—deep promises, a humble willingness to accept each other, and, above all, shared images of growing old together.

COMPOSITE SATURN IN GEMINI

To know a little bit about physics or music or astrology is easy. Anyone who stayed awake through a couple of years of high school can learn a few buzz words and a handful of basic concepts. If they keep the conversation moving fast enough, they may even be able to pass themselves off as experts. But to press ourselves to the limits of our potential in any area of learning, we need Saturnian virtues: discipline, focus, and concentration. With their composite Saturn in Gemini, this couple moves toward maturity by committing to an endless process of delving deeply into whatever interests them, including each other. They might benefit from taking classes together, for example—and to go instantly to the heart of this configuration, just imagine an elderly couple holding hands as they sit in the lecture hall of the local Jung Society. They're ninety years old and they're still learning. Even better, when they go home that night, they've got something new to discuss.

Not all Geminian learning takes places in academic settings. These two need to read books and share what they've discovered with each other. It's good for them to watch documentaries, visit museums, travel together to interesting places. Saturn likes detail and complexity, and it balances the Geminian temptation toward "sound bites." Thus, they may come to cherish occasions when they are apart and need to communicate by letters or email—the deeper exchange of ideas that usually comes from writing powerfully supports the evolutionary intentions of this configuration.

In the end, the real subject they are studying is each other, and language is their tool for that process. In direct conversation, they mature by learning to let each other finish sentences, avoiding interruption. This isn't about politeness; it's about creating an energy between them that encourages complex and serious thinking—another mark of maturity. Similarly, expanding their shared vocabulary is a great benefit to them simply because big words are often more precise than little ones. Saying "I felt humiliated, and I was startled by my vengeful reflexes" actually conveys the emotional nuances of an experience more clearly than saying, "I was so pissed off I wanted to kill the bastard!" Note also how the first statement naturally suggests the language of a self-confident grown-up, while the second one sounds more like the words of a young person. There's no shame in being young, and sometimes the salty language of the street can be very eloquent. Formality isn't the aim here, nor is the banishing of simple, direct language. The aim is banishing the *taboo* against serious, mature, precise speech, the kind that conveys the deepest truths we know. With that taboo removed, and with a life-long commitment to feeding and cross-fertilizing the fires of their knowledge, these two move rapidly toward claiming the dignity and grace of their composite Saturn.

COMPOSITE SATURN IN CANCER

The alpha and the omega of the sign Cancer is the notion of the *nest:* home and hearth, the place where we restore and nourish ourselves, each other, and anyone depending on us. There are quite a few letters in the alphabet between alpha and omega, of course! Cancer also refers to the larger process of healing. It is related to emotions in general and to the protective instinct. Anything that *feeds* us is in the Cancerian domain. With their composite Saturn in Cancer, this couple faces great works in all those categories. But it all comes back to building a home.

Saturn is often treated negatively in astrological literature, as if it were always about blockages and bad luck. We are often "blocked" where we're afraid, and often our fears are perfectly reasonable. To understand composite Saturn in Cancer, let's recognize that building a home is a profoundly serious, high stakes business. Broken homes are common, but they take a bite out of everyone they touch. If there are children involved, the stakes double. Once we start making a home with another person, we've risked deep wounding—and we've made a bid for even deeper happiness. Anyone who isn't a little bit afraid simply doesn't understand the nature of the game.

In the deep intimacy of home and hearth, people hurt each other. Most of the time, they do that because they themselves have been hurt, maybe when they were children, maybe later on. Recognizing this truth is the first discipline (Saturn) in the process of mutual healing (Cancer) for which these two have come together. When people behave cruelly or coldly toward each other, they are usually expressing pain and rejection they have internalized. Knowing that, we steel ourselves to relate to each other forgivingly and gently. When we have been hurt, we hang in there, looking compassionately for the wound behind the other person's misbehavior. When we have misbehaved ourselves, we discipline ourselves to have the humility and honesty to own it and to ask for forgiveness.

All that is hard work. Given the reality of our anger and pain, that hard work is also the foundation of any home that promises to endure. With their composite Saturn in Cancer, these two people have signed up to practice the ongoing disciplines of forgiveness and humility. They are healing something hurt inside themselves, and they are building a present and a future that are different from their past. With forgiveness, trust develops. There is an ever-deeper confidence in the stability of their bond. The "blockages" and "bad luck" are transformed into a precious sense of having found a home. They no longer expect perfection, only honesty, loyalty, and some wisdom. As the process unfolds, an aura of maturity arises around them. It attracts vulnerability in their friends, who often seek the comforting presence of these "elders." And they move into the future, soulfully and with their feet firmly planted on the ground of human emotional reality as it actually is.

COMPOSITE SATURN IN LEO

Why do birds sing? Ornithologists may talk about territoriality and mating signals, and they are probably on solid theoretical ground. But as you sit in the garden on a perfect May morning listening to all the exuberant whistling, it's hard not to feel that the birds are celebrating the sheer joy of making noise. Each bird has style and takes up some space, and seems to have fun doing it. Humpback whales sing their own songs too. And so do happy humans. We love that classic Leo realm: *self-expression.* We puzzle over which shirt to buy and how to present our hair. We worry about how we look in photographs. We like to make people laugh. Most of us have had fantasies about being in the movies. Many of us paint or write or play musical instruments. All of that is the roar of the astrological Lion.

With their composite Saturn in Leo, part of the soul-contract of these two lies in a commitment to develop the intensity, color and individuality of their self-expression. They've come together in this lifetime to support each other's maturation in that quest. They've agreed to learn the *discipline* (Saturn) of *letting it rip* (Leo). They are casting off the dead hand of repressive sorrow.

Their evolutionary work starts at the very rudimentary levels of appearance and behavior. With composite Saturn in Leo, this is where the foundation is laid: right in the body and its reflexes. Maybe they're out shopping. One of them tries on a flamboyant hat. And looks perfectly ridiculous. The other one responds positively to the *idea* of the bold hat—and reaches for another one that works a little better. The shopping imagery here is very casual, but all the core pieces of the puzzle are present. Leo wants to wear a colorful hat. Saturn brings in the elements of judgment and discrimination that make that hat a good choice in the long run. If we wear a dumb hat out in public and later realize it, it might be five years before we take another such risk. *Embarrassment represses us.* Here we see the core composite Saturn in Leo notion: these two are developing *a symbiotic partnership that enhances their ever-maturing capacity for creativity and self-expression.*

When we think of creativity, we don't always think of strange hats. A big part of the work can start there, though, in the realm of clothing—or more generally, in the realm of the language we use, the jokes we tell, the aura we create around ourselves: the *theater* of our lives. These two need to coach and support each other in those arenas. The process extends outward into *life-style*. They encourage each other to fulfill bright dreams: mountaineering, drinking espresso in Roman cafés, living large in general. It culminates as they support each other in the incredible soul-risk of authentic artistic self-expression: putting their naked hearts on canvas or the printed page or the ivory keys of the piano. With enough loud applause, gentle reflective criticism, and support, they will arrive at that goal.

COMPOSITE SATURN IN VIRGO

Analysis, discrimination, and cautious, critical judgment are classic Virgo skills. What they lack in excitement, they make up for in sheer utility. Every time you've kept your wallet in your pocket when faced with some urgent huckster exhorting you to Act Now, you've benefitted from Virgo's ability to sort out reality from hype. And that's always the key: reality versus hype. Or to put it more broadly, Virgo's core perception lies in the distinction between the Ideal and the Real. And Virgo sees both: *what could be* and *what actually is.* And it compares them, always drawn to the discrepancies, always concerned with pushing reality in the general direction of perfection. A side effect of those critical perceptions is that Virgo is profoundly alert to error and shortfall: hence its acute attention to the huckster's exaggerations and empty promises.

With Saturn in Virgo in the composite chart, the maturational challenges for this couple lie in learning a set of skills that allow discrimination, criticism and judgment to serve the evolutionary aims of their bond rather than destroying it. Every relationship and every human being has room for improvement. Many of us, with our hearts in the right places, can accept with good grace a nudge in the direction of virtue from time to time. But most of us would prefer not to receive a second nudge too close on the heels of the first one. We have a human need to feel accepted as we are, without modification and without "suggestions." We all need at least *some* unconditional love, in other words. Or some R-E-S-P-E-C-T, as Otis and Aretha put it years ago.

Given this Saturn placement in the composite chart, there is a powerful and pervasive evolutionary drive in the couple. That of course can potentially be good news. The question lies in how they use the energy.

Saturn's patience, forbearance and sense of timing must temper Virgo's focus on the "issues." Much of it comes down to learning when not to speak, when to practice *silent* forgiveness, and when to mix humor and the longer view into the perceptions of the moment.

One more point: a composite Saturn in Virgo can get a lot of work done. It tends toward responsibility, effectiveness, and duty. But it can also become too fussy over details and too quick to take responsibility for pointless, time-consuming tasks. Vigilance is appropriate here. If the couple moves in those kinds of unnecessarily hassle-intensive directions, a chronically pressurized and worrisome attitude creeps into the relationship—unpleasant enough in its own right, but it also interacts viciously with their vulnerability toward nickel-and-diming each other to death psychologically.

COMPOSITE SATURN IN LIBRA

We humans are proud monkeys with sharp teeth. Even the nicest, mildest man or woman who has ever taken a breath would sometimes challenge our patience in an intimate domestic situation. It's worse: there's nothing like sexual intimacy for bringing our deepest craziness to the surface. Unresolved issues with our parents? Fear of abandonment? Free-floating rage? Sleep with someone for more than five or six consecutive weekends, and there it all is, loud and clear—to our partner. To ourselves, we're just "right." And ready to shoot to prove it.

It's a wonder that any two humans can live together. How do we do it? That love works at all is a miracle.

One of the answers is that classic Libran skill: *diplomacy*. We humans have learned a bag of tricks for navigating around each other's minefields. With composite Saturn in Libra, these two have a soul-contract to push these skills into a wiser, more mature expression. They are learning how to honor each other's egos, walk softly around each other's Shadows, and to avoid unnecessary, costly friction. In a word, they are learning the *discipline* (Saturn) of *courtesy* (Libra). If they succeed, then 100% of their energy can go into the real work: deepening their level of trust and enhancing the mutual evolutionary benefits of their partnership. If they fail, then the story of their relationship collapses into a pattern of endless bargaining and bickering, punctuated with compromises that satisfy neither of them.

Two people with composite Saturn in Libra are a year into their relationship. A touchy issue comes up for one of them: the other one sometimes smells bad. The problem is of course perfectly correctable—a little soap and water, a fresh tee-shirt. But how to broach the subject? Being told that one's smell is offensive can *feel* offensive to the person hearing it. Words have to be chosen very carefully. The smelly person needs to be made to feel respected and supported, as if his or her virtues were Godzilla compared to the Bambi of this "slight odor, that perhaps suggests some serious defect in the cheap soap we're using."

We hope you smiled at that last line. It's difficult to think deeply about Libran courtesy without recognizing its profound connection to a sense of humor. With composite Saturn in Libra, humor is elemental to the strategy these two must employ for making their relationship work. It's the grease—or the grace. It's the magic that allows love and truth to co-exist. *With their issues reframed as clowns rather than as evil demons*, these two can talk about almost anything. Body odor, bad breath, PMS, "testosterone poisoning"—all of them can be brought into the open without anyone's feeling *equated* with them. Similarly, diplomatic and humorous language arises for handling the more important psychological issues that come up in intimacy: control, fear, anger, sexual curiosity about others.

Now imagine two people who've been on that sophisticated road for fifty years. Feel their grace and maturity. Feel how their love shines through the humor. Feel how they've learned the graceful *skill* of accepting each other's simple humanity. That's the evolutionary goal of composite Saturn in Libra.

COMPOSITE SATURN IN SCORPIO

There's a passionate sexual hunger in us all. When we're very young, we believe the hormonal message uncritically: if we could only have this person, we'd be satisfied forever. And if we don't get him or her, our lives might as well end here. A little time passes and maybe we've "had" a person or two. Almost inevitably, we feel gypped: those people turned out to be human beings! They weren't the everlasting sexual gods and goddesses we'd expected. They didn't leave us in a permanent state of orgasm after all.

At this point, we come to a crossroads. Some people become cynical, deciding that the only way to feed this passionate sexual hunger is through variety—spending their lives *beginning* relationships. Others become "realistic," which is to say they accept the depressing notion that these hungers are cruel biological jokes the universe has played on us. They take refuge in fantasy or simply give up, surrendering to solitude or dull love.

With composite Saturn in Scorpio, these two have signed a different soul-contract entirely. They aim to take a third road: enduring, endlessly transformative passion. Sounds good, but it's hard work. A lot of initial sexual passion derives from the newness and unfamiliarity of the partner. The *sexual* (Scorpio) *discipline* (Saturn) this couple is attempting pivots on sustaining that sense of newness and unfamiliarity. How? Once we "know" someone, what more is there to discover? That's the critical question. At a superficial level, the answer is easy: *not much.* But psychologically and spiritually, we humans are deeper than oceans.

But we hide that depth. We are frightened of revealing it. Often we've been punished for being "too heavy" or "too weird" or "crazy" or "bad." We've adjusted to a shallow society, and been blasted whenever we were even slightly maladjusted to it. With composite Saturn in Scorpio, these two have an inner agreement to be *open to anything* in each other.

It takes a lot of will-power to sustain that. Maybe your partner is attracted to someone else. That's nobody's favorite subject. But consider the rich vein of psychological information that opens up the minute two people put that kind of material on the table, without shame or any sense of taboo. For psychologically immature people, such attractions might be as simple as the third person's resemblance to a certain pop star—and even that reveals interesting questions: there are lots of attractive pop stars in the world. Why this one? As people grow in wisdom, those who catch our fancy are of course increasingly resonant with places in ourselves that are emergent or underfed, or suppressed and then "projected" onto the object of our attraction. How much precious "newness and unfamiliarity" can be brought to the surface this way! This is the third road that sustains the passionate heat between two souls.

We've used attraction to others as the illustration here. It's a good one, but far from the only one. Any hard subject could illustrate the principle almost as well: perceptions about each other's parents or families, speaking honestly about ageing and dying, what it would feel like if either person received a scary medical diagnosis.

That's the discipline of composite Saturn in Scorpio: endless commitment to truth, unwavering resolve never to shame one's partner for an inner condition, and determination never to be driven apart by fear or pride.

COMPOSITE SATURN IN SAGITTARIUS

Imagine a wise fool wandering in an alien city, asking strangers about the meaning of life. Most of them would give him a wide berth, thinking he was crazy—and never consider how much it revealed about their own beliefs that they took such a question to be insane! The few who did respond would likely represent a wide range of philosophical views. There would be Christian answers and Jewish answers and existentialist answers and Republican answers and cynical answers, and so on. In other words, all the major "religions" of the world would be represented. We humans have been worrying about the meaning of life since we first uttered a comprehensible syllable, and we still haven't come to many agreements. Even with their composite Saturn in Sagittarius, these two won't come to any final answers either. But they will try: their *discipline* (Saturn) is focused on *answering the unanswerable* (Sagittarius).

The dark expression of this configuration lies in deadening rigidity. They need to be wary of mind-dulling *agreements* between themselves, whether it's an agreement to be Methodists or New Agers or whatever else. Anything that dampens the *quest* violates their soul-agreement.

The Sagittarian road is a hard one. No "answer" can ever correspond perfectly to reality. For one thing, we are three-dimensional creatures living in a multi-dimensional cosmos: the "big truth" can never be captured in the frail nets of our limited minds. But even that familiar perspective has its traps. It can easily lead to a lazy, stable belief-system in which we make a religion out of not knowing and not *trying* to know. With composite Saturn in Sagittarius, there is a rigorous, unending *effort* to learn—and to learn in as accurate and grounded a way possible—why we are here on this planet.

How can these two do that? Let's start by saying how *not* to do it: by shielding themselves from anything that challenges what they already believe. With their composite Saturn in Sagittarius, for these two such a course is anathema. The path to the higher ground for them—and to the precious Saturnian maturity of their relationship—lies in intentionally exposing themselves to philosophical shock. One effective road in that direction is travel. When we travel outside our own culture, inevitably we encounter radically distinct ways of being human. Sagittarius has a natural correlation with journeying, but we need to throw Saturn into the equations here too. Saturn is always fascinated by the difficult and the challenging. The imagery falls into place when we think of this couple paddling up the

Orinoco rather than doing a safe, week-long wonder-tour of Europe—or when we extend that trip to Europe for a year.

Ultimately, with their composite Saturn in Sagittarius, the real "traveling" for this couple is more philosophical and intellectual than geographical. Picture them, two Christians heading for the *peyote* cult. Two Jungians off to see Disney World. A pair of Beethoven scholars trance-dancing at the rave. Physicists studying religion. Professors of rats-in-a-maze psychology reading this book. Those are the kinds of Sagittarian disciplines that keep them on course.

COMPOSITE SATURN IN CAPRICORN

Saturn rules Capricorn, so this composite configuration is very potent. With all the other Saturn placements, we can lay out some useful truths. What we cannot see is how *central* those truths are to the destiny of the couple. With composite Saturn in Capricorn, we know they are pivotal. This couple is capable of extraordinary feats. Both Saturn and Capricorn refer to similar strengths and intentions: serious accomplishments, discipline, focus, integrity. There is very little these two cannot do if they set their joint determination on a project. Like any other powerful force, this energy has to be used in a careful, reflective way, or it can become dangerous.

Say you've had the week from hell at work. Last time you noticed, it was Monday morning. Since then, it's been strictly pedal-to-the-metal. Every night you lay down to sleep, exhausted, and the next thing you knew the alarm was blaring and off you went again. You've been crawling toward the weekend like a thirsty cowboy heading for a watery mirage in Death Valley. Finally it's here: Saturday morning! And you are too wired and tense to relax. You know you *need* to relax—it's practically a duty, given your week. But you can't. And the more you make yourself try to cool out, the more impossible it becomes.

With composite Saturn in Capricorn, these two are magnets for responsibility. Together, they'll probably rise to those demands quite effectively. The questions they need to answer are, how do *we* personally want to use this energy? What would our life together look like if we were not beset by other people's needs—or other people's sermons about the nature of our duties? What's the great work we've actually come together to accomplish? (A valuable hint about a general answer to that question lies in considering the *house* where their composite Saturn lies—you can look that up in the next few pages.) All of these questions boil down to one central theme: who gets to choose the direction of this formidable Saturn-in-Capricorn force? Is it the two people who "own" it, or is the world around them—family, friends, the community, their jobs?

There is a great dignity in accomplishment. For all the usefulness of simply loving ourselves the way we are and not having to prove anything to anyone, we humans are still impressed by excellence in others. We admire someone for disciplining themselves to become a fine pianist, for example. Or building a successful business. Or raising a sane family in the ghetto. With their composite Saturn in Capricorn, part of the soul-contract for this couple is to direct that same self-affirming principle inward. *They intend to gain self-respect, dignity and a sense of their own natural authority through accomplishing something impressive.* They have a lot to give—and enough steam to make it happen. All they have to do is to make sure they are not wearing chains that someone else has designed for them.

COMPOSITE SATURN IN AQUARIUS

"Faith, I ran when I saw others run!" That's a Shakespearean quote—Henry IV, Part 1, Act Two, to be precise. We first encountered it in humbler circumstances: on a tee-shirt belonging to a friend who'd just run the Boston marathon. The words made us laugh, as they probably did the Elizabethan crowds who first heard them. They're also an excellent summary of the human condition. Literally—if you're walking one way down a street and suddenly are faced with a panicked crowd stampeding in the other direction, what are you going to do? Anyone who decides to investigate what frightened the crowd might be brave—but in the Darwinian scheme of things, such a person is also less likely than most of us to leave much of a splash in the gene pool. Survival is often enhanced by surrendering to our herd instincts. With their composite Saturn in Aquarius, this couple needs to overcome those reflexes. Their path in this world goes against the grain. The *Great Work* (Saturn) they have signed up to accomplish is *individuation* (Aquarius). Separating from the herd. Living life their own way.

Relationships are hard work, even with the best of intentions. Fortunately, human beings have been working at them for thousands of years. We've inherited a lot of hard-won learning. Our ancestors have passed their gifts down to us in the form of folklore and social customs.

Here are a few of the treasures: You don't know if it's true love until you've had your first fight. Monogamy enhances trust. Children stabilize a marriage. Couples sleep in the same bed. Marriage means you live together. Say a few kind things for every hard thing you tell your partner.

Like running away when you see others run, all of the above is actually pretty solid advice for most of us. But not necessarily for these two. With their composite Saturn in Aquarius, they have reached a point in the evolutionary journey where it is more important that they make every decision themselves, freely, under their own power and without any external influence. They must feel that every step they take together is purely voluntary. They are inventing their own rules.

That's dangerous business. The collective "folklore" we mentioned a minute ago is actually valuable stuff. It makes loving easier. To experiment with any of those principles requires a lot of *maturity*—or creates that maturity on the fast track! In their evolutionary effort, two powerful allies exist for this pair. One comes from Aquarius, and is a deep love of truthfulness. The second is Saturn's gift: a capacity for profound, grown-up commitment. As they experiment with the "rules," they will surely blunder from time to time. Those two allies can help them over the rough patches.

In the end, their shared evolutionary intention can be conveyed in the image of two delightfully idiosyncratic elders, having made their own way down life's winding road, loving each other well, wearing "grievously inappropriate" clothing for their age—and laughing at anyone it bothers!

COMPOSITE SATURN IN PISCES

We hit a switch at two in the morning, and instantly we have daylight. We touch the thermostat, and we can soon have the house at any temperature that feels good to us. Turn a dial and we have a symphony orchestra—or Jimi Hendrix reincarnating in our living room. Turn another one and our dinner is cooking. We live in an age of instant gratification, and that's pretty sweet. But some processes cannot be sped up or made easy. Building a relationship is one of them. Another is working the ancient set of evolutionary methods we call the spiritual path. With their composite Saturn in Pisces, those two slow, stubborn processes are closely linked. This couple has a soul-contract to *discipline themselves* (Saturn) to take *full responsibility* (Saturn again) for the evolution of their own *consciousnesses*

(Pisces), and in so doing, to create a deeper level of spiritual maturity in their relationship.

Some yoga classes are like Olympic events. Churches and meditation classes are full of people posing as holier than they actually are. It's not difficult to detect competitiveness among people "on the path." They'll intimate how long they've fasted, how many days they were out alone in the wilderness on their vision quest, or how many hours they can sit in meditation. All of that is just the usual human ego-circus. You laugh or you cry. The only piece that truly matters in such evolutionary endeavors is always invisible: it is the quality of surrender in the inner experience. But that surrender can be enhanced by a strong quality of *intention,* which in turn is supported by discipline and determination. An individual doing such work often benefits most by not talking very much about it—keeping the thirsty ego out of the whisky bar, in other words. But in this case we are talking about a composite chart, and so the "individual" is really a relationship between two people. Thus, we recognize that, with composite Saturn in Pisces, this couple's evolutionary aim must cover two bases. First, they need some kind of serious, joint spiritual practice. Second, they need to keep pretty quiet about it, except between themselves.

Serious, joint spiritual practice: what does that mean? Anything that feels right to them is the best answer. "Religious" people often delight in blowing each other to Kingdom Come over their differences, but the true mystics always recognize that, while there are many roads up the mountain, the mountain has only one single peak. And Pisces is the sign of the mystic, not the theologian. They can choose their own beliefs, and those beliefs actually matter very little here. What matters is their logging hours in the presence of God, by whatever methods they like. Doing so alone is fine—they remain individuals despite their relationship. But with their composite Saturn in Pisces, it is also important that they share this effort. It cannot be a secret between them, although it is useful for it not to be displayed for the world's eyes.

So here's an old couple with magic thick in the air around them, off on vacation. "Where are you going?" asks their neighbor. "Oh, nowhere special—just off to our cabin in the mountains, as usual." The neighbor persists, "What do you two *do* all day up there?" And they answer, "Oh, nothing much—we just sit on the porch and look through our eyes."

The key is that these two elders know *who* is looking through those eyes.

COMPOSITE SATURN IN THE FIRST HOUSE

Let's say that these two people decide to earn their living by shoplifting. This isn't exactly the career advice we would give based on having composite Saturn in the first house! But we'll learn something from this image, so bear with us. Maybe they're twenty-something, with body piercing, tattoos and purple hair. The minute they walk into the store the rent-a-cop's eyes get as squinty as Clint Eastwood's. He scrutinizes their every move. Their felonious career is doomed from the starting gate. Now instead let's imagine that our heros are in their seventies and dressed as if they've just left the country club. They could load their pockets and purses, and the rent-a-cop would tip his hat as they walked out of the store.

Take it a step deeper. Imagine that you are an actor on stage playing those two roles. Feel how differently you experience yourself? The emotional chords struck by being young and wild versus old and staid are entirely distinct. That rent-a-cop is reacting to more than simple appearances. He is also reacting to subtle cues: their carriage, their energy, their facial expressions. Those inner conditions create an outward appearance, which in turns triggers a corresponding social role. It's all one big ball of synchronistic wax.

With composite Saturn in the first house, these two people center themselves as a couple by embracing the ageing process. No matter their present age, it is profoundly helpful for them to imagine themselves together in their later years. With age comes a certain dignity, and that self-image is very supportive here. Let's add that making a relationship work is an *accomplishment* nowadays. It's something of which two people can be legitimately proud. That's Saturn energy too. The whole point is that there is a kind of *seriousness* in this relationship. That doesn't mean they're humorless or uptight. What it means is that together they are carrying the archetype of the Elder and the more they accept that role, the more their relationship gains clarity, faith in itself, and authority. If they do their work and choose to remain together, they have a destiny in their community: to represent the culmination of a long effort to do the work that love demands. That's a real gift for them to give their community. Early in their relationship, they'll start to get the message that this is what's expected of them: just a short way into their courtship, they'll be startled to realize that people are already imagining that they've been together a long while. They'll be asked if they've "set a date yet." They'll be asked for intimate advice. That's what Elders do, and with composite Saturn in the first house, they'd better get used to it!

COMPOSITE SATURN IN THE SECOND HOUSE

A simpleminded astrologer might imagine that with "malefic" composite Saturn in the house of money, these two people will experience a lifetime of poverty and financial reversals. In practice, that's not a terribly realistic threat. Far more probable is that, if they commit to this relationship, they'll work hard for every penny and gradually, soberly, build a solid material basis for the life they share. Likely, one or both of them will find an "inner financial wizard," perhaps quite unexpectedly. Sudden windfalls of wealth are not to be expected; slow, methodical growth is. That's the spirit of the ringed planet.

The second house covers bases that have nothing to with finance, but before we leave the subject of money, there's one more comment to make. Poverty is not only an objective condition of the checkbook. It is also an attitude. A wealthy person who is constantly worried about money is poor in spirit; a person in more modest circumstances living within his or her means and not thinking much about cash is in many real ways far wealthier. With composite Saturn in the second house, these two need to be wary about the pursuit of money taking up too much of their time and attention. It's very useful for them to practice the discipline of squandering money from time to time, just to keep it in its place. There are people to whom we could say that, and it would be catastrophic advice! But not these two—if anything, they'd err in the opposite direction, trading an abstract promise of a financially secure future for a day-to-day life of monetary stricture.

Going more deeply, the second house is always related to self-confidence. With Saturn there, especially at the early stages of a relationship, these two face the risk of simply *not believing in themselves sufficiently as a couple*. Instead of squandering some money every now and then, they could squander the relationship! Everything under the domain of the ringed planet takes time and patience. While it would be wrong for us to imply that every couple who happens to have a composite Saturn in the second house should commit to a lifetime together, we can say that sticking with the process of courtship is a good move. This is the kind of connection that could be a slow-cooker, building gradually into something that is more than either person imagined it to be at the beginning. As the story unfolds and various milestones of deepening commitment are passed, composite Saturn in the second house becomes a rock-solid foundation for a long, grown-up future together.

COMPOSITE SATURN IN THE THIRD HOUSE

Sound bites, catchy slogans, and bumper stickers serve purposes in the world—and probably in relationships too. Bright people use them as quick-reference summaries of complex ideas; dumb ones use them as a kind of intellectual butter-substitute. But there are communicative processes that cannot be simplified or made to happen in thirty seconds. With composite Saturn in the third house, the success of this couple depends upon their becoming masters of deep, detailed, patient verbal exchanges.

Intimate life is full of paradoxes. We can love people profoundly and yet be angry enough to think of hitting them. We can want children, and mortally dread the responsibilities that having them would entail. We can support our mate's relationship with his or her family, but still not want the in-laws here for the holidays. Try getting any of those situations to fit on a bumper sticker! Discussing situations such as those requires time. Both people have to speak in paragraphs and, ideally, they take turns doing so. It can only be successful if both partners recognize that *deep, serious communication is a priority*, and make time for it. It can never happen during the commercial breaks of a sitcom.

Saturn, on the negative side, is always vulnerable to blockages and frustrations. With composite Saturn in the third house, these two people are at risk of slipping into silence. That's a danger, but it's not their fate in any immutable sense. Here's how that problem can arise and how they can avoid it. Say we love our partner, but we're angry enough to feel tempted to hit him or her, as we described a minute ago. Maybe those feelings are so complex that we don't know how to express them. Maybe the relationship has not developed the essential composite Saturn in the third house *skill* of creating time for dialog. So we clam up. Maybe we're also sitting on that issue of our ambivalence about having children. And the in-laws have just told our answering machine that all seventeen of them want to come for Thanksgiving. Yikes! See how a backlog of unexplored issues can build up? Soon we just don't know where to begin. More silence ensues. Soon enough, the couple is either sitting on a volcano—or just so crippled with a depressing sense of being overwhelmed that the relationship runs out of gas.

All of that is optional. All of it has the same cure: getting past the current cultural climate of instant answers and sound bites, and committing to the Saturn discipline of structuring the relationship in a way that reflects a promise to speak and listen to each other patiently, regularly, and in detail.

COMPOSITE SATURN IN THE FOURTH HOUSE

In the world of intimacy, there is hardly a more powerful symbol than making a home together. It comes in stages, some of them unspoken and tender. Consider the sweet implications, for example, of one lover's first leaving a toothbrush in the other one's bathroom! They've begun the ancient fourth house ritual: two homes are becoming one. Moving up the ladder, a couple begins to live together—or "basically" live together! A couple buys their first home. Behind all fancy verbal posturing about relationships, home is really the bottom line. They do it or they don't do it. That's where a couple walks their talk, if they are truly committed to each other. Or where they face the truth of the limitations on their commitment. Legalisms aside, making a home together is essence of the life-partnership society calls "marriage."

These issues are pressing for most couples, but with composite Saturn in the fourth house, for these two, home is everything. It is the Great Work. It is the make-it-or-break-it issue of their bond. And to get it right, they will have to work hard.

Astrologers who think of Saturn as a bad planet would immediately imagine that this couple will experience misfortune or trouble around trying to establish their nest. We really don't need to be that pessimistic—but it is fair to say that making a home will demand a lot of focused effort and probably a lot of sacrifice on their parts. Maybe they live in a part of the country where real estate prices are sky-high. How long do they have to save to get the sort of place they need? What other sacrifices do they have to make? *Or do they realize that they need to move to another part of the country, perhaps sacrificing some career-potential, because having a home is so important to them?* That might be a very sound psychological calculus for these two, and a good example of how to satisfy Saturn's demands.

Maybe, given modern realities, one or both of them have kids from a previous relationship. How do they form a home under those circumstances? Maybe they live in different cities—if so, *who moves?* With composite Saturn in the fourth, underlying these kinds of vexations is the eternal question: how badly do they want this relationship? Will they take it seriously enough to pay the price? There's no shame in refusing. Not all relationships are meant to last. But ultimately, for these two to move into a shared future, these home-and-hearth questions will need to be addressed.

COMPOSITE SATURN IN THE FIFTH HOUSE

Wherever Saturn lies in a composite chart, a couple must practice discipline. Almost always, Saturn asks us to make the power of our wills dominant over our instincts, appetites and reflexes. The virtues of the ringed planet are stern ones: integrity, maturity, morality, and character. The fruits of a strong response to it are dignity, self-respect and accomplishment.

So what are we to make of composite Saturn in the house of *fun?* Because that's exactly what the fifth house entails: playfulness, joy, and celebration. At first, this composite Saturn configuration appears to be nothing but a massive self-contradiction. Until we think deeply about it.

Our first step in untangling this Saturn placement lies in recognizing that fun is not frivolous. Nor is it something that happens automatically when work stops. Life is very often difficult. As adults, we must accept that reality and deal with it. But in brokering life's difficulties, we become hardened. We get lines on our faces. We become business-like. Just think of the way you feel ten minutes after your alarm rings on Monday morning—and "feel" is actually not the right word there, because the truth is that you are not "feeling" very much at all in that moment: you are simply doing what you must do, putting one foot ahead of the other. The necessity of that grown-up response to life is self-evident. Perhaps less obvious is that we also need to recover from it! And that recovery is the heart of the fifth house: it represents the *evolutionary and psychological need for wild, Dionysian release.* It represents the cure for our necessary "adjustment to reality."

With Saturn in the composite fifth house, a couple must practice the *discipline of celebration.* They must actively and studiously make time for renewal and spontaneity. Underlying these observations is our awareness that such a couple is vulnerable to becoming too stiff and predictable. They can be dangerously out of touch with how tired they are, or with the terrible *mordida* demanded by dutifulness, responsibility and "doing the right thing." They need to remember how much fun it is to go dancing. They need to remind themselves of the simple pleasures of civilization: films, performances, happy restaurants. Bubble baths. Chocolates. And yes—even sex. Dutifulness and tiredness can kill even that.

These concerns are particularly pressing if the couple has children—another basic fifth house correlate. While we wouldn't pay too much attention to grim fortune-telling interpretations of "misfortune through children" with this configuration, we must still be concerned with the risks of the couple's becoming so focused on the needs of their family that they forget their own needs as lovers and as human beings.

Creativity is central to the fifth house, and with their composite Saturn there, these two benefit from a serious, long-term commitment to joint creative projects. Perhaps they landscape a garden together, complete with trees and a fish-pond. Maybe they form a band or become involved with a theater group, and strive for excellence and continuous improvement. Maybe they write a book together. The point is that the attainment of excellence in some shared creative expression can be profoundly engaging and compelling. They can wake up excited on a Saturday morning thinking about it. Behind the hard Saturnian concentration, behind that tremendous outpouring of energy and effort, they're smiling merrily, glad to be alive.

COMPOSITE SATURN IN THE SIXTH HOUSE

Everyone knows that falling in love is a magical world where the air is perfumed, skies are always sunny, and your beloved is the loveliest and most reasonable creature who ever graced your bedspread. And everyone knows that, given a bit of time, the facts of life strike: love is hard work and the merry hormones coursing through your bloodstream are not sufficiently enchanted to make reality disappear. One common metaphor for this intrusion of reality into a relationship is the question, "Who is going to take out the garbage?" It's a good one, so let's start there.

The sixth house has to do with the daily routines of life, garbage-patrol being only one of them. No one enjoys it, of course. And garbage is just one metaphor—what it stands for is the whole range of minor mechanical processes that allow life to continue: cooking, shopping, paying bills, returning calls and email, housecleaning. Even half of that work is a huge drain on our time and energy, which leads us to an elemental principle in trying to understand a couple with their composite Saturn here: if each one of them does half the necessary work, they'll each feel they're personally doing three-quarters of it! That perception leads to resentment, which leads to familiar domestic patterns of treachery—weaseling out of duties, manipulating our partner into doing more, and so on.

Probably no couple is completely immune, but the key is that for these two, *consciously building a fair and rational division of labor in the relationship is absolutely critical*. It won't happen automatically. It requires responsible, mature discussion and compromise. They need to talk about it, realistically assessing each other's natural talents and tastes and coming up with the least odious division of these tasks. And then they need to stick to their promises. That's the grease that allows these wheels to turn.

One of the reasons this skillful handling of daily routine is so important right from the beginning is that very likely, as their story unfolds, they will face some extraordinary, demanding situation that calls for them to make sacrifices for one another: an indigent parent moves in; there is illness in the family; one of the incomes is lost. If they have built the classic Saturn sense of being *an effective team*, they'll rise to this bit of karma. If not, it may be the straw that breaks the camel's back.

COMPOSITE SATURN IN THE SEVENTH HOUSE

An inexperienced astrologer could easily get off on the wrong foot interpreting this configuration—and probably thoroughly frighten the poor couple who had it! Saturn, "the greater malefic," in the house of marriage! Yikes! Run away! Fortunately for our heroes, this reading of the symbolism is totally wrong on two counts. First, there really are no bad planets—every one of them serves a potentially positive purpose, Saturn included. And second, the main meaning of the seventh house in a composite chart is *about relationships the couple has with other people*. It's only indirectly about the couple themselves.

Whenever we see a planet in the seventh, whether it is in an individual birthchart or a composite, we know that other people are the triggers for some kind of essential process. We cannot do it alone, in other words. In this case, we recognize that a couple with composite Saturn in the seventh house needs help. As a couple, they have soulmates. Those soulmates might be single, but they are often other couples.

Relationships are hard. People set out with good intentions and open hearts and often wind up in emotional train wrecks. But there are success stories too. Forget astrology for a moment and apply some common sense. When we're faced with a daunting task, and we have a rational fear of failure and don't really know what we're doing, naturally we take a moment to see how others have done it. We study success and emulate it. We put our feet where others have walked without landing on their heinies. That is exactly what these two, with their composite Saturn in the seventh house, must do.

To whom do they turn for guidance? Their composite chart tells us: their helpful soulmates are of a Saturnine nature. One very simple thought is that they are older. How much older? Enough so that everyone notices it. If our heroes are twenty-year-olds, maybe they look to a couple who are thirty. If they're fifty, that ten years might not be enough: their soulmates might be a happy couple in their seventies who've already weathered storms that are just brewing on the horizon for our duo. Age differences are a common correlate of Saturn, since it refers to "Elders."

But the deeper reality is that Saturn is about wisdom and tempered, digested experience. It's unlikely, but not out of the realm of possibility, that our couple finds guidance in people who are chronologically younger than themselves. In any case, their soulmates display the whole pantheon of positive Saturn qualities. They are mature people with seriousness, realism, and a deep sense of personal integrity. They listen well. If it's a couple, they are deeply and unambivalently committed to each other, and have a realistic sense of each other's strengths and weaknesses. They are disciplined and have a balanced relationship with their pleasures and appetites. They love each other, but you also get the sense that each has made peace with a kind of sacred inner solitude—and that they treasure that quality in each other. If one died, the other would weep—and survive.

Read that last paragraph again in the light of one more perspective: these qualities we see in our heroes' soulmates are the very qualities they themselves need to bring into their bond. They receive them as a gift from the outside, internalize them, and later, just by being who they are, they offer them back to the world.

COMPOSITE SATURN IN THE EIGHTH HOUSE

Single people who read pop-psychology books often speak of "fear of intimacy" as if it were a mental disorder. That's a common perspective nowadays, but anyone who's been in a serious, no-exit sexual relationship is more likely to view such fear as a sign of good reality-testing and normal brain function. Love is profoundly frightening. We all have hot-button issues and places inside ourselves whose existence we just don't want to admit. We're all capable of very dark thoughts. Who has no "inner murderer?" Who has never told a lie? Who hasn't been driven half-crazy by their sexuality?

Take it further. How would you feel with all that information hanging out, as obvious as a billboard? And what if the person reading the billboard is in a position to deal you a crippling psychological blow, if they so chose? What if they are as crazy as you are, and they have an agenda about changing you, controlling you, and making you over in their own image?

Spooky, huh? Welcome to the wonderful world of committed love, at least from the eighth house perspective! It puts "fear of intimacy" in a different light. With any planet in the composite eighth house, a couple has signed up to deal with these deeper psychological territories. With their composite Saturn there, they need to do that work in a "Saturn" way—or those issues will erode their ability to remain committed to each other.

"Commitment" is a key word with Saturn, always. And that is what is required here. How can we possibly trust another person enough to deal with deeper, more threatening kinds of issues? Certainly we are not going to do it with someone who is here today and likely to be gone tomorrow. Trust is founded on vows and promises—vows and promises that have been proven reliable by the only sure test: the passage of time. Two people can meet and truly love each other very quickly. Love can be telegraphed directly from one soul to another, and even though it doesn't make logical sense, most of us have experienced it. But trust is different: it must be forged in the furnaces of difficulties endured and promises kept. With composite Saturn in the eighth house, these two need *to win each other's faith*. That process cannot be rushed. We're dealing with scared, cautious, self-contained places in each of these people—in fact, *healing that particular fear of commitment in each other is what they've signed up to do together*. In that process, it probably takes a hundred promises kept to make up for one broken. It calls for the reassurance that comes from a partner's being consistently honest, committed and honorable. If we strip away all the cultural and social mythology and get right down to the bare bones of composite Saturn in the eighth house, we are talking about the ancient, archetypal reality of marriage, in a spirit of "until death do us part."

Anything less isn't strong enough medicine to make the process of surrendering the ego's defenses safe enough to endure.

COMPOSITE SATURN IN THE NINTH HOUSE

The ninth house is expansive, adventurous, and philosophical, while Saturn is rigorous and grounded. The combination is rich and paradoxical, and a little daunting. With their composite Saturn there, the successful maturation of this couple's relationship depends upon a sustained effort in a challenging direction: figuring out exactly why they are together, what the rules are, and what they believe the meaning of commitment to be.

Religions usually offer a lot of fancy talk about the sanctity of human commitments. Perhaps these two draw some comfort and clarity about their bond from such an ecclesiastical direction. Many astrologers would emphasize the connection between this configuration and traditional religious beliefs. That reading of the symbolism is valid but, while we can honor it, we need not be limited to it. In fact, the trouble with taking refuge in religious support for a bond is simply that it is always about somebody else's words and thoughts. We can say them without having really made them our own. Saturn, on the other hand, always calls for absolute integrity and objective self-analysis. When we are parroting words that aren't real to us personally, we've failed that test—or perhaps a kinder way of saying it is that we are passing tests just fine, but in a lower grade.

So, what is the moral, philosophical basis of this bond? With composite Saturn in the ninth house, that's the question. And it is, to put it mildly, an *essay* question! No quick, pat answer will work. Should your partner fail you grievously, is there anything you have a right *not* to forgive? Discuss. Under what conditions, if any, would you declare yourself free of the vow you've spoken? Discuss. Do people "drift apart," and is that a valid basis for ending a relationship? Do you have the right to keep any secrets at all from each other? Should honesty ever be sacrificed for the sake of kindness? In committing to each other, what are the precise limits and definitions of your commitment to each other's families? Discuss, discuss, discuss.

Ideally, those "discussions" should begin early in the relationship. If two people with this configuration cannot agree on some elemental principles, their bond will very likely fail. Saturn is merciless that way. It can become a black hole if we don't rise to its challenges. And of course no two people will agree on everything! That's not even the aim. Two people can vote for opposing political candidates, united by their higher commitment to respect each other's differences. We doubt that two people can remain together very happily, however, if one believes in sexual fidelity and the other one doesn't. Let them agree on a "religion," walk their talk, and then commit to the reality of endless adjustment and deepening as their lives together unfold.

COMPOSITE SATURN IN THE TENTH HOUSE

Saturn is very strong here. One common interpretation is that this couple is very career-oriented. That pronouncement is not in fact very reliable. Truth is, two people, neither of whom think of a job as anything more than a way to put food on the table and toys in the toy box, can come together with Saturn in their composite tenth. They won't immediately be transformed into dynamos of blind ambition, nor should they be. Their evolutionary work, as individuals and as a couple, maybe very well lie elsewhere.

Another common reading of composite Saturn in the tenth is that a couple with this configuration are likely work together professionally. While there is a little pull in that direction, again it's not a very reliable prophecy.

So what does it mean? Our first step in answering that question is to recognize that, as a culture, we are very work-oriented. That bias has tainted the astrological view of the so-called house of career with an overly professional perspective. The reality is that the tenth house refers to our role in the tribe—the way we look to people who don't know us very well. Work is part of that, but so are a lot of other factors that define us socially, such as our relationship status, where we live, our political and religious affiliations, our ethnicity: all the hats we wear. Taking it up a notch, let's recognize that part of being sane and self-actualized is finding a meaningful role to play in the world. At the risk of making it sound silly, we can call this our "cosmic job description." And that brings us to our point: with composite Saturn in the tenth house, this couple *has* such a job description. In a nutshell, they are to be *Elders*.

Strangely, being Elders has nothing to do with age! Elders guide and advise the "younger people" in the tribe: that is their age-old role. In a composite chart we are talking about a relationship, and so we recognize that these two human beings have signed up to demonstrate to their community how committed love works. They can be natty little conventional types or wild-eyed radicals—in any case, they have a community, and all communities are full of men and women facing the eternal questions of human sexuality. Right from the beginning, their crowd will take their relationship seriously, taking cues from them, watching them carefully. People who believe in love will be rooting for them to make it. Meanwhile, those who look askance upon the idea of two people in a serious life partnership will be doing the opposite: feeling that this relationship is a threat to their lonely belief-system, they'll do their best to sabotage it. In either case, we see the powerful symbolism these two wield.

Many combinations of two people have composite Saturn in the tenth house. Realistically, not all of them are supposed to be together in life. For these two, the stakes are high: the pressure of social expectation alone makes it virtually impossible for them to be in a casual relationship. Like it or not, they will become *symbolic* of intimacy in their community—symbolic of success or symbolic of failure, but always symbolic. That's inherent to the tenth house: it is always public. Ultimately, there is a burden they must decide whether they want to carry: the burden of showing others the way. There is no shame in choosing not to carry it. But if they succeed, the mind immediately races ahead to the magnetic image of two old people walking hand in hand, keepers of each other's histories and secrets, tempered by love, their rough edges smoothed by the crashing waves of decades of intimacy, honesty, and commitment. One wordless look at them and even a stranger has received a blessing.

COMPOSITE SATURN IN THE ELEVENTH HOUSE

Imagine a couple attends a weekend relationship workshop. A positive use of their time or not? It is, of course, a pig in a poke. You never know. Maybe the class is brilliant and helpful—or maybe it's taught by some empty-headed idealist who's yet to experience a romance hitting its first anniversary. In either case, there is one reliable prediction we can make: at the class, *our heroes will encounter other couples who are willing to work seriously on their relationship.* And with composite Saturn in the eleventh house, that's soul-food. These two need the support of that kind of community around them.

The eleventh house is linked to our social network—the faces we recognize, our crowd, our tribe. It's often connected with the word "friends," but that's misleading nowadays: the eleventh house isn't always so intimate. If you are a member of an astrological society or a church or even a group of country-western dancers who put on their cowboys hats the first Saturday of every month, you are familiar with the eleventh house context. With composite Saturn in the eleventh house, this particular couple benefits from having "Saturn" people around them, especially ones who take a "Saturn" attitude toward their own relationships.

If we read a traditional astrology book, those statements might actually seem a little depressing. Why? Because "Saturn people" would probably be represented as abysmally boring. Predictable. Humorless. Literal-minded. Tired, sexless creatures dressed in drab clothes, wearing practical shoes. Yuck! That's a good description of the dark side of Saturn, but that's not what this duo needs—what they need around them is the energy of maturity, honor, commitment, and integrity in relationship. Those virtues are not in any way the opposite of having a good time. In fact, they probably *help* in that department. Solid love is freeing. There is something exhausting and distracting about people "on the make." Being around someone in the midst of heartbreak is tiring too—if we love them, we want to help, but the conversations do tend to sound like familiar litanies. With the "sexual question" more or less settled, the range of joy in life is free to expand beyond the enormous gravitational field our hormones create.

For this couple with composite Saturn in the eleventh house, the company of people in solid, tried-and-true relationships is like fresh air. They can of course support each other in hard times, comparing notes about the bumps in the road of love. When they hit bumps themselves, how precious it is to have people around who are rooting for the relationship rather than expecting it to fail! By contrast, think of the way divorce and breakup can become "contagious" in a group—one couple parts and there's an epidemic. To support their commitment, these two people must simply find their place in the community of long-haul lovers.

COMPOSITE SATURN IN THE TWELFTH HOUSE

Mystical realities are symbolized by the twelfth house, and Saturn is linked to solitude. It's a natural combination—mystics are forever seeking lonely mountaintops and wilderness hideaways. They love getting away from the noise, distractions and temptations of the social world. But with composite Saturn in the twelfth house, we're talking about a relationship: not a solitary condition. How can these pieces add up? Simple: these two people *need to get away together.* They need regular doses of radical, uncontested privacy.

Couples naturally regenerate by withdrawing. Even the most inveterate party animals sooner or later share a private joke before returning their attention to the crowd. Most of us who are closer to the midrange of the introversion-extraversion spectrum feel some relief when guests leave our home, even if we love them and enjoyed ourselves. With composite Saturn in the twelfth, we're simply seeing an exaggerated version of this principle: for this couple, learning to create and defend their own privacy plays a pivotal role in the maturation of their bond. Without those skills, something drains out of the space between them. Their love gets lost in the maze of other, lesser loves: friendships, family life, and so on. It doesn't need to be that way; they can have the solitary time they need and enjoy those other relationships too. Diplomacy—and clear boundaries—are the secrets.

The spiritual life of a couple is always complex, but when there is a composite planet in the twelfth house, it becomes pressing. "Religion" is public and can be shared by a couple, but the twelfth house isn't really about religion. It's more about the notion of direct contact with the next dimension—and that may sound exotic, but anyone who has ever prayed or meditated has had the experience of it. Ditto for anyone who has ever simply walked into a sacred space—a cathedral, an Anasazi kiva, a Zendo—and been blown away by the feeling of the place. The point is that these two need to experience such things together, and the ticket that gets them in is shared solitude. Perhaps they walk into an empty cathedral together. They are quiet. They separate and wander through the alcoves. One looks up and sees the other a hundred feet away, sitting quietly in a pew. The other one sits down too, but not too close—eyes closed, but after a while he or she becomes aware of the partner's presence. Eyes open, a smile, an unspoken understanding—and they both walk out of the building into the sunlight. Only then do they begin talking, and maybe nothing that happened "inside them" is even mentioned. No need to say it. It is simply understood. That is the heart and soul of composite Saturn in the twelfth house. Those silent, shared understandings weave a bond between the souls.

Now, imagine they'd succumbed to social pressure, and brought their noisy nieces and nephews along on the trip . . .

CHAPTER THIRTEEN: THE COMPOSITE URANUS

Uranus spends about seven years in each sign of the zodiac. Result: a lot of people who wind up in relationships with each other have the planet in the same sign. And since composite charts are based on midpoints between planets, their composite Uranus will be in that same sign too. Some astrologers therefore dismiss such planetary symbolism as "just generational." That's a wrongheaded approach, in our opinion: the fact is that if two people, plus their composite chart, all have the planet in the same sign, the effects are quite visibly reinforced.

When people are born with their natal Uranuses in *adjacent* signs, which also happens a lot, then the composite Uranus will fall in one sign or the other—and then it "sides" with the person who's got it in that same sign, giving us at least a hint of a "Feudal System" dynamic, as we described in Chapter Three.

In any case, where the composite Uranus lies, we can hope for some fascinating fireworks. This is the planet of rebellion. It carries the gene for human *zaniness*. Always, it represents an area in a couple's life together where, if they are going to be true to their hearts, they're going to get into some interesting trouble. Society—which may mean their culture, their community, their ethnic context, or their families—has one plan for them; their souls have another. Who will win? That's uncertain. It depends on their own courage, creativity and self-awareness. But one point is sure: if they get it right, they'll "look wrong," and if they get it wrong, they'll "look right." What feeds them as a couple may seem offensive to other people. Or it may seem grossly impractical, crazy, or simply silly. If they are true to themselves, pressure on them to change will mount. Naturally, such pressure can draw them closer together, make them stronger as a unit. Or they can succumb to it, falsifying their lives and creating an uncomfortable feeling of "going through the motions" in the area of life defined by the position of their composite Uranus.

There's a wild card feeling about this planet. Where it falls in the composite chart, especially in terms of its house placement, there is a tendency for strange and unexpected developments to unfold. Underlying that apparent chaos is a basic Uranian principle: "cosmic matching funds." If the partners are true to themselves, typically that means painting themselves into a corner somehow—breaking out of the "safe" patterns established by society is dangerous, impractical business. It seems that, if the couple is willing to do that anyway, the universe will create odd and unusual circumstances that support going forward against the odds. But only if they've determined to do it anyway!

COMPOSITE URANUS IN ARIES

One day in Jodie's yoga class, her teacher said, "And whoever has had the most assertiveness training can come take these foam blocks." Silence! We were all completely derailed. What were we supposed to do? There were enough blocks to go around, but no one wanted to look aggressive or greedy by taking one first. None of us had Uranus in Aries, but it felt like a Uranus in Aries moment nonetheless.

The Lord of Individuality in the sign of the Warrior! Does that mean this couple should start a revolution? Not necessarily, but they've got some thinking to do about the whole function of courage, willpower and assertion in their lives and in their relationship.

Sometimes it seems that in no area of life do we get more socialization than in how to handle our Aries function of will, assertiveness and anger, beginning with but not limited to The Terrible Twos, the time of our first Mars returns. A long discussion of gender politics is beyond the scope of this book, but men are probably socialized to be more tough and aggressive than they actually are, and women are probably socialized to be less so.

But the questions run deeper than that. What's worth getting angry about? What requires a show of force or an act of will? What should our boundaries be? The answers vary more by culture than we might think. In some cultures, *not* sleeping with your host's wife was an insult. In others, showing the soles of your shoes is an offense. Fans have been known to kill one another at soccer matches. These are *learned* responses, not innate ones.

A couple with composite Uranus in Aries needs to work out for themselves where they will draw their own lines in the sand, when they'll rattle their sabers and when they'll use them. And if they're doing a good job with this composite Uranus placement, their decisions may puzzle or even shock other people, but that's not our couple's problem!

COMPOSITE URANUS IN TAURUS

The sky is our father; the earth is our mother. We are all natives of this planet; it is our natural habitat. We are all mammals, all primates, intelligent ones but primates nonetheless. Our bodies were designed for use, and work best when they are fed properly, move wisely, and rest and play and cuddle enough.

How quickly we forget these basic facts of our existence. In much of the industrialized world, most of our lives are spent in little boxes with four walls. We've polluted the outside air. Many people barely spend a moment outdoors, eat atrocious diets, never stretch, never move, and don't sleep enough.

For Uranus in physical, earthy, kinesthetic Taurus, that is madness.

This composite Uranus sign needs to revolutionize its treatment of its primate self. Here we may find a couple who sleep on their screened-in porch in the open air, who go camping, who practice yoga daily. These partners may refuse to join the rat race and maintain the crazy pace we Americans demand of ourselves. They may walk or bike to work, rather than drive. They may spend time and money on regular massage and other types of bodywork—recovering the power of touch is important for them. They may experiment with their diet until they find the one that most fills them with vitality.

As we write these words, there are about five inches of snow on the ground. Both of our cats have gone outside just long enough to sniff the air, set a paw in the snow, shake off the offending white flakes and retreat into the warm house and their cat beds. But on a temperate day, they tend to come in only long enough to eat and get a quick pat. They are just doing what cats do: following their instincts. A couple with composite Uranus in Taurus needs to do the same thing, and honor their instinctive side.

COMPOSITE URANUS IN GEMINI

Gemini, the Storyteller, the Journalist, the Observer. First of the Air signs, with all of Air's mental and conceptual outlook. The eternal student, the messenger with winged feet, the glib and curious youth, in love with ideas and with youth itself.

What happened when the generation with natal Uranus in Gemini got to college? An outpouring of insatiable curiosity about the rest of the world and the life of the mind. More than once, we've heard professors tell us that there was unusual brilliance in the student body during those years, brilliance of a degree they hadn't seen before and haven't seen since. A lot of other things happened, too. Student unrest. Journalism as a revolutionary tool. Teaching as a subversive activity. Peter Pan joined a rock and roll band. And a number of young people claimed they wanted to keep their options open as long as possible, and that they valued Experience over Stability: no job, no possessions, no commitments except to a life of maximal freedom and wonder.

Times change, and time catches up with us all. There's no shame in the maturing process. Yet a couple with composite Uranus in Gemini needs to make sure that their life together remains *interesting* to them both. That may mean using their brains, their feet, their library cards or their Frequent Flyer miles. It may mean taking a class rather than nodding off in front of endless reruns on television. And, all other things being equal, they should opt for a fascinating vacation before they recarpet the family room.

Let's say that our couple heeds the Pied Piper call of their composite Uranus in Gemini, saves their money, uses all of that sign's verbal ability to parley their way into six months off from their respective jobs, rents an RV and goes traveling across the continent. They home school their kids on the road. The neighbors think they're strange. Their state's school system doesn't approve, but can't very well stop them. The kids' grandparents may border on apoplectic. *Yet that couple has done more for their marriage in those six months than six years of living just like everyone else would do.*

COMPOSITE URANUS IN CANCER

Where Uranus lies, we need to break the rules and follow our own path. We tend to individuate both *from* and *through* the typical characteristics of the sign where our Uranus is located, and this is just as true for couples as it is for an individual. What do we associate with Cancer? A flippant answer might be Mom, home and apple pie, but let's look at this placement a bit more closely.

Cancer has to do with *nurturing,* both physical and emotional. It has to do with *a rich inner life.* It prefers *a secure nest* in which to accomplish all of the above. A couple with composite Uranus here needs to make conscious decisions about these areas of their shared lives.

Nurturing: this can apply to how they nurture each other, pets or a garden, but the most typical meaning is children. Should these two have children? As is typical where Uranus lies, they will get a lot of well-intended advice here that won't work for them. As someone once said, "It's wonderful to have children, and it's wonderful not to have them." Which side of this fence our couple comes down on should be entirely up to them. If they decide to have children, the same Uranian logic applies to how those kids are raised: according to how this couple best sees fit. If they don't have children, no one should be allowed to shame them or pressure them about it.

Nurturing is food, too. Perhaps they need to arrive at their own diet plan, and we don't mean a reducing diet, but such things as joining a local food co-op, growing their own vegetables, or exploring a vegan lifestyle.

A rich inner life: self-actualization is important for this couple. In an ideal world, they would be able to make decisions about their relationship based on the top levels of the psychologist Abraham H. Maslow's hierarchy of needs: love, creativity, self-actualization, personal growth, spiritual pursuits. Many of us are too busy dealing with the lower levels—survival, food, clothing, shelter—to have time or resources to devote to the higher levels, yet the higher levels are grist for the mill for Cancer. Perhaps this couple needs to limit their wardrobe in order to free up some money for yoga seminars. Perhaps they need to settle for lower incomes in order to develop their art.

A secure nest: what constitutes security for this couple may not be a retirement plan, a home in the suburbs, and the accumulation of material goods. They may experiment with housing arrangements, or strive to live as simply as possible.

Obviously, there can be trade-offs among these features of Cancer: nurturing, a rich inner life, and security, since it isn't always easy to attain all three. These partners need to choose for themselves what the right balance among these factors is for them.

COMPOSITE URANUS IN LEO

Comfort. Acceptance. Warmth. Humor. Self-expression. And a certain display of personal style and flair that derives from all of the above (and we don't mean in the clothing department). That's what Leo's all about. A planet in this sign has learned all it can from self-flagellation, and requires *joy* to evolve any further.

This couple needs to say "yes" to life, and to help them do so, they need to play. If the various, joy-affirming, life-enhancing reasons why it's *good* to be alive—chocolate, orgasms, hot tubs, nature, pets, music, hiking, jokes, etc.—are amputated from their relationship, they're in trouble.

Your own list of fun might have been different than the one in the above paragraph. If you're a couple with Uranus in Leo, then more power to you! Go enjoy life however it most pleases you to do so. Yet because Uranus is involved here, what you relish may be puzzling to the mainstream. Baseball trading card conventions? Rebuilding ancient 486 PCs? The Society for Creative Anachronism? Never mind the raised eyebrows at the office; just dive right in. One hint: Leo planets also thrive on applause, so if you can get some positive feedback from the folks who share your offbeat tastes, so much the better.

But how you're having fun is only half the battle. The other half is claiming your right to have as much of it as you need. We live in a culture of maniacal overworkers, partly by choice, partly by necessity—or perceived necessity. Europeans *average* three to six weeks of *paid* vacation *every year*. Think about it.

A couple with composite Uranus in Leo should remember: on our deathbeds, we are usually more inclined to value whatever we did that opened our hearts, not how many hours of overtime we put in.

COMPOSITE URANUS IN VIRGO

Here is a classic Virgo word: *should*. What a couple is "supposed" to do seems eternally opposed to what they actually want to do. The situation has that primordial Virgo signature: the tension between the ideal and the real, between "should" and "want." It's fashionable in some circles nowadays to hold the position that we *shouldn't say "should"*—a position fraught with some humorous paradoxes, needless to say. But without "should," we would have no room in our lives for those solid Virgoan qualities: conscience, altruism, and civil behavior.

The challenge facing the couple with their composite Uranus in Virgo lies in successfully throwing out the bath water while preserving the baby. Maybe they've accumulated a ton of empty plastic bottles. They "should" re-cycle them. Fair enough: our ability to survive on this planet depends upon our willingness to live in more ecologically savvy ways. That's just self-preservation, and only idiots, manufacturers of plastic bottles, and certain elected officials would argue with it. Maybe these partners with composite Uranus in Virgo have good professional jobs. They "should" keep those jobs as if life itself depended upon them, and give up this crazy idea of cashing in their chips, going to Nepal to study Buddhism and eventually opening a Buddhist center somewhere.

Hmm.

Whose voice is speaking there? At one obvious level, the answer is that it is the voice of the world—the collective, anti-Uranian chorus of everyone who has ever given them "common sense" advice about how they "should" live their lives. At a deeper level, that limiting, boring, repressive voice is coming from inside them. And that is often the most tangled thread for people with composite Uranus in Virgo to sort out—their *internalized* "tribal" voice, that intimate part of themselves that purports to speak for their souls . . . and actually has a lot more to do with the values motivating the characters they saw on television before they were ten years old.

We are nothing without values and principles. The task facing this couple is to make sure that those values and principles are in fact their own.

COMPOSITE URANUS IN LIBRA

Libra, the traditional sign of marriage. What could this independent planet mean here?

Let's start by stating that Libra is also the sign of fairness, moderation, reciprocity and the formation of aesthetic relationships as well as human ones. Libra needs balance, both in and out of relationships.

Remember that Uranus in a sign rebels both *against* and *through* the matters of that sign. Here the relationship itself, and the very notion of relating, are subject to scrutiny by the Lord of Independence. This couple needs *to choose to be together*, not drift into a union through habit and because of societal expectations.

They may well question some of the age-old traditions around love, and come up with their own answers. Something about their relationship itself needs to break the rules. Which ones? We don't know. It may be as simple as the man's not always walking on the half of the sidewalk closest to the traffic, if the couple is heterosexual. It may be as profound as never living under the same roof—they may have a horror of feeling joined at the hips.

They may have married across socioeconomic or racial boundaries. They may take separate vacations. They may go through a private ceremony of re-commitment once a week. Whatever they do, they shouldn't take the relationship as a given, but as a living, breathing art, a work in progress, a balancing act.

How this couple deals with its friendships may also be affected by composite Uranus in Libra. Choosing their friends, and deciding on their friends' roles and importance in the relationship, can be a brave new world for these partners. So can their taste in the arts. What decorates their walls may shock or startle a less conventional couple, but for these two, beauty really is in the eye of the beholder.

The challenge for this couple is to make the relationship a day by day performance art, deliberately chosen, and not hide behind a wall of "niceness."

COMPOSITE URANUS IN SCORPIO

A few years ago in Canada we saw an interesting piece of graffiti: "Psychological Revolution Now!" In a bumper-sticker kind of way, that phrase captures the spirit of composite Uranus in Scorpio. This is the sign of making the unconscious conscious. To that end, it is intense, brooding, passionate and self-analytical. It wants depth, and employs psychological perceptiveness and honesty to get there.

When you were growing up, you might have been told not to discuss religion, politics, sex or money at the dinner table or at parties. Later, magazines might have advised you not to discuss your sexual pasts, insecurities, or attractions outside the relationship with one another, and to be very careful indeed about criticizing each other's families.

In general, that's probably good advice, even in these permissive times. For a couple with composite Uranus in Scorpio, however, that advice just doesn't work very well. If they sense polite evasions or skillful minimizing, they'll feel compelled to probe beneath the surface of those defenses. Friends with less revelatory dispositions may be appalled at what these partners discuss with one another, but that's what works for composite Uranus in Scorpio.

With a few caveats. It *is* possible to go too far in such conversations, and neither partner should carry it to the extent of bullying or shaming the other one. Also, this composite Uranus sign is not a license to go probing unasked into the psyches of people outside of the couple.

Scorpio also has to do with our reactions to death and dying. These partners would do well to have some frank talks about those issues, and figure out how they want to handle their estates, whether they want living wills, or what sort of funeral arrangements each might prefer. What each of them thinks happens to the essence of the person after the body dies is another good subject for discussion, and for sharing individual opinions.

The challenge for this composite Uranus sign lies in the couple's making their own individuated response to the areas of life most of us term "taboo:" sexuality, death and dying, the occult, and the deep unconscious, without either pointlessly going too far or retreating into shallowness.

COMPOSITE URANUS IN SAGITTARIUS

What do you believe in? Love? God? Buddhism? What helps you make your life meaningful? Progress? Education? Ecology?

Sagittarius has to do with generating a certain philosophy of life or world view, with choosing what stars we steer by. It is a sign that needs to move toward a belief system, to have faith in something.

But with Uranus in Sagittarius, the whole question of what beliefs shape our lives and why is brought sharply into focus. The search for meaning can be extreme or, if sufficiently frustrated, can even turn to cynicism and expediency—those are "religions," too. Here are a few others:

Aim for the American dream: a nice house, two cars and two children.

Look out for number one.

Attend the church of your choice.

A rolling stone gathers no moss.

College and graduate or professional schools are the best route to a better-paying job.

Live fast, die young and live a good-looking corpse.

We could spend all day naming these religions great and small, but the point is that the couple with Uranus in Sagittarius should accept none of them blindly. They should believe nothing without questioning it thoroughly first.

Travel helps this sign grow, so perhaps this couple will shun that house-holding American dream in order to stay mobile. They may skip extra education for hands-on experience. And they might "leave the church of their fathers," join it, or start a new one all their own.

Like its opposite number, composite Uranus in Gemini, composite Uranus in Sagittarius needs a wide variety of experiences, but ideally they should all contribute to the evolution of this couple's worldview. Whoever said "the road of excess leads to the palace of wisdom" undoubtedly had a lot of Sagittarian energy!

COMPOSITE URANUS IN CAPRICORN

What could it mean for this couple to individuate both *against* and *through* the energies of the sign of the Wise Elder, the Executive, and the Prime Minister?

Capricorn seeks accomplishments, Great Works. It can exude a natural authority. Its drive is to become a master of manifestation in the material world, the outer world of form.

The mini-generation of people with the Lord of Independence in this pragmatic sign will be called upon to re-examine the roles of integrity, achievement and self-containment in their lives. What will they want to accomplish by the end of their time on the planet? What mark might they want to leave behind them? A reformed company? A sane family? A work of art? A political or legal change in society? There's no way to tell for sure, but we can be fairly sure that it won't be "business as usual" with this couple, and we can be positive that it shouldn't be.

To accomplish what they need to do, these partners will have to break the rules, and that may be difficult for them. It must have been hard for Gandalf, the wizard in *The Lord of the Rings,* to refuse the head of his order Saruman's request that the wizards ally themselves with the Dark Lord, Sauron. Gandalf made that refusal at not a little personal cost. Yet he did the right thing, and helped save Middle Earth from Sauron thereby. It must have been hard for Mr. Spock, the Vulcan science officer in the original *Star Trek*, to leave his own Vulcan people and join a human crew, not to mention sacrificing himself to save the ship and its personnel in one of the *Star Trek* movies.

Remember those bumper stickers from the 1980s and 1990s: "Subvert the Dominant Paradigm"? Those are Uranus in Capricorn bumper stickers! What did Gandalf and Spock do, in the above examples? They started out working within the dominant paradigm, then left it. Interestingly, by doing so they happened to serve not only their individual growth, but the common good.

Finally, this couple is called upon to define the meaning of true success, accomplishment and integrity for themselves, not according to societal measures.

COMPOSITE URANUS IN AQUARIUS

The Lord of Individuality is powerful in his own sign, and that means he'll be a powerful force in the lives of this couple. Whatever house he occupies will be a charged and busy one in their lives.

We're about to say something that will sound like a play on words, but we mean it quite literally and sincerely: this couple must figure out the individuation process of their relationship by themselves. Workshops on finding their true selves, or discovering the heart's core of their marriage, however well intended or skillfully presented, will not work very well for them. They are striking out on new relating territory alone, with no idea what might lie ahead. The trusted old maps simply don't apply to their terrain.

How does that feel? It can be not only bewildering, but stressful. *Adaptability* and *openness to the new* are key here. We're reminded of a young adult science fiction novel that Jodie treasured in her childhood, *The Universe Between*, by Alan E. Nourse. In this novel, a portal to a new universe had opened up, but everyone we first sent there went insane, because the laws of our physics simply did not apply there. It's been a long time since Jodie read this book, so she may not have remembered these examples precisely, but they'll serve to give you the general idea. Rectangles could have five sides, not four, yet still be rectangles. Right angles didn't have to be ninety degrees, yet still were right angles. Mathematicians in the other universe could divide by zero with impunity, while trying to do that here produces nonsense equations. Finally, we figured out why our envoys were all coming back as gibbering nervous wrecks, and we started testing potential envoys for their adaptability in dealing with strange new realities.

That's what it can be like to have composite Uranus in Aquarius: unnerving! All the rules for relating just don't apply any more. The trick is for this couple not to let that unsettle them, not to buckle under the stress nor cling to old ways that won't work for them, but rather to adapt by creating their own rules.

COMPOSITE URANUS IN PISCES

Pisces, sign of the Mystic and the Dreamer and the Visionary. Or, if responded to less skillfully, the Escapist. The goal of this sign is to experience itself as consciousness, not just personality, to experience other realities as just as real as this one. To that end, compassion and imagination are major tools.

How this couple walks the border between reality and fantasy is at issue with composite Uranus in Pisces. They are working on a revolution in mysticism, in whatever form that might take for them. They'll have some trouble living as purely rational, scientific, atheistic, empirical thinkers, because the whole thrust of Uranus in Pisces is counter to that mind set. For Pisces, reality is fluid. "Question Authority" is an Aquarian bumper sticker, but "Question Reality" is a Piscean one! Thus, there can be a delightful irreverence about the "real world" to this couple, a shared sense of the cosmic joke, and a refusal to take officiousness very seriously, whether they find it in organized religion, the New Age, or government offices.

They may need to be careful about not rebelling against consensus reality to the point where they lose their ability to function in it. Meditation, creativity, compassion and humor are all constructive ways to explore consciousness, but there are destructive and addictive ones, too. Another shadow side of composite Uranus in Pisces might be a sort of learned helplessness, a shared assumption that reality is simply too overwhelmingly harsh and difficult to deal with. That's not true! This composite Uranus sign needs to learn to be graceful about accepting the endings, the transitions and the unknown in their lives, but that doesn't mean surrendering their internal locus of control.

The challenge for this couple is to enjoy developing their unique take on the transrational side of existence, and to let their imagination and compassion flourish, without retreating into unhealthy escapism.

COMPOSITE URANUS IN THE FIRST HOUSE

The classic astrological interpretation of this placement would be that, regardless of how conservative or mild these people may be as individuals, as a couple they give an immediate first impression of uniqueness, zaniness or downright eccentricity and unpredictability. In extreme cases, that first impression may include detachment, alienation, contrariness or even sociopathy. They don't give off the same "vibes" as everybody else. Wherever they are, they don't seem to fit in. Something about them just sticks out like the proverbial sore thumb. Security officials question them at airports. They get pulled over for more than their share of "routine" license checks. Stand-up comedians target them in the audience. What's happening here? The Lord of Individuality is part of the face this couple wears in the world. Their shared mask is imbued with the energy of the Rebel and the Non-conformist. Of course this astrological signature can draw attention and projections.

But that's not the entirety of what this composite configuration *should* do. This couple shouldn't stop at merely *looking* different. The Ascendant has been called "the identity in action." This couple needs to act—Ascendant—according to the imperatives of the unique—Uranian—entity that they form together. Frankly it's hard to say exactly what a composite first house Uranus should do, because that's the couple's own decision. About all we can state with any certainty is that it means questioning all the current status quos for a relationship, and making up their own minds whether those status quos work for them.

There are a million unwritten rules for how we are supposed to relate, and every culture and subculture has its own. The man drives, pays the bills and maintains the family computer. The woman grocery shops, cooks and does the laundry. They vacation together and attend all parties together. They alternate whose families they see at what holidays. They eat three meals a day whether they're hungry or not.

But not without *questioning* all of the above, if they have composite Uranus in the first house. Perhaps that means not getting married. If they do, perhaps it means changing both of their last names to an entirely different third name, or not living together. Maybe it means changing their religion, breaking family traditions, or keeping a telescope on the roof of their house and a pool table in their living room.

It's when those unwritten rules are never questioned, and are slavishly followed, that this composite Uranus house placement starts to *act out* the couple's individuality, rather than to *act upon* it. Perhaps, in an ideal world, these two were meant to leave New York City and run a ranch in the Montana outback. Perhaps some failure of nerve has kept them from doing so. What do they do instead? Dress the whole family in cowboy outfits, and endure raised eyebrows or worse from all over Manhattan. Suppose they buy that ranch after all; will they still get stopped by security at the airport? Probably. It's hard to have this composite Uranus placement without some ambivalent reactions—so those reactions might as well be to the life that this couple truly *chose* to lead.

COMPOSITE URANUS IN THE SECOND HOUSE

Fluctuating and unstable finances! With composite Uranus in the traditional house of money, that's what the fortune-teller would predict for these two. Why might that be? To answer that question, we have to look more closely at the concept of money as a symbol. Symbolism is not literalism. What might money symbolize?

Energy. The power to survive in the world. The freedom to live one's life as one chooses. That for which we trade our time and skills and effort. That which we trade for something we find valuable enough to buy.

Now we're getting warmer. The second house also shows that which we value, that which we hold dear, that which we consider a precious resource. If we have enough of that resource, we feel confident in our ability not merely to survive, but to thrive. If we don't have enough of that resource, we feel bereft, and our self-esteem, as well as our chance of survival, heads south.

Society fills us with an unreasoning need to buy things. Canny retailers put impulse items by the cash register and on their shelves' end caps, or put loss leaders in their windows. The media is full of ads about the latest product that's all the rage, that's better than sliced bread, that will transform our sex lives, our bank accounts, our productivity, our leisure hours, our "cool" factors. In Western society, this materialistic brainwashing starts in our infancy and doesn't stop until our deathbed.

Our point here is not to bash the advertising industry: we live in a consumer society too, and we probably like our toys as much as the next person. Our point is that most of us *think* we need a lot more stuff than we actually do. If you don't believe us, go visit a yard sale, or a place that rents storage units. But what do we actually need? What do we actually value? Talk to a couple whose house burned down. Ask them what they grabbed on their way out the door. Chances are that if there's anything on the list besides their kids, their pets and their hard drives, then the rest of the list begins with something like photographs. Heart-stuff. Items with sentimental value. What do they most regret not having been able to save? Chances are it's not their channel zapper or their clothing.

"Sentimental" value has a lot to do with the second house. What do you hold most valuable? After your loved ones, what would you save from a fire? Think about it. A musical instrument or a CD? Then music is one of your core values, and a core resource, too. Your grandfather's diary? Then family is a core value and a core resource.

"Where your treasure is, there your heart is also." A couple with composite Uranus in the second house needs to define *for themselves* what that treasure is, what their values are, and honor those values. Maybe their treasure is time to travel together. Then they might need to resist advertisers' pressures to buy the latest stereo equipment, window treatments, a microwave, a riding lawnmower and patio furniture, and start saving for an RV, or for a month off with a Eurail pass. Mom and Dad might think their house is sparsely furnished, and the neighbors might think their lawn is ill-kept, but so what? Whose house and lawn are they, anyway?

Suppose our couple has misdefined their treasure. Remember those "fluctuating and unstable" Uranian finances? Look carefully at what that couple has lost—was that loss a blessing in disguise? An unconscious Uranian yard sale? Look just as carefully at their "impulsive" purchases; do they say anything about that couple's real treasure?

COMPOSITE URANUS IN THE THIRD HOUSE

The Lord of Rebellion in the house of speech. True or false: does this couple "have a mouth on them," as we say in the South? All couples communicate, both with one another and with the outside world. But this couple has a greater tendency to have a smart mouth, or tendencies toward foot-in-mouth disease, than most do.

How does society say that we should handle communication within a relationship? It has rules, of course, regardless of the fact that some of them are contradictory. Don't fight when you're tired. Don't go to bed angry. If you can't say something nice, don't say anything at all. Honesty is paramount. Everything should be put on the table for discussion. What you don't know can't hurt you. Some of these rules vary from culture to culture. We hear from British friends that they are far less likely to discuss their past relationships with their mates than Americans are, and that British couples tend to fight about whose family of origin was saner, while American couples seem more likely to fight about whose family was crazier.

Confused? So is a couple with composite Uranus in the third house. Only Uranian rules should apply to them, and those rules are worked out by their own trials and errors, not handed down by their parents or picked up from their friends. Maybe they have a serious conference about the state of their relationship once a month. Maybe they figure if it ain't broken, don't fix it. Perhaps they never write down their dinner dates with friends or holidays with family. Perhaps their appointment diary runs two years ahead, and copies of it hang in the kitchen and by every phone in the house. It can take time to arrive at the communicative style that works for them, and what works for them may change. And if it doesn't resemble the communicative style of any other couple on the planet, so what?

What should they talk about? Whatever they please. Above all, neither of them should feel censored by the other in any way.

What about how these partners communicate with people outside the relationship? Again, they need to make up their own rules, and they'll dislike any feeling of being censored or edited. Yet each culture does have some mores about what's appropriate to discuss in a social context, and these two may get a reputation for their blithe disregard of Emily Post and Miss Manners in that regard. Sometimes common sense or self-preservation indicates it might be better to keep one's mouth shut, too. From time to time, this couple may have a perfectly good and self-serving reason to watch their language. If they wind up blurting out something "inappropriate" regardless, they might be wise to observe carefully what that thoughtless remark got them out of, or into, and how that might relate to their individuation as a couple.

COMPOSITE URANUS IN THE FOURTH HOUSE

Uranus, Lord of rebels, of geniuses and revolutionaries. Planet of misfits, mad scientists and sociopaths, too. Doesn't sound very homey, does it? No, not if by "homey" you mean the traditional nuclear household of Betty Crocker and apple pie, Leave It to Beaver and Donna Reed. For baby boomers, their parents and a lot of Gen Xers, that televised family mythos was the norm. Dad worked; Mom stayed home and raised the kids.

Let's look at some statistics about households. The Bureau of the Census's 2000 Census showed that only 69% of American households—defined as people living under the same roof—had at least two members related by blood, marriage, or adoption. Married couples without children formed the largest segment of those households. In 2000, the average U.S. household size, family or non-family, was 2.59 persons, while the average family size was 3.14 persons. According to www.learnframe.com, almost 80% of U.S. families are either dual-income or single-parent households, and *only 7% of families* fit the stereotypical Ozzie-and-Harriet model of a never-divorced working father and a stay-at-home mother.

That mythic family model no longer corresponds to the American majority's reality at all, if indeed it ever did. Yet some of us feel unmoored, as if something is not quite right, as if we are somehow not "normal," in proportion to how far our own households deviate from that internalized norm.

How did you feel reading those statistics? Relieved? Intrigued? Startled? Annoyed? The facts don't fit the myth. Where did the myth go? What are our households supposed to be like now? That's a composite Uranus in the fourth house feeling: *the old family mythology doesn't work, and we have to create our own households.*

There's no telling how this couple will react. Maybe they'll live apart. Perhaps they'll join an intentional community or a commune or a three family household. They might try a long distance relationship or a commuter marriage. They could live on a houseboat, on a space station, in a gypsy caravan or in the house next door. The only certainties are, first, that *they must intentionally choose their own living arrangements*, regardless of how traditional or *avant garde* those arrangements are. Perhaps our couple settles in Norman Rockwell suburbia, but they have hippie parents who live in a treehouse. Perhaps they have Norman Rockwell parents, but they've moved into a huge yurt with one big happy family consisting of five of their dearest friends, three cats, two ferrets and a possum named Mulroy. No matter: they must be willing to defend their choice of whatever hearth works best for them.

COMPOSITE URANUS IN THE FIFTH HOUSE

Simply having fun together is an essential ingredient for lasting love. It balances the hard inner work that love requires, and it helps us face the stresses and frustrations of everyday life. With their composite Uranus in the fifth house, these two people need to have a good time, just like the rest of us—but they need to do it their own way. In simple terms, they'll probably develop some odd hobbies or avocations, and in that process, some strange friendships as well.

Here's the deeper story: there are people who love to watch football games, and others who find them boring and predictable. One person loves opera; another one says she'd rather listen to fingernails scraping a blackboard. Just simply discovering the truth about what kinds of playful activities actually have a revivifying impact on this couple is their challenge. Chances are good that the answers lie outside the realm of conventional behaviors. Not everyone is attracted to the idea of stamp-collecting, but for these two, despite the "geek" factor, it might really be perfect. What about searching for arrowheads or photographing polar bears? What about exploring caves?

And here's a still deeper version of the story: from the cradle, we are *told* what is fun and what isn't. We are expected to enjoy parties more than work. We are told that by a certain age, we should "outgrow" certain fashions or certain kinds of music. Who says? Always with composite Uranus in the fifth house the core idea is that there is tension between how the couple has been trained to enjoy themselves and the reality of what they actually need. If they respond weakly, they will dutifully "have fun" just as they have been told by their social class how to do—and gradually wither from sheer soul-tiredness. A conservative couple with this configuration might need simply to admit to themselves that they *hate* going to their exclusive country club. A wilder couple might realize that they actually don't want to listen to this "very chic" jam band or hip-hop group anymore—the music just isn't moving them the way (gulp) old Frank Sinatra records do!

Uranus in the fifth house is really all about the freedom to have fun in a way that really works. And that is a lot more difficult than it sounds. The process starts with very honest conversation, and the conversation itself must start by making sure that the couple is *really* all alone in the room—no figures of authority or arbiters of "cool" are lurking inside them, listening and judging.

COMPOSITE URANUS IN THE SIXTH HOUSE

Uranus is naturally rebellious, and the sixth house is about exactly the kinds of daily duties and boring requirements that bring out resentment in most couples: housecleaning, shopping, changing the oil in the car, mowing the lawn. Almost universally, people imagine that they are doing more than their "fair share," that their partners underestimate how hard they're working, and that the other person is getting away with shirking the odious tasks that make life possible. The root cause of this tension is easy to understand: simply sustaining daily life is a huge, time-consuming job. It all seems trivial and dull, but the hard, sad fact is that it takes up most of our waking hours.

With their composite Uranus in the sixth house, this couple must be both vigilant and creative regarding their division of labor. Vigilance is needed because, with this configuration, it is very easy for the couple to slip into a stubborn pattern of "stand-off" about every day responsibilities, each one rebelling against their duties. The result is obvious: the need for routine housecleaning starts to look more like the need for demolition and urban renewal! These problems gather interest, in other words. If this couple is not vigilant about their own tendency toward rebelliousness here, the situation can spin out of control. Taxes and bills aren't paid. Important phones call aren't returned. And the condition of the cat box begins to impact their social lives.

Creativity—always a Uranian quality—plays a helpful role here. Maybe they both hate housecleaning with a passion. Well, maybe they've got a friend who'll gladly do it in exchange for cat-sitting and the right to borrow their truck when she's gardening. Maybe they can play poker, with the chips representing Get-Out-Of-Dishwashing-Free passes. Always, with Uranus, the right answer is essentially one that no one in the history of the world has ever considered before. These two may not be able to escape the practical, physical requirements of life, but they can approach them in novel, conscious ways—and probably get a laugh out of their answers, to boot!

COMPOSITE URANUS IN THE SEVENTH HOUSE

The seventh house is traditionally the part of the chart that describes intimate relationships. That's still quite valid. But all composite charts, by definition, are about relationships. There is no symbol anywhere in one of them that *isn't* of a "seventh house nature," so to speak. Thus, when we observe a planet in the seventh house of a composite chart, we must overcome the reflex to think of it narrowly as "describing the relationship," even though it does that to some extent. Instead, we must think about the *relationships of the relationship*—the friends, soulmates, rivals, partners, and so forth who help the couple fulfill their evolutionary intentions.

With Uranus in the composite seventh house, these external partners play a crucial role in the primary relationship. Elemental to understanding of any seventh house planet in any human astrological context is the fact that we cannot do what we came here to do without the help of the people it describes. For the couple with composite Uranus in the seventh house, there is a need for feedback about leading their own lives as a couple, about designing their own unique relationship, that comes to them from sources outside themselves. The people who carry this message are Uranian. They are independent, original, highly individuated, even quirkish or eccentric. They are very much their own persons. They may well be controversial, and our couple's association with them may raise a few eyebrows.

What is the nature of the gift these Uranian soulmates bring to the couple? Maybe they teach by example: perhaps they dropped out of the corporate rat race and opened their own B and B. Maybe their input is more direct and challenging: a couples therapist who encourages these partners to move away from their crazymaking families. In any event, the Uranian soulmates will have a lot of insight about how we needlessly distort ourselves and our partners to make a relationship work, and how we might behave in ways that are more authentic for us.

COMPOSITE URANUS IN THE EIGHTH HOUSE

Sex is so paradoxical: in human relationships, it complicates everything while making everything possible. Everyone knows that sexual bonds are stormier than simple friendships. But every couple understands the way sexual contact can mysteriously rebuild the deep sense of connection that the storms sometimes wash away. With their composite Uranus in the house of sexuality, these two people have a specific challenge: they must chart their own unique course through this maze of ancient mammal-programming and transcendent soul-experience.

Wherever Uranus lies, we must think for ourselves. The social scripts we've inherited just won't work meaningfully for us. And yet it is harder to find an area of human life that is more hedged by custom, taboo and conventionality than sex. Because we also consider sex to be "a private subject," we tend not to think of it as so controlled by outward forces. But try on the following bits of gossip (and know that for a couple with their composite Uranus in the eighth house, each of them is example of the kind of "group-think" they need to learn to recognize and escape).

They haven't made love for six months. Uh oh, right? (But who says a committed sexual relationship might not benefit from a period of abstinence?)

They've been together for ten years and I hear they still have to do it every night. (Compare this with the previous statement, and see how even sexual frequency is constrained by social expectations.)

They say they're not having trouble, but I hear they're taking separate vacations. (Why not? A little absence can make the heart—and perhaps other parts as well—fonder.)

They're both near fifty years old, but they did it in an elevator. (That's only for hot young couples, right? Who says?)

He claims he's not jealous, but she spends quite of lot of time with Thomas. (And why shouldn't we honor our partners' soul-connections with other people, even attractive ones?)

The point is, sex is a psychological labyrinth. Societies have always created a set of "suggestions" for how to live with it—and enforced them with the threat of mockery, shaming, or worse. For this couple with their composite Uranus in the eighth house, half of those suggestions are wrong. Their task is to figure out which half.

COMPOSITE URANUS IN THE NINTH HOUSE

"Sudden, weird or unexpected journeys." That would be one traditional reading of composite Uranus in the ninth house. And it may be prove accurate. Let's just look at it from a deeper viewpoint.

Uranus is always about getting free from the beliefs and expectations of the people around us. To understand it truly, we need to add that those people got to us pretty early—like about ten seconds after we were born. We've internalized their version of reality. For these two people, the belief-system of their families and communities is too limiting. It would stifle them, even poison them. They absolutely need to get away from it. Travel is one way to accomplish that aim, although any fool can get on an airplane. It's more than the physical miles—they need some miles in their minds, too. They need to see and feel different cultures. They need to understand how the basics of relationship are handled in other societies. Here we are speaking of relations with family and in-laws, gender roles, flirtation and fidelity issues, sexuality, children—the whole nine yards of committed intimacy. Other cultures are not necessarily wiser, although they may contain a few answers never learned or seen at home. The real point is actually the beneficial impact of the culture shock itself. It can shake them out of their assumptions.

As this relationship unfolds, this couple is likely to develop an interest in some rather exotic topics. One we can point to with confidence is astrology! Every society has an "official" version of the truth, composed of "serious" and "grounded" topics, brokered by "reasonable" or even "scientific" attitudes and values. The Uranian impulse is always to question those authorities, to look at everything freshly and differently. These mental impulses of curiosity need to be honored too—the individuality of the couple is enhanced by them.

Morality is a ninth house issue too. Certain moral principles, such as loyalty and honesty, are elemental to the reality of adult love. But there are an awful lot of "moralisms" that do not apply across cultures, or even to every happy, sane couple. Again, the Uranian key must turn in the lock: to make sure that the moral standards to which they subscribe are ones in which they actually believe. Until only recently, for example, divorce was considered "immoral." Or a couple who elected not to have children were violating some basic principle. Or that God "Himself" frowned upon the man who cooked and the woman who worked! Most of us laugh at these assumptions nowadays. If it weren't for couples with their composite Uranus in the ninth house, we would probably still be bound by them.

COMPOSITE URANUS IN THE TENTH HOUSE

From a traditional astrological perspective, there are two prophecies for the couple with composite Uranus in the tenth house. The first is that their reputation, public image, and professions would be a little weird. The second is that they should expect many sudden, unexpected changes to befall them, disrupting any plans they might have had for a quiet, more conventional life together. As is typically the case with such astrology, there's a kernel of truth in these predictions. Let's see if we can understand them more psychodynamically.

Whether we are raised by nannies in a country club or on the hard streets of a ghetto, society has a certain pre-planned biographical trajectory all picked out for us. That's true of us as independent individuals or as couples. Leaving aside any evaluations we might make of those pre-packaged lifestyles, it's fair to say that for the couple with composite Uranus in their tenth house, such a life together would feel wrong and empty. *But they are still under relentless pressure to live it.* Sorting out their own direction, and fighting for the right to live it, is the key.

The tenth house is usually related to career, but not every couple with a composite planet in the tenth actually works together professionally. The term *lifestyle* often proves a lot more relevant—how will they "style" their lives? By whose dictates, assumptions, and values? It's a fair bet that if they answer those questions in an evolutionarily positive way, they'll be violating the expectations of a lot of people. Another fair bet is that if they *don't* have good answers for those questions, the universe will de-stabilize their "safe" circumstances, providing them with another crack at finding the right answer—that's one of the dynamics that underlie the traditional prophecy of "sudden, unexpected changes."

Taking it a step further, if a couple with Uranus in the tenth house succeeds in claiming their own freedom and individuality in terms of the outward, obvious shape of their life together, there's a good chance that they'll figure out a way to get paid for having done that. Planets in the composite tenth house don't always manifest in terms of career—but there is a tendency for them to move in that direction, if the more elemental work of individuation has been successful. At the deepest level, we recognize here a soul-intention to make some kind of difference in their communities, to become agents of change in the collective, to affect the very myths and symbols by which their community knows and understands itself.

COMPOSITE URANUS IN THE ELEVENTH HOUSE

For these two people, time promises more than the usual mix of wrinkles and wisdom. It will also make them *stranger*! They are on a diverging course from the social mainstream. The longer they remain together, the more they come to question the usual assumptions about happiness, sanity, even reality itself. Increasingly, if they are true to themselves, they become forces for change in their communities—even if they don't think about it or intend it. Their lives take on a certain symbolism. They influence people by their very existence, like the first female airline pilots or black baseball players.

They may not have started out that way! Depending on factors in their birthcharts and backgrounds, when they first come together as a couple, they may very well have been "normal." And of course the word "normal" has a flexible meaning, depending on who is defining it at the moment. Always, however, "normalcy" is connected to some manner of *shared sense of reality*—anathema to Uranus. This is the planet that thinks for itself, that breaks the rules, that is resonant with genius and revolutionaries. This couple may come together as "normal," modern, television-watching existentialists—and become Pentecostal Christians. Or they may come together as culturally conservative Southern Baptists—and take refuge as Buddhists. Maybe they meet as brokers on Wall Street—and opt for the simple life on an old New England farm. The point is that they trigger rebellion in each other. The chemistry they generate moves them away from everything expected, safe, and known. They leave the map.

Chickens and eggs: early on, as this process begins to unfold, they start attracting some "unusual characters" into their social circle. Are they attracting them because of their own "inner unusualness?" That's a fair guess. Or do these strangers have a "corrupting influence" on them? The latter will probably be a common interpretation of their story among the people they leave behind.

In either case, in coming together, they have signed up for a roller coaster ride. It will carry them into the thin, cool ionospheric air of true individuality. They'll both shake their heads and look back at where their old lives were headed. Each will say to the other, gratefully, "I *know* where I would have been without you."

COMPOSITE URANUS IN THE TWELFTH HOUSE

Hearing a traditional interpretation of Uranus in the twelfth house could be bad for these partners' blood pressure. "Something really weird and bad will happen to you and you won't see it coming and it will shatter everything in the blink of an eye." Yikes! How can anyone live with such a prediction? It's ominous—and so vague that, if they believed it, a mix of fear and fatalism would come to pervade everything they did. Yet astrologers have long recognized that the planet Uranus does figure in all life's longshots. Winning contests? Yes—and getting hit by lightning too. The twelfth house is often related to trouble and loss, which is why this particular configuration leans away from hitting the state lottery and more toward being nervous when we hear thunder.

So what is really going on with composite Uranus in the twelfth? Here's the higher ground—and, as usual in evolutionary astrology, the basic idea is that the gloomier traditional predictions are much more likely to manifest if we fall short of getting the real lesson. This couple is ready to *individuate spiritually*. Very probably, together they must "leave the religion of their births." That, or go so much more deeply into it that they become virtually unrecognizable to the community around them. Together, they begin asking questions. Together, they begin to question the "spiritual authorities" with whom they grew up. Together, they attract radicalizing, mind-expanding experiences of undeniable authenticity.

When we speak of "spiritual authorities" and the "religion of their births," we need to use some imagination. The terms may be literal and obvious. But let us envision two people raised in the belief-system of modern psychology or   psychotherapy—who begin to find it soulless and empty and turn to shamanic practices. Or two, raised to worship money, who become Peace Corps volunteers in Haiti. In both cases, there are many who will think they have lost their minds—and that is a judgment upon which one can count if the higher Uranian road is taken! Underlying all this is not the notion that one set of beliefs is better than another, but rather that they have come to a point together where they must think and choose for themselves. They are ready to *take responsibility for the reality of their own perceptions*, rather than having those perceptions explained to them by priests, psychologists, imams, or New Age gurus in Los Angeles.

What about the harsh lightning-bolt predictions? Easy. If they need a wake up call, they'll get one. Life is too short for games we have outgrown.

CHAPTER FOURTEEN: THE COMPOSITE NEPTUNE

Like Uranus, Neptune moves slowly through the zodiac. Its speed varies, but on average it takes about fourteen years to get through a sign. For that reason, it's very common for people in sexual unions to have their natal Neptunes in the same sign, and thus to have their composite Neptune in that sign as well. If their Neptunes lies in different signs, then there's an excellent chance that their composite Neptune shares its sign with *one* of their natal Neptunes, in which case we would need to pay attention to some of the "Feudal System" logic we outlined in Chapter Three.

"Mystical" is better word for Neptune than is "spiritual." It's narrower and more specific. How we conduct ourselves behind the wheel of a car on the freeway is a spiritual question—but one hopes that we're not in an altered state of consciousness at the time! And Neptune is very much about such states. Instantly that language turns our attention in the direction of intoxicants, sacred plant medicines and so forth—definitely Neptunian territory. But the meaning of the planet is bigger than that. It also includes conditions of consciousness that are induced through spiritual practices such as meditation, fasting, chanting, yoga, sacred drumming, and so forth. And in every one of these activities, there are certain common features: consciousness becomes less identified with ego; there is a feeling of surrender to something much vaster than ourselves; and "reality" as we define it consensually—the three-dimensional, "reasonable" world—loses some of its compelling authority over us.

Not every couple professes a religion or even any particular theological belief-system. But every couple, just as every individual, benefits from a sense of surrendering to wonder, vastness, God, the mystery of life—pick your favorite metaphor. All that is under the domain of the composite Neptune. "The family that prays together stays together," as the billboards inform us. But praying—and churches, religions, meditations, and the rest—are somehow a little too safe, too glib and pat, to convey the realities of this planet. One of the keys to an authentic understanding of Neptune's action is an appreciation of its *sheer weirdness*. When our three-dimensional consciousnesses contact n-dimensional reality, fuses tend to blow. Logic and reason fall apart. Things stop making any sense. And something ancient and gloriously pre-scientific in us loves it.

Where Neptune lies in the composite chart, the couple is invited to *surrender to the inscrutable weirdness of God.* It's an area that calls for radical faith, and an openness to being guided by forces we don't understand. Any control issues we have as a couple are going to have a rough ride.

Throughout history, mystics are forever surrendering. There's beauty in that, but also darkness. Where composite Neptune lies, the couple might give up too much, unconsciously conspiring to make a virtue of "doing without." And the horror is that, if we go down that road, we're often "doing without" something we actually, legitimately need for our journey together. Even the most ferocious individuals, with a fire-breathing, dragon-slaying, eat-nails-for-breakfast composite chart, may not be immune. Where Neptune lies, we might just go to sleep, lapsing into uncharacteristic passivity and lassitude—unless we stretch our psyches and senses toward that divine weirdness that's calling us.

Please note: Neptune entered Leo around the beginning of the First World War. For obvious reasons, there aren't a lot of lovers around with the planet in the earlier signs of the zodiac! Below, you'll read about Neptune in the signs Leo through Pisces.

COMPOSITE NEPTUNE IN LEO

Neptune was in Leo between 1914 and 1928. As lovers, this generation came of age between approximately the mid-1920s and Word War Two. *And they sure had terrific clothes!* That may sound like a silly remark, but it carries us toward the heart of Neptune in this sign. Leo the Lion is about *display.* It is about appearance and manifestation. It is about our *right to exist*—boldly, colorfully and without apology. It is about our right to take up some space, to insist upon being taken seriously. The dance these lovers did—and will do again when the next crop of them starts appearing in 2078—is easy to misinterpret in shallow terms, or in terms of vanity and self-importance. And of course those are the shadows of Leo. The myth this generation of lovers spun has an empty concern with mere appearance as its dark side. But underlying it, as always, is a divine intention. And that intention is *theatrical.* It has an enormous sense of humor about itself, and about life's grand drama.

This group of souls watched the Great Depression. They experienced the Second World War. They were lovers in dark, dangerous times. Those historical realities provided a stark background for the sheer color of Leo. A plucky spirit of confidence and faith pervaded the myth of love then, despite the horror. Or maybe even because of the horror.

How can we dance when bombs are falling? Bravado like that can be faked. It can be a kind of "whistling past the graveyard." And undoubtedly there was some of that kind of simple posturing in this generation. But the real heart of it is pure Neptunian mysticism: the knowledge that physical life is always short and uncertain, but that our spirits are eternal. The knowledge that there is something glorious, even divine, in us all—something that can laugh at death, shine brightly in the deepest darkness, and never be defeated.

And incidentally, that "something" looks good in an elegant hat.

COMPOSITE NEPTUNE IN VIRGO

Neptune passed through Virgo between 1928 and 1942, and so lovers born during approximately that period of time show a Virgo Neptune in their composite charts. As always with the slower outer planets, there is a generational signature here, as well as individual meaning. The basic underlying mythos and mood are ones of caution, with a great emphasis upon self-sacrifice and service. Love asks a lot of us. A willingness to give—and even a sense of the joy of giving—are essential to it. As an ideal, composite Neptune in Virgo carries that energy. Implicit in it is an instinct that lasting intimacy requires sacrifice, that each person must do his or her part—plus ten percent—if the bond is to endure. It is easy to see the spiritual implications of this kind of attitude: a sexual bond characterized by such egoless devotion and surrender works almost like the vows of obedience, humility and service taken by monks and nuns throughout history.

Neptune, however, also warns of places where we might give up too much. In that regard, its interaction with Virgo can be dangerous. A couple with their composite Neptune in Virgo must guard against becoming invisible to each other—and even perhaps to themselves—as they move into the deeper complexities of a shared life. Virgo has a particular affinity for the *details* that allow our existences to go forward: paying the bills, keeping the house clean, doing the laundry. All of those things are necessary to life, but most of us have recognized that they're also inclined toward endless proliferation. When are we ever done? When have we ever gotten everything finally in order? The answer of course is never. And that means we must all learn to recognize when "enough is enough," and it's time to sit back and appreciate the larger view: the joy of life, the meaning of life, the texture of life. Composite Neptune in Virgo runs the risk of being steamrollered by the endless onslaught of minutia. It can drown in a sea of lists. Each lover can became a cog in an efficient machine whose ultimate purpose has been forgotten.

Service is a very real expression of love, and these lovers are here to serve each other. That is the Virgo path. If the love remains always in their eyes and their hearts as they face the endless complexities of life, they are on the higher ground.

COMPOSITE NEPTUNE IN LIBRA

Neptune passed through Libra from 1942 to 1956.

There is, sometimes, a kind of sweet perfection in human love. Two people can watch over each other, nourish and nurture each other, and simply be better together than either of them could ever be alone. And they can *know* that and own it, humbly and gratefully. They can view each other's faults charitably, in the light of forgiveness and with a sense of their own weaknesses and limitations. They can appreciate each other, like each other, and be the guardians of each other's highest aspirations. Without lapsing into denial and phoniness, they can see the best in each other, concentrate on that, and turn their hearts away from judgment, "psychology," and anything else that might separate them. They can commit, above everything else, to keeping their attention on each other's spiritual realities. They can love each other's souls.

Romantic? Yes indeed. And that set of attitudes and values is the core of composite Neptune in Libra. So why did the generation of people with their composite Neptune in Libra practically make a national sport out of divorce? Actually, it makes sense: the *expectations* this generation put on love were extraordinarily demanding. Unless there was real soul-magic in a relationship, they tended to feel shortchanged. *"Something was missing"* became their refrain, as they moved from relationship to relationship.

So why was something always missing? The answer brings us to the lazy, passive side of Neptune—the side of the "mystic" that is vulnerable to giving up the very things it most needs. With a Libran composite Neptune, there is a driving need actively *to feed and preserve the sense of soul-contact* between the two individuals. Something as simple and pleasant as making a custom of dining by candlelight can help significantly. We all know the magical, soulful feeling that candle-glow can produce, especially if the couple takes their time about it, sits there a while after the food is gone, and maybe takes a moment simply to look into each other's eyes. Shared spiritual practice can help. So can putting themselves in sacred situations—cathedrals, temples, the presence of real Teachers.

Perhaps most central for the couple with composite Neptune in Libra is the conscious use of sexual energy: making love, at least sometimes, in a way that honors sex as a sweet sacrament of soul-communion, and avoiding the pervasive cultural pressure to turn it into mere recreational biology, pornography, or God's joke.

COMPOSITE NEPTUNE IN SCORPIO

Neptune passed through Scorpio from 1956 to 1970.

Passion. What is it? White-hot emotional intensity. A bond that can never be broken. Eternal devotion that burns beyond the grave. The ability to read each other's minds, inhabit each other's skins. The stormy affair. Antony and Cleopatra, Tristan and Isolde. Abelard and Heloise, Romeo and Juliet. Lancelot and Guinevere. History mythologizes such couples, and the arts all but deify them. Notice how often this theme turns up in novels, music and film. Different centuries, different costumes, different mores, but the same archetype is at work in all of them.

Passion is overwhelmingly seductive. It can be profoundly dangerous, this quest to feel your own heart beating in your lover's chest. We are beyond Libran romanticism here. Like a hurricane or some other great force of nature, passion can turn our lives upside down, shatter us and transform us completely. Think of the devastatingly handsome vampire. The demon lover. La belle dame sans merci. Passion of this depth and force invokes the shadow, yours and your lover's and even that of the society around you. Lose your heart in this cataclysmic way, and you can lose your sanity, your honor, your country and your life along with it. They don't call it "fatal attraction" for nothing.

A couple with composite Neptune in Scorpio can risk their hard-won equilibrium for such love regardless of how experienced and psychologically sophisticated they are. Passion is everything. Passion is the Holy Grail, that by which we transcend the realm of mortals.

And passion at that volcanic level is very, very difficult to sustain for any length of time. Why?

Intensity is exhausting. Have you ever had a four-hour fight with your mate? We mere mortals get tired. We have jobs, kids, families, responsibilities. Moreover, when our shadow is evoked and exposed, which happens in a relationship of this nature, we get scared. Defenses form against the person who can rip the lid off our insecurities and secrets, who knows where our vulnerabilities lie. We need to re-establish boundaries. We need to lie low and lick our wounds for a while.

Nonetheless, a couple with this composite Neptune sign needs to feed the soul-passion between them. Carefully. Scorpio is a Mars-ruled sign, so not letting anger build up and fester will go a long way toward helping sex stay as fervent and bond-building as it can be with this placement. Risk revealing too much, rather than clamming up and letting the relationship go on automatic pilot. On the other hand, beware of soap-operatic arguments that don't resolve anything. Strive to settle conflicts fairly as well as quickly. Try to remember that one reason your shadows are emerging is so that they can be seen, accepted and perhaps at least partially integrated, not shunned or denied or subjected to psychological character assassination.

COMPOSITE NEPTUNE IN SAGITTARIUS

Neptune passed through Sagittarius from 1970 to 1984.

The Holy Grails for this couple are gaining a far wider perspective on the world than the one they were born with, and aligning their behavior to some sort of agreed-upon ideals and principles of right action. These partners need to feel that it's part of the Divine Plan that they are together. Without a sense of wonder that Spirit brought them together and continues to take an active interest in the relationship, some of the magical heart will go out of it.

What can produce that sense of wonder?

Journeys, both literal and metaphorical. Vision quests. A pilgrimage to a sacred site. A trip to Europe, a trip to the Edgar Cayce center, or a weekend jaunt. Embarking on the local Jung Society's "Journey into Wholeness" together.

Learning. These two should not be strangers to their local continuing education departments, planetariums and museums.

Philosophizing around the fireplace on a winter's night, or around the picnic table on a summer one, or at the coffee shop after church.

And a total change of pace once in a while! If they're bored with their lives, they may interpret it as being bored with one another, and that, combined with the Sagittarian hunger for new experiences, may make these two sacrifice the relationship.

Other problems can arise if God is speaking personally to one of these partners, and the other one disagrees with what the Lord Almighty said. Did you smile when you read those words? That's good: a sense of humor goes a long way with composite Neptune in Sagittarius. Neither partner has a monopoly on their connection to Spirit, and one shadow of Sagittarius is proselytizing. Not everything is a "lesson," and nobody has the moral high ground all the time.

COMPOSITE NEPTUNE IN CAPRICORN

Neptune passed through Capricorn from 1984 to 1998.

Love is a discipline. Love is a point of honor. Love is a reflection of our integrity and our maturity. All of us are free to make a vow of love, or not to make it. But once made, to break such a vow shames us and trivializes us. For that reason, no one should be pressured into taking such a vow. A grown man or woman, after long reflection, chooses freely whether to make that promise. A person may go through life without undertaking it; that is fine. That is his or her own business. There is no pressure to accept the task. Just be serious. Do it right or don't do it at all: that is the essence of composite Neptune in Capricorn. That is the Mythos that underlies the relationships these couples create.

They are relatively young now, as we write. Neptune entered Capricorn in 1984 and remained there into 1998. These people arrive at their sexual maturity in a world characterized by highly chaotic change in terms of life-long partnerships and marriages. They add a timely and needed element of realism, seriousness and sobriety to the mix.

Some astrologers relate Capricorn to "traditional values." We have to be careful of such a label blinding our imaginations. Couples with their composite Neptune in Capricorn will not necessarily be more conservative than the general population. They will simply be more realistic. Again, the core idea is that life-long commitment isn't for everyone—in fact, Capricorn is the "Hermit," and so very probably there will be more people in this generation who simply choose to live more solitary lives. And those lives might not be "monastic" either: it is realistic to recognize that sex exists outside of committed relationships. Accepting that fact without a second thought—or a thought of "traditional values"—simply reflects the core Capricornian wisdom: first see reality as it is. Then make your grown-up choices within that context, and stick with them.

When this generation has finished its work, we may well see a world in which fewer people choose commitment, but the commitments will be better, more realistic, more stable ones.

COMPOSITE NEPTUNE IN AQUARIUS

Neptune passed through Aquarius from 1998 to 2011.

In human intimacy, think anything. Try anything. Put no blinkers on your imagination. The rules of the game are simple: hurt no one if you can help it, and love as much as you can. Beyond that, let's throw away the last ten thousand years of history and tradition and just start over again.

Extreme? Maybe—but look at the results of the last ten thousand years: there really isn't that much to lose! This is the spirit of composite Neptune in Aquarius. The iconoclastic genius of the Water-Bearer collides with the unbounded capacity of the human imagination. Once it triggered the Italian Renaissance. As we write, it is happening again. Neptune entered Aquarius in 1998. It remains there until early 2012. As these children grow up, they will rewrite the rules. They will create new, liberated visions of human potential and possibility in general, and they will create a new blueprint for intimate relationship.

Could a marriage exist between three people? Could people marry, but choose to live on opposite sides of the country? Could a marriage be created with a twelve month renewable contract? Could wedding rings be replaced with wireless file-sharing hardware linked to brain implants in the two (or three) people's cerebrums? And could *anything less* than that even be considered "marriage" in this modern world? Why be old-fashioned?

Some of these are probably very bad ideas! But remember: it is the nature of radical creativity that it makes a lot of mistakes. And that radical creativity is the essence of Neptune in Aquarius. Mistakes must be accepted as part of the process of discovery. With composite Neptune in this sign, undoubtedly there will be a lot of heartbreak—love's "experiments" always involve real people with eternal human vulnerabilities. But this generation will carry sex forward into a post-patriarchal mythos of global culture. Their errors will be spectacular. Conservatives will fulminate and comedians will have a field day. But the world they leave behind will have a new mythology of love.

COMPOSITE NEPTUNE IN PISCES

Neptune passed through Pisces from 2011 to 2025.

Composite Neptune in its own sign is powerful, and can be a powerful force in the spiritual and secular lives of this couple.

Here, the partners' path to the Divine is a classically mystical path. Meditation, reflection, compassion, imagination and openness to the transrational are all important here. This couple may have had more than their portion of shared ESP experiences, too, as God gives them extra encouragement to look within. Their presence in one another's lives heightens and potentiates all that which we associate with Pisces in each other, for good or ill. Mysticism—and absent-mindedness. Visionary imagination—and woolgathering. Sensitivity—and learned helplessness.

They need to honor the divine in one another. To be able to go into an altered state in each other's presence. To participate in a kind of shared receptive trance. When this composite Neptune is functioning well, they may find that their meditations are deeper in one another's presence than they are when alone. They may feel a profound and mysterious connection between their spirits that's very hard to explain in words—it can be and is experienced, but can't be described.

As with every planetary placement, darker possibilities exist here too. They are more psychically sensitive in each other's presence, more mystically aware, more compassionate, more tuned in, and their need for meditative time is increased by being around each other. Yet that self-same heightened meditative and psychic awareness in this couple may be something that they choose to numb, not to develop. If they decide to go down that route, they will be spacier in each other's presence. They'll find it harder to concentrate. They'll forget things. Any flirtations with mind-altering substances may deepen, until they feel more and more helpless about coping with day to day realities and responsibilities.

A shared, or at least mutually supported, spiritual practice becomes all the more important here. With that in place, this couple can share in transporting, almost hallucinatory experiences of deepening sensitivity, compassion, otherworldly awareness and soaring imagination.

COMPOSITE NEPTUNE IN THE FIRST HOUSE

The first house is very willful, even self-centered. Neptune is the opposite, so there is a deep paradox here for this couple. Are they headstrong, or are they drifting like leaves in the wind? Let's add that any planet in the first house is extremely powerful, so this paradox is perhaps the central mystery of their bond.

Let's start with what we know for sure. Outwardly, with composite Neptune in their first house, there is a feeling of something a bit out of synch with this world about these two. They seem transcendent—or spacy, depending on your point of view. There may be even be something glamorous about them. That doesn't always mean physical beauty either. Just as easily, it can correlate with a certain vibration of intrigue or fascination. Going a bit deeper, we find that people have widely varying perceptions of them: they're smart; they're dumb; they're sophisticated; they're just weird. Stop and think for a minute, and you begin to see the deeper reality: when others look at these two, what they're seeing says more about their own biases than it does about this couple. They are like sponges for the projections of other people. They would be a movie director's dream: they could play the parts of any kind of couple.

Another sure-fire layer of the mystery is that, from the moment they came together, these two people have been having experiences that defy rational explanation. A week into the relationship, they phoned each other but got busy signals because they'd called at exactly the same moment. A wild thought enters the mind of one of them, and two seconds later the other one says the same words out loud. These kinds of minor psychic phenomena occur so frequently for this couple that they hardly notice them. A deeper way of saying that is that they seem to *trigger mystical or psychic development* in each other. And that's the key to our first house Neptune paradox.

Yet bumping into the next dimension occasionally and at random is a lackluster use of a composite Neptune in the first house. The soul-contract between these two people is centered on the willful, intentional exploration of these kinds of spiritual phenomena. Together, they need actively to pursue the kinds of experiences that deepen their innate mysticism: meditation classes, visits to sacred sites, yoga, encounters with spiritual teachers. Such choices will press the buttons of some of their friends and family members—and that's where the first house "ego" energies come into play. As the cliché has it, you can't make an omelet without breaking some eggs. And the danger with this Neptune placement is that, instead of taking this active role in pushing the edges of the envelopes of their consciousnesses, they might just drift along, taking in the show, carrying the expectations of people around them, and letting this astonishing opportunity slip through their fingers.

COMPOSITE NEPTUNE IN THE SECOND HOUSE

Confusion and dumb choices about money—that would be the standard framework for an interpretation of composite Neptune in the second house. Neptune is otherwordly, and in financial affairs two and two make four, so the combination is typically seen as an unhappy one. Throw in another fact: in money matters, we are usually swimming with the sharks, and Neptune's gullibility can makes it an easy mark—thus, the configuration is seen as ominous of a vulnerability to being "conned" or cheated out of what is rightfully ours.

As usual, the conventional interpretation is worth a moment's consideration. Those lapses in practical judgement are in fact dangers for a couple with composite Neptune in their second house. But there are many other layers of meaning to the configuration.

Even in money matters, there is more to say: for one thing, this duo might very well make a lot of money by cashing in on the *joint power of their imagination and creativity*: that's Neptune as well. Maybe they could write together or make movies, or simply design beautiful objects: clothing, furniture, houses. If they keep one eye on practical reality, they might also improve their financial fortunes by trusting their *unique capacity to sense future trends* before they happen. Maybe in a few years, moving to the "incredible energy vortexes" of Nebraska will become the "in" thing to do—if these two start buying up real estate outside Omaha, we'll buy some too!

There are deeper waters here, ones that have nothing to do with money. The psychological arena that the second house represents is self-confidence. With their Neptune here, these two need to concentrate on *believing* in their innate spirituality and imagination. What that means in practical terms is that they *invest* in those qualities in themselves, treating them like something they value as precious. If they take their spirituality seriously, they will feed it. They will spend the money it takes to sit with teachers. For example, they'll attend classes, go on vision quests, get psychic readings and counsel, do energy work and conscious bodywork, visit sacred places. Above all, they'll *take the time* to tend to their souls. This integration of conscious, intentional spiritual growth will become one of the main sources of their dignity and confidence in their relationship. Similarly, they will take their joint imaginative powers seriously. They will, for example, buy a good video camera and take a filmmaking class together. They'll have musical instruments in their house. They'll paint together. They'll design a home. And again, they will *take the time* to develop these creative dimensions of the life they share.

With composite Neptune in their second house, for these two it all comes down to taking their spirituality and their creativity seriously. That faith is the trigger that allows the blossom to shoot through the stem.

COMPOSITE NEPTUNE IN THE THIRD HOUSE

Communication is the lifeblood of any relationship. Without it, there is no connection between people. One method of communication is, of course, language. It's not the only form, but let's start there. With composite

Neptune in their third house, finding a clear path to each other through words can be a challenge. Easily, meanings can be misconstrued. Take the seemingly simple sentence, "You've lost weight." Here are some possibilities for what that might mean in the ears of the partner: You are looking great. Or you are too fat. Or you look unhealthy—or you look healthy. Or I've been secretly harboring resentment at your recent weight gain. Or I love you and am attracted to you. Or I only value you as a sex object.

One dimension of compatibility in a relationship is that the words and phrases in my dictionary have more or less the same meaning in your dictionary. For the couple with composite Neptune in their third house, that verbal compatibility can be elusive—unless they handle the challenges of this configuration effectively. How can they do that? Let's start by recognizing that there are other forms of communication besides language. The key is that, for these two, these alternative methods of staying connected are actually a lot more effective. They provide a context in which language is less of a trap for them. In a nutshell, these other forms of communication are non-verbal: body language, touch, direct emotional rapport, psychic linking. With composite Neptune in their third house, this duo is actually very strong in those departments. Very likely, they delighted in that early in their relationship—communication was almost supernaturally easy in their salad days. They seemed simply to be reading each other's minds. The heart of what we are saying is that those early perceptions were valid. The trick is that they need to keep trusting them, then build on them as a foundation for all their verbal processes.

How? Well, when one says, "You've lost weight," the other one, ideally, sits with the words for a moment before responding or interpreting them. Looks into the partner's eyes. Visualizes a tube of light linking their hearts. Is open and receptive. *Lets the psychic link work*, in other words. Lets it be the foundation for all other forms of communication—not a substitute for them, but the foundation.

We sometimes marvel at wartime stories in which two people who have no language in common come together in marriage. How can they do it? The challenges must be enormous—and yet we suspect that many of these couples have composite Neptune in their third houses, and that much passes between them through channels our ancestors of three million years ago knew very well. For these two, here's a recommendation: pretend that you are such a wartime couple. At least once a year, go somewhere alone together and leave the English language at home.

COMPOSITE NEPTUNE IN THE FOURTH HOUSE

Dating and courtship are a labyrinth, but if a couple successfully threads its way through the initial stages of the process, sooner or later a pressing question looms on the horizon: should we try to make a home together? That's fourth house territory, and with Neptune there our first statement is cautionary: these two need to be careful they don't let that issue drift away in the fog. Wherever Neptune lies in the composite chart, there is a risk that the couple will "transcend" something they really need. For these two people, once they've gotten their relationship on solid ground, making a home together is a natural step.

This is delicate territory, since many people become attracted to each other but ultimately have no evolutionary need to live together. Some of them will have composite Neptune in the fourth. Living together is a serious step, and it shouldn't be rushed. But within those parameters, any couple with a planet in the fourth house sooner or later has to deal with the question of whether they are going to be "a family" or not—that's simply the heart of the matter with this house. And it can be a very joyful, fulfilling step, if both people desire it and they handle it wisely.

With Neptune in the composite fourth house, any "nest" these two make together needs to be Neptunian. In a nutshell, that means dreamy. There are homes you walk into and immediately feel calmer and more open emotionally and psychically. Achieving that "look" is not purely a matter of interior decoration. In fact, at the highest level of understanding, we must recognize that the actual spiritual practices these two employ together are the hub of the wheel. For them to make a home that supports their relationship, it is deeply helpful if they, for example, do yoga there. Or sit in meditation. Or say grace before their meals. Or pray. Those kinds of activities create a lasting energy in any building in which they occur. A cathedral feels different to us energetically than a bus station.

First things first—but second things second. A few lines back we emphasized that creating a Neptunian space isn't a question of interior decoration. Still, with Neptune in the composite fourth house, these two can support their bond by paying attention to the physical appearance of their home as well. Probably the single most useful comment is that peace and quiet are very supportive of meditative attitudes. They really benefit from living in a place that allows them that freedom from intrusive noise. Secondly, let's emphasize the helpfulness of candles, oil lamps, and electric lights that can be dimmed. Some people are helped by spiritual or religious images—sacred icons, representations of saints, paintings that carry the imagination into the next dimension. A fountain or a fireplace can add Neptunian ambience to a home, as can peaceful music. But always remember: these are only outward supports. Anybody can spend a few hundred dollars at the local New Age emporium and make their place look like a medicine man's boudoir. The real key is inward spiritual practice in the home.

Finally, let's take one practical peek in the direction of the Shadow. With Neptune in the composite fourth house, these two should probably be wary about being deceived in real estate transactions—the dreamiest, most peaceful house in the world won't help them find inner peace if the cellar tends to flood, the foundation is rotting, and there are termites in the walls.

COMPOSITE NEPTUNE IN THE FIFTH HOUSE

Lovemaking is fifth house territory. With composite Neptune there, this couple probably has an interest in the subject! So far, we're confident that our interpretation is on solid ground. But how do they *maintain* their interest in sharing their sexuality with each other? This is one of life's persistent questions—people constantly fall into mutual attraction, but how often does such an attraction survive even one serious conversation, let alone a few weeks of relationship?

Sexual response can be destroyed by betrayal, anger, or violence. It can be destroyed by shame. It can be eaten alive by unresolved psychological issues. But it can also be destroyed by more immediate, concrete sexual dysfunction or incompatibility. A planet in the fifth house always gives us some clues regarding the natural erotic style of a couple. With these two, there must be a Neptunian dimension to their lovemaking. That means there must be at least sometimes a sense of their using sexuality as a doorway into mystical, sacred space. If they can't make love with each other's *souls*, their bodies soon lose interest.

How can they experience sex that way? How can they keep it truly sacred? As with most things Neptunian, this is more a question of consciousness than a question of any particular outer behavior. Still, we can say that very likely there is sometimes eye contact through the point of orgasm. Very probably, sexual expression is sometimes very gentle and tender, with more emphasis on energetic, emotional connection and less on earning the gold medal in some pornographic Olympics.

As individuals, they may or may not have any interest in experiencing sexuality this way. That's a question that can only be answered from their individual birthcharts, not from a composite chart. But with Neptune in the composite fifth house, we know that this *relationship* needs that kind of sexual experience. It may be the natural meeting point between two very different sexual styles, or it may provide a missing piece in what is an otherwise baffling sexual frustration.

Once this couple has established this primordial erotic foundation for their bond, they'll find that it spins off other joys in unexpected, delightful ways. It is, for example, the trigger for *shared creativity*. There is some art-form trying to come through them, something that neither of them could accomplish in a complete way without the other one's specific talents and perspectives. They'll also find that their ability simply to have fun together—another fifth house theme—will be greatly enhanced.

One more note. Traditionally, the fifth house is related to "debauchery." Getting into trouble with addictive or compulsive behaviors is a danger, and many a couple with Neptune in the composite fifth house has gone down that road together. What underlies this problem is pain—a pain that comes from the absence of the core psychospiritual eroticism that is the true meaning of this configuration.

COMPOSITE NEPTUNE IN THE SIXTH HOUSE

The sixth house is often related to the idea of *service*. And in fact a couple with their composite Neptune there may very well be drawn in an altruistic way to be of some use in their community. But we can be a lot more specific about the nature of this service: one of the forgotten meanings of the sixth house is *lineage*. Most of us have been served by a mentor at some point in our lives. If that happens, then typically, as we mature, we go on to mentor someone ourselves. And presumably someone mentored our mentors, just as those we mentor will eventually pass on the gift themselves. Extend that pattern into the forgotten past and the unseen future, and you've got lineage. The individuals comprising it may not be remembered literally by name, but that doesn't make them any less effective or precious.

A couple with Neptune in the composite sixth house, whether they know it or not, is part of such a tradition. What exactly is being passed down the line? The answer lies in the general category of Neptunian energy and Neptunian initiations: it pertains to consciousness itself. And specifically, given that we are speaking here of a composite chart, the tradition to be conveyed is one of *conscious, spiritual mating and bonding.* Being a conscious lover in a committed relationship is not easy or totally intuitive; there are "tricks of the trade." There are hard-won answers to tough questions, such as knowing when to get in our partner's face about something, and when to forgive and forget. And conscious lovers have been on this road for a million years, gradually accumulating better answers. It's all that, *and the vibration behind all that,* that are being conveyed in this Neptunian lineage.

Thus, with this configuration, we are alerted to a couple, probably a little older than our heroes, appearing in the courtship-days of our subjects. There is something magical and attractive about this older couple—they *know something.* And somehow, that "something" is passed on. How? The phrase, "monkey see, monkey do" comes to mind. So does the Sanskrit term, *darshan.* In some primordial human way, the older couple teaches the younger one something about how to keep soul-consciousness alive between two people in the face of the mundane realities of living together in the world. And the older couple expects nothing in return—the giving is as joyful as the receiving.

The wheels turn, and eventually we find our heroes, a little older now, exercising a strange and mysterious attraction over another two people, younger than themselves. And the flame, incalculably ancient, burns on.

The wonder is that all this might have happened over something as mundane as a "chance meeting" in a grocery store.

COMPOSITE NEPTUNE IN THE SEVENTH HOUSE

The seventh house always gives us insight into our "significant others." For a couple, this isn't about *their* relationship. It's about their closest friends. Very typically, it describes other *couples* with whom they have some kind of connection. Many traditional astrologers would view this particular configuration in a negative light—that our two heroes would be deceived by their friends, or that they would tend to form alliances with unsavory characters, given to drug addiction, dissipation, financial indigence, drunkenness, and flaky theorizing.

The horror is, all that could be true. There are, as we will soon see, happier potentials, but let's consider these dark prophecies first. They are not random words of despair; astrologers have seen these patterns. They are real. What astrologers often don't say is that they are also optional!

Neptunian people are often drawn to *escapism*—that is the underlying pattern in all the dispiriting comments we've made so far. So what motivates people to escape? The basic answer is pain. And pain always lies at the crossroads of two vectors. Outwardly, there is something that hurts us. And inwardly, there is a *degree of sensitivity* to that hurt. Kick a rock, and it won't bother the rock! Rocks don't feel much. The more sensitive a person, the more susceptible he or she is to pain. Thus, Neptunian people—who are the astrological epitomes of sensitivity—are overrepresented in drug and alcohol treatment programs, escapist religions, and bars at closing time.

With Neptune in their composite seventh house, this couple has some unresolved karmic business with people in those conditions. Maybe they can help them. If they can do that without being drawn down the drain themselves, good for them. But they do need to learn that sometimes people in that condition aren't interested in truly being helped. All they want is a free ride, a shoulder on which to cry, and to borrow a few dollars until "Monday."

Our heroes are kind, but they are going to have to learn to cut some people loose. That will hurt them, but it needs to be done.

What about the higher ground? Some people are born with highly elevated levels of sensitivity, and they respond brilliantly to them. These are the *creative visionaries* of a culture, and, with Neptune in their composite seventh house, this couple will probably know a few of them. Maybe they are poets or musicians or painters. Others among their higher-order Neptunian soulmates are psychics, meditation masters, and healers—the spiritual lighthouses of the community. In all cases, these relationships serve a critical role in the intimate life of this couple. They help keep their feet on the higher ground, assisting them in maintaining that sweet sense of other, higher worlds interpenetrating this physical one.

COMPOSITE NEPTUNE IN THE EIGHTH HOUSE

In attempting to overthrow the old Goddess cultures, one of the charges hurled by the patriarchal propagandists was that witches had intercourse with the devil. It was, of course, a lie, purely and simply. But the *origins* of the lie are interesting. Many of the world's older religions recognized that sexuality, under certain circumstances, could provide a doorway into higher conditions of consciousness. Two people, joining their energies that way, could be stronger psychically than either of them could be alone. Adding sexual energy to certain meditation practices was like putting rocket fuel in the engines—doorways into other worlds would open. For these two people, with Neptune in their composite eighth house, such doors are available today. Their soul-contract is to pass through them together. Whether they know it or not, they are part of that ancient tradition.

When this couple came together, an alchemical process of transformation was launched deep inside each one of them—a process they could not understand or even recognize, except as an enticing sense that the sex looked "promising" in this relationship. Still, evolution never happens automatically. There are needles to be threaded here, and ways to get the process wrong. Always with Neptune, the darker possibility lies in a sort of lackadaisical "transcendence." Down that road, people basically just become lazy and unmotivated, not claiming the treasures that are available to them. Eventually the heightened sensitivities devolve into various forms of escapism. For these two, we could imagine sexuality following what would seem at first to be a conventional, predictable course—hot and compelling at first, then mellowing into something more akin to the normal realities of stable relationships. All those changes would seem unsurprising and expected—but then, instead of sexuality stabilizing in the usual long-term way, it would continue to go down the drain until it essentially disappeared all together. And that *isn't* normal. That is Neptunian dysfunction.

So what happened? They key here is that for these two, with their Neptune in the composite eighth house, if sexuality doesn't open magical, psychic doors for them, it will simply fade away. And the happy news is that it can open those doors. That chemistry is basic to their relationship. It is what *wants* to happen between them.

How can they help that process along? Negatively, they must recognize certain no-no's: ideally, they should never treat sexuality as the world does: as something between a joke and a form of recreation. If they are not feeling emotionally connected with each other, they should refrain from sexual expression until they've had a talk about what's separated them. They need to be wary about overriding psychic walls between them with alcohol or drugs—again, talk works better. Positively, eye contact during sex is probably the single biggest conscious-triggering yoga. All the magical processes come down to a commitment always *to see Spirit* in each other during sexual contact. It is very helpful if they speak together about the inward experiences they have during sex; that makes them more "real"—or more precisely, it integrates them into the shared reality of their relationship. Similarly, there are books that have been written about these conscious sexual traditions. Some are in the shamanic, "medicine" traditions. Some are Tantric. Just knowing consciously that they are part of that lineage can help them further believe in the reality of their own experiences with each other. In a nutshell, they simply need to keep the divine present between them. That energy will carry them into worlds they've never imagined—and anything less will bore them, first into mechanical responses, and then into either boredom-induced celibacy, separation, or affairs.

COMPOSITE NEPTUNE IN THE NINTH HOUSE

At first glance, the combination of mystical Neptune with the religious ninth house seems perfectly natural and easy. Our understanding is richer when we recognize that mystical spirituality and religion are not interchangeable ideas. In fact, the history of religion shows a disturbing tendency for true mystics actually to be seen as a threat, even persecuted, by God's "official" spokespersons. With Neptune in the composite ninth house, this same battle rages inside the dynamics of this couple. One of their soul-contracts is to resolve it.

The loftiest aspect of the ninth house is the notion of the endless quest for understanding. It is less about certainty than it is about good questions. With Neptune there, the natural area on which these questions focus is the nature of consciousness itself. What is the relationship between mind and cosmos? That's an inquiry so vast that ten thousand years of theology haven't answered it. Our two heroes won't answer it either—but their relationship will thrive on the process of trying.

How? By seeking information. Data. Grist for the mill. Has there ever been a religion that didn't contain at least a piece of the truth? These two benefit from learning a bit about all of them. And when we say "religion," we need to understand the word broadly. Any set of beliefs through which people interpret the world is a religion. That means not only Christianity and Islam and so on, but also existentialism, political views, cynicism, materialism. All of them are "religions" in some sense, and for these two, a good aim is the achievement of fluency in all those religious languages.

The ninth house is also connected with travel and cross-cultural experience. Whenever we see a planet there in the composite chart, it's a good bet that the couple benefits from getting away from the culture of their birth, at least temporarily. They need that "fresh air" in their perspective. When the planet is Neptune, we see something more specific: the need for shared journeys undertaken for intentionally, consciously spiritual purposes. There is an ancient word for such journeys: pilgrimage. These too have a soul-stretching impact upon this couple.

If they slip into Neptunian laziness and give up their natural path, then they will probably find themselves adhering to a numbing "religion" that substitutes dogmatism for thought or experience. That could be any of the obvious candidates—Fundamentalism by any of its names. But just as easily, they could slip into making a religion of "not knowing" or "not caring." Those perspectives are lazier, but they can be defended with the same ignorant zeal that marks any Bible-thumper.

COMPOSITE NEPTUNE IN THE TENTH HOUSE

The Lord of Mysticism in the house of career . . . So should this couple start a psychic hotline together? Found an ashram? Not necessarily, although either of those events might happen.

Neptune symbolizes altered, non-linear, transrational states of consciousness. It's helpful to remember that there are many varieties of such states. Some of them take us close to Spirit and are blissful. Some of them simply blur the boundaries of our egos, impair their functioning, and are scary or dangerous or weird. When we are deep in meditation, we are in Neptunian awareness. When we are just about to fall asleep, we are also in a Neptunian state. When we are lost in a movie or a book, we are experiencing another world as just as vital and real as this one—Neptune again. If we're watching the six o'clock news, and a stranger's trauma floods us with such compassion that our eyes fill with tears, that's also a Neptunian experience: we identified with something beyond our own ego. Have you ever picked up the phone to call a friend, only to hear the friend's voice on the line because he or she was calling you? More Neptune. When we're a drink or two over our limit, that's yet another altered state of consciousness, and a potentially dangerous one.

The tenth house is not just the house of career; it is also the house of reputation, of public identity, of public image, of one's role in the community. With Neptune here, this couple's "cosmic job description" should not be defined merely in material terms. We don't often see ads for professional mystics in the classifieds. Yet this is an earthy house, and an externally oriented one that needs some concrete manifestation. How to integrate this internally oriented planet, this planet of inner work, into the extraverted workaday world?

The key lies in remembering that one way or another, this couple has a soul intention to *symbolize* Neptune, our awareness of consciousness, in their larger community. What happens if they get it right? There are many possibilities. They may symbolize Spirit, and our various means of connecting with it; perhaps they are deacons in their church, or meditation teachers. They may symbolize intuition or heightened sensitivity to that which lies beyond the veil; maybe they host a psychic when she comes to town, or they host an Edgar Cayce study group. They may represent compassion—they volunteer at the local soup kitchen. They may embody the Neptunian realms of fantasy and imagination; they're film-makers. Or they may serve as a bad example: drifters, drunkards, addicts, or become so entrenched in learned helplessness or victim consciousness that they can't stand on their own two feet.

COMPOSITE NEPTUNE IN THE ELEVENTH HOUSE

As the wheels of life turn, these two will become increasingly "Neptunian." That's just the nature of anything in the eleventh house; it gets stronger with age. Good news or bad? It doesn't depend on Neptune itself—it depends on how this couple handles it and responds to it. At its best, this configuration promises an ever-deepening sense of a soul-linkage between them. One way of thinking about that is the notion that it takes them a while to discover that they are soulmates—that if they hang in there, that feeling that they are "supposed to be together" really takes hold. Here's another perspective: where do soulmates come from anyway? How do souls create that healthy interdependence, something strong enough to survive even death and rebirth? The assumption is that at some point in their distant past, they came together and formed that bond. Well, why not now, in this lifetime? Can't the soulmate contract come into existence anymore? Our second perspective is that these two are offered the opportunity to create that bond, over time, in this lifetime.

Either way, to get it right, a couple with their composite Neptune in the eleventh house requires certain supports. Some they create themselves. Right at the top of the list is a strong, shared *inner intention* to put their relationship on a spiritual basis. So much of this comes down to letting mystical or perhaps religious language be natural and comfortable for them. Lines such as "Here's something I want your soul to hear" come to mind—and of course we must recognize the soul-eating peril of misusing such language! My soul probably doesn't need your soul to hear that it's about time the garbage was taken out.

These two benefit a lot from shared prayer or meditation, or at least shared silence. A long walk in the woods can be as sacred as a long sit in a church or temple. Two Muslims can share an appreciation of a Christian cathedral, and two Christians can feel their souls touch in a Sufi dance.

The eleventh house correlates with group activity. Here, with their composite Neptune in the eleventh, we recognize the benefits that come to these two from having some kind of spiritual community around them. That may be formal, as for example with a church or an ashram. But just as easily it can be informal: a crowd of friends who can all say the word "God" without immediately following it with the word "damn!"

With such support, our couple will natural move in that sweet soul-connected direction this configuration promises. Without it, they are drawn to lower reaches of Neptune's potential: shared addictions, escapism, a gradual sense of the relationship's running out of gas. Sometimes the balloon simply bursts and the bond collapses: the relationship ends, "not with a bang but a whimper." Or, far worse, it continues: a study in gray mist, going nowhere.

Far better to head for the sweet higher ground, with a little steadying help from their friends—and a lot of help from themselves.

COMPOSITE NEPTUNE IN THE TWELFTH HOUSE

If these two have any doubts about the reality of psychic phenomena, they had better be prepared to shed them. With their composite Neptune in the twelfth house, the computers between their ears are definitely networked! Thoughts in one person's head will turn up in the other one's head without the intervening necessity of speech. The same for feelings and moods—there's a constant tide of emotion flowing between them, blurring the boundaries of their private inner worlds. Early in their dance together, they experience dozens of these kinds of little miracles. They phone each other at the same moment. They run into each other at the same out-of-the-way restaurant. Out of the blue, they both say the words, "I was thinking—" cutting each other off mid-sentence. And of course it turns out that they were thinking the same thing.

This magical dimension of their bond must be cultivated. It's not just there for entertainment purposes. Something spiritual is triggered in the chemistry of their interaction. It's as if they are more evolved together than they are separately. Together, they experience a taste of the Higher Mind. Should they walk into a temple or a meditation room together, they naturally tend to be quiet, feeling the energy or an angelic presence. There's really no way for us to know the language they will use to describe these experiences—only that the experiences are there for them to have. The mystery we call "God" is trying to make itself felt between them. It's as if together they're a radio receiver tuned to that ancient channel. But one was the antenna and the other one the transistors.

Quiet time alone as a couple is essential for keeping a composite Neptune in the twelfth house tuned. Some days they simply need not to get out of bed! Some evenings, how sweet it is for them to let the home be lit only with candles, or to turn the lights down low. A bit of meditative music in the background can subtly turn their consciousnesses toward the inner planes. Even one of them meditating can have a contagious effect, creating a resonance of silence in the other. These "temple" feelings must be cultivated and encouraged, because the alternative is a kind of loss of focus in the bond. Always with Neptune, we must beware of a lackadaisical side to the planet, one that gradually trends down toward laziness. They might tune each other out. They might disappear into the television. The very energy that creates so much magic at the beginning of a relationship can turn in these darker directions so slowly and subtly that they hardly notice the attrition.

The bottom line is that their soul-contract is a bid for the higher mystical ground. Together, they have what it takes to arrive there. They get a glimpse of it, for free, right at the beginning. Then they have to work to make it permanent.

CHAPTER FIFTEEN: THE COMPOSITE PLUTO

Pluto takes about two and half centuries to orbit the Sun, spending an average of twenty years in each sign of the zodiac. The result is that in romantic relationships, it's very common that both people have the planet in the same sign. Since composite charts are based on midpoints between planets, their composite Pluto will be in that same sign too, although of course the house symbolism and planetary aspects will probably vary widely between them. As we saw with Uranus and Neptune, some astrologers are inclined to dismiss such Pluto sign symbolism as just generational. But actually the effects are dramatically reinforced.

When people are born with their natal Plutos in *adjacent* signs, which also happens frequently, then of course the composite Pluto must fall in one sign or the other. In that scenario, it "sides" with the person who's got it in that same sign. That gives us at least a hint of a "Feudal System" dynamic, as we described in Chapter Three.

So what does Pluto *mean?*

The astrological power of this icy little world, so far from the Sun, is astonishing. A couple of years ago, as data came in that further shrank the already-diminutive diameter of the planet, there was a big flap in the media about whether astronomers were going to downgrade Pluto to the status of an asteroid. Most astrologers just laughed and shook their heads. More than a few remarks were made about not envying the future Pluto transits of those who were foolish enough to risk mocking the Lord of the Dark. The International Astronomical Union has since relented: Pluto's status as an official planet seems secure for the time being.

And well it should be. Few astrological symbols give us such trenchant insights into ourselves and, through its placement in the composite chart, into our relationships with each other. For all of us, as individuals and in partnership with each other, there are *places we don't want to go*—hell-worlds inside us, where we keep our wounds and our secrets. These are places where parts of our souls have been carried off, Persephone-fashion, into the Underworld. In fact, our dear friend and colleague, Jeffrey Wolf Green, has developed a popular and powerful system of astrological analysis in which Pluto is actually *equated* with the soul. Our system and his reconcile easily—all we need do is remember that the soul (Jeff's view of Pluto) tends always to be wounded (our view of Pluto). In either case, there is a need for us to undertake a daunting journey of soul-recovery, down through our blindness and our resistance, into the stormy places inside us all.

Every couple has a composite Pluto. Thus, every couple has a wound they must face. On the surface, this might seem illogical. The composite chart exists at the instant we meet—in fact, it existed potentially as soon as we were both born. How can there already be a wound between us when we haven't had a chance to hurt each other yet? It's a fair question, and we can't answer it by referring to wounds we each bring to the relationship separately. Those wounds are discernible astrologically, but they're discernible in the two natal charts, not the composite chart. The answer, as we explored in Chapter Four, lies in the notion of the pre-existing karmic pattern of the couple—what and whom they were together in prior lifetimes. Always, our assumption here is that souls simply don't enter into real intimacy in this lifetime without some prior history. We certainly meet people in this lifetime with whom we have no prior connections, but those relationships tend to be formal, transitory and fundamentally forgettable.

Where composite Pluto lies, soul-healing must happen. The alternative is for the relationship to be distorted and haunted by forces that always lie just beyond the reach of rational comprehension. "Soul-healing," by the way, can be translated pretty effectively into pigeon-Greek as *psyche therapos*. And what an irony that many of today's psychotherapists don't believe in the eternal soul—it's like podiatrists who weren't convinced of the reality of the feet!

Not every couple needs psychotherapy, in the modern, narrow sense of the word, or would benefit from it. But all couples, in their own way, must sooner or later make the journey down into the dark. The benefits of that journey are not simply the resultant diminishing of negatives. Once Pluto work is done, there is a great release of energy into the relationship. Much sheer *Eros* that was tied up behind the repressive mechanism is released, empowering the pair to *do everything they do* with more verve, intelligence, creativity, and panache. Once we get to the higher potentials of Pluto, we are actively creating meaning and works of lasting significance in our life together. This is a planet that, once moving, can shape history.

Note that in the sections that follow, you won't read about Pluto in Aries, Taurus, or Gemini—Pluto hasn't been in those signs for so long that virtually all the lovers who experienced that configuration have passed from the earth. We've included sections about some generations of lovers who do not yet exist, at this writing—those with Pluto in Capricorn and

Aquarius. We've not included Pluto in Pisces because it's so far down the road.

COMPOSITE PLUTO IN CANCER

Cancer the Crab, that most delicate of creatures, is drawn inward, to the heart, to the feelings, to the safest and most impenetrable of shells within which to nurture oneself and others. Although we must remember that we are considering just one symbol that applies to hundreds of millions of relationships, couples with their composite Pluto in this sign carry a wound that had something to do with the loss of their shell, the loss of protection, the failure of nurturing, with feeling overwhelmed and utterly vulnerable.

Perhaps this couple's home burned down or was taken from them. They might have lost their life savings. Perhaps they lost their families. Maybe those who were supposed to nurture them abused them instead. We have to be imprecise about the specific origin and details of the karmic wound here—but remember that a close consideration of the composite lunar Nodes as described in Chapter Four will carry us light years closer to specificity.

For this analysis, it's sufficient to remember that with composite Pluto in Cancer, this couple has experienced something akin to the ground crumbling beneath their feet. That which they thought was their ultimate refuge has failed them or betrayed them. Their sense of safety in the world, their ability to trust, their willingness to lower their defenses and allow true adult to adult intimacy, were all damaged long ago. Thus, we find a complicated relationship with the acquisition, maintenance and shedding of shells, and with nurturing. Perhaps that shell is a house. A gated community. A family, the bigger the better, but where everyone either lives at arm's length from one another emotionally, or where no one is allowed to have any boundaries, any shells of their own. Entrenched and bristling defense mechanisms. Some all-encompassing belief system that leaves nothing in doubt. A recession-proof job or retirement plan. Often, all that which lies within that shell is "nurtured," sometimes regardless of whether that nurturing is necessary or appropriate, or abuse in disguise. All that lies beyond the shell is viewed as foreign, suspect, and probably dangerous until proven otherwise. The underlying logic is that if I have the *perfect* shell, I am safe: no one will rip it away from me and hurt me.

The "cure" for the Cancer Plutonian wound in the composite chart lies in the area of nurturing, healing and caring for one another and for others outside the relationship, outside the shell. This means realizing that there is no guaranteed safety in this world, and that no one is ultimately responsible for anyone else's happiness. It means self-revelation: taking *calculated risks of emotional nakedness* with one another. It means truly listening instead of rushing in with a solution. Sometimes it means "tough love," too, rather than merely colluding with each other's defense systems.

COMPOSITE PLUTO IN LEO

Leo the Lion draws attention to itself, and doing that is not always a formula for longevity. While we must be cautious and general here, since we are dealing only with a single symbol that applies to hundreds of millions of relationships, it is safe to recognize that couples with their composite Pluto in this sign carry a wound that had something to do with being set up and knocked down by their communities. Those words cover a lot of bases, of course. Movers and shakers in history, lifted high, then brought down through political reversal or treachery—yes, that could be. Or simply souls raised amid privilege in some "bullet-proof" bourgeoisie who was then clobbered by loss or catastrophe. That's consistent too. We cannot help but be distressingly vague about the specific origin of the karmic wound here—and take comfort in remembering that a close consideration of the composite lunar Nodes as described in Chapter Four will carry us light years closer to specificity.

For our purposes now, it's sufficient to remember that with composite Pluto in Leo, something hurts very badly in this couple. Their spontaneity, their joy in life, their ability to trust life and to feel comfortable in the human family, were all damaged long ago. Thus, we find a kind of approach-avoidance relationship with pleasure: a compulsion to feast—and then worry about calories. Benders, followed by penitent abstinence. A desire to be famous—and thus feel defended and powerful—followed by a fearful compulsion to undo the fame and escape into anonymity, loss or shame. Perhaps the single most characteristic mark of this Plutonian wound lies in a vulnerability to establishing an impressive facade which has nothing to do with the actual nature, tastes, or desires of the soul. The underlying logic is that if I am the epitome of importance and "coolness," I am safe: no one will hurt me.

The "cure" for a Leo Plutonian wound in the composite chart lies in the area of authentic creative self-expression. The couple must find a way to leave tangible evidence of their values and their inner processes in each other's hands, and then in the hands of the world. Their souls must shine forth, and be seen and appreciated *as they truly are.* They must experience *authentic success and appreciation*—and the word "authentic" is the key. Merely playing the role of success is the empty path, just another defense against being truly seen, and thus hurt.

COMPOSITE PLUTO IN VIRGO

Virgo the Craftsperson strives for *perfection,* and its tools include two highly detailed and laser-sharp pictures: one of reality as it actually is, the other of an ideal reality, reality as it could be if it had been perfected. Since few things in life are perfect or even perfectable, this dynamic is unlikely to lead to contentment. While we must be cautious, since we are dealing with a configuration that applies to hundreds of millions of relationships, we can generalize that couples with their composite Pluto in this sign bear a wound that has to do with having fallen short of some deeply-held ideal. Many scenarios could fit this description. Journeymen who never became masters of their trade. Servants unable to rise above their station. Soldiers or politicians whose missions failed. Athletes who lost a big game. Commoners never raised to peerage, unpublished writers, architects or masons whose designs for a medieval cathedral were rejected. We have to be imprecise about the specific origin of the karmic wound here—and remember that a close consideration of the composite lunar Nodes as described in Chapter Four will help us become more specific.

For our purposes now, it's sufficient to remember that with composite Pluto in Virgo, a deep sense of inadequacy is at work in this couple. Their self-esteem, their ability to see positive outcomes, their belief that the cup could be half full rather than half empty, their capacity to accept a good-enough although flawed reality—a job, a body, a person, a relationship—were all wounded long ago. Thus, we find a complex set of issues regarding criticism, guilt and shame. They may judge themselves, one another and the world too harshly, and dole out punishment for not being perfect: self-destructiveness, risky behavior, negativity, consistently underestimating themselves and selling themselves short. On the opposite side of that coin, they may defend against those feelings by becoming grandiose, blaming everyone and everything other than themselves for what's wrong with their lives, and being unable to bear criticism. The underlying logic is that if I don't try, I will be safe from a repetition of that crushing failure.

The "cure" for the Virgo Plutonian wound in the composite chart lies in the area of recognizing that perfection is an unattainable goal. *Working towards growth and improvement*, on the other hand, is both attainable and healing. With clear-eyed Virgo realism and a big dose of tolerance, this couple should work on themselves, work on the relationship, and find some way to contribute together to the larger human good.

COMPOSITE PLUTO IN LIBRA

Libra wants peace, harmony, equilibrium, symmetry, and accord. That Libran principle applies to both relationships and aesthetics. Although composite Pluto in Libra is a configuration shared by hundreds of millions of relationships, we can still say that couples with their composite Pluto in this sign bear wounds that stem from some fundamental loss of peace, from radical inequalities and divisiveness, from failure to compromise, from some breakdown of elementary human courtesies.

Perhaps they suffered from the horrific breakdowns of the human social contract that can happen during wartime. They could have been the victims of prejudice and other inequities: Jim Crow laws, lynchings, the caste system. Perhaps such injustices prevented their relationship from attaining its deepest levels; how easy is it to marry across racial or religious lines? Maybe it included the painful realization that not all conflicts have a win-win resolution—America was going to be a free and independent nation or remain a British colony; there was no middle ground. We have to be imprecise about the specific origin of the karmic wound here; still, an analysis of the composite lunar Nodes as described in Chapter Four will help us become more specific.

For our purposes now, it's sufficient to remember that with composite Pluto in Libra, a profound and pervasive tension, rooted in that loss of peace, is at work within this couple. Their centeredness, their ability to be moderate and calm, to believe in true equality and reciprocity, and to do what Jung called "hold the tension between the opposites" was damaged long ago. Therefore, we observe free-floating anxiety, indecisiveness, a tendency to compromise too much or too little, to try to gloss over conflicts and harsh realities, to strive for peace at any cost, to prefer a cool appropriateness to honesty or real connection. The underlying logic is that if I never rock the boat, I'll be safe.

The "cure" for the Libra Plutonian wound in the composite chart? We're reminded of the bumper stickers, "If you want peace, work for justice," and "Commit random acts of kindness and senseless beauty." It's a resolution that this couple will help contribute to an aesthetically aware, truly civilized, charitable, courteous society. Striving for justice includes stating one's own needs, hearing the needs of others, and granting equal importance to both.

COMPOSITE PLUTO IN SCORPIO

Scorpio's primary aim is the generation of consciousness about the dark. The dark side of our character; the human capacity for evil. The human unconscious. Everything that can make us uncomfortable, that can poke holes in the human ego's certainty that it's always in the driver's seat. This is deep, charged, and not particularly popular territory. Composite Pluto in Scorpio is a configuration shared by countless couples, yet we can generalize that couples with their composite Pluto in this sign carry wounds that stem from a denial of the dark, a refusal to deal with some of the grittier truths about human nature, the turning of a blind eye to the human shadow. They might have been whistle-blowers who were scapegoated or attacked, in the ancient tradition of Kill the Messenger. Perhaps their own blindness contributed to their victimization by bullies and tyrants, or perhaps someone else looked the other way while they were being abused. Perhaps, on the other hand, this couple were the perpetrators rather than the victims, and all the while insisted that their hearts were pure, that the other guy started it. We can't know the specifics of the karmic wound here; still, an analysis of the composite lunar Nodes as described in Chapter Four will help us become more clear.

For our purposes now, it's sufficient to remember that with composite Pluto in Scorpio, a brooding intensity fills this couple, a fascination with the dark, a reflexive suspiciousness about others' real motives, a desire to ferret out ever more complex, charged and uncomfortable truths. This is not necessarily an *identification* with the shadow, although in some cases that may occur, as may a denial of it or a projection of it onto others. It is, rather, *a need to examine and understand* the human shadow, in ourselves and in others. The danger here is of looking at the world exclusively through that Plutonian lens, to the point where despair and hopelessness arise, where the shadow looms so large that it blots out faith in the possibility of the human capacity for good as well as evil. The underlying logic is that if I assume the worst, I won't be blindsided again.

The "cure" for the Scorpio Plutonian wound in the composite chart lies in recognizing that we all participate in the collective shadow. No one person or group has a monopoly on it, and the collective shadow includes both victim and victimizer. The human psyche contains both dark and light. This couple should face the complexity of their own natures, that can both feel and cause pain, with equal amounts of courage and compassion.

COMPOSITE PLUTO IN SAGITTARIUS

Sagittarius, sign of the Pilgrim, the Anthropologist, the Gypsy, the Scholar, the Philosopher. The motif of the quest connects these symbols, the quest for perspective, knowledge, experience and understanding. The sign is idealistic, colorful, pattern-seeking, pattern-recognizing. For Sagittarius, life *must* contain some grand meaning. Composite Pluto in Sagittarius is a configuration shared by millions of couples, yet we can state, cautiously, that this composite Pluto indicates that the couple carries wounds that come from a *loss* of meaning, from dashed hopes, from restrictions and restraints, from the pratfalls that grandiose idealism, naïveté, inflation and restlessness can suffer. Missionaries attacked by cannibals? Cowboys captured by Indians? Scholars muzzled by the Inquisition? We can't know the specifics of the karmic wound here; still, an analysis of the composite lunar Nodes as described in Chapter Four will help us become more clear.

For our purposes now, it's sufficient to remember a hunger for freedom, purpose and expanded possibilities fills this couple, along with the fear that hunger can't be satisfied. There is a yearning for some greater significance. There can be a frustration with God, that the mechanisms of the universe are not more clear. Sometimes this frustration is so painful that the opposite reaction forms, and Pluto in Sagittarius insists that it knows exactly how many angels can dance on the head of a pin, how much they weigh and what their names are. This "knowledge" can be used to justify, rationalize or explain all sorts of behavior, and can contribute to reality-testing errors that more Saturnian types would be far less prone to make. There can be cynical or condescending indignation about the proclivities of more earthbound, less far-sighted and great-spirited souls. The underlying logic is that if God speaks to me directly, I will be spared the pain and embarrassment of mere mortal error.

The "cure" for the Sagittarius Plutonian wound in the composite chart lies in this couple's willingness to believe, their admission that belief is not knowledge, their tolerance of their own and others' uncertainties and mistakes, and their readiness to embrace the new, the foreign and the untried.

COMPOSITE PLUTO IN CAPRICORN

This is the sign of the Great Work. Of hard-won accomplishments, Herculean labors and great undertakings, whose fruition demands Capricornian virtues: realism, pragmatism, efficiency, self-reliance, integrity and productivity. While we must be cautious and general here, since we are dealing only with a single symbol that applies to hundreds of millions of relationships, it is safe to recognize that couples with their composite Pluto in this sign carry a wound that involved some great work that failed to reach its full manifestation. An unfinished symphony. A pioneer settlement that had to be abandoned. An unratified treaty, a bankrupt enterprise, no medal in the Olympics. Perhaps the cause of the failure was lack of persistence, poor reality testing, hostile circumstances or sheer fatigue. We can't know the specifics of the karmic wound here; still, an analysis of the composite lunar Nodes as described in Chapter Four will help us become more clear.

For our purposes now, it's sufficient to realize that a mood of great seriousness, stoicism, purposefulness and formality pervades this couple. Their confidence in their ability to achieve something meaningful, and to overcome harsh outer circumstances, has been damaged. Thus we can find exaggerated issues around survival, power, and the need for control, a reflexive pessimism, a tendency toward worst-case-scenario thinking and guardedness. Vulnerability, emotional, financial or practical, is avoided at all costs. Feelings are suspect, rationalized, or dismissed—including one's own feelings. A kind of brittleness sets in. Without an emotional compass, all that drive to accomplish can be aimed in ultimately unsatisfying and empty directions. The underlying logic is that if I don't make any mistakes and take all possible precautions in every situation, I will remain safe from a hostile outer environment and from unpredictable, unreliable, irrational human beings.

The "cure" for the Capricorn Plutonian wound in the composite chart lies in Great Works—but only if this couple recognizes that all of that Capricorn self-discipline and drive are best used to manifest some inner ideal in the outer world, rather than to build barricades against the feeling life and the uncertainties of human existence.

COMPOSITE PLUTO IN AQUARIUS

Pluto enters Aquarius in 2023, and relationships showing a composite Pluto in that sign will start showing up perhaps fifteen years later. At the time we're writing, that's definitely back-burner material! But we can use the symbolism to peer into the future.

As always, there is a divine intention behind this Plutonian configuration. It has to do with liberating human individuality within the context of love. There is an age-old tension between intimacy and freedom. Love is so precious, but it costs us so much. How many people throughout history have held their tongues about something they felt or believed simply to avoid conflict with their partner? Or to avoid hurting their partner? Love is full of compromise. Kindness must trump truth sometimes. But there is a dark side to all that, and for this Pluto-in-Aquarius generation of lovers, their task is to devise a culture of intimacy that is more compatible with human individuality, honesty, and freedom. They will create art-forms about it. They will vex their more conventional Pluto-in-Capricorn parents. And they will re-define the eternal, archetypal institution of marriage—by whatever name it is then known!

Pluto always casts a dark shadow. It pervades the cultural soup and makes itself felt in every life. Each generation of lovers must deal with it, along with their own more individual wounds and defenses. With Pluto in Aquarius, the shadow is coldness, distance, and detachment. *Alienation*, in a word. Love goes bad sometimes, and knowing how just to walk away is a necessary survival skill. But if we are too good at it or tend to use it too quickly, it can spell loneliness. Now imagine a planet full of people who all have an Olympic level of that skill—there's the Shadow of composite Pluto in Aquarius.

COMPOSITE PLUTO IN THE FIRST HOUSE

Outwardly, there is a feeling of dramatic intensity about a couple with their composite Pluto in the first house. There is something sexy about them. You feel like opening up around them, telling them secrets. And you are not the only one: if these two ever wrote a book about the shady sides of their friends' lives, there would be a lot of embarrassed people in the community. The Plutonian energy in their outward "mask" asks for that kind of confessional response—even when these two might prefer not to know.

The inward story is different. The first house is about the freedom to make our own choices. These two are wounded in that department. We view that wound as *karmic*; that is, as leftover damage inside them from a previous lifetime together in the reincarnational sense. If the idea of reincarnation doesn't work for you, it's easy enough to just stay with the present tense and not worry about the origins of the wound. What matters anyway is healing it, not explaining it. Using reincarnational language, we can see that they were tricked out of their freedom. Their relationship was not allowed to unfold naturally. Perhaps they were imprisoned in some sense, but very likely the bars of that cage were not literal. Much more likely, they were connected with what appeared to be worldly power. But is a leader ever truly free? Typically, those in positions of control lead very structured lives. Furthermore, they often have to make bitter, morally complex decisions—who, for example, can ever succeed in politics without making repugnant compromises? Something of that Machiavellian nature hurt these two. They danced close to the "Dark Side of the Force." They carry those scars forward into their present experience.

How can that manifest? They may become overbearing as a couple. They may exert unnecessary and inappropriate levels of control over their friends and family. There may be an aura of darkness, uncomfortable intensity, or even something tragic about them.

The healing of this composite Plutonian wound lies in these two people learning to *do exactly as they please*—wisely! Their aim is a kind of "enlightened selfishness," where they share their hearts with each other, decide what choices will give them the most pleasure, and then go forward unencumbered by any other concerns. The underlying idea is that deep down inside them, at the level of their instincts, is a natural, spontaneous goodness. As they learn to trust life—and themselves—again, their inner compass needle swings back toward this naturalness and simplicity. In getting there, they may make some waves, but they will recover their innocence. In being kind to themselves, they build a solid foundation for their kindness toward others—one that is rooted in firmer bedrock than philosophy or morality. One that is rooted in natural instinct.

COMPOSITE PLUTO IN THE SECOND HOUSE

Our word *plutocrat* means someone with a pile of cash. Gems and precious metals come from under the ground, so it makes sense that the "lord of the underworld" would be pretty flush—that's very likely the origin of the Pluto/money connection. Given that the second house is traditionally the house of money, it's no surprise that financial astrologers love this configuration! And indeed it's fair to say that a couple with their composite Pluto in the second house may very well find that their financial fortunes improve as their relationship becomes more committed. They may even eventually deal with large sums of cash, and the complications and opportunities that reality can generate.

Underlying that surface there is a wound. To grasp its nature and its impact upon their present life together, we need to recognize that the second house means a lot more than money. It actually refers to the entire material basis of survival—money, certainly, but also what money buys: food, shelter, safety, protection from environmental extremes, clothing. These two are wounded there. We view that wound as *karmic*; that is, as leftover damage inside them from a previous lifetime together in the reincarnational sense. If the idea of reincarnation doesn't work for you, it's easy enough to just stay with the present tense and not worry about the origins of the wound. What matters anyway is healing it, not explaining it. Using reincarnational language, we can see that in a prior lifetime together, this couple experienced some trauma connected with survival. A detailed analysis of their composite lunar South Node will open up the story for us, but just seeing this Plutonian configuration is enough to lead us to speculate that they may very well have experienced poverty together. It's plausible they have actually experienced famine together, or perhaps the indirect results of war or some environmental fluctuation that rendered survival dubious. The key is that this prior-life memory has created a *feeling of foreboding* in the couple, as if something bad will surely happen to them again. This subtly undercuts their faith in themselves as a couple, and that's really the psychological key: the healing of the Plutonian wound is linked to their learning to trust that their relationship can survive. They need to let go of the feeling that somehow they have bought a ticket on the *Titanic*. Achieving material security can actually be a very helpful, healing step for them. It would be ignorant and insensitive to frame such a goal as "unspiritual." Hungry people need a meal; later, we'll give them the philosophy!

There's another karmic possibility, statistically less probable, but one we need to consider. That's the idea that these two, in the karmic past, were not hurt by poverty, but by its opposite: great wealth. That's a rarer condition, obviously. But it can still be damaging to one's dignity and self-confidence. Outwardly, a wealthy life is an easy one. Laziness and a lack of the drive toward true self-actualization can take a terrible toll. Furthermore, whatever we accomplish, people will tend to downgrade it, imaging that it was the result, not of our own strengths, but of our resources and connections.

In both cases—lack and too much abundance—we see the same underlying Plutonian second house wound: self-doubt. In a nutshell, these two have come together as a couple in this lifetime in order to prove themselves to themselves. They are gaining dignity and a sense of their own solidity and legitimacy as a couple. There is only one way to do that: their relationship must succeed.

COMPOSITE PLUTO IN THE THIRD HOUSE

These two will say anything! They may not be that way as individuals, but if you get them together, you know that the conversation is going to head for the deep end of the pool. Maybe it will start out as humor—one of them makes a risqué remark or offers some teasing "psychological insight" that actually cuts close to the bone. In the blink of an eye, talk has gone into taboo territory. Maybe humor is bypassed entirely. One says, "You're looking older lately. Are you all right?" The other one nods and adds, "And you've gained a few pounds. What's going on?" Thirty seconds later you're pouring out your heart. Or walking out the door, feeling invaded and violated, with them left sitting there wondering what happened.

Underlying those confrontive surface behaviors, there is a wound. To grasp its nature and its impact upon their present life together, we need to recognize that the third house means a lot more than language. It also refers to the entire basis of *perception*—how we see the world, how we filter our perceptions through the stained glass of our biases, interests, and psychological orientations. These two are wounded there. We view that wound as *karmic*; that is, as leftover damage inside them from a previous lifetime together in the reincarnational sense. If the idea of reincarnation doesn't work for you, it's easy enough to just stay with the present tense and not worry about the origins of the wound. What matters anyway is healing it, not explaining it. Using reincarnational language, we can see that in a prior lifetime together, this couple experienced some trauma connected with how they viewed the world, what they said, and the reactions of others to them. A detailed analysis of their composite South lunar Node will open up the story for us, but just seeing this Plutonian configuration is enough to lead us to speculate that their mouths got them into a lot of trouble. They almost certainly crossed swords, perhaps unwittingly, with the representatives of the "official version" of reality. Maybe that involved a prior life in which they were connected with a religion deemed *heretical*. Maybe they were *siblings* in a family headed by a tyrant, and rather than keeping silence, they spoke up and were punished.

In any case, two phenomena arose in them, and they are dealing with them in the present lifetime. First, there is a lot of edge and anger in them around "their right to tell it like it is." This can lead them to use too much linguistic force in their statements to others and, most centrally, in their own dialog about their relationship. They need to learn gentleness, especially with each other. They need to learn that crackling one-liners that work wonderfully in a stage-play are generally catastrophic grandstanding when two people are treading in delicate emotional territory.

The second phenomenon is more subtle. In the past, they were punished for speaking what they perceived as the truth. This has led to a fear of repeating that pattern. Thus, despite the outward appearance of extreme candor, we can actually find a vulnerability to "lies of omission," or even to flat-out lying, when *fear of punishment* is a factor. And of course lovers, despite their fancy talk to the contrary, do typically punish each other for honesty. The deep healing for these two with composite Pluto in the house of language is, gently and slowly, to move to a place in their relationship where they trust each other enough to lay scary truths on the table.

COMPOSITE PLUTO IN THE FOURTH HOUSE

With composite Pluto in the deep, interior world of the fourth house, there is an undercurrent of psychological intensity that flows like blood through a vein in this relationship. Looking in from the outside, the surface of the pond might seem placid enough—but there are surely finny, improbable creatures swimming in the depths. Squint at them with the eye of a psychologist or a detective, and immediately the wheels start turning: something is going on here, something is not what it seems to be. These two have a secret.

And it's good that they do! Every shrink worth a penny is zealous about maintaining confidentiality—and every shrink worth a quarter knows that the deepest therapy in the world happens in the secret world of a serious, committed sexual relationship. With composite Pluto in the fourth, these two *do* have secrets—and they need them! Their bond is an alchemical cauldron in which a very private process of soul-healing is happening. It is profoundly helpful for them to speak honestly with each other about the families in which they grew up. For this relationship to work, that psychological territory must be sorted out. We don't need to make dark assumptions about their families either—only to observe that the unusually high level of honesty that is appropriate to these two people wasn't supported in their early training and socialization. Either they resolve that pattern, or they reproduce it.

Underlying all this is a wound. We view that wound as *karmic*; that is, as leftover damage inside them from a previous lifetime they shared together in the reincarnational sense. If the idea of reincarnation doesn't work for you, it's easy enough to just stay with the present tense and not worry about the origins of the wound. What matters anyway is healing it, not explaining it. Using reincarnational language, we can see that in a prior lifetime together, these two were almost certainly in a family together. Possibly they were married, but the clan-relationship might not have been sexual; just as easily they were simply kindred. And something catastrophic happened. A detailed analysis of their composite South lunar Node will open up the story for us, but just seeing this Plutonian configuration is enough to lead us to speculate that in coming together in this lifetime, they remind each other of unresolved, painful issues from a previous one. As they come to trust each other more deeply, they'll open up some "unfair" interpretations of their own—and each other's—families. And even if the interpretations are truly unfair, they are still connected with reality—the difference being that it's not the *present* reality they are seeing. It's the one from the prior lifetime. And, in a nutshell, it's never too late for therapy! *Psychological healing and reclaiming their faith in the idea of family* is their soul-contract.

COMPOSITE PLUTO IN THE FIFTH HOUSE

Pluto is dramatic and the fifth house is expressive. Put two and two together, and what you've got with composite Pluto in the fifth is a formula for fireworks. And fireworks can be a lot of fun! Much depends on where the explosions are happening. In a nutshell, the pyrotechnics need to be directed into these arenas: creativity, a pagan celebration of living, and passionate sexuality. Otherwise, they'll land in the realm of exhausting psychodrama, vexing attractions to other people, and children from hell.

To remain healthy, composite Pluto in the fifth house requires that these two people really make "seizing the day" a priority, especially in terms of life's more ephemeral joys: dancing "as if no one is looking;" making space for play, enjoying a little too much food with their soul-friends from time to time. It is helpful for them to concentrate on always encouraging each other sexually, and never shaming or repressing each other. Letting their relationship feel like the scene of the liberation of their libidos, not as a prison for them, is critical. If they can find a creative medium to share, so much the better: acting, music, painting.

Why so much emphasis on getting the ya-yas out? Underlying those expressive, playful behaviors, there is a Plutonian wound trying to be healed. To grasp its nature and its impact upon their present life together, we need to recognize that there is a basic human need for ecstatic release. It's the only force that can balance the undeniable pain of life. These two are wounded in the house of pleasure. We view that wound as *karmic*; that is, as leftover damage inside them from a previous lifetime together in the reincarnational sense. If the idea of reincarnation doesn't work for you, it's easy enough to just stay with the present tense and not worry about the origins of the wound. What matters anyway is healing it, not explaining it. Using reincarnational language, we can see that in a prior lifetime together, this couple experienced some trauma connected with the repression of their natural instinct for pleasure and release. A detailed analysis of their composite South lunar Node will open up the story for us, but just seeing this Plutonian configuration is enough to lead us to speculate that, in a prior life, they were hungry for each other sexually, but that the situation or local customs prevented the full exploration of those energies. Perhaps they were shamed by bad, repressive religion. Perhaps they had a brief and socially catastrophic affair that left them both damaged. Maybe they experienced a childhood together under tragic, "growing up too fast" circumstances.

In any case, in the present lifetime, they have signed a soul-contract to try to develop a right relationship with the human need for pleasure. If they are committed to each other for the long haul, they still need to try to live each minute as if it were their last. And if they come to a place where the joy of their bond has seriously dissipated, they must recognize that there is only one ultimately real reason to stay together: because they want to!

COMPOSITE PLUTO IN THE SIXTH HOUSE

When truly dreadful things happen in life, we find out who our friends are. It can be a bitter phrase or a very sweet one, depending on whether the people we count on fail us or prove reliable. With their composite Pluto in the sixth house, this couple is very likely to deserve a gold medal in troubled times—they'll come through for us like saints. They are also a magnet for such situations. Together, they'll see more than their fair share of life's difficulties, if not in their own lives, then in the lives of those around them: disease, family dysfunction, existential and economic reversals. Simply calling this "bad luck" is a defensible perspective, but here's a deeper one: these two are *servants of humanity*. God will use them where they are needed. When they came together, an alchemical process was triggered that made them far more useful to others together than they ever could be as separate individuals.

Within the context of this basic soul-contract, they have choices to make. The first and most elemental is simply this: how will they serve? It is wise for them to seize the initiative here. Simply stated, here's the menu. They can exercise a set of helpful skills of which they are justly proud and which give them a sense of fulfillment. Or they can be outmaneuvered by circumstance into washing out the johns, mowing lawns, and being at the beck and call of various petty tyrants. In either case, it's Plutonian sixth house energy: service.

Underlying these surface behaviors, there is a wound. To grasp its nature and it impact upon their present life together, we need to recognize that sixth house "service" has a lot of meanings. Some of them are bitter, and these two have been wounded there. We view that wound as *karmic*; that is, as leftover damage inside them from a previous lifetime together in the reincarnational sense. If the idea of reincarnation doesn't work for you, it's easy enough to just stay with the present tense and not worry about the origins of the wound. What matters anyway is healing it, not explaining it. Using reincarnational language, we can see that in a prior lifetime together, this couple experienced some trauma connected with a grievous weight of unwanted responsibility. There are duties from which we cannot in good conscience escape: a dependent child or aged parent may simply, objectively need us, for example. Going out a little further on the limb, let's recognize that slavery has been pervasive in human history. Perhaps these two were literally in chains together—and if it's not factually true, those words at least provide the right metaphor.

Karma tends to repeat; this is why we emphasize the danger of the joy of this relationship being diminished by pressing, exhausting duties—old patterns might manifest again, either in the form of circumstances or, more likely, in the form of an old tendency to accept burdens which they *could in fact ethically refuse in the present context*. Let's also add that the real shared soul-intention here is to find meaningful service, and transmute the karma into something higher, sweeter, and far more rewarding.

COMPOSITE PLUTO IN THE SEVENTH HOUSE

Watch a couple with Pluto in their composite seventh house for a few weeks, and you start entertaining some interesting questions about them. Who's that guy in the trench coat hanging outside their door? He looks like he's either a gangster or a spy. Who's that woman in the dark glasses? Is she a hooker or a rock star? Oh—those are their best friends, Mugsy and Bubbles. They're really sweet . . . once you get to know them.

OK, we're exaggerating a bit. But not much. Ostensibly, we all *choose* our friends—unlike family, those are voluntary relationships. But friendship, like deeper forms of intimacy, is partly karmic too. We may have evolutionary business with people who seem to be inexplicable "choices." With composite Pluto in the seventh house, this couple has a series of soul-contracts with a group of Plutonian people. And Pluto is, of course, the Lord of the Underworld.

One expression of this phenomenon is that our heroes may in fact find themselves drawn to and involved with some people who are actually doing a dance with the Dark Side of the Force. Naturally, there are dangers in that, and they do need to be careful of being dragged into trouble. But let's hasten to add that "darkness" is much in the eyes of the beholder. Cautious or prissy people use the label in a profligate way. Anyone exploring sexuality outside conventional contexts might be fairly called "Plutonian," for example—and that just means they're breaking taboos, not natural law. Ditto for people who are fascinated with crime, psychedelics, war, deformity, torture. The list of subjects that make people uncomfortable is long. It is also well-mapped, so that we don't commit a *faux pas* in the polite cocktail party of human civilization. With composite Pluto in the seventh house, the simple fact is that these two people have soulmates who are exploring these edgy areas. For this couple to do what they came here to do, they need the help of these honest, intrepid individuals.

Ultimately, the seventh house is about *trust.* These two are wounded in that department. We view that wound as *karmic*; that is, as leftover damage inside them from a previous lifetime together in the reincarnational sense. If the idea of reincarnation doesn't work for you, it's easy enough to just stay with the present tense and not worry about the origins of the wound. What matters anyway is healing it, not explaining it. Using reincarnational language, we can see that this couple was somehow deceived in the past. At the psychological level, we are looking at the results of a feeling or experience of *intimate betrayal*. This is why, in this present lifetime together, they are so drawn to psychologically honest people—these people, who are obviously not hiding anything, are the ones they can trust, and who play such a critically healing role in helping this couple return to a place of having faith in other human beings. The wonderful paradox is that in learning to trust others, they build a foundation for trusting each other more deeply.

One final note. Because karma tends to repeat, we can also count on the fact that whoever betrayed them in the prior lifetime will show up again in this one—and may well be no more honest now than then.

COMPOSITE PLUTO IN THE EIGHTH HOUSE

Drama finds these two. Psychological intensity radiates from them. When they walk into a room, there's a witchy, almost shamanic energy just beneath the surface: you'll see it when they catch each other's eyes in a conversation, or when someone in the social group makes a comment that is obviously wishful thinking or a comforting lie. They may not say anything, but you know they caught it—and checked it out with each other. These are Plutonian qualities, and Pluto is the natural ruler of the eighth house, so its signature is very strong in this relationship.

Going further, you get the feeling that there is real passion between these two individuals. It's a sexy energy, but the sense is that what drives their passion is deeper than the natural hungers of the body: they seem more *engaged* with each other than most couples. They know each other better than people typically do, even ones who have shared a bed for many years.

If you received dire medical news, to whom would you turn? These two are on the list. Their shared energy invites *realness*—in turning to them, you would expect compassionate understanding, but more importantly, you'd feel an assurance that they wouldn't fall apart or resort to clichés because they just didn't know how to handle the situation.

Underlying all this honesty and intensity is a wound. We view that wound as *karmic*; that is, as leftover damage from a previous lifetime they shared together in the reincarnational sense. If the idea of reincarnation doesn't work for you, it's easy enough to just stay with the present tense and not worry about the origins of the wound. What matters anyway is healing it, not explaining it. Using reincarnational language, we can see that in a prior lifetime together, these two almost certainly faced some kind of nightmare together. There is a feeling of shared tragedy between them. Probably it involved death, quite possibly each other's deaths. There's a fair chance it involved the impact of *evil* upon them—and, by "evil," we mean humanity's oldest enemy: the capacity that some people have to enjoy inflicting pain and damage upon others. There's been no shortage of that energy in human history, and there's a good chance these two were on the receiving end of it together. A detailed analysis of their composite lunar South Node will open up the story for us, but just seeing this Plutonian configuration is enough to lead us to speculate that in coming together in this lifetime, they remind each other of unresolved, painful issues from a previous one. This has given them a kind of soul maturity and a real ability to relate to people *in extremis*. But they also desperately need the healing comfort of the kind of honest, bonded intimacy and *shared understanding of our fragility* that they have potentially found in each other.

COMPOSITE PLUTO IN THE NINTH HOUSE

In the couple with composite Pluto in the ninth house, there is a driving hunger to penetrate down to the honest heart of whatever matters face them. The ninth house always ultimately seeks *understanding*, and Pluto intensifies that motivation as well as aiming it toward uncomfortable perspectives—places where the human heart naturally tends toward avoidance and rationalization. The configuration is therefore quite consistent with a shared *scientific* attitude, as well as a kind of streetwise sense of what makes people tick. In philosophy or religion, it inclines toward hard-hitting psychological perspectives rather than fluffy fairyland "answers." There is a quality here that a casual observer might interpret, quite incorrectly, as cynicism. It's not that, really: just a profound desire not to be hoodwinked by glib, slick perspectives or teachers.

Seeking truth is dangerous business. What we find might hurt us. Those whose identities are built around lies and falsehoods are inclined to punish us for it. Karmically, there is a shared story here that includes being wounded somehow by the *collective beliefs* of a culture. A shared prior life experience that included religious persecution or prejudice is quite possible here—but so is any story where the finger of "public morality" is wagged judgmentally. With the "travel" associations of the ninth house, we may be looking at a shared piece of unresolved prior life material that had to do with geographical and cultural dislocation: pioneers, immigrants, refugees. As always, details emerge only as we bring in all the various past-life indicators, building upon the foundation laid by the lunar Nodes.

One last piece: with Pluto in their composite ninth house, part of the soul-intention of the couple in this lifetime is to *return to the physical place where the karmic wound was laid down*. A kind of cathartic healing comes simply from seeing it again. It's like a woman returning to the scene of a rape, or a Woodstock-generation soldier returning to Viet Nam. Where is this place? We can't know from looking at the composite Pluto, but the couple will find it—it may haunt their imaginations, or figure in their own intuitive processes when they first fall in love. They may even be drawn there "by chance" while they are "vacationing."

COMPOSITE PLUTO IN THE TENTH HOUSE

Plutonian topics, are by definition, nervous subjects we talk about carefully, if at all: sex, disease, death, money, ageing. In social relations, we approach them with great diplomacy and almost Oriental indirectness—or with the marvelous, buffering illusions of emotional honesty that humor creates. The tenth house, on the other hand, is absolutely public. Nothing can hide there. It represents what we appear to be to the social world. It's the tribal definition of our identity: our work, our relational status, the hat we wear in the eyes of people who don't really know us in any other way.

So, with their composite Pluto in the tenth house, these two people are dealing with a paradoxical combination of forces: something that is normally kept hidden is as obvious as a pornographic hot-air balloon floating over a funeral parlor. At the soul level, these two signed a contract: together, they are going to bring something shocking and uncomfortable to the attention of their community. If they get it right, they'll make a difference in this world. They'll bring something to light that needs to be seen. And if they get it wrong, they'll be targeted for *projection*—people will gossip about them, or worse.

Underlying these patterns, there is a Plutonian wound trying to be healed. We view that wound as *karmic*; that is, as leftover damage from a previous lifetime together in the reincarnational sense. If the idea of reincarnation doesn't work for you, it's easy enough to just stay with the present tense and not worry about the origins of the wound. What matters anyway is healing it, not explaining it. Using reincarnational language, we can see that in a prior lifetime together, this couple was hurt by the worldly powers of the day. An evil king. Dark government. Fascism. Institutionalized persecution or prejudice. Perhaps they were killed; perhaps they were driven into poverty or hiding. A detailed analysis of their composite lunar South Node will open up the story for us, but just seeing this Plutonian configuration is enough to lead us to know three things. The first is that deep in their karmic memory banks is a fear of being seen or noticed—and this fear runs counter to their soul-intentions in this present lifetime. They simply cannot let it make decisions for them. The second point is that, this time around, they need to stand up bravely and effectively for something that will make people nervous, uncomfortable and angry—telling the truth about what's happening to our ecosystem, for example, or describing the sweatshop realities that keep us supplied in toys and cheap clothing. The third point is that if they don't make a positive response to the destiny's call, then they'll surely slip back into the old karmic pattern: somehow, some way, someone will decide to make them a victim—again.

COMPOSITE PLUTO IN THE ELEVENTH HOUSE

We humans are all a little scared of the dark, but some of us are a bit less afraid than others. With their composite Pluto in the traditional house of friends, this couple is drawn to claim membership in a Plutonian tribe—that is, among people who are engaged in exploring perspectives and experiences that make the general run of the population jumpy. That phenomenon can take a lot of forms. At the sophisticated end of the spectrum, we might find them attending a psychological lecture. More simply, we might see them standing in line to take in a horror flick. Why? Because such movies represent an artistic attempt to deal with questions of darkness in the world, and Plutonian types are overrepresented among those who attend them.

Another dimension of the eleventh house is that any planet there tends to grow in power over time. Simply said, the longer these two stay together, the more intense and spooky they will become! There are reasons for that evolutionary trend, and we'll understand them in a moment.

Underlying those developmental patterns and social behaviors, there is a wound. To grasp its nature and its impact upon their present life together, we need to recognize that the eleventh house refers to the impact of *tribal collectives* upon individuals who are swept along by them—just think of the mad energy of 30,000 people screaming at a football game, and you've tuned into the right channel. These two are wounded there. We view that wound as *karmic*; that is, as leftover damage from a previous lifetime together in the reincarnational sense. If the idea of reincarnation doesn't work for you, it's easy enough to just stay with the present tense and not worry about the origins of the wound. What matters anyway is healing it, not explaining it. Using reincarnational language, we can see that in a prior lifetime together, this couple experienced some trauma connected with pressures from the collective. A detailed analysis of their composite lunar South Node will open up the story for us, but just seeing this Plutonian configuration is enough to lead us to know that either they were targeted by a group, or that they themselves were swept into beliefs or actions that compromised them.

Together, their soul-contract is to heal this wound. That work is difficult. It comes later in their relationship; their first years together are essentially about building a foundation of trust and a network of supportive relationships in the world that will allow them, when the time is right, to uncover the core karmic pattern. We don't know its specific form, but we do know this: once they've dug it up, they'll realize that, systematically, they have allowed the social and cultural world around them to make too many decisions for them. As they evolve together, they reach a point where they feel that they can either wither or reclaim their lives. If they make the latter choice, which is of course the right one, their truth will go off like a bomb in the context of their community: they will break the rules.

COMPOSITE PLUTO IN THE TWELFTH HOUSE

A friend who had nightmare wartime experiences as a solider once said simply, "Some things can never be forgiven." The look in his eyes brooked no debate. That wasn't because of hostility or defensiveness on his part; that was because of a pain so deep and so personal that any comment would have been nothing but warm, wet, meaningless air. A client lost her husband and two children in an airplane crash. What can you say? That's transiting Pluto for you? No. All you can do is sit together and try to feel your common humanity. Life is bigger than us. Life eats us. Those are facts so real that sometimes silence, patience and faith are the only responses with any dignity.

Pluto in the twelfth house is an astrological reference to such extremity. With that configuration in their composite chart, there is an ingrained depth of compassion in these two. There is also a deep sense of life's tragic dimension. Underlying this poignant feeling is a wound. We view that wound as *karmic*; that is, as leftover damage from a previous lifetime they shared together in the reincarnational sense. If the idea of reincarnation doesn't work for you, it's easy enough to just stay with the present tense and not worry about the origins of the wound. What matters anyway is healing it, not explaining it. Using reincarnational language, we can see that in a prior lifetime, these two almost certainly faced some kind of ultimate loss. In some sense, they lost everything, even hope. A detailed analysis of their composite lunar South Node will open up the story for us, but just seeing this Plutonian configuration is enough to lead us to speculate that in coming together in this lifetime, they remind each other of unresolved, painful issues from a previous one. They are haunted and deepened by this ghost from the past. Maybe they were refugees. Maybe they experienced the death of a child. Perhaps they were victims of a genocide. We don't know. But we do know that in this lifetime, they trigger certain vulnerabilities in each other: gloomy, unfocused feelings of foreboding, possibly depression, a propensity toward shared patterns of numbing escapism—into overwork, drugs, alcohol, soporific media addiction. Those are the traps. Those are the soul-cages.

What about the higher ground? First, we must honor the *maturity of compassion* in these two. With composite Pluto in the twelfth house, they can bridge across the isolation that is felt by people in serious psychological or existential extremity. Thus, they are natural counselors with the energetic stripes of people who've really, truly "been there themselves." God will use them to comfort others, and that is part of their soul-contract. More personally, they've made a deal to face this wound together. They may not "remember" it specifically, but sooner or later issues will arise in their relationship that reflect their adaptive numbness relative to the unresolved wound. If, for example, they lost everything materially in the past life, they will recognize that they've made too much of a virtue of poverty in this lifetime—or that they've paid too much for their fear-driven financial security. If they lost a child, they will fear having children—or experience exaggerated anxiety in terms of their children's well-being.

Ultimately, of course, all of us will lose everything we have. That is the nature of life. Sooner or later, death comes and we leave this world. And what comforts us then? The only real answer is our knowledge of our innate spirituality. And, in the final analysis, a deeper, shared sense of that eternal divinity in each one of us is the aim of these two souls. When someone faces grievous loss, we cannot preach to them—and those who do are typically coming more from a place of fear than a place of faith. But we can know that, finally, a spiritual perspective on loss is the only one consistent with sanity and soul-survival. No one can be rushed into it; for these two, with their composite Pluto in the twelfth house, it's better late than never.

CHAPTER SIXTEEN: THE COMPOSITE LUNAR NODES

We tease out the past life story underlying a present life relationship by analyzing the Nodes of the Moon, both in the composite chart and in the charts of the two individuals. In many ways, this process is the heart of modern evolutionary astrology. The full interpretive process is complex, entailing a revisioning of virtually every configuration in the composite chart from this new nodal perspective. In Chapter Four, we presented a detailed overview of the relevant strategies and techniques. There, we learned about the richness of past life detail that arises from going beyond looking only at the lunar Nodes themselves. We learned how important it is to understand the message of the *planetary ruler* of the South Node, and to analyze any planetary aspects to the nodal axis.

Every planet in the composite chart hints at a piece of the karmic drama. What we've not been able to do in these pages is to keep perspective on the individual importance of each of those planetary placements. For one couple, a Libran Mars may be the key to our understanding of their prior life dynamics. For another, it might be a minor detail. Determining the right perspective depends absolutely upon grasping the message of the lunar Nodes. They are what put the planets in context.

In the pages that follow, we present "cookbook" interpretations of the composite lunar Nodes in terms of each of the twelve signs and houses. We believe these ideas can provide you with a good interpretive foundation—but you've got to build the temple on that foundation yourself. If a couple has, for example, a composite South Node in Pisces, you can count on there being an underlying pattern of drifting. They might surrender too much of what they legitimately need for their lives. But *in what prior-life context* did they develop that pattern, and where might it hurt them again? Go to the houses. Maybe their South Node lies in the ninth house. If you turn to that section, you'll read about prior-life experiences in a *religious* context. Put that together with the Piscean information, and you've got the outlines of an answer: perhaps they were involved in a religion (ninth house) that encouraged too much surrendering (Pisces). Maybe their South Node lies in the fourth house, not the ninth. Then, as you'll see, the evidence points more toward self-sacrifice within the context of *family* or *clan*.

The trick lies in seeing the *psychological and motivational issues* **represented by the South Node's** *sign* **expressing themselves in the** *circumstantial context* **of the South Node's** *house*.

Then of course we need to add the message of the South Node's *planetary ruler,* weaving its story into the package. Perhaps this couple with a Piscean fourth house South Node has composite Neptune in the second house. As the ruler of that Piscean South Node, Neptune might introduce pressing concerns of a financial nature in a past life: wealth or poverty was the specific trigger that pressed them into that high degree of self-sacrifice for the family. But which one was it—wealth or poverty? Well, that leads us to wonder whether Jupiter (wealth) or Saturn (poverty, more likely) is aspecting that Neptune. Or maybe there are other planets in the composite second house, giving us a clearer picture.

You can see how quickly all this ramifies into complexity—and, thus, into rich detail. Again, to learn the interpretive procedures, please review Chapter Four. Here, our intention is simply to provide you with solid starting points in terms of the basic meanings of the Nodes in the signs and houses.

One final consideration: in what follows, you will notice two distinct biases. We focus on negative interpretations of the South Node and positive interpretations of the North Node. That is quite intentional. It is not that the South Node is "bad" and the North Node "good." But the composite South Node, while it definitely alludes to some real strengths in the couple, also primarily focuses our attention on areas where they have issues *left unresolved* from the past—issues which tend to haunt them in the present. By thinking negatively about the South Node, we focus our attention narrowly and effectively on those issues. Similarly, the North Node represents answers and solutions to those prior-life dilemmas. Concentrating on positive interpretations there is the whole point: that's where the healing liberations and attitudinal paradigm-shifts can happen.

COMPOSITE SOUTH NODE IN ARIES
(Composite North Node in Libra)

Interpreting the Moon's South Node is like taking a defining moment out of a prior life drama, and putting a stethoscope on the condition of the two human hearts in that instant. We know what they were *feeling*—but we have no idea what they were seeing, thinking, or doing. We take the emotional message and, using hints from other places in the composite chart, we attempt to discern the outlines of the actual story. With the composite South Node in Aries, we know that these two people were feeling the effects of a lot of adrenaline! In some sense of the word, they were involved with *war.* Often, given the human enthusiasm for war as evidenced in our collective history, we can take that allusion to the violence of battle literally: these two may very well have actually been in a do-or-die situation of combat together. But "war" can also be a metaphor for any human situation involving danger, intensity and competition: climbing mountains, sailing a Spanish caravel through uncharted waters, even being locked in business or political competition.

One interesting question lies in determining whether these two were on the same side or enemies in this "war," although the distinction is less important than it might seem at first. It's very common for beings who actively hated each other in a prior life to become attracted to each other in this lifetime—and then of course to have their ancient issues make themselves felt in their present life interactions. Hard aspects between the Nodes in their personal birthcharts tend toward this latter interpretation. Where we see softer aspects, we can make the assumption of *comradeship under fire*, with its attendant emotions of fierce loyalty—and often a rather startling ignorance of each other in a multidimensional human way. People huddling in a London underground station with *Luftwaffe* bombs raining down may feel real love for each other in a primal human way, and yet have almost nothing in common.

In any case, knowing that the North Node lies in Libra helps give us perspective. The evolutionary intent of this couple lies in the general area of *calming down,* and specifically in making peace with each other. We might even add simply getting to know each other, and taking their time with that process—the Arian air of urgency tends to press these relationships into premature intimacy, and sometimes premature apocalypse! To accomplish that aim, they need to understand the insidious way each one of them conspires with the other to keep their existential situation more *dramatic, intense and exhausting* than is good for either one of them. They need to learn to listen to each other. They must weed out a kind of competitiveness that creeps in through the cracks in their self-awareness. They need to resist turning each other into cartoons, and instead take the time to know each other really well as nuanced, complex human beings. They benefit from exposing themselves to civilizing influences:

painting, music, graceful people. Above all, they need to absorb the notion that love is a bigger concept than passion.

COMPOSITE SOUTH NODE IN TAURUS
(Composite North Node in Scorpio)

Taurus is the most primal of the Earth signs. It echoes the nature of those earthy denizens of our planet we call the members of the animal kingdom—and the natures of all of us two-leggeds who haven't strayed too far from remembering our natural roots. Taurus is about instinct, and all the simple truths we know in our bones. Like an animal, it is concerned with the basics: food, warmth, shelter, and love. It prefers the familiar. It avoids the unexpected. With the composite South Node of the Moon in Taurus, a couple's karmic past may very well have been agrarian, or otherwise connected to nature. They might be carrying soul-memories of shared membership in a so-called "primitive" culture—Hopis or Druids or Ashanti. That's far from certain, but it is consistent with the Taurean signature. So is any "simple" life: the farmer, the craftspeople, the fishermen. We'll often see a natural way with animals in such a couple, or real ability as gardeners or naturalists. Commonly, there is some capacity to work with their hands together.

Generalizing a bit further, we can observe the Taurean South Node signature in any shared lifetime that was motivated by the desire to keep life *stable* and *predictable*—and therein lies the pitfall. An attachment to stability and predictability has suffused the logic of this soul-bond; in the present life, they run the risk of *stasis*. One manifestation of that issue in the context of modern society lies in being overly concerned with financial stability, to the point of "paying too much for money." Another lies in the avoidance of natural developmental conflicts within the context of relationship: being so preoccupied with being happy together that the work which actually maintains happiness in a relationship is avoided.

There is plenty of simple, instinctual goodness in Taurus. It represents a kind of natural morality, without elaborate philosophical embellishment. By instinct, something inside us knows that killing for pleasure is wrong, or that it is wrong to take sexual advantage of children. Thus, a kind of *unstudied righteousness* exists in this couple. One down side to that positive quality is naïveté—a vulnerability to the predations of more

Machiavellian types. We might be looking at the "city slicker" tricking the "simple Indian" out of possessions, land or sexual favors.

All of this leads us to understand the significance of the Scorpio North Node for such a couple. Their evolutionary intention lies in making peace with life's complexity, irony, and moral ambivalence. They are ready for a psychological leap forward. In this lifetime, they intend to dance with their Shadows, and to integrate parts of them. This is a very delicate step for their evolving souls. Emphatically, the aim is not to become "bad"! Rather, it is to make peace with their own pre-existing "inner Scorpions." Like Adam and Eve, it is time for them to "eat of the fruit of the tree of the knowledge of good and evil." Together, much of this work revolves around accepting their own needs for power, their sexual hungers, their jealousies, their control issues—all the "dirty games" people play. They must learn to accept these qualities in themselves and, even harder, in each other. In this lifetime, as a couple, they are going *beyond goodness*. They are going into *wholeness*, which is really the highest form of love—a love that excludes and shames nothing. In the jargon of psychology, they are learning to withdraw their projections, which means to recognize in themselves the qualities they are most inclined to judge in others. In the end, what they are aiming toward is an intimacy so profound it will startle them.

COMPOSITE SOUTH NODE IN GEMINI
(Composite North Node in Sagittarius)

Quick intelligence and lightning reactions—those are Geminian qualities. Think of a fast-paced conversation, and how rapidly your mind free-associates. Now think of driving a car in heavy traffic on the freeway: again, stimulus, response. These improvisational skills, this sense of making it up as you go along, is absolutely basic to our understanding of the Twins. With the composite South Node in Gemini, the past-life experiences whose mood still overshadows our couple embrace all those speedy mental energies and inner states. In the past, these two were shaped by situations that required light-speed reflexes, and a capacity to recognize opportunity and seize it faster than a cat can bat at a passing hummingbird. This focused their psychic energies in a rational, cerebral, rather stressed-out way—a necessary adaptation to their circumstances then, but perhaps too narrow a way of being human for them today. And yet, as soon as they meet again in this lifetime, the gravitational field of the old associations makes itself felt.

Gemini often refers to *siblings*, and while we shouldn't be rigid about anything, it's easy to imagine these two as brothers or sisters in a prior lifetime. Throw in a tale of their being abandoned at an early age and having to live by their wits, and you've got the right Gemini South Node feeling. The sheer speed and flexibility of Gemini also links it to *youth*. Being literal would be inappropriate here, but the composite South Node in Gemini does often correlate persuasively with karmic experiences that are uniquely linked to the perils and opportunities of youth—it would strain credulity, for example, to imagine a traumatically premature marriage occurring at age forty! But it could be indicated by a Gemini South Node linked to relationship symbolism in the composite chart.

In the present life, the couple with the composite South Node in Gemini must guard against a state of chronic overextension, where they have plenty of effective tactics but no overarching purpose or strategy. There are relentless pressures toward chatter and running around in circles. They will resolutely believe those pressures to be external, but that's really just the hangover of the karmic mood. The truth is, those pressures are mostly psychological and internal.

The composite North Node in Sagittarius, the sign of the philosopher, emphasizes the present tense need for this couple to think deeply and intuitively about what is truly important in their lives. Values, beliefs and personal philosophies need to guide them. Religion, in the broadest sense, might help them keep perspective. A helpful "yoga" is to spend some time every year in something like a retreat together, talking about where they are in their lives and in their relationship—and where they would like to be at the same time next year. Travel is an excellent Sagittarian vitamin for them, in that it helps extricate them from the clutches of their immediate dramas. They may also be guided by their intuitions to visit the scene of the prior life Geminian trauma. The eerie experience of simply seeing the place, and half-recognizing it, can have a liberating impact on the relationship.

COMPOSITE SOUTH NODE IN CANCER
(Composite North Node in Capricorn)

Tell a decent mother and father that their child is in peril and immediately nothing else matters. It's such a natural reaction that if we were to see any other parental response, most of us would probably feel judgmental. Certain instincts are so elemental to our humanity that they bypass the higher brain functions. Most of them have a lot to do with species survival, and form the basis of our moral and legal systems. Cancer, ruled by the Moon, is the astrological epitome of instinct in general, and especially of the instincts associated with home, hearth and the protection of the vulnerable. With their composite South Node in Cancer, this couple carries the profound mark of having been "family," and probably of being linked by parenthood—either as parents together or in a parent-child relationship. Should we see a chronic patten of one nurturing the other, we have a compelling clue about who was the parent and who the child! If instead we see equality but also a deep, easy familiarity, then it's more likely we're seeing two who were partnered in a domestic situation. In either case, from the outset there's typically a deep, unreasoning and unquestioning feeling of *loyalty* and *bondedness*.

Always with the South Node, it's helpful to be concerned with the potentially blinding or limiting effects of the karmic past, however laudable it might be. Family is generally a cautious institution. So much focus naturally rests on the demands of nurturing that a deadening stability can arise. We can see complex, passionate human beings reduced to roles and functions. There can be a kind of paradoxical invisibility—people who see each other every day in predictable circumstances are often less alert and savvy about each other than strangers conversing on a train. Unconditional love, forgiveness, long-suffering acceptance of each other: these are precious qualities common with the composite South Node in Cancer. But they can breed psychological pestilences! These two people must strive to see each other as multidimensional adults. They need to guard against the temptations of working out the relationship a little too effectively, letting it get too comfortable. They need to come to conscious decisions about where the boundaries should exist between themselves and their kinship groups. Similarly, they need to navigate carefully around the risk of friends, especially needy ones, becoming their "children." Even pets can be an issue here. The point is that, with the composite South Node in Cancer, these two carry a tendency *to escape from facing each other as naked souls through the device of focusing attention on the needs of others.* Naturally, having children together, while it might feel desirable and in fact be quite appropriate and rewarding, underscores these risks unless they've first had sufficient time to establish their adult bond.

Their composite North Node lies in Capricorn, suggesting a kind of "toughening" occurring in this lifetime. This is the sign of the Elder. It represents a developmental stage beyond parenting and nesting. There's more hard truth in it, and more willingness to be alone and separate. The evolutionary intentions for this couple embrace a kind of *maturation* in their bond. They are learning to love each other's solitude, and to defend it. They are learning how not to be "cute," both in public and privately with each other. The nurturer is giving way to the truth-sayer.

There is no incubator of psychological wisdom—and dysfunction—more powerful than family. These two have been there, and they've learned a lot. With their composite North Node in Capricorn, the time has come for them to move out of the narrow framework of the inward-looking family and to share this wisdom with the larger community.

COMPOSITE SOUTH NODE IN LEO
(Composite North Node in Aquarius)

Leo is the Lion—the King of Beasts—with dominion, at least in folklore, over all other creatures. The folklore is easy to appreciate—one look at even a small house cat, and we see the "royal" qualities our ancestors noticed in the feline branch of the animal kingdom. With the composite South Node of the Moon in this sign, thinking of the couple as "royalty" in a prior life gets our minds aimed in the right direction. With symbolism, it's of course essential to avoid the pitfalls of literalism: this doesn't mean the pair necessarily sported crowns in another lifetime. But they were surely in a position of some privilege, and probably envied to some degree by others. Sometimes people attain such positions of prominence through effort and accomplishment, but throughout history it's often been the circumstances of birth that determined one's place in the social pecking order. Thus, the imagery of *privileged birth* enters our equations. Given the often grim realities of poverty and powerlessness throughout history, a lot that's positive can be said about the implications of a Leo South Node! But always, with this Node, our bias is toward the pitfalls rather than the joys of any situation. Being born into privilege entails severe social expectations in terms of role, marriage, work, values and behavior. It can be a straightjacket, stifling the natural intentions of the soul.

In the present life, the couple with their South Node in Leo may not be born into wealth or hereditary privilege, but they will tend to *shine* somehow anyway. Often, they carry the burden of being the "perfect couple" in the minds of others. Many times, together, they are able to create considerable *success*: money may be part of it, but we should also be sensitive to the idea of success in creative areas or other vocations where the bank account isn't always the final criterion of having "made it." A simple observation, but one that carries important clues, is that they often like to present themselves in dressy clothing, and look not only good but also *natural* that way.

Understanding Leo's South Node traps is easy in the light of the North Node, with its Aquarian evolutionary intentions. Aquarius always carries the energy of true freedom; it is the astrological reference to real individuality. Immediately, we understand the vulnerabilities inherent in the Leo karmic pattern: the creation of a kind of success that is shaped more by a capacity to fulfill the expectations and values of others than by authentic soul-expression. Easily, these two can manifest a kind of empty theatricality in some area of life. Typically, they haven't set out to do that. It "just happened." But a deeper analysis reveals the core issue: they allowed themselves to be swept along by the currents of other people's projections.

The Aquarian solution? *To do as they please!* To cultivate a blasé attitude regarding the opinions of others. To find the inner freedom to make "bad" decisions in terms of the eternal "pecking order" logic of human society.

COMPOSITE SOUTH NODE IN VIRGO
(Composite North Node in Pisces)

Poor Virgo gets teased a lot. That's just an astrological manifestation of pop culture, with its tendency to project negatively onto anything threatening. In common with the rest of the zodiac, there is something sacred and precious here: jokes about Virgos alphabetizing their socks notwithstanding, this sign carries the human drive toward competence, precision, and humility. It is the archetype of the Servant, with all the attendant implications of helpfulness. It's the part of us willing to make the effort to get *good at something*. Still, since we are looking at the composite South Node of the Moon, it behooves us to look at Virgo a bit dubiously in this context. For a couple with their South Node there, it's time to move beyond the blinding and limiting dimensions of the sign of the Virgin. What are they?

Perfection is a harsh and exacting standard. No one can ever live up to it. And yet this couple, in a prior life, attempted it. And, of course, failed. To call this their "fault" is like lamenting the existence of gravity or taxes. But they internalized a feeling of inadequacy and its dark cousins: shame, guilt, and a penitential, self-punishing attitude. Repressive, shame-based religion may be the culprit—but just as easily we might be observing the results of cultural puritanism, racial or ethnic shaming, the ego-shattering impact of discipleship under an overly exacting master, or sexual abuse. We may possibly be looking at "real" guilt, in unresolved response to some actual dark deed. That latter point must be handled with delicacy, since most of the time a composite Virgo South Node is more reliably correlated with the "phony" guilt created by unnaturally demanding external standards. As usual, details of the karmic story only emerge through a more complex analysis involving the house position of the Node and its planetary ruler, its aspects and so forth. All we see here in terms of the Virgo South Node itself is a self-doubting, hassling, endlessly fussing mood that can leach the joy and magic out of life, if it's allowed to stand.

The Moon's North Node, and thus the evolutionary intention of these two souls, lies in Pisces. To understand the meaning of this configuration, we must start with a line that almost inevitably goes in one ear and out the other: *God's love is absolute*. What that signifies is that there is nothing a human being can do to affect God's love—being absolute, it is beyond conditioning. Thus, God doesn't give a merry damn whether we feed the hungry children of the world or murder people at random. We state the principle in shocking terms like that in the hopes of awakening ourselves to the sheer, liberating Piscean power of the idea. This couple has reached a point in the journey where they need to *let go of their identification with struggling to evolve*. They need to play—to "become as little children." They need to get out of their own way.

That said, let's add a dangerous concept: these two need to meditate together. Why is that so dangerous? Because, by instinct and karmic reflex, they will interpret meditation as more struggle, more of their endless shortfall. But this Piscean meditation is relaxing. It ends when we're tired of it. It has no aim or goal. And in the end, meditation and everyday consciousness become the same long dance under the benign eyes of a God who loves us already.

COMPOSITE SOUTH NODE IN LIBRA
(Composite North Node in Aries)

We humans are dangerous primates, with aggressive qualities, strong emotions and sharp teeth. Can anyone imagine a relationship—or a civilization, for that matter—thriving without a generous dose of respectful compromise, tact, and courtesy? Let's throw in grace, empathy and love's blessed ally: a sense of humor. These are all Libran qualities, and with the composite South Node in Libra, no matter how heated this couple's negotiations may become, an inner compass needle pulls them back toward this pleasant civilized mood. In the karmic past, they were very clearly partnered in some way. To assume that they were, if not married, at least lovers is probably a safe bet. In significant ways, this is a relationship that dawns in this present lifetime already worked out and established. Furthermore, given Libra's natural associations with the more sophisticated aspects of civilization, they probably carry into this world a soul-momentum of interest in the arts, in justice, and in the dissemination of all that is lofty and uplifting.

So what's wrong with all that? Nothing! But we do need to recall that the core meaning of the Moon's South Node is that it represents patterns that have already served their purposes, and which lead to evolutionary stasis unless challenged. The "fair" middle ground can be dead for everyone. Compromise can mean answers that please no one. Courtesy and respect can hide truth, and provide cover for the parts of these two people that fear it. Aesthetic experience—music, film, television, beautiful clothing and beautiful people—can be used in escapist ways, helping to avoid those nose-to-nose, eye-to-eye moments that are the heart of shared soul-process. These are the traps facing the couple with the composite South Node in Libra. For all their long soul-history together, there are ways in which they barely know each other. So much reality has been hidden behind walls of "appropriateness." Justice, reason and dignity have robbed them of love. The mask associated with their place in society has hidden their true faces—even from each other.

Now, with the composite North Node in Aries, the evolutionary intention of this couple lies in embracing fire, stormy passion and, when necessary, anger. It's time they got to know each other, warts and all. One piece of good news is that they are building on a deep foundation of trust. Their love is hardy enough to cope with some stress and strain. In fact, stress and strain are far less threatening to it than the prospect of the bond foundering on a lack of drive and heat. Together, they benefit enormously from shared adventure—anything that gets them into situations that frighten them a bit. They don't need to take foolish risks, but they do need to see how they look to each other in situations where their conventional roles are stripped away. They need to learn that their love is strong enough to digest anger, even bitter anger. They need to make room in their discourse for each other's wilder sexual edges. They are learning that love doesn't mean agreement or even harmony. They are, at last, making room for each other's separate individualities. As partnered souls, they are evolving toward a time when they *could* let each other go—and, paradoxically, it is that realization which allows them to remain together.

COMPOSITE SOUTH NODE IN SCORPIO
(Composite North Node in Taurus)

There are parts of life that can make our blood freeze in our veins: human depravity and incomprehensible human suffering. A child in fearful agony. Dreadful bodily dysfunction. Sadistic violence. A person's state of mind one minute before jumping in front of a train.

None of us want to get very close to those places, but sometimes, unbidden, they get close to us. Terrible, dark events do happen, and when they do, they leave marks on the souls that experience them. The couple with the composite South Node in the sign of the scorpion has known such extremity. One possible response to such experience is to become numb, but Scorpio does not symbolize those kinds of dissociative responses. They lie more in the dark side of the Aquarian vein. Here, we see the imagery of the heart as an open wound, shocked and dumbfounded, but still taking in the nightmarish perceptions.

There is an atmosphere of seriousness here, and a corresponding vulnerability to loss of perspective, gloom, and suspicion, especially regarding the lighter, more playful dimensions of human experience. There is also wisdom and, potentially, compassion. The key here, from the evolutionary point of view, lies in recognizing that souls often evolve rapidly when faced with extreme hardship. A couple captured and chained on a slave ship, even one that sinks en route, may learn more about life and themselves in a year than a more fortunate couple learns in a safe lifetime together. Still, such a path of soul-growth obviously entails serious wear and tear on the attitude, and the persistent scars that tragedy always leaves in its wake.

Taking it one step further, we must recognize the *fascination* that the dark side of life exercises upon our psyches. A quick perusal of what's playing at your local movie houses will quickly confirm the existence of this weird, ambivalent attraction. Strange as it may seem, the very realities we most fear seem to pull at us the most. Along with the wear and tear, it is this *attachment* to heaviness that constitutes the deepest obstacle for the couple with the composite South Node in Scorpio. The gravitational field of their unresolved karmic wounds pulls them into ever deeper waters—even when the higher path is a simple, pleasant stroll along the beach.

And that brings us to their composite North Node, which lies in Taurus. Here the evolutionary emphasis lies in the area of calming down—of getting over the processes that brought them to their present state of agitated, psychologically complex wisdom. As always with the North Node, the work is challenging, and it goes against the natural grain. *These two have come together to comfort each other.* In earthy Taurus fashion, that comfort must be concrete—a timely hug rather than a pithy insight. A bath and nap, not a serious talk. This couple benefits a lot from living away from a city, if possible, or at least in getting out of town as often as they can. Animals have a lot to teach them; it would be good for them to have a cat or a dog, with the homey comforts these creatures imply. They need to move their relationship toward a simple, instinctual acceptance of each other. We hear so much about how complex relating is; however, for two people with the composite South Node in Scorpio, that's the last notion they need to emphasize. What they need is more the idea that life is *easier* with a partner, and that of course we humans are happier with a mate than without one! That last line may not apply to everyone on the planet, but for these two it conveys the right attitude. Calm, naturalness, and a return to the senses are the path forward.

COMPOSITE SOUTH NODE IN SAGITTARIUS
(Composite North Node in Gemini)

Sagittarius is the sign of the *Quest,* and with their lunar South Node there, this couple had already logged many a searching mile together by the time they met in this current lifetime. An exuberant spirit of *possibility* suffuses their relationship. It's as if their backpacks were loaded, the secret map carefully folded in their pockets, and the wandering road open before them. In the karmic past, they've shared a commitment to seek an understanding of life, and they've known instinctively that such understanding can only be gleaned through the total immersion of one's senses in all creation. Thus, they share a patterning of breaking out of predictable molds, of doing the unexpected and the extreme. In prior lifetimes, they've shipped out together for far shores. They've left their homes behind and gone on crusades. They've met under the date palm when the moon rose in the wee hours to join the caravan. Their prior lives together would make a great movie.

Sometimes, the underlying Sagittarian hunger for an understanding of life has been eclipsed behind their sheer appetite for adventure. Even then, the furnaces of philosophy were being stoked and fed—and that point is even more true when their adventures have led them into spectacular miscalculations and errors, as they often did! Other times, this philosophical hunger has been more obvious: together, these two have been deeply marked by *religion* and by adherence to compelling *belief-systems.* They may have shared monastic lifetimes or been involved with religious movements. With influences from Pluto or Mars, we may recognize that they might have been martyred together. Often, the religious impulses in Sagittarius combine with its geographical restlessness to produce utopian beliefs involving mass migration to a New World. They may, for example, have been Mormons heading for Utah, Jews returning to Israel, or dissident Protestants heading for colonial America.

With the South Node, we must always be especially alert to the darker side of these old patterns. Even where they are intrinsically healthy, there's still something tired and worn-out about them. Believing in values and philosophies can be blinding. Even believing in our relationship can dull our sensitivity to the need for processes of negotiation and adjustment. It's a short step from faith to a kind of unconscious editing of life's true complexity. In common with many religious people, in prior lives these two have fallen into patterns of collusion regarding the denial of truths that ran counter to their expectations—and it's a short step from fundamentalist Islam or Christianity to fundamentalist New Age thinking today. Karmically, the issue they've come together to resolve is their *compulsive addiction to certainty.*

That brings us directly to their evolutionary intention, as symbolized by their composite North Node of the Moon in Gemini. Here, we find a basic focus on listening and receiving, and a willingness to be surprised. *They need amazement and wonder, and ideally it starts at home with their openness to surprising each other.* Two people, shoulder to shoulder, agreeing on everything—how deadening! The soul-growth of this couple depends on vigorous, respectful disagreement, followed by long conversation. Without differences, they have nothing to teach each other anymore. Let the Buddhist sleep with the Christian. Let the Existentialist try to love the astrologer. Their formula this time around is endless dialogue, fueled by floods of unexpected, mind-stretching experience, and seasoned with an appreciation for their differences.

COMPOSITE SOUTH NODE IN CAPRICORN
(Composite North Node in Cancer)

Necessity is a stern teacher. We rise to it, or we are destroyed by it. With their composite South Node of the Moon in Capricorn, there is a grown-up, no-nonsense attitude in this couple. Their survival skills are superb. They can add two plus two and come up with four, even when the numbers would put tears in anyone else's eyes. In prior lifetimes together, they have squarely faced hard reality and steeled themselves to do the right thing. Nowadays, our pop psychological culture places a great premium on being in touch with our feelings. And of course only an ignoramus would argue against that idea. Still, circumstances arise in which the higher ground demands that we set our feelings aside and take a course that our conscience can accept in the long run. Anyone who has ever resisted a temptation understands this territory—and our couple with this South Node configuration understands it very well. Together, in prior lifetimes, they have faced grim moral and practical requirements. Perhaps they were pioneers eking out an existence in an unforgiving land. Perhaps they gave birth to a crippled child—or to a large, hungry brood of healthy ones. They've known grinding poverty—or the relentless demands of power and position. As always, we can get a better handle on the actual circumstances through a consideration of the house that contains the South Node, along with the various associated planetary configurations. What we see here is simply the basic Capricorn signature: strength, self-denial and character, bred in a harsh environment.

Slogging along, putting one foot ahead of the other, becomes a habit. So does self-denial. So does hopelessness. After a while, we stop noticing pain or need. With their South Node of the Moon in Capricorn, friends can rely on this couple. If they have children, the kids will have their physical needs met. If they move into a new neighborhood, they might find themselves chairing the Neighborhood Watch committee. If they work together, as they might very well do, their business runs efficiently—and survives downturns that catch their competitors unaware. They are a magnet for duty and responsibility, and they handle them with maturity, realism and aplomb. As those duties and responsibilities proliferate, our couple rises to the challenges without outward signs of distress.

But are they having any fun? Are they soothing the ancient wound that binds them together in this wintry landscape of necessity? Are they giving themselves permission to feel, to cry, to need? Are they reaching out to their streetwise inner orphans? Those are the questions that bring us face to face with this couple's composite North Node of the Moon in Cancer. *These two have come together for mutual healing.* In the karmic past, they did not have the luxury of tears. We certainly don't need to shame them for that, only to recognize that they were adapting realistically to inhumanly harsh realities. Their intent now is to soften. They have made a soul-contract to integrate weaker, more emotional, gentler parts of themselves into their relationship, and then into their lives as individuals. They must cry those old, unfallen tears, and do so in each other's arms.

Underlying the karmic mood of the couple with the composite South Node of the Moon in Capricorn is an abiding hunger to be safe—at last. That hunger is inseparable from a need to establish an emotionally secure home. Physical and financial safety are part of it, but even more central is the feeling of emotional safety that comes from being committed to their relationship for the long haul. Their guardian angels smile when they see these two planting trees together instead of seasonal marigolds. They jump for joy when these two feel safe enough to express sorrow or fear or need or other "weaknesses" to each other. Perhaps the ultimate barometer of that security is the feeling that it might be "safe now" to have children. Or at least a spoiled cat!

COMPOSITE SOUTH NODE IN AQUARIUS
(Composite North Node in Leo)

Could an ancient Egyptian have imagined a world without a pharaoh, or a medieval European a world without kings and dukes? The wheels of history turn. We look back over the pages of the history books and so much seems inevitable, as if there really were "wheels" of history, turning like gears in some impersonal mechanism. But the truth is that the world changes because of individual people shaking things up. Those people are almost always a tiny minority of the population. Very typically they pay a price for the gift they give us—the figures of authority in the pre-existing culture are fiercely opposed to anyone who challenges the status quo. When these "revolutionaries" reincarnate, they'll often have the South Node of the Moon in Aquarius, the sign of the Rebel or the Exile. When we see that South Node signature in the composite chart, we know that in a prior lifetime, these two people were outsiders together, existing in tension with consensual reality. There was a feeling of "us against the world," although often the "us" could also be defined as a movement of which they were a part. In other words, we might be looking at a couple who were among the slaughtered Cathars in thirteenth century France—or slaughtered civil rights activists in twentieth century Alabama.

If we are going along with the herd, believing what we are told to believe, our brains don't get a lot of exercise. But if everyone we meet imagines us to be wrong, that "muscle" between our ears gets a lot stronger. For our couple with the composite South Node of the Moon in Aquarius, there is an instinct to do things their own way, to question the received wisdoms of their culture, and to follow less-trodden pathways. They think for themselves and tend to be drawn toward the familiar ground of subcultures that are at odds with the social mainstream. Far more than most of us, they truly write their own script. Still, because of their unconscious karmic soul-conditioning, they may reflexively ignore the comforts and wisdoms of "normalcy." They may become so identified with a set of colorful, rebellious *ideas* that they lose touch with their own natural feelings and instincts. They may needlessly alienate or isolate themselves from the human family. Furthermore, because they may share soul-memories of persecution or even torture, they carry a *dissociative* tendency—basically a reflex to "go away" emotionally. That too can drive them into a cerebral orientation which, while intellectually impressive, can also entail the opening of a gulf between the mind and the soulful "belly" of our common humanity.

With their composite North Node of the Moon in Leo, the couple with this configuration shares the Lion's soul-intention: To roar! To be heard! Something was left undone in the karmic past. *Part of the reason they've come together again in this present life is to finish their business from long ago.* The exiled heretic must make its presence felt in the world. To be "right" is one thing; to be heard is another. The first requires mental freedom and a willingness to question authority. This couple has those bases covered. The second goal, actually being heard, requires a different set of skills—ones they did not master in their prior lifetime together. Most of them are more *theatrical* than mental. They must find ways to look plausible and convincing, especially to the "unconverted." They must *build effective bridges* this time around. They need to be appealing, non-threatening except where absolutely necessary, and to radiate confidence. Even the message their *clothing* sends must be calculated. Ditto for their language and word choices.

Don't be misled by the emphasis upon outward appearances here, even though much of it is quite intentional. There is an inward breakthrough happening for the couple with the composite South Node of the Moon in Aquarius as well. For them, it is time to "come in from the cold." As they have been judged by others, they have become judgmental. As they have been isolated, they have separated themselves from the larger community. Their soul-contract is to find a way to make a positive difference in the lives of people who, formerly, would have burned them at the stake. This represents motion in the only direction higher than truth, and that is the direction of forgiving, unconditional love. Together, they are moving beyond *rightness* into *effectiveness.*

COMPOSITE SOUTH NODE IN PISCES
(Composite North Node in Virgo)

Mystical traditions universally encourage us to look beyond the appearance of the world. They teach us the ancient Piscean truths: our true natures are not these transitory physical bodies; our true home is not this endless, three-dimensional passion play. For our couple with the composite South Node of the Moon in Pisces, these ideas are the glue that joins the two of them together. But if they truly observe the world as if it were a dream, does anything they do matter? Feeding imaginary starving children—or slaughtering imaginary rivals: does either action carry any significance? Is compassion any more relevant than hatred?

In prior lifetimes together, this couple has experienced a hallucinatory *loss of self.* They have seen the world as a dream, and felt themselves moving like ghosts through it. There is a good chance that they have entered into spiritual practices together: long meditations, devotional ritual, fasting. That they have been in monastic orders together is a fair guess. Those perspectives make them sound officially holy, and perhaps they deserve that title. Just as likely, we may see them drinking together in a prior life bar, or floating together through socially-defined roles in frivolous elegance, or experiencing the dull dream of lives defined purely by the expectations of others. It is very possible that all the scenarios above apply to them—and that the monastic existence came *first.* That might seem counter-intuitive, but spiritual practice is serious medicine. A soul that is not ready for the changes becomes disoriented.

Before we look at the actual evolutionary intentions for the couple with the composite South Node of the Moon in Pisces, we should spend a moment counting their treasures. They've brought with them into their secret world a deep, authentic sense of magic. Their psychic connection is extraordinary—they often feel as if they are reading each other's minds. Together, they have an incredible faculty of imagination and creativity. They "get the joke" about human egos, their own included, and that helps them keep perspective on their conflicts.

What they have come here to do together this time is symbolized by their composite North Node of the Moon, which lies in Virgo. One big part of this intention leaps out when we realize that Virgo is an Earth sign: these two have a soul-contract to get down to earth. They are learning to function in more effective, orderly, efficient ways. Virgo is the *Servant*—but we need to be careful of that language. The aim here is not to become servants in any literal sense, nor is it necessarily so lofty as becoming servants of humanity. It is really about simply becoming skilled enough at something to be of use to other people. Accepting specific responsibilities and discharging them competently is central to Virgo. *Making little things matter* is a huge part of the work of the Virgo North Node.

Underlying these practical impulses to be helpful is an evolutionary strategy. With the composite South Node of the Moon in Pisces, this couple has become curiously self-absorbed. They have fallen into the dreamlike trap of the "spiritual path," with its subtle reinforcement of the ego. They've reached a stage in their evolutionary trajectory where they need to take that ancient medicine: *service*. They need to make other people's dilemmas more central and compelling to them than are their own dilemmas. In becoming useful to others, they are profoundly useful to themselves.

COMPOSITE SOUTH NODE IN THE FIRST HOUSE
(Composite North Node in the Seventh House)

Freedom: we all value it—and dread its constant companion, which is uncertainty. In every truly free situation, we must make choices. Sometimes we're free to choose between pleasant, positive courses. Other times, we're between a rock and hard place. Most of the time, we have no idea what kind of outcomes our choices will bring. Will marriage bring joy or sorrow? What about having a baby? Or moving to the coast? With the composite South Node in the first house, these two have felt the weight of that kind of freedom over and over again. When they have been together in prior lifetimes, they have typically faced circumstances that demanded decisive action. They've hardened themselves to burn their bridges behind them. Very often, their choices have affected not only themselves, but also the lives of others. First house energy correlates with *leadership*—and while leaders often appear to be clear and certain, their inner reality is often far shakier: they must make life-shaping decisions without any way of knowing if they are right or wrong. This has created a self-contained, inscrutable quality in this couple, as if no one outside themselves can see their inner processes with any clarity. They can be impressive and radiant together, yet elusive.

Choosing—or not choosing—a mate is one of our ultimate, inalienable human freedoms. Once the hormonal veil of falling in love begins to lift, we recognize that, in loving, we give up a lot of precious freedom. With their composite South Node in the first house, these two have often come to that crossroads—and chosen to go down separate roads. They've been too strong to surrender to each other. Their prior life conditioning had pumped so much energy into their natural authority and their compulsion to take personal responsibility that the delicate interpersonal balancing act of partnership was incomprehensible to them. With this nodal configuration, it is even quite possible that these two have been rivals, enemies or competitors in previous lifetimes. If so, we will see plenty of evidence for that tension in the present lifetime as well.

Their composite North Node lies in the seventh house, the traditional house of marriage. While it would be dogmatic to say that they must marry in this lifetime, it is fair to recognize that their evolutionary intention lies in the direction of partnership and cooperation. Countering that intention is the weight of the karmic pattern, pulling them toward self-sufficiency and clueless isolation. These two need to learn to listen to each other, to depend on each other and to surrender to each other. The core evolutionary issues between them are *trust* and *commitment*. The great Intelligence of the universe has provided them with a set of dreams and desires which they can only fulfill together. Each one has talents and skills the other one lacks. Each holds half of the treasure map. Only by seeing through each other's eyes and listening through each other's ears can they do what they've come into this world to do.

COMPOSITE SOUTH NODE IN THE SECOND HOUSE
(Composite North Node in the Eighth House)

Calling the second house the house of money is like saying orchestras make loud noises—it's true, but it leaves out all the music! *Resources*, not just dollars, are the issue here. Food and shelter are on the list. So are skills that empower us to survive—and that includes everything from the ability to start a fire without matches right up through professional talents that pay the bills in a complex, high tech culture. With their composite South Node in the second house, issues around these resources have left a mark on this couple. Depending on the extremity of the South Node's sign and planetary connections, it is possible that these two have known literal starvation together. It is possible that they have been exposed, perhaps fatally, to extreme climatic conditions. Reliably, in prior lives, they have known the distorting impact of financial extremes on their well-being. Poverty may have taken its grinding toll on them—but great wealth can twist lives almost as easily, creating a spiderweb of expectations, manipulations, and mistrust. All these prior-life experiences have threatened their actual *survival*, physically or spiritually or both. And that has left a mark of fear, self-doubt, and insecurity upon their souls.

What resources support committed love? Obviously, food, shelter and a few dollars in the bank all help. But we must also recognize that loving is difficult, and that it requires mental health and maturity as well. Reading history, we recognize that the concept of "marriageable age" separated significantly from puberty only in the last century or two. That's in the industrialized world; in the Third World, it's still common to see people, especially female people, married in their early teens. From a modern reincarnational perspective, it follows that in prior lifetimes many of us have been cast off in the matrimonial boat without the oars of maturity. Patterns are then established between people which reflect their childish lack of self-knowledge, their inevitable sexual ineptitude, and the role-playing behaviors that attempt to veil the vacuum. Even when love is potentially real between two people, this kind of karmic experience leaves a mark: with the composite South Node in the second house, *the relationship doubts itself.* It can feel doomed, or like a ritualized trap.

How do these two get on with fulfilling their soul-intentions? With their composite North Node in the eighth house, they are attempting to surrender sexually to each other in full, self-aware maturity. There is a pent-up need to consummate their love. Sex, for these two, can function as a kind of evolutionary yoga. Paradoxically, they must bring their spiritual maturity to their sexual relationship and, at the same time, allow the ancient mysteries of committed sexuality to trigger maturation and gender-wisdom in each of them.

Kids kissing in the backseat are all excited, but we know they'll be broken up by the end of the school year. What do the wise old lovers, with eyes that go back forever, know? With the composite North Node in the eighth house, these two are moving toward the answer.

COMPOSITE SOUTH NODE IN THE THIRD HOUSE
(Composite North Node in the Ninth House)

Maybe you're driving in the middle of six lanes of heavy, fast traffic. Maybe you realize that you've got only a quarter of a mile to get over into the right lane. Maybe at that moment the person riding shotgun next to you asks about your philosophy of life.

Probably you ignore him. If you think about anything other than navigating through the traffic, you will likely have an accident. If you make any response to his question, it's certainly short, and probably humorous or cynical.

Life gets like heavy traffic sometimes. Things are moving so rapidly and unpredictably that we simply do not have time to reflect. We are thinking, but the thoughts are focused on immediate concerns. We are practical, concrete and reflexively logical. With their composite South Node in the third house, this couple carries the mark of that kind of mentally-driven reactivity. In prior lifetimes together, their pattern has been one of *acceleration, improvisation* and *rapid adaptation.* Perhaps they were orphaned siblings together, picking pockets in the marketplace to survive—with a belly full of hunger pressing harder than a moral analysis of thieving. They have remained alive by recognizing opportunity and seizing it before it shifted away from them. They have collaborated and communicated well; they've mastered teamwork like two brilliant basketball players sneaking the ball into the paint. Often, this configuration suggests literal sibling connections in a prior lifetime.

Trouble is, they could run on sheer momentum in this lifetime. As always, the South Node represents a pattern that has served its purpose. We need to recognize its dead-end qualities and move forward. If they fail in that challenge, then their lives together will be swept along by currents outside themselves. They'll be fast and efficient and maybe astonishingly productive, but they won't have a real strategy. They'll communicate glibly, but never get down to the soul of things between them.

The good news is that they do not need to remain locked in the gravitational field of that composite South Node. With their composite North Node in the philosophical ninth house, their evolutionary intention is to go "sit on a mountaintop" together. They need to talk about why they are alive in the first place. What are their values? What kinds of lives do they want to look back on from the perspective of old age? What happens when their souls are included in the existential strategy sessions? *Religion,* in some sense of the word, may help give them perspective on these questions. Almost certainly, as they move toward this more reflective style of thinking, they will realize that one fundamental goal that unites them is the desire to *travel*—and instinct will then guide them to the literal scene of a shared prior lifetime in which events happened too fast for reflection and integration: back to that "marketplace," where they contrived to survive.

Seeing the "scene of the crime" can have a liberating effect on them, which is why we must view travel in sacred terms for these two: it is one of their spiritual disciplines in this lifetime.

COMPOSITE SOUTH NODE IN THE FOURTH HOUSE
(Composite North Node in the Tenth House)

Cities only came into existence a few thousand years ago. Nations are practically a brand new concept. Throughout most of human history, our fundamental sense of place in the world was defined by kinship groups: families, clans and tribes. Those are fourth house realities. When we are thinking about a couple with their composite South Node in that house, we must think carefully. The idea that they came out of "family systems" in the karmic past is surely true. But so is the idea that they probably walked around on two legs! What we need to recognize here is that these two were *defined* by family, and that the impact of familial expectations and familial mythology upon them was severe and limiting.

One immediate hypothesis is that, in a prior lifetime, this couple was literally born into the same family—that they might have been siblings, in other words. For emotional reasons, it's often hard for people in a sexual relationship to think of themselves in those terms, but it can easily be the case. We can say the same for other possible kinship connections between them: one was the other's grandparent or niece or nephew. In any case, there is typically a quality of *unquestioning, total loyalty* between people who share this composite South Node. Often, there is an uncanny sense of familiarity between them right from the start of their present relationship. Living together feels very natural, and tends to happen quickly.

The karmic trap lies in the ease with which their individual identities can be subsumed by the requirements of the "family system." That pitfall can take two forms. The first lies in being crushed beneath the expectations of their literal families: enmeshment in the family dramas, and enslavement to the life-limiting realities of the family myth: "We Smith women always marry drunks;" "We Simon men always wind up working on cars for a living." The second lies in their creating such crushing expectations all by themselves—having children too quickly, having too many of them, or becoming so preoccupied with being a couple they forget to be individuals with separate lives.

With the North Node in the tenth house, there is a great soul desire to come out into the world. Together, these two *know something* which can be of use to strangers. It's time to offer their gifts to the world, not hide them in their private, unexpressed imaginations. The essence of their evolutionary strategy lies in simply launching themselves into the white water of life lived in the context of community rather than in the withdrawn context of family. Prioritizing their professional lives is often a very big part of this intention, in practice. "Will we move across the country to take these great jobs—or stay where we are to be close to mom and dad?" In this case, moving would reflect the evolutionary intention, while staying home would reflect the now deadening karmic pattern.

COMPOSITE SOUTH NODE IN THE FIFTH HOUSE
(Composite North Node in the Eleventh House)

Creativity, children and issues around *hedonism* are a trinity of factors that define the karmic circumstances in which this couple found itself. The balance among the three is generally discernible through a consideration of the rest of the nodal factors, although all of them are worth exploring in every case.

Where we see significant involvement with the Moon or Saturn, or with the signs Cancer and Capricorn, look especially to karmic entanglements involving children. This is a very common pattern. For all the joys and rewards of raising kids, it's useful to remember that over and over again in human history, people have sacrificed much that was potentially important to them on the altar of parenthood. Unintended pregnancies have always been plentiful—and often bound people into premature, ill-fated marriages. Once children exist, their needs tend to eclipse the needs of their parents. This may be natural, but it can also be tragic. With our bias toward the South Node always leaning toward suspicious perspectives, these darker readings of the impact of children in prior life experiences are generally productive. In the present life, the couple may simply reproduce the old pattern. Or there may be a lot of tension and questions around whether to have children, with obscure fears and resentments complicating their decisions.

With the composite South Node in the fifth house, the couple may very well have been involved with the arts in some form in a prior life as well. Perhaps they were partners in such endeavors, or met there. One of the easiest ways to confirm that possibility is to see if the pattern is reproduced in their present life together. If they are drawn to creative work together in this lifetime, it clinches the karmic roots of the behavior. Generally, artists serve an experimental role in a society, going out to the ragged edges of emotion and experience that other, more cautious citizens find fascinating but too risky to assay themselves. Thus, we have an observable linkage between the creative life and the "issues of hedonism" to which we alluded a few lines back. Freud famously observed that the libido never forgets a pleasure. Most addictions and compulsions are far easier to create than to shake, and this couple may very well have fallen into prior-life patterns involving debauchery or dissipation together. And of course they need not have been artists to go down that road!

"Love affairs" is another classic fifth house correlate, and often play an important role in the nodal interpretation. Love affairs can lead to pregnancy of course, tying in this theme with all the issues around children. Even without thinking of children, it's worth considering that this couple "broke rules" to be together in a prior life.

In the present life, with the Moon's North Node in the eleventh house, the core of the healing process for the couple revolves around learning to *think strategically* together. It's about taking a longer view, realizing that they have time to make decisions and develop their dreams. They benefit enormously from pressing toward long-term goals: saving to build a home together or to have a major adventure. If children are on the radar screen, it's helpful for them to delay pregnancy for a while, putting it more under their own intentional control. In matters of creativity, there's a need to nurture their *development* as artists over time—perhaps taking instruction from masters and honing their craft over decades. In terms of friendships, positively, they need to develop discernment in terms of which kinds of people help them become what they most want to become—and, negatively, to recognize people who, while fun, lead them nowhere or worse.

It would be profoundly misleading to think that a couple with their composite North Node in the eleventh house is trying to get past the need to enjoy life! It's really more that they are learning to be a little smarter about wringing the maximum amount of joy out of living, given the twin realities of pleasure's dark, compulsive side and of our need to live strategically given life's brevity.

COMPOSITE SOUTH NODE IN THE SIXTH HOUSE
(Composite North Node in the Twelfth House)

Responsibilities have defined the relationship of these two human beings for many lifetimes. Always, their own personal needs have been eclipsed by the dark moon of duty, self-sacrifice and humility. This is the traditional house of servants—and they may have literally been servants together. Given enough planetary harshness around a composite South Node in the sixth house, and we might even imagine them as slaves. (By "planetary harshness," we mean hard aspects involving Pluto or Saturn, for example.)

Bondage is not always coerced. These two may have chosen their chains, and done so without masochism. In the days before birth control, a couple might simply find themselves swamped with children, with all the attendant duties and necessities. They—and probably the eldest siblings—would then live lives defined by the needs of the young ones. A beloved mate can become ill or incapacitated; again, duty calls. In that case, the flow of service is tilted from one partner to the other, creating karmic impressions of imbalance, and perhaps resentment in one and guilt in the other.

A disciple or an apprentice is profoundly bound by duty and obedience toward the master. Again, this is a voluntary situation, but no less restrictive for that. Autonomy is sacrificed; devotion and surrender are the themes. And once the student "graduates," he or she is then compelled by another set of duties, those of passing on the torch to the next generation in the lineage.

Traditionally, loving self-sacrifice is considered to be good karma. And even the suffering of a slave is viewed as "burning away bad karma." In a slightly blasphemous nutshell, God owes this couple something! All that service has created an imbalance in their universe. There must be a flow *back* to them in this lifetime. They must receive something. This brings us directly to their soul intention as a couple, which is symbolized by their composite North Node in the mystical twelfth house. Now, in the present life, it is pivotal that they wean themselves away from their karmic compulsion to lose themselves in a labyrinth of duties and responsibilities. They have served others; now they need to serve themselves. How? By withdrawing from their total engagement with the needs of others, and ensuring that they have plenty of solitary, soul-nourishing time as a couple. Spirit wants to give them a gift of magic and insight. More precisely, they have already purchased such a gift with their karmic pattern of service. All they have to do is claim it. Where? In the silence. On the mountaintop. In the wilderness. In the cathedral. In their peaceful bed together.

There is nothing they have to do *first.* They only need to get out of their own way—and think carefully before complicating their lives any further. What about their existing responsibilities? Given the nature of their karmic pattern, we can assume that such duties do exist unless the relationship is just beginning. Certainly, we all have obligations we cannot in good conscience ignore. But, in this symphonic universe, very often for a couple with the composite South Node in the sixth house, those people towards whom they are feeling responsible have actually reached a developmental stage where trying to help them actually does more harm than good. Some little birds never learn to fly unless they are tossed from the nest. The higher ground is not always defined by duty and self-sacrifice.

COMPOSITE SOUTH NODE IN THE SEVENTH HOUSE
(Composite North Node in the First House)

When people are involved sexually in the present life, it is natural that they imagine themselves to have been lovers in a previous incarnation. For obvious psychological reasons, it is unsettling to imagine that the person with whom you are presently having sex was once your mother or father! God bless our forgetfulness, but of course metaphysically we must recognize that the long dance that souls do with each other often involves playing many different roles: siblings, enemies, kind strangers, aunts, uncles, comrades, and so on. Even this couple, with their composite South Node in the traditional house of marriage, were not necessarily married in a prior lifetime. They may have been partners in some other way. But of all possible house positions for the South Node, this is the one with the most reliable natural correlation with literal matrimony. Very likely, with these two, we are looking at the reincarnation of a prior-life marriage.

If they've done it before, why do it again? Always, with the South Node of the Moon, we know that the answer lies with something left unfinished, wounded, or incomplete from the past. We understand that the soul-contract underlying the current relationship can only be fulfilled once the old patterns are recognized and released. What are they? Start by imagining a man and a woman, both single, both living sanely and independently. They become involved. Within a few years, he has "forgotten" how to cook. She has "forgotten" how to get the oil changed in their car. Both loses pieces of their wholeness, *projecting* them onto the other person. Some of this division of labor is natural and healthy, one of the practical comforts of partnership. But there is a fine line between such division and pathological fragmentation. *In the karmic past, these two lost themselves in each other.* They became mutually dependent in ways that inhibited their own individual growth. Probably, they were known as a "cute couple" and widely viewed as in a happy relationship. Thus, they carried not only each other's projections, but also the projections of their community—and the fact that those projections were positive does not diminish the distorting impact of other people's expectations upon them.

Where to go from here? The aim is not to break up or to stop loving each other. Instead, it involves making more room for the true self in their dialogue. With their composite North Node in the first house, together they are aiming for a kind of *enlightened selfishness.* They are separate souls, on separate journeys. Sometimes they will need different experiences. Often, it boils down to each of them being in different places on a Thursday evening—or in different continents on their vacations this year. The fear must be taken out of separation. A respect for each other's autonomy needs to be seen as a precious gift of love. Naturally, as they evolve in this first house direction, there will be some butting of heads. And their guardian angels will be cheering! Love revels in human differences; it can thrive on creative tension between people. Light and dark give meaning to each other. Female and male become conscious of themselves in each other's presence. Oneness is a deep wisdom, but Spirit knows itself through duality. For these two, the time has come to let there be some breathing space between them. And in that separation, their love evolves into a deeper spiritual maturity.

COMPOSITE SOUTH NODE IN THE EIGHTH HOUSE
(Composite North Node in the Second House)

Storminess, strong emotion, and enormous intensity define the mood of this couple. With their composite South Node in the eighth house, their relationship has been forged in fire—and probably in nightmare. Whether in a prior lifetime together the relationship itself became a nightmare is an open question. We certainly don't need to assume that—drama can bring people closer or drive them apart, depending on how they respond to it. But we can safely assume that together they have had experiences which were extreme, as revealing as a psychic X-ray, and probably tragic.

The eighth is the traditional house of death. Mortality is not the only issue here, but it probably figures prominently in the prior-life picture. Perhaps nothing creates such strong emotions in us as death—just think of the movie scenes that have put tears in your eyes. Imagine two young men drafted into war seeing mangled, decaying corpses for the first time. Imagine two medieval women loading the dead onto the plague-wagons. Imagine a man holding his dying wife in his arms, hearing the cries of their newborn infant.

What do such shared perceptions do to the relationship between two people? How do they respond? The answers, of course, are as varied as the individuals. Perhaps we see profound, emotionally naked *bonding*. Maybe we see *shell-shocked denial*. Maybe evolution is accelerated; possibly it is stalled, overwhelmed by the horror of its experiences. And in every case, the mark of deep wounding is left: fear, grief, anxiety.

And fantastic sex. This is not a spurious remark. One of the greatest enemies of deep sexuality is emotional distance. Everything in the eighth house pulls in the opposite direction: toward soul nakedness. Even when the couple were not in fact lovers in a prior life, with their composite South Node in the eighth house, they will probably feel that way. Their level of familiarity with the normally hidden layers of each others' psyches startles them from the outset of their present relationship. Whether that familiarity was forged in a bed or in a battle-trench is immaterial.

The soul-contract this time around? Their composite North Node lies in the second house, which is typically seen as the house of money. Actually, it is pertinent to a far broader range of concerns, all of them related to *the resource base upon which survival depends*: food, shelter, appropriate skills and social alliances. One piece of the puzzle for this couple is that to heal the wounds of the past, they absolutely must create an environment which feels *safe* to them. To be precise, it must not only seem safe according to the logic of the human intellect, but it must also feel safe to the "inner animal." The human intellect understands that most of us feel safer in this world if we have established financial security, live in a reasonably secure home, and have a supply of existential "parachutes:" life insurance, health insurance, a retirement plan, and so on—and it would be positively diabolical to suggest to this couple that such concerns were somehow unspiritual. Their "inner animal" needs the assurance and comfort of quiet and stability; it benefits from living in a natural environment, if possible. It likes to see food available. It wants escape routes.

If this couple can create that reassuring second house environment, then in that ambience of security they begin to regain confidence in themselves and in life.

And that is the whole point.

COMPOSITE SOUTH NODE IN THE NINTH HOUSE
(Composite North Node in the Third House)

Kids in school learn that Christopher Columbus "believed the earth was round," contradicting the flat-earthers' fear that if we sailed far enough out into the ocean, we would sail catastrophically off the edges of the world. Even though the historical truths are more complex, the childhood imagery conveys a visceral sense of the power of belief—and therefore of the ninth house. If we believe in something, we can accomplish great feats. Belief empowers people, just as surely as believing in nothing weakens them. With their composite South Node of the Moon in the ninth house, this couple's soul-memories are characterized by the life-shaping impact of compelling belief. Given the realities of human history, we can make one more conjecture: most of the belief-systems that have shaped cultures in the past have been at least partly *religious* in nature. Thus, with considerable certainly, we can affirm that this couple has been powerfully and indelibly marked by religion. Were they in "holy orders" together? That is a possibility. We would look to other dimensions of nodal analysis to confirm it—the planetary ruler of their South Node lying in the twelfth house (monasteries) would encourage such an interpretation, for example.

But we need not assume an ecclesiastical past for these two. Religion can impact life in many other ways. One very natural line of reasoning weaves another dimension of the ninth house into the picture: *journeys*. How often in history has religion caused people to travel and experience other cultures? We might invoke the notion of their going off on the Crusades together, or on a pilgrimage to Mecca, Rome, Macchu Pichu, Benares or elsewhere. We might imagine the Puritans coming to the New World, or Mormons heading west. Or Jews banished in the diaspora.

With the composite South Node, it always sharpens our inquiries if we look askance upon the prior life orientation, seeking any limiting or distorting effects it might have upon the present experiences of the couple. The *need to believe* fogs our ability to see what is before our eyes. Arguing with "true believers" is demonstrably impossible; they cannot imagine themselves wrong, regardless of the evidence. They will kill, and fail to see the humanity of those they are killing. They will deny the evidence of their own senses. They will "sail off the edges of the world" without stopping to consider their folly. How many pioneers simply disappeared into the wilderness? How many pilgrims and crusaders never made it home again? This couple has been blinded by their own zeal in the past. They've jammed themselves into the tight shoes of unnaturally repressive moralities. Out of "faith," they've lost their groundedness in instinct and common sense.

With their composite North Node of the Moon in the third house, this pair of human beings shares a soul intention in this lifetime to believe only what they can actually see and experience. They are returning to direct knowledge, sensory wisdom, and discovery. Their guiding star is *curiosity*. They benefit from learning experiences, especially confusing ones! That may sound strange, but it comes down to this: if they meet an impressive Buddhist teacher, they immediately need to seek out a Christian or a Muslim or a Physicist. Giving life permission to be complex—and then comparing notes, sharing perceptions and endlessly conversing, with no perspectives taboo or forbidden: that is the way forward for this couple.

COMPOSITE SOUTH NODE IN THE TENTH HOUSE
(Composite North Node in the Fourth House)

A reasonable criticism of reincarnation is that far too many people "remember" lifetimes in which they were somehow famous or participated in pivotal historic turning points. Logic dictates that nearly all of us have lived mostly humdrum lives and, once gone, were forgotten relatively quickly. There is of course no shame in that anonymity—souls can do deep evolutionary work in absolute obscurity. But the same logic that compels us to accept that most of us aren't listed in the history books also declares that some of us must be listed there! The most obvious astrological indication of that condition is having the South Node in the tenth house—the traditional house of honor. When it's the composite South Node, then we take the next logical step: the couple was well-known and somehow *symbolic* to their wider community. Saying that they were "Antony and Cleopatra"—or "Bonnie and Clyde," for that matter—gets us roughly on the right track.

Still, there aren't enough famous couples to go around, so we need to penetrate the mystery of the tenth house a little more deeply. The issue here is not whether or not we are remembered historically. It is the question of becoming part of the collective mythic symbolism of a community—and it doesn't matter if the entire community is subsequently washed away to sea and forgotten, nor if the entire community consisted of 92 people in an isolated medieval German village.

With their composite South Node in the tenth house, this couple is marked by a prior life experience of *prominence and leadership* within whatever their society was. Given historical realities, the chances are excellent that they were *born into* this prominence—famous dukes outnumber famous serfs by a wide margin here. Fame and power have obvious attractions, but always with the South Node of the Moon, our approach begins with recognizing that, from an evolutionary point of view, something is hung up here. There are unresolved issues from the past that haunt these two in the present tense. Is there a negative side to power? Are there soul-cages built into prominence and high birth? For this couple, we must consider the damage done to them by constant role-playing, feigning affection for people whom they neither liked nor trusted, and constantly jockeying for position. And we must be cautious regarding their legacy of skills when it comes to improving their present-life status: they might pay too much for their careers and their status, for example.

One of the most uncomfortable perceptions we need to consider with this nodal structure is that perhaps, in a prior life, these two married without any particular love for each other. Such "political" marriages are common historically. These partners must make sure that what they are feeling for each other in this lifetime is real, and that they are not carrying the projections of their community—every time they hear someone say, "you two *belong* together," they need to recognize that any such decision is purely their own.

With their composite North Node in the fourth house, the soul-contract between these two, first and foremost, is to go down into their deep hearts together. The fourth house is where "psychology" starts to unfold within us: our innermost feelings and needs reside there. They aim to put a high premium on honesty and reflectiveness, and thus truly know each other. Our domestic needs are symbolized by the fourth house as well. If, in their inward searching, they choose to love one another as partners, then the goal here is to create a home together. Literally having a place to live that reflects their natures and their long-term commitment is a large part of this. Perhaps they buy a house. But a house is just a building. A home is a place of nurturance, safety, and the sentiments created by shared history. Opposite the tenth house, it is the place most removed from the world "out there." It is the secret world, behind the walls. And it is where this couple may freely choose to go. But remember: their soul-contract is actually to make that choice, not to go there out of duty or anyone else's expectations.

COMPOSITE SOUTH NODE IN THE ELEVENTH HOUSE
(Composite North Node in the Fifth House)

Ready for a little math? Stand back: here comes The Forrests' First Law of Group Dynamics. To determine the IQ of any group of human beings, take the average IQ of the members and *divide it by the number of people in the group.*

Okay, maybe it's not rocket science, but the formula does explain a lot of human history. The power of the lowest common denominator is always palpable in crowds. The darkest expressions of the principle are visible in lynch mobs, marauding armies, and in newsreels of fanatical preachers, mullahs, and rabbis. One can even feel it in a more benign form at major athletic events—thirty thousand people howling for blood is a formidable display of monkey-power.

With their composite South Node of the Moon in the eleventh house, we are looking at the life-shaping impact of that collective social force upon the soul-memories of a couple. Somehow, in a prior life, they were swept along by broad historical or cultural currents. These currents carried them away from authenticity, away from their actual soul-intentions, and away from their natural values. *They lost their individuality in the context of the will of the group.* Our fanatical images from a few lines ago may be quite relevant, but we don't necessarily need to assume such drama unless there are also serious Plutonian or Martial signatures connected with the Moon's South Node. Given Venusian signatures, for example, we might be looking at the far more insidious impact of "polite society" on a couple—the civilized pressure to "marry well," to live "normally," and to believe what others believe. Given Jupiter signatures, we might be looking at the way what we call success can rob people of their direction in life, and even of their souls. As always, in other words, details emerge only in the larger nodal context.

What we can count on, regardless of context, is that in this present lifetime, these two human beings intend to claim more freedom from outside influences. That much is perhaps obvious, but their fifth house

North Node takes us in some directions we might not anticipate quite so readily. The fifth is the house of joy. We learn a lot about it simply by affirming that it refers to the natural human need for *fun*—the pleasure principle. *For this couple, it has become imperative from an evolutionary point of view that they do as they please.* That's harder for them than it might seem. Why? Because, with their South Node pattern, they are vulnerable to accepting collective beliefs about what will please them—the new car, meditating in Sedona, losing weight . . . whatever their cultural susceptibilities and socialized values dictate.

The necessary foundation of their healing process lies in recovering their capacity *to know and recognize their own desires*, and to act upon them. This process often starts out with very simple things: listening to music that's not particularly popular, vacationing in places no one has ever heard of. As they evolve together, they will increasingly experience a desire to *express themselves creatively.* Perhaps they take up painting or acting together. Maybe they write poetry. In so doing, they find themselves in the *company of artists.* And at that evolutionary juncture, they have reached a crossroads—and a serious rite of passage in terms of discrimination. On one hand, there are their natural soulmates—artists who are truly life's experimentalists, affirmative of exploration and risk, celebratory of life, and slow to judge others. These individuals represent the polar opposite of "group think." They therefore apply a lot of useful tension to the couple's South Node pattern by encouraging them simply to be themselves, spontaneously and unselfconsciously. On the other hand, they will surely encounter "artists" who epitomize that outworn, conforming tribal consciousness. There's nothing so conservative as the *avant garde.* There's no one less cool than someone overly concerned with looking cool. If they fall in with these people, they've fallen back into the old South Node pattern, except that now it's congratulating itself on being something other than what it really is.

COMPOSITE SOUTH NODE IN THE TWELFTH HOUSE
(Composite North Node in the Sixth House)

Terrible loss and soul-growth: so often, they are a matched set. A marriage ends, a career collapses, our doctor proffers ominous news—and we turn to Spirit. The change can be completely authentic. Hospices are often full of luminous eyes. With their composite South Node in the twelfth house, this couple has known loss and grief in a prior lifetime together. They have probably also forged a bond rooted in deep, shared spirituality.

A close consideration of the sign of the South Node, along with the planets ruling it or in aspect to it, can fill in the details of the story. Just knowing that the moon's South Node lies in the twelfth is enough to invoke imagery of bereavement, imprisonment, wasting illness, and the loss of whatever gave these two joy in a prior lifetime. It is also consistent with the notion that they "met in a monastery or a convent," or in the context of some mystical institution—a mystery school or a secret society, for example. Clearly, as this world became emotionally unacceptable to them, they put their faith in the next world.

Much that is rich and inspiring flows from this fountain of tragedy. The connection between these two people is profound. Still, with the South Node, our focus must always be on the issues left unresolved from the prior lifetime and on the ways those issues might interfere with the actual soul-contract in the present life. "Loss of self" haunts this couple. Easily, they can fail to claim the outward, existential supports of simple happiness, instead losing themselves in their inner lives. They could disappear into their imaginations, feeding them with endless film or reading. They could dissolve into escapist spiritual practice. The underlying soul-memories of pain can trigger a dependency on alcohol or drugs. They can move through their lives like grieving ghosts.

With their composite North Node in the sixth house, the soul-contract between these two people involves coming back into their bodies. The sixth has much to do with health and the physical realities of life. Exercising together is helpful. So is making a happy ritual out of their meals together. Even more helpful is touch; these two need simply to hold each other.

The sixth house is also about service and our need to feel competent and useful to others. With their North Node there, this couple's soul-contract involves giving a gift to the world. Despite their shared pain, they also carry real wisdom. Certainly, in a prior lifetime, they at least began to integrate the lessons of unthinkable loss. Probably, in response to that pain, they found true teachers. They were given guidance, both from human sources and spiritual ones. They carry something precious inside them: an understanding of life, and very likely the karmic memory of specific spiritual practices and perspectives. Thus, along with their hurt, there is gratitude—and that gratitude naturally wants to express itself as generosity toward other people. Their pain wants to abandon this world, while their gratitude wants to serve it. Their shared evolution in this lifetime depends completely upon tilting the balance of those two conflicting emotions toward service.

PART FOUR: THE COMPOSITE CHART IN ACTION

CHAPTER SEVENTEEN: THE FITZGERALDS

The ghosts of the seminal American novelist, F. Scott Fitzgerald, and his wildly creative wife, Zelda, will forever haunt the parts of the astral world where God recycles the Roaring Twenties. It's rare that two human beings can so perfectly represent and encapsulate an age. Scott and Zelda stand out like Caligula, Queen Victoria or James Dean, their names inseparable from an era, and their glory and their tragedy taking on the iconographic quality of myth.

In *Skymates: Love, Sex and Evolutionary Astrology*, we explored the Fitzgeralds' marriage from a conventional synastric perspective. We looked at each of them as separate individuals through the lens of their birthcharts. We considered the interaspects and house transpositions that bound their charts together. And we tried to coax a sense of "wholeness" out of the symbolism in an effort to glimpse the texture of their secret world.

For easy reference, we are reproducing the Fitzgeralds' birthcharts again here on pages 414 and 415. To avoid undue repetition, we'll assume that you've read the previous volume and are thus familiar with their story: how they swept the world off its feet with their dashing style and their fairy tale romance—and how, in the end, madness, unbridled passion, and alcohol brought them first to their knees, then early to their graves. From now on, we'll focus exclusively on their composite chart, which is represented on page 416. It is set up for Montgomery, Alabama, where they first met.

A composite chart is ultimately no different than a birthchart. Like a birthchart, it details the kinds of experiences that best nourish the spirit of a particular pair of human beings. It describes their available resources, their joint strengths, and their potential weaknesses and blind spots. Like a birthchart, it illuminates the happiest, most rewarding patterns of experience for the relationship, while it cautions us about darker possibilities. If there is any trick to working effectively with composite charts, it lies in remembering that the "entity" of the composite chart is only a distant cousin to the personalities of the two separate individuals. It has a life of its own—and needs of its own. You have to see it, first and foremost, as standing on its own two feet.

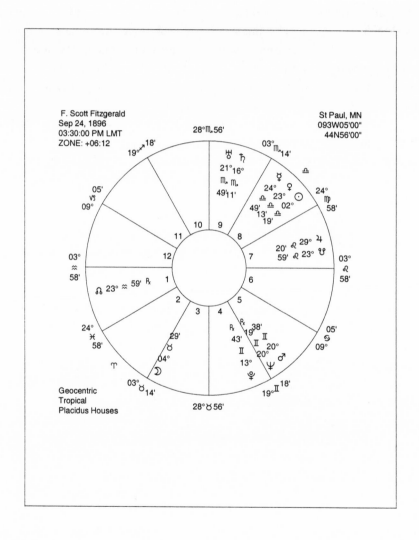

F. Scott Fitzgerald
Sep 24, 1896
03:30:00 PM LMT
ZONE: +06:12

St Paul, MN
093W05'00"
44N56'00"

Geocentric
Tropical
Placidus Houses

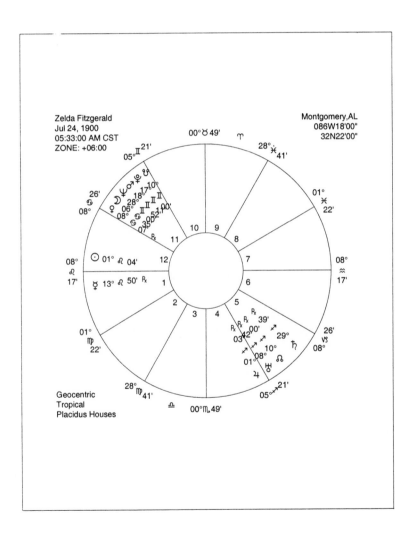

Zelda Fitzgerald
Jul 24, 1900
05:33:00 AM CST
ZONE: +06:00

Montgomery,AL
086W18'00"
32N22'00"

00° ♉ 49'

28° ♓ 41'

01° ♓ 22'

08° ♒ 17'

26° ♑ 08'

05° ✶ 21'

00° ♏ 49'

28° ♍ 41'

01° ♍ 22'

08° ♌ 17'

26° ♋

08°

05° ♊ 21'

Geocentric
Tropical
Placidus Houses

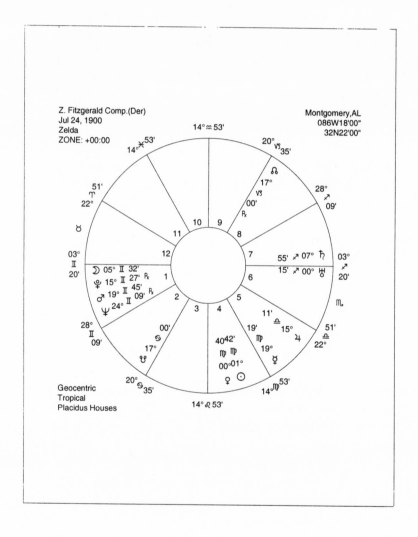

Z. Fitzgerald Comp.(Der)
Jul 24, 1900
Zelda
ZONE: +00:00

Montgomery,AL
086W18'00"
32N22'00"

14°≈53'

Geocentric
Tropical
Placidus Houses

Sun and Venus

Beginning an interpretation with the Sun is a useful approach. It represents the couple's core identity and their ultimate source of vitality. If two people fail to take care of their Sun, their bond simply withers. They become petty; they lose faith in themselves as a couple, and they turn dull and predictable.

If they get the composite Sun right, they can endure almost anything, even dumb mistakes. With the Sun healthy, we are resilient. We bounce back from love's darkest hours.

Zelda and Scott had their composite Sun in Virgo in a nearly precise conjunction with Venus. Their identity (Sun) as a couple was dependent upon exposure to healthy Virgo experiences: craftsmanship, competence, meaningful responsibilities, accurate self-appraisal. At the archetypal level, *perfection* is the endpoint of Virgo; its shadow is a collapse of confidence in the face of that goal.

The Venus-Sun conjunction is a common feature in composite charts drawn for people with romantic connections. The "goddess of love" (Venus) fuses (conjunction) with their shared identity and self-image (Sun). They naturally *think of themselves as lovers.*

Would the Fitzgeralds' Venusian love survive the pitfalls of time? The composite chart cannot answer that question, but having their Sun-Venus conjunction in Virgo does set a condition: their love would last only if they nourished it with Virgoan virtues and experiences—a long-term commitment to personal growth, humility, lots of meaningful, hard work, and serious attention to reality. And if they fell short? Then they would fall prey to Virgo's shadow, losing faith in their marriage and descending into self-punishment and mutual psychological assassination through criticism and antagonism.

Significantly, the Fitzgeralds' Sun-Venus conjunction lies in the fourth house (the deep unconscious; roots; the "house of the home"). Scott and Zelda were meant to draw much of their solar vitality from experiences of withdrawal from the noisiness of the world into the sweet shelter of a "home base." As a couple, they were in desperate need of roots: a solid domestic life and perhaps a family. The fourth house is the truest astrological expression of commitment 'til death do us part. It refers to *bonded relationships.* That means relationships that *cannot* be broken. The vow must be radical for it to work at all.

What actually happened? Those solar needs were at best only partially met. Despite their wealth, the Fitzgeralds never really had a home, living instead in hotels and transitorily in rented houses. In 1924, to gain hiatus from their hectic Manhattan lifestyle, they sailed to France—but immediately duplicated there the same screaming social pace they had maintained in New York City.

They did have a daughter, Scottie, in 1921—but the child was raised primarily by nannies. Subsequently Zelda had several abortions. By appearances, it seems they punished themselves (Virgo shadow) by withholding home and family (fourth house) from themselves, thereby robbing their relationship of an elemental source of renewal and energy.

It would be dogmatic to suggest that children and a traditional home life are essential to the happiness of every couple! But in the Fitzgeralds' case, we can be certain that roots of that sort could have had a healing, vitalizing effect on their partnership. Reduced to its elements, the message of their composite chart is crystal-clear: their solar vitality depended upon enacting the fourth house archetypes of nest and clan. Instead, they apparently succumbed to the darker, self-punishing side of Virgo. They never developed the *skills* (Virgo) of home life, thereby allowing their confidence (Virgo again) in their union to erode—and opening the way for the self-sabotaging aspects of that sign's negative manifestation.

The Ascendant, and the First House Moon, Mars, Pluto and Neptune

An individual with a fourth house Sun is typically hard to get a fix on. Often such a person is shy or withdrawn, as if we saw only a facade behind which lurked a very different character maintaining an impeccable poker face. If we were very sensitive, that is the way it would have felt meeting Zelda and Scott Fitzgerald. As a couple, they were essentially indrawn and quiet, even humble—but you wouldn't know it to look at them! They wore a mask about as subtle as a ticker tape parade.

The Fitzgeralds' first house—representing the face they presented to the world—is highly charged. Their Ascendant is Gemini, which typically suggests an active, engaging, open outer "persona." But their Ascendant is heavily modified by the presence of three planets in the first house: the Moon, plus a triple conjunction of fiery Mars, intense Pluto, and glamorous, slippery Neptune, all of them in Gemini as well. Put it together, and these two buzzed and sparkled in any social arena. Such a combination guarantees that lunar *imaginativeness and whimsy,* Martial *verve,* Plutonian *drama,* the *aura of magic* associated with Neptune, and above all, Geminian *animation* and *glibness* would characterize their social behavior.

The Gemini Ascendant, under these modifying circumstances, simply adds an aura of youthfulness, verbal dexterity, and avid engagement in experience. Likely, their intelligence as a couple was quite palpable. And since Mercury rules Gemini, this Ascendant adds more juice to that planet—which is already critically powerful for other reasons. It rules (*disposits,* to use the old technical term) all the Fitzgeralds' first house planets. It also rules their Virgo Sun. And Mercury itself is placed prominently—it's in Virgo and in the expressive, playful fifth house. Thus, this frenetic, restless, eloquent planet played a central role in portraying the tone of Scott and Zelda's life together. Unsurprisingly, their quickness and verbal fluidity (Mercury) was as legendary as their mesmerizing charisma (that huge first house). These qualities blended synergistically with the appealing whimsy of their Gemini Moon. A friend, Edmund Wilson, describes their impact upon people in these terms: "The remarkable thing about the Fitzgeralds was their capacity for carrying things off and carrying people away by their spontaneity, charm, and good looks. They had a genius for imaginative improvisations . . . "

Perhaps the most obvious statement we could make is that the Fitzgeralds are remembered as figures in American *literary* history—a classic Mercury signature. As the ruler of their Ascendant, we would expect Mercury to be deeply imprinted upon the image they projected outwardly onto the social world.

Scott and Zelda's fabled unpredictability, as well as the fertility of their imaginations, we can also trace to Mercury's centrality, along with their prominent first house Gemini Moon. They were always changing, always making it up as they went along. Mars in the first house added passion and an edge of anger, belligerence, even violence—in 1925, Scott described their "four-day rows."

And Pluto? Among other things, this is the planet through which individuals embody the forces of history. It is here that we observe the uncanny way the Fitzgeralds came to symbolize the *Zeitgeist* of the 1920s—in the first house, their Pluto really showed. But Pluto means more than that. It is also a place where we are challenged to go down into the psychological dark, to face unpleasant truths, insights and realizations. Sometimes this material is pertinent to the traumas of childhood, in the fashion of psychology. Always, it reflects the scars on the soul whose origins we can only understand in metaphysical terms.

We'll learn more about the specific nature of the karmic wound the Fitzgeralds brought into the world with them, when we get to the analysis of their lunar Nodes. For now, it is sufficient to recognize that there were three areas in which deeply honest self-scrutiny was absolutely necessary, lest they be brought down by their own character flaws in the fashion of Greek tragedy. The first area was simply egoism and the abuse of power: classic first house Shadow material. The second derives from Pluto's conjunction with Mars. It was the caustic effect of an attachment to anger and passion upon the human soul. The third had to do with Neptune—and warns of dire consequences if they didn't bring Plutonian psychological honesty to bear upon their relationship with their own glamour and, perhaps above all, upon their need *to escape from psychological or emotional pain* through addictive or compulsive behaviors.

Let's add that with Pluto in their composite first house, there was an "intimacy zone" around Zelda and Scott. Anyone who got near them would be inclined to reveal their deepest secrets. Typically, the Fitzgeralds would learn a lot more about the people around them than anyone would learn about them, except for when they revealed their own natures through the transparent window of their actual behavior.

Sun/Moon (Dis)Integration

A colorful Geminian mask. And behind it, a quiet, possibly insecure fourth house Virgo core. *The introvert wearing the mask of the extravert.* The tensions are obvious. Even if we were to miss them at first glance, a glance at the aspect grid would quickly correct our oversight. The Fitzgeralds' composite Gemini Moon was less than four degrees away from a perfect square to their Virgo Sun: the aspect of friction. What they *appeared to be* outwardly (their first house stellium) and what they *really needed* in order to sustain their spirits (their fourth house solar configuration) were working at cross-purposes. Integration was the aim, but it wouldn't come easily or automatically—and it would depend absolutely upon their establishing a sacrosanct home base, away from the glitzy temptations created by their first house "ticket to everything." Home was to be the alchemical furnace in which the ironies and paradoxes of their relationship were made to dance together. It could only happen there.

Understand this elemental Sun/Moon clash, and you've found the key to unlocking Zelda and Scott's composite chart—and the painful story of their marriage.

Scott: "We were the most envied couple in about 1921 in America."

Zelda: "I guess so. We were awfully good showmen."

Those lines, taken from a transcript of a talk with their counselor, Dr. Rennie, in 1933, capture the power of their outer persona . . . and also the falseness *they themselves perceived in it* when viewed from the deeper perspective of their fourth house Virgo center.

Balance was possible. Squares are not "bad" aspects; only challenging ones. The Fitzgeralds could, for example, have evolved a pattern of quiet home life in an isolated locale and punctuated it with stimulating blitzes into the cosmopolitan worlds of New York and Paris. That is what an evolutionary astrologer would have suggested, had they consulted one. The secret with squares is to feed both sides of the question, creating reasonable compromises between contrasting legitimate needs, and raising both pieces of the puzzle to their highest potentials. Their Moon needed stimulus; their Sun needed a steady home base. These are not truly opposites!

Even though the dominance of mask over core is what led to the erosion of their marriage, it would be misleading to imagine that the Fitzgeralds' colorful, impassioned behavior is what killed them. Just as easily, they could have starved their outer Geminian self, living a quiet, responsible, middle-class life—and wound up just as alienated from each other.

The whole is greater than the sum of the parts, and it is the whole that must be fed.

Here's an excellent rule of thumb to apply when you find yourself stumped with a composite chart: *just pretend that you're looking at an ordinary birthchart belonging to one individual human being.* The idea of some intangible entity or meta-personality hovering bodilessly in the ether between two partners may be confusing. But *people*—you see them every day. You're accustomed to watching them, figuring them out. You have a lifetime of practice there. So start your interpretive work with the composite chart by trying to imagine that it represents a flesh and blood individual. Who is that person? What's his style? What are her secrets? Why did that soul come into this world? Then apply all those insights to that bodiless entity that may have been befuddling you a moment before.

If the Fitzgeralds' composite chart were the chart of a person, what would he or she be like? Witty, sharp, charismatic, theatrical . . . yet somehow slippery, distant and unavailable. Those words translate into plain English the astrological ambiguities we've just analyzed in terms of their Sun-Moon square. And that translation moves us from a baffling world of abstract symbolism to familiar daily life—a world where you have reservoirs of wisdom based on your own years of living among the human family. And a world in which you've already met people whose feet would fit the shoes we just described! What would you say to them, should they ask you for counsel?

If the Fitzgeralds' composite chart were a person, one observation leaps out: he or she would be awfully tough to get to know well. Pleasurable, light social contact would come readily. But achieving real intimacy and true knowledge of his or her inner workings would challenge the wiles of the most cunning psychologist.

The elusive quality of the Fitzgeralds' ambiguous "extraverted introvert" composite chart is confirmed by the words of their (temporarily) close friend Gerald Murphy: "I don't think they cared very much for parties . . . and I don't think they stayed at them very long . . . They usually had their own funny little plans—they'd be with you for a while and then they'd disappear and go on to some other place—and then you'd see them again somehow—they'd seek you out again."

Scott himself, perhaps saying more than he knew, wrote: "There never was a good biography of a good novelist. There couldn't be. He is too many people if he's any good."

Democracy, Feudal System or Culture Shock?

Scanning the birthcharts, comparing them to the composite, we're now ready to wrestle with the question of which one of our three major interpretive "bins" we should reserve for Scott and Zelda Fitzgerald.

Each of them has a very strong Gemini signature, with three planets each in that sign. Each of them has a major Venusian influence. Both of those qualities match the composite chart and thus could suggest a rather homogenous expression of "Democracy." But this is just one piece of the puzzle.

The fourth house focus of the composite hooks nicely into Zelda's Cancer Moon-Venus conjunction, but it doesn't find much resonance with Scott's chart—implying the possibility of a bit of "Feudal System," leaning toward Zelda. But, again, this is just one piece of the puzzle.

All the observations above effectively rule out "Culture Shock." There is just too much of both Zelda and Scott in this composite for that "bin" to be relevant.

Confused?

Take your glasses off. Don't look for any more details. Let it get fuzzy, so you just see the broadest patterns. What we want with this mode of analysis is the big picture, and only that. Sun, Moon, and Ascendant are our most reliable sources for that kind of perspective.

The composite chart shows the Sun in Virgo and the fourth house, the Moon in Gemini and in the first house, and Gemini rising.

Zelda's chart shows the Sun in Leo and the twelfth house, the Moon in Cancer and in the eleventh, and Leo rising.

No matches.

Scott's chart shows the Sun in Libra and the eighth house, the Moon in Taurus and in the third, and Aquarius rising.

Again, no matches.

Take a step back. What *elements* are represented in these primal triads?

The composite—two Air signs and one Earth sign.

Zelda—two Fire signs and one Water sign. No matches at all.

Scott—two Air signs and one Earth sign. *A perfect match to the elemental balance of the composite's primal triad.*

And there you have it: with the Fitzgeralds, we see a distinct tilt toward the "Feudal System," with Scott supported and Zelda disadvantaged. The composite chart "feels" more like him than it does her. "Democracy" has some relevance too—as usual with our three diagnostic categories, it's not totally clear which box to put them in. But "Feudal System" fits better than any other—we just have to tilt our language in bit in the direction of the "king" being in control, but that the "vassal" is not without some clout!

Lucky Scott? Absolutely not. To make this marriage work, he'll need to develop a lot of sensitivity toward Zelda, making sure that her voice is heard and that his life does not eclipse hers.

Let's continue with our analysis.

Saturn and Uranus

Consistent with our deductions so far, there is further astrological evidence that the Fitzgeralds might well have existed in a state of relative isolation from intimate human contact—or at least that such authentic contact would arise only as a result of substantial efforts on their part. In Sagittarius, we see a conjunction of Saturn and Uranus. It straddles their seventh house, the traditional house of marriage. Saturn is solidly placed in that house, while Uranus is down a little below the horizon, in the sixth house. Its conjunction with Saturn makes it relevant to the seventh house, and we'll investigate it in those terms first.

In the context of an individual birthchart, a traditional astrologer would say that Saturn ("the Lord of Solitude") in the house of marriage means loneliness and frustration in intimacy, while having Uranus (independence; individuality) involved there signifies marital instability and erratic sexual behavior.

In a composite chart, the *couple itself* would experience that isolation and instability *in its relations with other people*—if we are to trust the fortune-teller.

A healthier, more accurate reading of the configuration would not be so fatalistic. As always, there are higher possibilities, but reaching them requires determination. The fortune-teller's prediction of instability in friendships and dangerous degrees of isolation becomes reality only if Scott and Zelda are unwilling to make honest effort—always Saturn's evolutionary requirement.

Couples, like individuals, usually benefit from the perspective and support that comes from friendship. Marriage is not always easy, but just watching another couple face their own dramas can help it along. We can learn from their mistakes, benefit by their realizations, compare notes. This interdependency is especially productive when our composite chart shows seventh house planets, as did the Fitzgeralds'. In metaphysical terms, we can say that *they, as a couple, had soulmates.*

Their seventh house influences at once show the *natures* of the Fitzgeralds' soulmates and the *lessons* they needed to learn from them.

To form and maintain such supportive bonds, the Fitzgeralds would have needed to develop self-control, dignity and seriousness (Saturn at its best), and a free-spirited willingness to hook up with people of whom others might disapprove or upon whom they might look askance (Uranus at its best). Loneliness and frustration (Saturn) and erratic, crazy behavior in relationships (Uranus) are just the shadows those two planets cast. Predicting such circumstances would only make them that much more likely to manifest. But recognizing that they could easily arise is wisdom—provided we also indicate the path to the higher ground.

An evolutionary astrologer would have suggested that the Fitzgeralds make a strenuous effort to sustain certain human bonds and to be willing to make sacrifices for them—that's Saturn—and also simply to be themselves there (Uranus), without pretensions or any of the walls erected by the human need to be perceived as cool. The astrologer would also give them some clues and "signs" by which they could recognize these kindred souls. All of this advice would be phrased as a strategy for their psychological survival as a couple.

Did the Fitzgeralds succeed? Only partially. They did form a close bond with an expatriate American couple, Gerald and Sara Murphy, who were living in France. The Murphys were *older* than the Fitzgeralds, *quieter, less flamboyant*, which fits the Saturn profile. And yet they were colorful—they had left a prosperous familial commercial empire, choosing instead to live abroad on a relatively modest income, studying art. That eccentric behavior bears the stamp of Uranus. The Murphys had Saturnine sobriety mixed with Uranian rebelliousness, and thus they bore perfectly the "soulmate signature" foretold in the Fitzgeralds' composite chart.

At first the bond between the two couples was profound. In a letter to the Fitzgeralds written on the occasion of a temporary leave-taking, Gerald Murphy wrote: "Ultimately, I suppose, one must judge the degree of love for a person by the hush and the emptiness that descends upon the day after the departure . . . We four communicate by our presence . . . so that where we meet and when will never count. Currents race between us regardless: Scott will uncover for me values in Sara, just as Sara has known them in Zelda through her affection for Scott."

Those last lines especially emphasize the soulmate quality of the interaction between the Murphys and the Fitzgeralds. Through their mutual sharing, *each couple helped the other to see itself more clearly,* thereby promoting the intensification of self-awareness characteristic of this kind of human love.

Sadly, within a single year the Fitzgeralds' crazed "mask" and its wild behavior had at least partly soured the bond with the Murphys. Drunken driving, violent quarreling and endless competitiveness took their toll. Sensing the defensive quality of Scott and Zelda's histrionics, Sara Murphy wrote, "If you can't take friends largely and without suspicion—then they are not friends at all." And in reference to a situation in which Scott, drunk, threw a fig at one Princesse de Caraman-Chimay, a guest at a Murphy dinner party, she added, "We cannot—Gerald and I—at our age and stage in life be bothered with sophomoric situations like last night."

Note that the Fitzgeralds here appeared to be rebelling against normal adult responsibilities. That pattern fits perfectly the darker potential of Uranus's presence in the composite's sixth house (although it conjuncts the composite's Descendant). Wherever this planet lies, we have a tendency to question authority and to avoid "doing as we are told." This is necessary from an evolutionary point of view, but once we throw away the rule book, we are on our own. Earlier, speaking of the Fitzgeralds' fourth house Virgo Sun, we emphasized the benefit that would have come to Scott and Zelda had they established some kind of domestic normalcy. Uranus in the sixth is dead square that Sun, implying that rebelliousness against responsibilities could undercut the very center of their marriage. That's what happened, both with the Murphys and elsewhere. Let's also recognize the higher ground: these two were never going to fit into a totally conventional model of 1920s home life. They needed to approach their definition of responsibility with creativity, originality, and respect for each other's freedom and individuality. Those are higher Uranian qualities, and they *can* be integrated effectively with getting the dishes done.

The Murphys' support, so critical to the stability and sanity of the Fitzgeralds' marriage, was squandered. With their solid Saturnine sense of responsibility and their simultaneously colorful Uranian style of living, the Murphys held out an ideal to Scott and Zelda: they had a proven blueprint for the kind of marriage toward which the Fitzgeralds were aspiring. Had the Fitzgeralds been able to learn the lesson the Murphys offered by their simple presence and their love, Scott and Zelda might have achieved the integration of their pyrotechnical lunar mask and their conservative solar core, thereby balancing the opposing forces that threatened to tear them apart.

It is worth noting here that such a seventh house configuration in the composite chart *guarantees* that the soulmates will in fact appear. What is does not guarantee is that the couple will trust them and accept them and surrender to them sufficiently for the alchemical processes of love to work their magic.

Tragically, the Fitzgeralds refused that gift. Why? The question is fundamental. To answer it, we must return to the most elemental observations about the Fitzgeralds' composite chart. We must return to the Sun.

Back to the Sun

In their deepest solar self, Scott and Zelda Fitzgerald were shaped by the archetypal fields of Virgo and the fourth house. As we have seen, the maintenance of their solar vitality as a couple ultimately rested upon their ability to deal precisely, effectively, and competently (Virgo) with the dual fourth house territories of *personal psychology* and simple *home life.* Should they fail, then their vitality would gradually erode, tossing them into a Virgoan spiral of escalating self-doubt and self-sabotage.

That they took the second course is a matter of history. That the first course was open to them is the keystone of modern evolutionary astrological theory.

As the solar core of the Fitzgeralds' marriage fizzled, they increasingly attempted to compensate for the resultant Virgoan insecurity by pumping up their first house mask. It was that thin defensiveness that finally made sincerity with the Murphys—and everyone else—impossible. And with their mounting desperation, that walled-in tension began to resemble madness. When, for example, Scott flirted with dancer Isadora Duncan, Zelda wordlessly threw herself head first down a flight of stone steps. One night Scott allowed Zelda to challenge him to a series of dangerous high dives from the Riviera cliffs into the sea. Both anecdotes reveal the self-destructiveness characteristic of Virgo when its intense evolutionary drive turns to self-punishing shame.

The fourth house is a realm of unbridled subjectivity. It can be a source of creative inspiration. It can also represent a kind of psychic black hole into which the healthy adult personality can collapse. As the Fitzgeralds' marriage gradually succumbed to self-imposed strangulation, it is no accident that Scott and Zelda both fell into pathological fourth house states, out of touch with outward reality: he, to alcoholic torpor; she, to schizophrenia.

Could they have done differently? Of course. That at least is the only legitimate astrological answer to the question. Slowing down a bit, giving themselves more privacy, establishing a home life—all of these were pieces of the puzzle. Any one of them would have helped establish an existential framework within which the Fitzgeralds might have undertaken the real fourth house work: self-administered psychoanalysis, triggered by and supported by the reality of psychological surrender to hearth and home. Their Venusian love for each other, had it been coupled with humility rather than humiliation, might have catalyzed a healing of the dark forces within each of them, the forces that instead drove Scott to the gin bottle and Zelda to the madhouse.

Remember that we are looking at the "Feudal System" here, so there is a danger that Scott would have too much influence over the shape of the marriage. Note that when we were attempting to sort out which "bin" to place them in, we briefly noted the resonance between Zelda's Cancer Moon-Venus conjunction and the fourth house Sun-Venus conjunction of the composite. For a moment, we considered the possibility that the relationship would emerge as a "Feudal System" tilted toward her. But then that thought was eclipsed by the perfect resonance between the elements in Scott's primal triad and those in the composite chart. Still, Zelda, far more than Scott, had a natural feeling for the joys of domestic life. In a "Democracy," she would have been the *natural caretaker* of that critical part of the relationship. But under the logic of the Feudal System, "circumstances" sided more with Scott. Swept along by his own destiny and shaped by his own limitations, he never heard the voice that could have saved the marriage. Perhaps that voice never spoke, and was only felt inside Zelda's heart.

Ultimately, fourth house work is spiritual. That is, it pertains to deep consciousness. Zelda and Scott might have healed each other's haunted spirits. Instead they bought drinks for the drunkard, while taunting and dazzling the madwoman.

Jupiter

A relatively minor feature of their composite chart, at least at this level of analysis—Jupiter in the fifth house—adds corroborative evidence to what we have already seen.

Joining chart-ruling, all-powerful Mercury in the celebratory fifth house, Jupiter further underscores themes of playfulness, creativity, joy—and possibly of debauchery. The relevance of those themes to the realities of Zelda's and Scott's life together is irrefutable. They were both artists; they often lived large and playfully, and they tended toward excess. On the brighter side of the equation, this placement affirms that they could affirm their basic faith in their bond by celebrating it and sharing creative projects. On the dark side, demons of immoderate indulgence lay ready to pounce. Where Jupiter lies, we often have a "gift from the gods." For the

Fitzgeralds, that gift was centrally linked to their shared creative potential. We need to be careful here not to confuse this statement with the obvious fact that these two people were artists. What this configuration refers to is their potential for *joint* creative work—and the joy and faith that would come to them through that process.

The fifth house also relates to children, and the apparently squandered delight that could have come to Scott and Zelda through their bond with their daughter—not to mention the children who were never born.

The South Node's Tale

The Fitzgeralds were public figures. As such, they lived in a house of glass. Libraries the world over have alphabetical files of their darkest secrets and their most trivial failings. For that reason, everything we have explored so far can be tested against their actual history, even very intimate material. But now we come to "the chart behind the chart." Now we come to the Nodes of the Moon and their various planetary correlates. In doing that, we enter a less directly verifiable world: the realm of reincarnation.

As we described in Chapter Four, past life material, while inherently slippery, does make itself felt in "testable" ways in the present tense. It works exactly like the unconscious wounds connected with forgotten childhood damage. In the same way, traumas left over from prior lifetimes have a predictable—and observable—impact upon our lives today.

(Please note that, if you are uncomfortable with the notion of past lives, almost all of what follows can be understood in genetic, ancestral terms too. Call it an expression of the interactions between data stored in a couple's DNA, if you prefer. Then the past life material can be taken as an evocative metaphor.)

We begin with one arbitrary assumption: Zelda and Scott Fitzgerald had indeed shared at least one prior lifetime together.

Every one of us has a composite South Node with everyone else on the planet—it's simply a mathematical construction that exists potentially between any two charts. Most of the time it's an empty symbol: our species has not existed long enough for everyone to have even had time to shake hands with everyone else! And of course, given lower population levels in the past, far fewer bodies were available, so the "lines" for them were longer and they moved slowly.

But when we see two people meeting as strangers and moving quickly into a complex, intimate relationship, we feel safe in assuming that it is not the first time their souls have touched. The Fitzgeralds passed that test—we'll assume their South Node is active and meaningful.

Scott and Zelda's South Node lies in Cancer. Immediately, this suggests that their karma together existed in some kind of *family context.*

The Moon always rules Cancer, but its placement in the always-prominent first house further emphasizes this "lunar" dimension to their bond: *hearth, home* and *clan.* A Cancer South Node and an inherently strong Moon: these factors thus reinforce each other. Clearly, these two have been "related" in the past. The overlapping symbolism of both Cancer and a *strong* Moon suggest that possibility quite vividly.

The South Node lies in the second house, which brings in circumstantial themes connected with money—or with what money represents, which is food, shelter and the material basis of survival. Psychologically, it refers to feelings of personal insecurity.

That Node-ruling Moon lies in Gemini, where it is mightily reinforced by its conjunction with the Gemini Ascendant and its association with three other powerful, edgy Gemini planets in the first house: Pluto, Mars, and Neptune. Thus again there is a pattern of overlapping symbolism. The natural associations of all this Geminian energy are *communication, improvisation* and *mobility.* They relate to *curiosity* and to *speed.* Because of the latter two qualities, they also connect with the theme of *youth*—young people tend to be quicker, more nervous, and often more curious than older ones. *Heresy* is a traditional association with these Geminian symbols. Why? Because they both "ask too many questions." *Language skills* are spotlighted. Another traditional connection is that Gemini and the third house both relate to *siblings*—to brothers and sisters.

One of the tricks for prising the karmic story out of the astrological chart lies in finding places where the various archetypal fields invoked by the symbols *overlap* each other—where separate symbols seem to be saying the same thing in different ways. We can usually count on such symbolic overlaps' pointing to important material. Under the Cancer and Moon symbolism, we've seen a strong reference to prior life *family bonds* as a theme that binds Scott and Zelda together—and "family," of course, refers to a wide range of possible relationships: aunts, uncles, cousins, children, grandparents, married couples, and so on.

Now, under the Gemini and third house symbolism, we see a possible reference to *siblings*.

And we've hit paydirt: we now must seriously entertain the notion that *Zelda and Scott were siblings in a prior life.*

Gemini and the third house symbolism further emphasize a theme of improvisation and intelligence, probably in the face of shifting, uncertain circumstances—remember that the second house placement of the South Node suggests concerns with material survival and the accompanying feelings of insecurity that often go along with such situations. They also highlight a tremendous acceleration of shared thinking and an enhanced communication function, probably in response to those same challenges: these kids were having to *invent responses to complex circumstances.* They did it together, as a team, relying on each other. Thus, this past life pattern of youthful, high-stakes decision making leaves its mark in the present composite chart.

The fact that the Moon (ruler of the South Node) lies in the first house does more than highlight the lunar themes. The first house has its own specific layers of meaning: *leadership, decision-making, personal responsibility* and *initiative.* Generally, people strongly impacted by first house symbolism find themselves in positions where others are counting on them—or, at least, where they have no one to count on but themselves. In the first house, we are either simply on our own or "the buck stops with us."

Wait a minute! Everything else pointed to Zelda and Scott being *children* together, either brothers, sisters, or a sister and a brother. Note the ambiguity: *children generally don't fit the first house paradigm.* Children more commonly have parents and extended families; they are protected and nurtured. They don't have to lead or take any ultimate responsibility. Adults watch out for them.

Confusing? *Reframe the confusion as understanding*: we've hit paydirt a second time. These two, as young siblings, were very much on their own, improvising their own survival. Scott and Zelda begin to look like orphans—or like kids in what we would today call a dysfunctional family or at least a highly debilitated one.

What's the worst case scenario for a child? Most of us would say *abandonment.* And what planet represents worst case scenarios in general? What planet rules nightmares and catastrophes? The answer lies just ten degrees from their Node-ruling Moon: it is Pluto—and the conjunction of "the Lord of the Underworld" with the Moon adds a theme of trauma and extremity to our emerging story. As siblings in a lifetime long ago, Scott and Zelda faced a child's worst nightmare—abandonment—and they faced it together with pluck, curiosity, and improvisational intelligence, although underlying all that were terrible feelings of self-doubt and concern with survival, as reflected in that second house placement of the South Node.

Sound familiar? Outward "you and me against the world" bravado, hiding a core of sheer terror?

Pluto, in turn, is conjunct Mars, further spotlighting the stress and tension of the situation. And both Mars and Pluto are ominous of *violence* and *rage*.

Did Scott and Zelda run away from a violent home? Was their family sundered by the collective violence of war or persecution? (Remember we did see the Gemini signature of *heresy* in the mix . . .) Did some Plutonian physical catastrophe—volcanic eruption, earthquake, famine, plague—leave these two as hungry waifs in the ruins?

Any one of those scenarios could be made to work consistently with the symbolism. And, really, any one of them would tell approximately the same story from a psychological perspective. That's enough for our purposes. With that, we can get a kind of parable—a story that, while not necessarily factual in a rigorous sense, *parallels* the facts with sufficient accuracy to be *thematically applicable, illuminating and useful.*

Despite the horror of this story, an essential part of it centers on the Fitzgeralds' *victory* over these dreadful, unnatural circumstances. Together, they seem to have gotten through it. They were *winners.* They engineered their survival creatively, intelligently, and perhaps, violently. They landed on their feet. And, with Geminian symbolism so prominent, we can assume they achieved this through cunning, verbal dexterity, and an amoral use of sheer quickness.

Yet we must remember one immutable principle: the karmic story that emerges through nodal analysis represents something at least partly distorted or wrong. Perhaps it is a mistake we made in the past that still haunts us today—something we have come back together in new bodies to resolve. It's either that, or it's something we actually got "right," but the process left us damaged: some acts of courage and heroism leave real scars on the psyche. Sometimes winning hurts us. Sometimes we make the best of a bad deal. With Scott and Zelda, we're inclined toward the second hypothesis: they got through, but they got hurt.

How? How did their victory hurt them? The question is really an easy one, provided we remember to forget about astrology and just engage our human wisdom for a minute. Think about it: what happens to kids who have their world collapse, even the ones who survive. How long does it take them to trust anyone again? And "trust" is a big word—it means not only trusting other human beings, but also trusting life, even trusting God. How long does it take for the human heart to thaw, once it has frozen as the price of staying alive? And what if we have hurt others so that we can live? What kind of deal do we have to make with our consciences to do that? How long does that deal take to undo? How long does it take to get over the "high" of war and violence? Once we have made a justifiable moral compromise, how hard is it to return to a stricter standard? How long does hyped passion take to drain out of the system? Earlier in this chapter, when we first mentioned the Fitzgeralds' first house composite Pluto, we wrote: *For now, it is sufficient to recognize that there were three areas in which deeply honest self-scrutiny was absolutely necessary, lest they be brought down by their own character flaws in the fashion of Greek tragedy. The first area was simply egoism and the abuse of power: classic first house Shadow material. The second derives from Pluto's conjunction with Mars. It was the caustic effect of an attachment to anger and passion upon the human soul. The third had to do with Neptune—and warns of dire consequences if they didn't bring Plutonian psychological honesty to bear upon their relationship with their own glamour, and perhaps above all, their need to escape from psychological or emotional pain through addictive or compulsive behaviors.*

Now, through our nodal analysis, we can understand those words with vastly more precision. When Zelda and Scott came together, they triggered shared karmic memories in each other. These memories were emotional, as always, rather than factual or informational. For them, it was immediately "you and me against the world." Immediately, they knew that together they could "conquer the world." They knew they could "trust no one." They were hardened into a posture of anger and withdrawal. They were attached to passion and escapism, and inclined toward paranoia. And they were brilliant, forceful and highly verbal.

There's one more big piece to the puzzle: Jupiter in Libra and the fifth house squares the nodal axis. Any planet square the Nodes represents something that *blocked* or *vexed* the couple in a prior life, something therefore left unresolved from the past, and a "skipped step" that must now be gotten right if they are going to proceed in their evolution.

Being in the fifth house, the Fitzgeralds' Jupiter is really in its element. The "King of the Gods" enjoys a good party! At its best, this configuration refers to a celebration of life—the Fitzgeralds' famous affinity for the "high life." At its worst, a fifth house Jupiter is ominous of *dissipation*. That trap had obvious relevance to them in their present life, but now we must recognize that it also represents something that touched them long ago, in another lifetime. A vulnerability to dissipation "blocked" or "vexed" them back then, and was something "left unresolved" as they entered this lifetime. Thus, we have another glimpse into the forgotten past: as a couple of siblings in another life, improvising their survival in a world gone hard, cold, and hostile, Scott and Zelda got hooked on a few pleasures—and the siren-song of those pleasures haunted them in the present life. The easiest concrete metaphor here would probably be the abuse of alcohol, although the abuse of anything—or everything—pleasurable would fit the imagery. That they brought this *addictive, compulsive, ecstasy-driven, escapist* karma forward into their life together as Zelda and Scott is of course exceedingly plausible, based on the observed realities of their biography.

Let's also recognize that as a "skipped step" this fifth house Jupiter takes on another very poignant interpretation. The fifth house is, among other things, the house of children—and these two, in a prior life, were robbed of their childhood. *They never got to be young*, at least not in a healthy way. In this present lifetime together, they carried forward a need to have something akin to "a second childhood." To celebrate and enjoy themselves in a wide-open, pagan way would be perfectly appropriate. They would also benefit from having children, and giving those offspring the kind of experience that they themselves did not have in the prior life. Generosity of spirit toward their own kids would be an act of healing for them. But the darker side of this Jupiter aspect lies in the Fitzgeralds' pent-up need for extremes of ecstatic release. With the glamour and money they attracted, combined with the permissive spirit of the Roaring Twenties, Scott and Zelda were like two sailors hitting a fleshpot port after six months at sea.

All this is the past. And the Fitzgeralds' challenge—and yours and ours—is to stop getting on with it!

The North Node's Answer

So how did F. Scott and Zelda Fitzgerald intend to go forward? That question brings us to their composite North Node, which lies in Capricorn and in the eighth house.

As always, we need to recognize that for every couple the North Node is the ultimate challenge, for the simple reason that it is *precisely opposite everything they know and believe by reflex.* There is absolutely nothing natural about North Node activity! Always, it asks us to go where we have never gone before. Always, we are clumsy and prone to error there. And invariably, it holds the key to an ultimately meaningful relationship and to a self-affirming feeling of motion and growth—not to mention a resolution of the ancient karmic dilemma.

Capricorn represents *maturity, hard work,* and *self-discipline.* It is linked to *character, personal honor,* and the ability to *resist temptation.* Like all the other signs, it has a dark side: repression, self-denial, the need to control everything. But as the sign of the North Node, we don't need to think about the dark side at all—unlike with the South Node, where we need to focus more exclusively on the darker side. Here, we only need to recognize that getting to Capricorn's higher ground is the answer to Scott and Zelda's questions and the aim of their shared soul contract.

The composite North Node lies in the eighth house. One of the main meanings of this sector of the chart, especially in the context of synastry, is sexuality. Here, the word doesn't simply refer to specific physical acts, but rather to the larger context of mating and bonding. A couple who are three weeks into a passionate affair know a little bit about the eighth house, but to really understand it, ask a couple who've been together for a few years. Ask them about how sexual love is tempered by disappointment and hurt—and by forgiveness and healing. Ask them about the pearl of sex that hides inside the oyster-shell of simple romantic heat.

We should emphasize that there is no evidence that the Fitzgeralds' prior-life relationship was sexual. We don't even have any impressions of gender. Their loyalty toward each other had a "comradely" feeling, more than the psychological intimacy characteristic of sexual bonds. In this lifetime, with their North Node in Capricorn and in the eighth house, they aimed to continue their traditional of loyalty to each other, but to carry it into a more mature expression.

Let's add that when souls are accustomed to a sibling relationship, the maintenance of sexual charge and sexual activity in the present life is often problematic. Passion, with all its renewing impact, can fall by the wayside once the hormonal and emotional hype of courtship fades.

Capricorn always refers to some kind of "great work." In the eighth house, that great work has something to do with the deeper kinds of bonding experiences available to human beings past the age of puberty. In order to find the focal point of this evolutionary activity, we need to consider the planetary ruler of the North Node: Saturn. Always, simply by the nature of rulership, the *planet* that rules the Node will have a nature similar to that of the *sign* of the Node. The result is that the planet itself doesn't tell us anything we didn't already know: we've already seen that the Fitzgeralds' soul intentions had to do with discipline and effort. Where the planetary ruler of the Node might actually open some doors for us is with its sign, house, and aspects, especially any conjunctions.

In the Fitzgeralds' case, Saturn lies in Sagittarius. The natural associations are *religion and law, moral and ethical principles, and belief-systems,* as well as *travel, cross-cultural experience, and anything that stretches them.* Any of these areas could be healthy goals and meaningful types of evolutionary activity for Zelda and Scott. But our technique here with the North Node is similar to the one we employed with the South Node: we look for *overlap between the themes of the sign and the themes of the house,* knowing that such overlap represents the heart of the matter.

That overlap leaps out: there is symmetry between Capricorn's moral focus on resisting temptation, and the Sagittarian orientation toward moral and ethical principles. There is also a natural synergy between Capricornish hard work, and education and effective engagement in expansive experience. Once again, the strategy of seeking overlap has brought us to a central point: the Fitzgeralds' soul contract was *to build a sexually bonded life together in which they could take pride, and to achieve moral dignity and self-respect through great works.*

The overlap jumps out when we consider Saturn's house position. It lies in the seventh, which is the traditional house of marriage. *Thus, the moral "great work" of self-discipline and maturity which the Fitzgeralds had signed up to accomplish was to build both a marriage and a set of supportive, long-lasting friendships of which they were proud.* To share life, ethically, morally, and for the long term. To resist the temptations which can corrode the heart of intimacy. Sexual fidelity, rather obviously, is high on the list. But we must also recognize the discipline and maturity it takes to resist pettiness, defensiveness, and cheap shots. We must honor the commitment to choosing the path of simple fairness with a partner, even when we can get away with less. Underlying this austere, demanding symbolism is M. Scott Peck's notion that "Love is not a feeling." (Of course any fool knows that love is a feeling! But what Peck meant was that *love is more than just a feeling*—it is also a vow to treat one's partner with dignity and sensitivity, even when no one is feeling very loving.)

Going further, we recognize that the seventh house in a composite chart always refers to the soul partners of the couple—that is, to other people outside the primary relationship. Again, with their North Node ruler in the house of relationships, we see a reference to the fact that the Fitzgeralds *needed help*. To achieve the kind of lasting, ever-expanding marriage to which they aspired, they needed guidance. In modern language, they needed *role models*: older couples who had gone before them and achieved what they themselves were trying to achieve.

Uranus is conjunct Saturn, adding a detail: these partners would help the Fitzgeralds move beyond their own unconscious, internalized cultural assumptions about marriage. These soulmates would help them experience more freedom, rather than less, as a result of their commitment to each other.

Let's remember Jupiter too. Any planet square the South Node is of course also square the North Node. It represents not only a problem in the past, but also one in the present. *We must resolve the square in order to gain access to the North Node.* That's simply the price of admission to North Node work. Without "squarely" facing the issues symbolized by that nodal aspect, we're simply stuck there. To go forward, the Fitzgeralds needed to get past their visceral instinct to "eat, drink and be merry, for tomorrow they might die." They needed to face and break their deep-seated pattern of escapism and addiction to ecstatic release. Self-discipline has obvious relevance in those sober arenas, but we can also take a gentler tack. Jupiter wants to express itself creatively (Libra; fifth house). The full expression of their potential for *shared* creativity would give them a lot of joy—and it would also take some of the load off the darker side of the equation.

Be careful here: it is tempting to brush this insight aside, knowing that the Fitzgeralds were in fact both highly creative people—it seems as if they "got it right," in other words. But remember that we are talking about *shared* creativity, not work they did as individual artists. Part of building the idealized marriage their souls intended to create depended upon their capacity to cooperate artistically, and to trigger previously unknown imaginative potentials in each other. It is worth noting that F. Scott Fitzgerald's name became legendary, while Zelda was mostly forgotten. To what extent did Scott's "Feudal System" edge eclipse his wife's voice, driving her toward madness? And, equally importantly, what work might have emerged from the incubator of their shared Jupiter-function?

In looking at the synthesis of the composite North Node's sign, house and ruler, we immediately focused on their points of overlap and mutual reinforcement. That's an effective technique, but let's recognize that there are more details present there. They help us flesh out the picture.

Saturn's position in Sagittarius emphasizes the beneficial impact of *cross-cultural experience* on Zelda and Scott. Since Saturn rules their North Node, traveling would be simply be good for them, and they clearly did quite a lot of it.

In general, we should emphasize how partnership can *enhance* freedom. With the subjective feeling of safety provided by a healthy relationship, aren't we more open to risk? Aren't we more likely to travel? Take professional risks? Trust people? Learn things? The answers to those questions are not necessarily universal or obvious. But the point is that we can imagine positive answers to them—and that's the kind of marriage toward which Scott and Zelda were aspiring.

First the hard work, then the joy: it's an old formula.

Conclusion

Could an evolutionary astrologer have saved Scott and Zelda Fitzgerald's marriage? It is tempting to react reflexively to that question and say "Of course not!"

Perhaps that's the correct answer. The giddy, self-flattering "high" of their early years must have been blissfully addictive—and like most addictions, it led inexorably to a painful crash. But were there seeds of wisdom in this man and woman, even amidst the glorious fantasy of their first years together? We cannot know. Were they bound inextricably to the nose-diving patterns of their biographies? Or was the equilibrium between insanity's gravity and love's uplifting touch so delicate that a featherweight could have tipped the scales of fate?

These questions are imponderable.

No astrologer need wrestle with them. Our work, in unraveling the message of a composite chart, is not to make pronouncements, be they baleful or full of hope. Our work is only to help, only to offer a gesture toward the higher road and to point an incisive finger at the Shadow in all its seductive guises. Beyond that, the couple itself must choose.

Maybe an astrologer could have helped Zelda and Scott. Maybe he or she, arriving at precisely the right instant, wielding the weight of a feather, could have upset the balance, planting seeds of peace and regeneration.

Again, we cannot know. But if astrology ever regains a place of honor among the allies of humanity, it will be because of individuals like you, reader, lying in bed wide-eyed late at night, struggling to find the words that might have made the difference.

Do such words exist? Not if we believe in ironhanded fate. But perhaps "fate" is an empty concept, only a lie, only a device we use to hide from a notion a thousand times more awesome: that the featherweight which truly tips the balance of our lives is not mechanical destiny, but rather our own innate capacity to make choices.

Maybe Zelda and Scott Fitzgerald, even deep in their pain, given a little help and a little hope, could have wielded that feather. No matter how true or how false that statement might be, if you're the type of human being who's cut out to be an evolutionary astrologer, you probably at least half believe it.

And for anyone who feels that holding out that kind of faith is like writing letters to Santa Claus, we quote a letter from Scott to Zelda. These words were written in 1934, in desolation, while she was in the mental asylum and he was trying—and failing—to ration himself to an ounce of gin per hour.

"The sadness of the past is with me always. The things that we have done together and the awful splits that have broken us into war survivals . . . stay like a sort of atmosphere around any house that I inhabit. The good things and the first years together . . . will stay with me forever, and you should feel like I do that they can be renewed, if not in a new spring, then in a new summer. I love you my darling, darling."

CONCLUSION

Once upon a time there was a very holy man, a Swami renowned far and wide for his great saintliness. Everyone sang his praises and enumerated his many virtues. People traveled far and wide to seek his darshan. One day a troubled young man decided to pay the Swami a visit, and set off to find the holy man's very isolated home. When he knocked on the door after a lengthy and arduous journey, a woman answered. He humbly told the woman that he was looking for the swami and would like nothing more than an audience with him.

"Him!" said the woman. "Why do you want to see *him?* I'm his wife, and I can tell you a few things about this so-called holy man." And she proceeded to describe all the Swami's faults in detail, with many devastating stories of his various misdeeds. Finally the young man said, "Well, I must have the wrong house. I'm very sorry to have bothered you." And he left, wondering what he should do now, and how to find the Swami. A few minutes later he passed a man upon the road, and stopped to ask directions to the Swami's house.

"Why, I am he," said the Swami. "I'd be happy to speak with you. I'm going home now; would you care to accompany me there?" And he pointed in the direction of the house that the young man had just left, the only house for many miles around.

The young man was so startled that his manners abandoned him, and he blurted, "But sir, I just met a woman there who said she was your wife, and she also said the most dreadful things about your character."

The Swami beamed. "You've met my wife! Isn't she *wonderful?* Without her, I'd never be who I am today."

This story, shared with us by a friend, helps illustrate that nothing impacts our souls so profoundly as our meetings with "significant others." Nothing else so shakes up our lives or so recalibrates our existential compasses. Nothing except love so opens the evolutionary doorway—or offers us such an opportunity to demonstrate how stuck we are.

In *Skymates Volume Two: The Composite Chart*, we hope that we have cast some light on how best to navigate the evolutionary processes that intimacy can trigger. We hope that we have assisted you in seeing specifically how the "whole is greater than the sum of the parts," and how psychospiritually complex the waltz of two souls can be. We hope that you, like ourselves, have felt humbled by the exquisite intricacy of the process. We hope that you have felt some wise laughter at yourself—and maybe a tear in the corner of your eye from time to time.

Sometimes, through transits and progressions, we can actually foresee one of those life-altering human encounters. They are so spiritually pivotal that astrology tends to signal them rather reliably. It's illuminating to watch people's responses when we announce that they are likely to "meet someone" soon. Some get excited at the news. Others turn pale. And typically the older the person is, the paler they become!

Not to be cynical about it, but by the time we've made a few trips around the romantic mulberry bush, we understand a basic truth about life—that "meeting someone," however much joy it may bring to us, is also going to rattle us right down to our bones.

Sexual love is so many things all at once. Since the beginning of human time, it has been a source of creature comfort and ecstatic release. It has also typically led to the births of children, and thus been the foundation of family. And as soon as "lovers" become "family," sexual partnership has always been required to evolve beyond its natural predilection for privacy. The magic, secret world of the young lovers begins to send tendrils into the community—and the community holds them tightly. The couple has been recognized as a new nexus in the clan network. Economic and social realities descended upon them. After a while, the stormy passions of love's beginnings typically faded. The cultural mythology kicked in, assuring the couple that the ending of their brief sojourn in paradise was to be expected. It was time for them to turn outward, to assume their rightful responsibilities, and to consider their early body-and-soul encounters as a naïve sweetness to be simultaneously treasured as a precious memory—and half-dismissed as immature fantasy.

Those days are gone. The idea of settling down to a life of numbing, soulless boredom together is appalling to most modern people. Not to say that it doesn't still happen! All of those eternal quagmires remain—kids, economic entanglement, participation in the social network. Easily, a couple can find itself mired in the same old mud pits that have been ensnaring men and women for millennia. Caught between a rock and a hard place, they soldier on together as their grandparents did. The difference is that for their grandparents, all the social mythology told them that this state of affairs was normal. That probably comforted them a bit. Nowadays, we experience it as either a personal failure or as an existential tragedy.

And maybe it is.

We feel robbed. And maybe we were—although the thief may be there in the mirror.

In this world of change, it's so easy to think of sexual love as one of the few human constants. But that isn't the truth. Everything changes. As soon as our understanding of sexuality expands beyond the most utilitarian notions of "Tab A in Slot B," we recognize that intimacy is inseparable from mythic and cultural realities. And nowadays at that level everything is different. Single people of all ages have a respectable place in the world. They can make a living, raise children, hold their heads high. Sex without marriage raises eyebrows only on the margins of mainstream culture. Divorce is common, and carries almost no stigma. With the practical and social pressures to remain in an unsatisfying relationship so reduced, we find ourselves increasingly faced with broken relationships. That reality is lamentable for the pain it causes—and profoundly exciting for the possibilities it creates.

If we no longer settle for deadness in our intimate lives, that leaves only one possibility: aliveness, of course. *But aliveness means evolution.*

A little while ago, we spoke of people's responses to the prediction that "they would soon meet someone." Some were excited; others turned pale. And we observed that typically the older the person was, the paler they became. There is obvious humor in this, but there is also a deeper truth. It's easy to say that Mother Nature plays hormonal tricks on us in order to ensure a steady supply of babies. But we prefer to say that God created human sexuality for more reasons than mere procreation. Sexual love can upset us, but behind that fact is a deeper truth: love is an evolutionary catalyst, and it works by first giving us a taste of something greater than ourselves—then holding that memory before us like a carrot at the end of a stick.

In chasing that carrot, we find ourselves stumbling over our own egos, our own wounds, our own self-importance. Gradually we chip away at all of them, trying to get to that carrot. The carrot perhaps never gets any closer—but its nature changes before our eyes, turning from naïve hopes of eternal ecstasy into a deeper appreciation of life's exquisite evolutionary machinery. And we learn that the chase itself is precious. We learn to treasure the process. We are changed by it, lifted up to the higher ground. We come to understand that intimate disagreements trigger growth in us, and that growth triggers deeper happiness. We accept one of life's greatest paradoxes—that "living happily ever after" is a contradiction in terms. Times of stress and sadness and anger are times of revelation. Without them, there is no growth; without growth, there is only deadness. Thus, without the sadness of love, in the long run there can be no happiness either.

In these pages, we have tried to describe how to avoid deadness; we have tried to describe the path toward that intimate aliveness we all crave.

If these two volumes of *Skymates* can help any loving couple to hang in there with a little more self-awareness, informed compassion for each other, and faith in the wondrous enterprise upon which they are embarked, the two of us will curl up in our bed together with a deeper feeling of happiness and gratitude.

Thanks for being part of the journey.

Love and Mischief,

Steven and Jodie Forrest
Chapel Hill, NC
Autumnal Equinox, 2004

APPENDIX

CALCULATING OR ACQUIRING THE COMPOSITE CHART

Or any other kind of chart, for that matter.

First, there are some free services online at both www.astro.com, Astrodienst, and at www.astrology.com, the astrology section of Ivillage. If you have trouble navigating either site, please go to our Links page for some pointers: www.sevenpawspress/links.html

If you want chart calculation software that does composites and interaspect grids, we distribute Alphee Lavoie's AIR Software. Please go our webpage about AIR, www.sevenpawspress.com/soft.hml. If you want to do some online comparison shopping of many different astrological software programs, please go to our home page, www.sevenpawspress.com, and follow the link you'll see there to Astrology Software Shop. They have comparisons, reviews, demos, screenshots and tech support all waiting for you. Cards on the table: if you buy a program from either AIR Software or Astrology Software Shop, we get a small cut of the price.

If you'd rather buy charts from us than get them free online or order your own astrological software, we have a computerized chart calculation service; please see our webpage www.sevenpawspress.com/cmpchart.html. We also offer two personalized, computerized synastry reports for which we wrote the orginal Skymates-based text, "The Sky We Share" for couples, and "The Single Sky" if you haven't found a partner yet.

For those reports and other reports that we offer, please see our webpage, www.sevenpawspress.com/written.html.

MORE ABOUT OUR WORK

For more information about our work, our other books (astrology and fiction), books by other authors, taped lectures and workshops, and a schedule of our workshops and apprenticeship programs, please go to our website at www.sevenpawspress.com

Not online yet? You can request a brochure from us at POB 2345, Chapel Hill NC 27515, or by faxing 919.929.7092, or by leaving a voice message at 919.929.4287.